Natsume's
BOOK of FRIENDS

Shojo Beat

Natsume's BOOK of FRIENDS

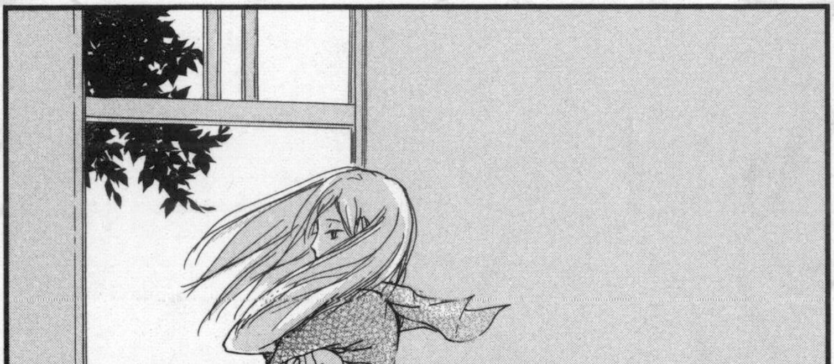

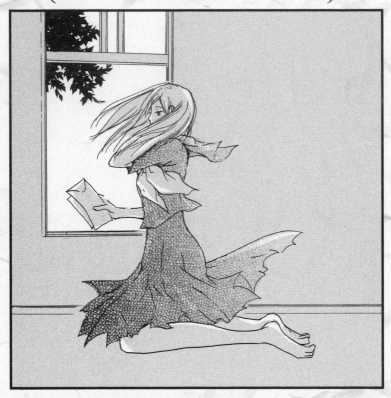

STORY and ART by
Yuki Midorikawa

VOLUME 8

Natsume's BOOK of FRIENDS

VOLUME 8 CONTENTS

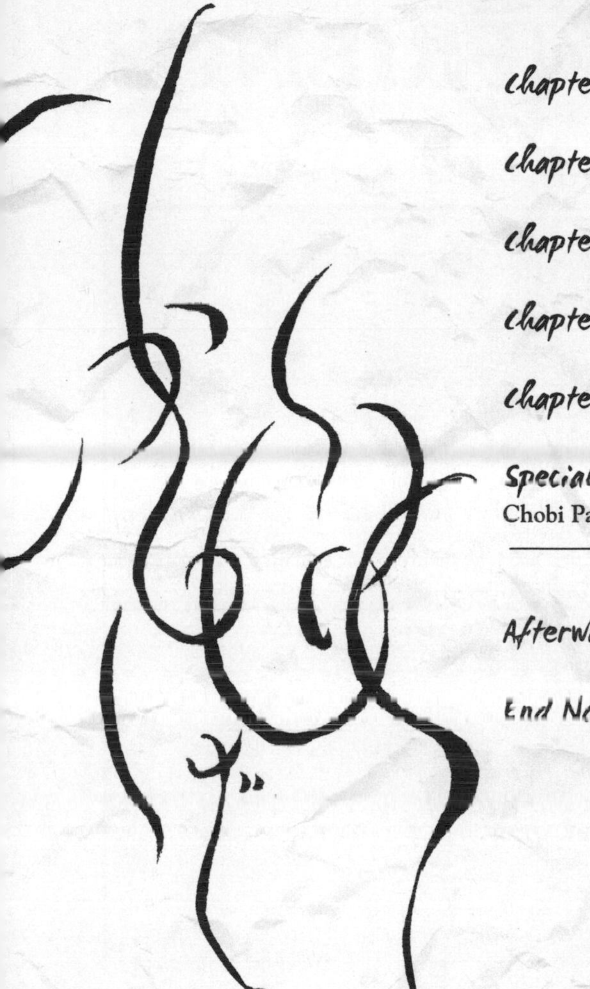

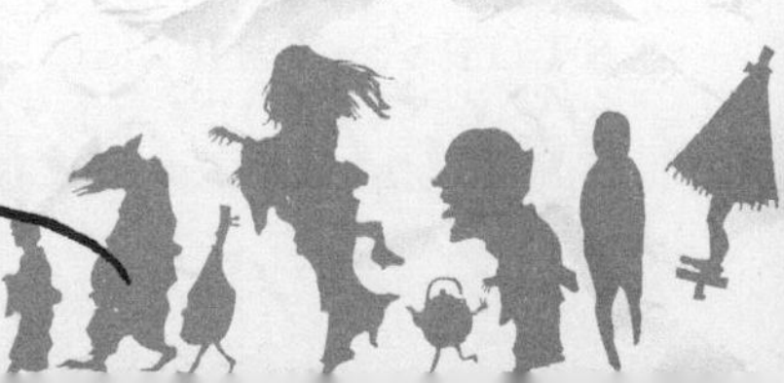

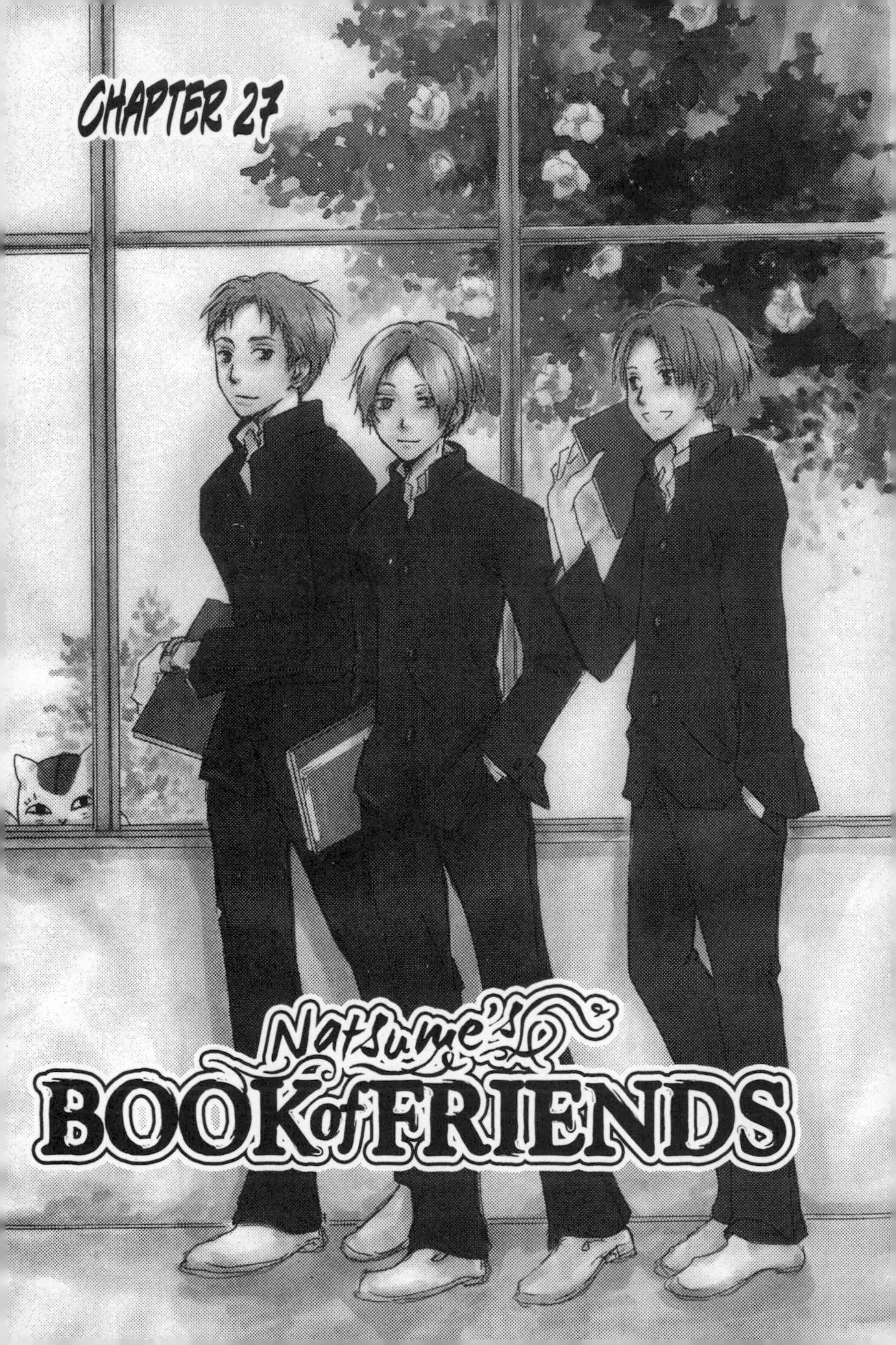
CHAPTER 27
Natsume's
BOOK of FRIENDS

Natsume's BOOK of FRIENDS
CHARACTER GUIDE

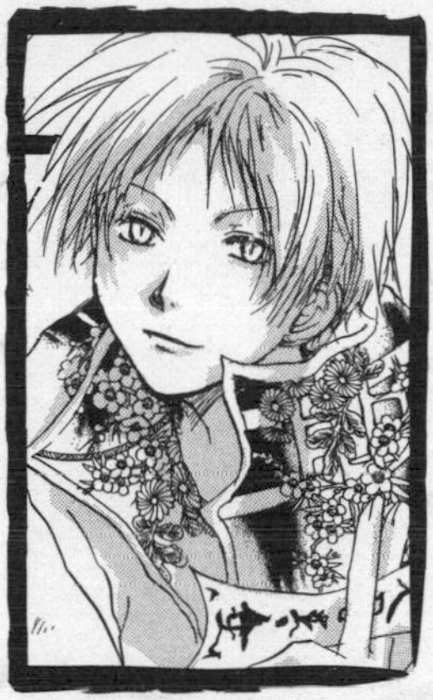

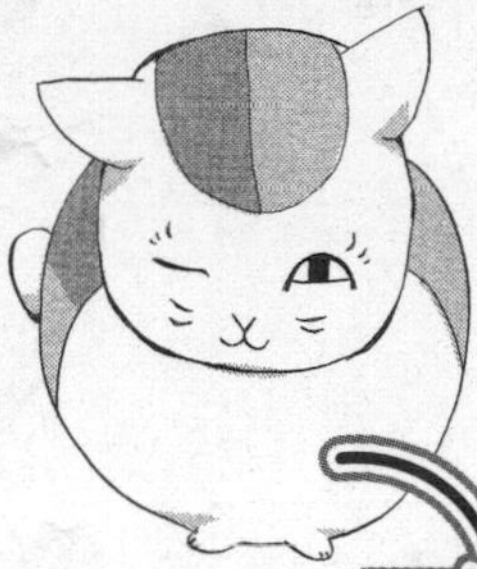

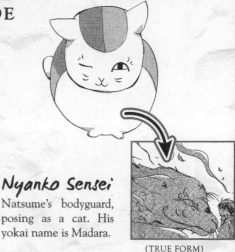

Nyanko Sensei
Natsume's bodyguard, posing as a cat. His yokai name is Madara.

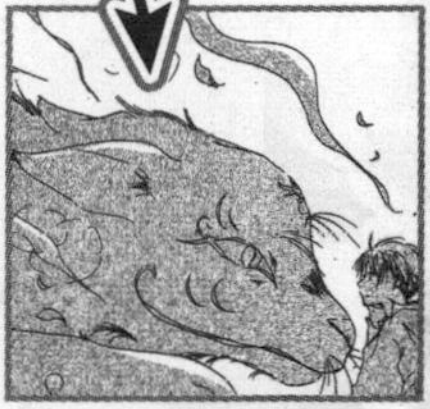

(TRUE FORM)

Takashi Natsume
A lonely orphan with the ability to see the supernatural. He inherited the *Book of Friends* from his grandmother and currently lives with the Fujiwaras, to whom he is distantly related. Like his grandmother, he's powerful enough to subdue yokai with a single punch.

Kaname Tanuma
Natsume's friend, the son of the priest at Yatsuhara. More sensitive to yokai presence than normal people.

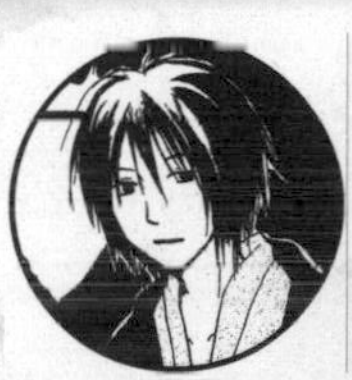

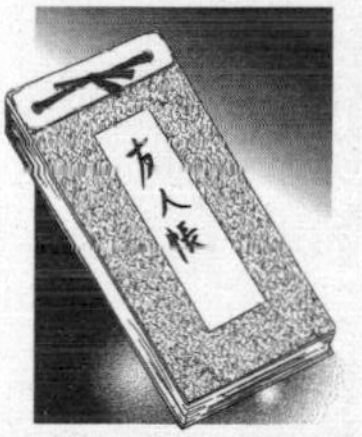

The Book of Friends
A collection of contracts put together by Reiko, Takashi's grandmother, that grants her mastery over the yokai who sign.

THE STORY
Takashi Natsume has a secret sixth sense—he can see supernatural creatures called yokai. And ever since he inherited the *Book of Friends* from his grandmother, the local yokai have been coming after him. Takashi frees Nyanko Sensei from imprisonment and promises he will get the *Book* when Takashi dies. With his new bodyguard, Takashi leads a busy life returning names to yokai.

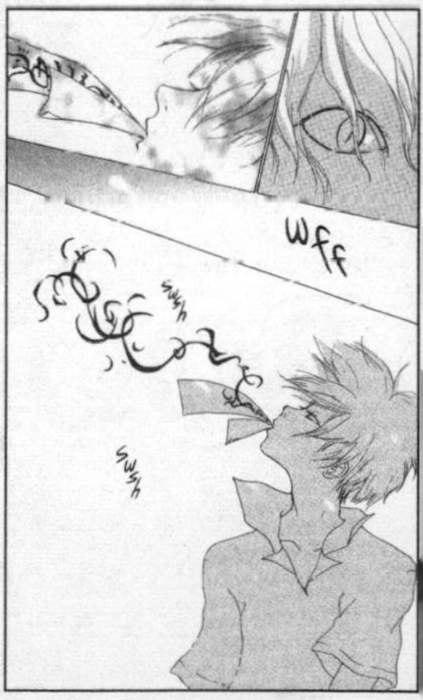
Wff

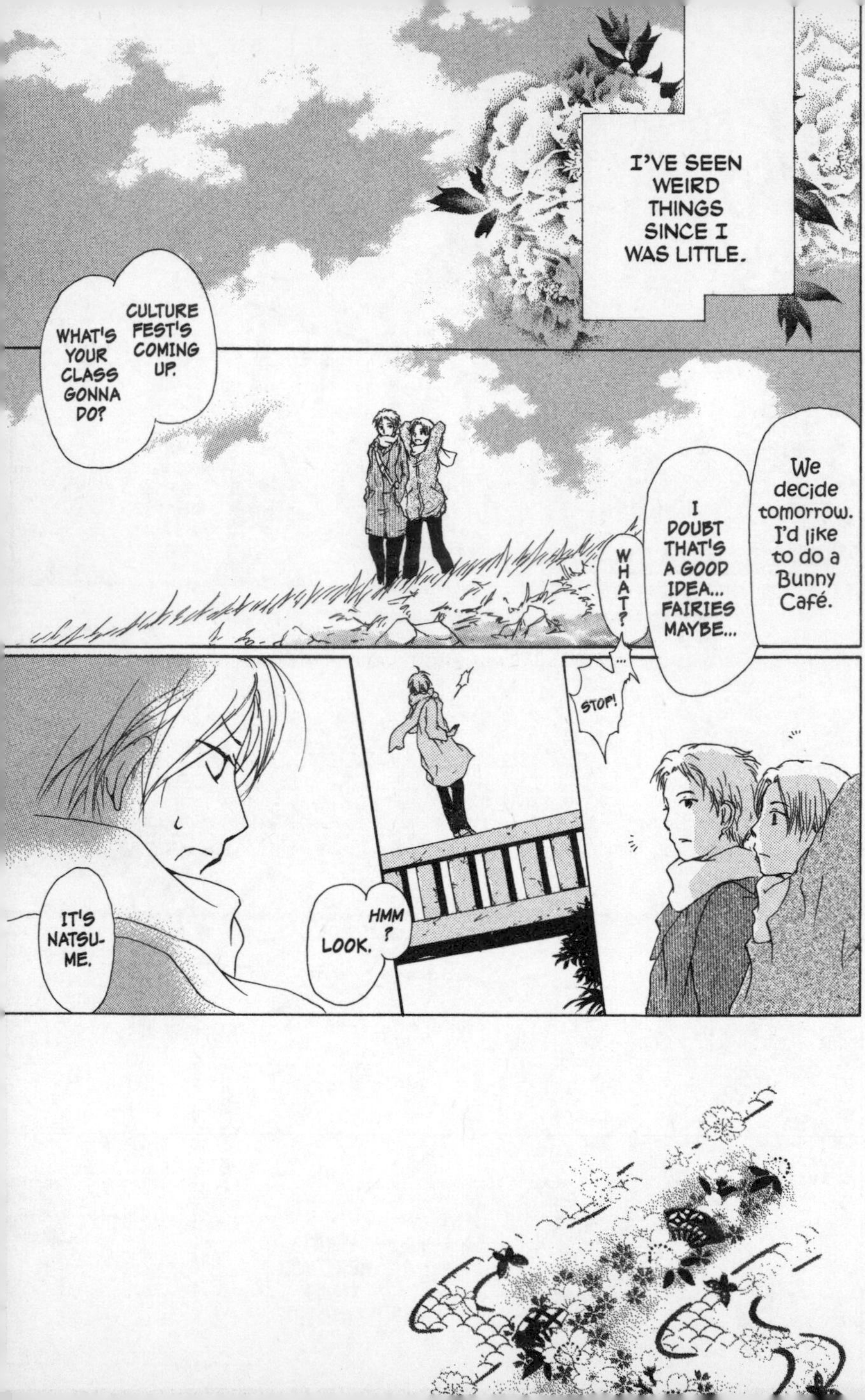
I'VE SEEN WEIRD THINGS SINCE I WAS LITTLE.
CULTURE FEST'S COMING UP.
WHAT'S YOUR CLASS GONNA DO?
We decide tomorrow. I'd like to do a Bunny Café.
I DOUBT THAT'S A GOOD IDEA... FAIRIES MAYBE...
WHAT?
...
STOP!
HMM?
LOOK.
IT'S NATSU-ME.

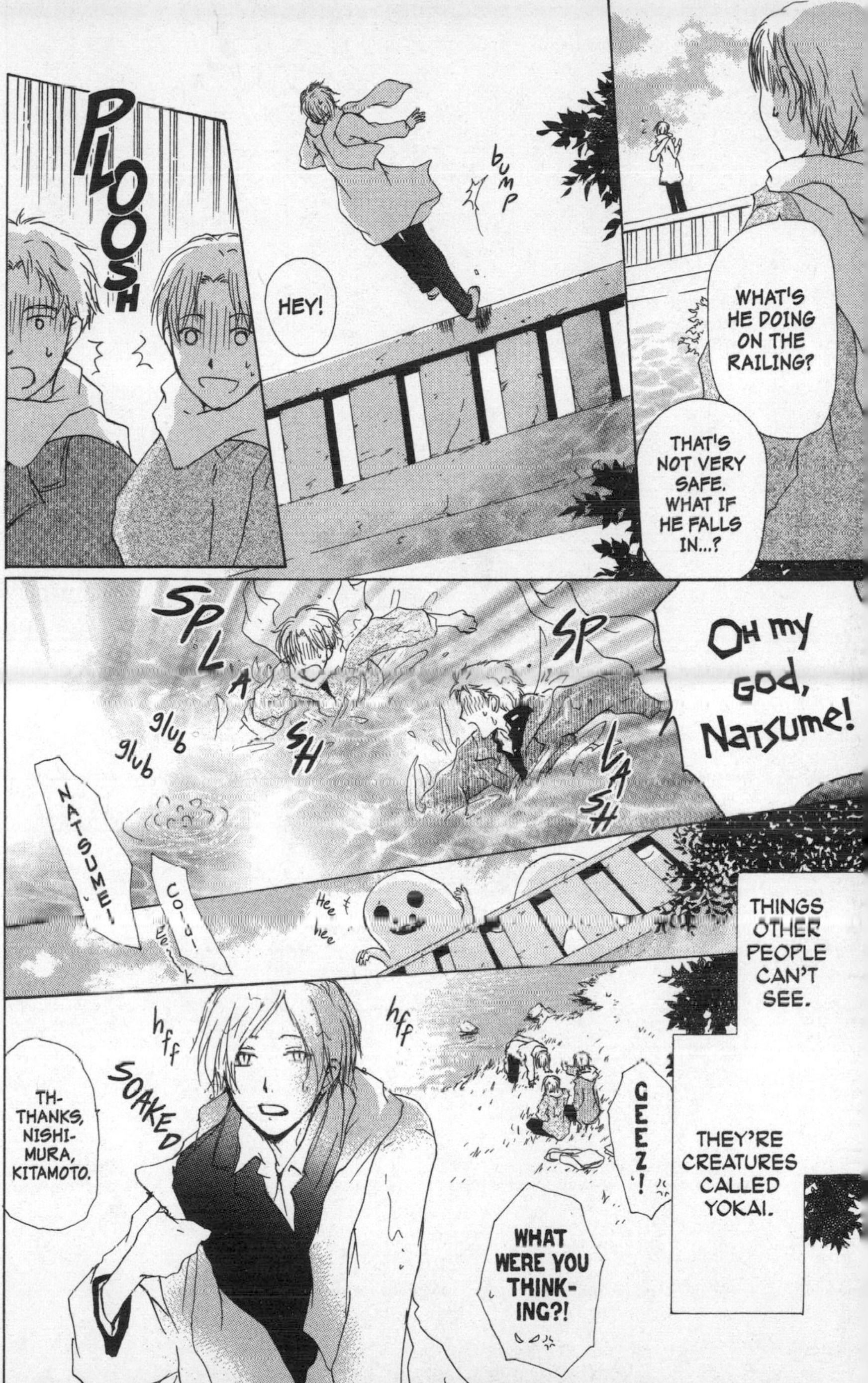
WHAT'S HE DOING ON THE RAILING?
THAT'S NOT VERY SAFE. WHAT IF HE FALLS IN...?
bump
HEY!
PLOOSH
OH my god, Natsume!
SPLASH
SPLASH
glub glub
NATSUME!
Cold!
Hee hee
THINGS OTHER PEOPLE CAN'T SEE.
THEY'RE CREATURES CALLED YOKAI.
GEEZ!
WHAT WERE YOU THINKING?!
hff
hff
SOAKED
TH-THANKS, NISHIMURA, KITAMOTO.

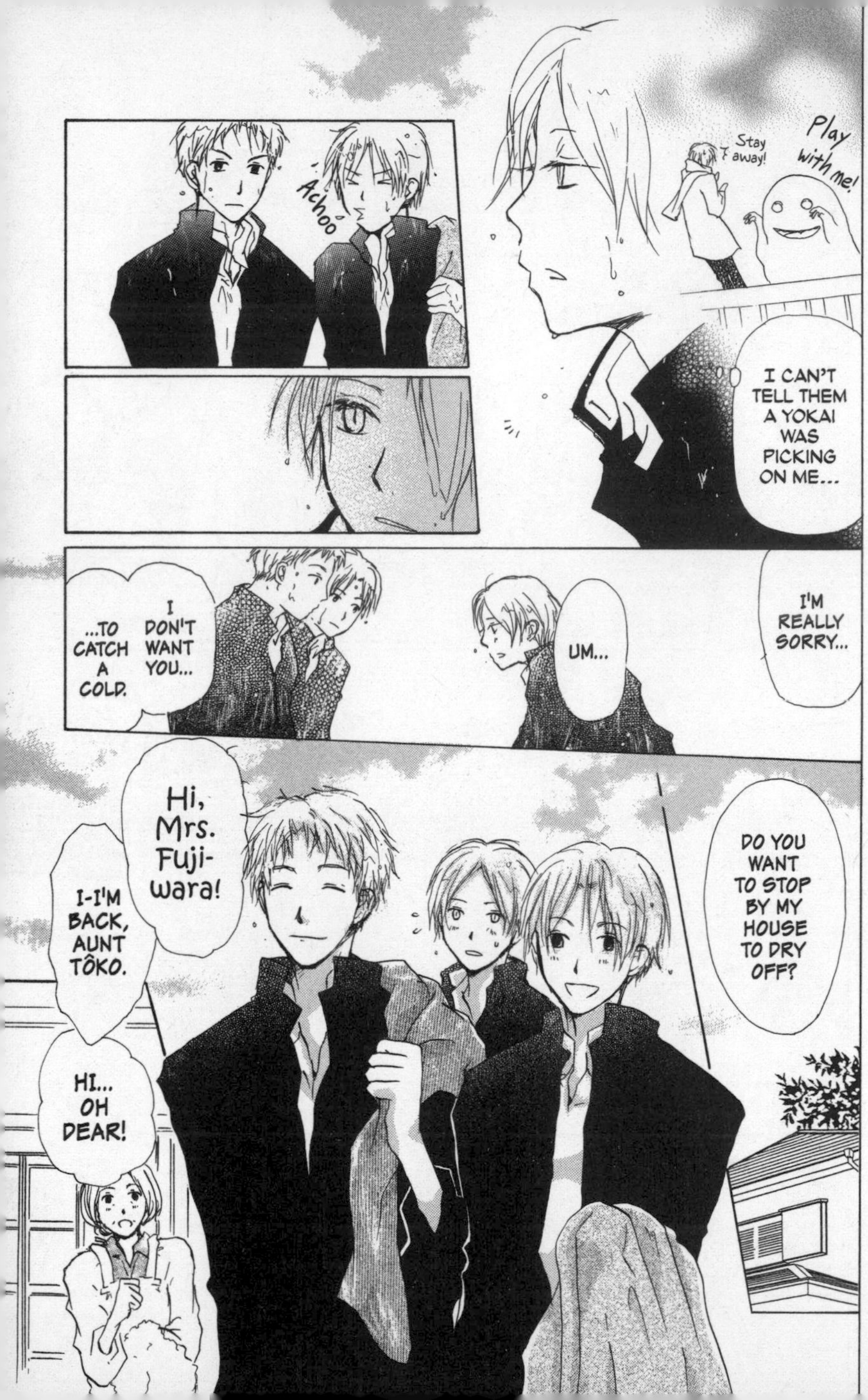
Play with me!
Stay away!
I CAN'T TELL THEM A YOKAI WAS PICKING ON ME...
Achoo
I'M REALLY SORRY...
UM...
I DON'T WANT YOU...
...TO CATCH A COLD.
DO YOU WANT TO STOP BY MY HOUSE TO DRY OFF?
Hi, Mrs. Fuji-wara!
I-I'M BACK, AUNT TÔKO.
HI... OH DEAR!

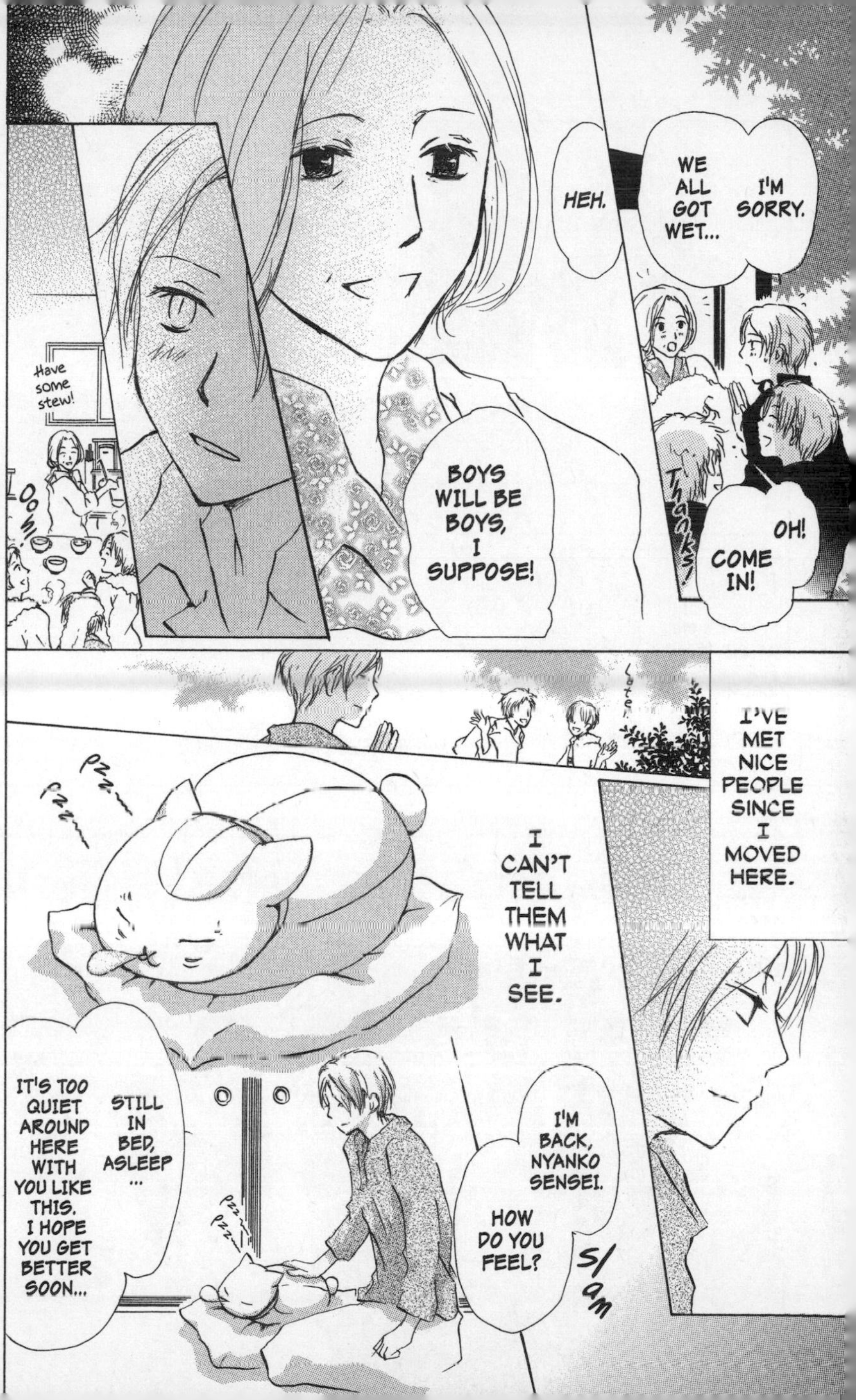
I'M SORRY.
WE ALL GOT WET...
OH! COME IN!
Thanks!
HEH.
BOYS WILL BE BOYS, I SUPPOSE!
Have some stew!
I'VE MET NICE PEOPLE SINCE I MOVED HERE.
Later!
I CAN'T TELL THEM WHAT I SEE.
pzz pzz
Slam
I'M BACK, NYANKO SENSEI.
HOW DO YOU FEEL?
pzz pzz
STILL IN BED, ASLEEP...
IT'S TOO QUIET AROUND HERE WITH YOU LIKE THIS. I HOPE YOU GET BETTER SOON...

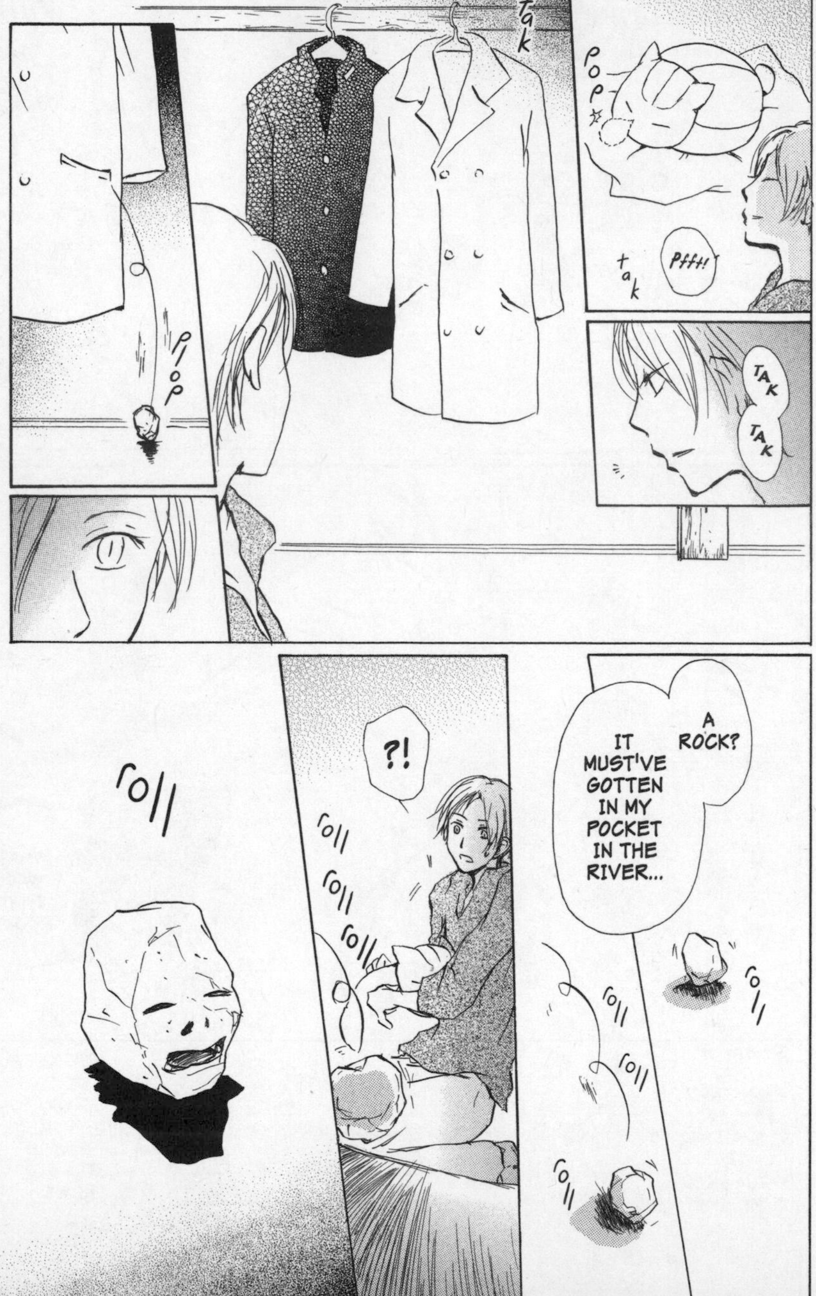
Pop
Pop
Pfft!
tak
TAK
TAK
tak
plop
A ROCK?
IT MUST'VE GOTTEN IN MY POCKET IN THE RIVER...
roll
roll
?!
roll
roll
roll
roll

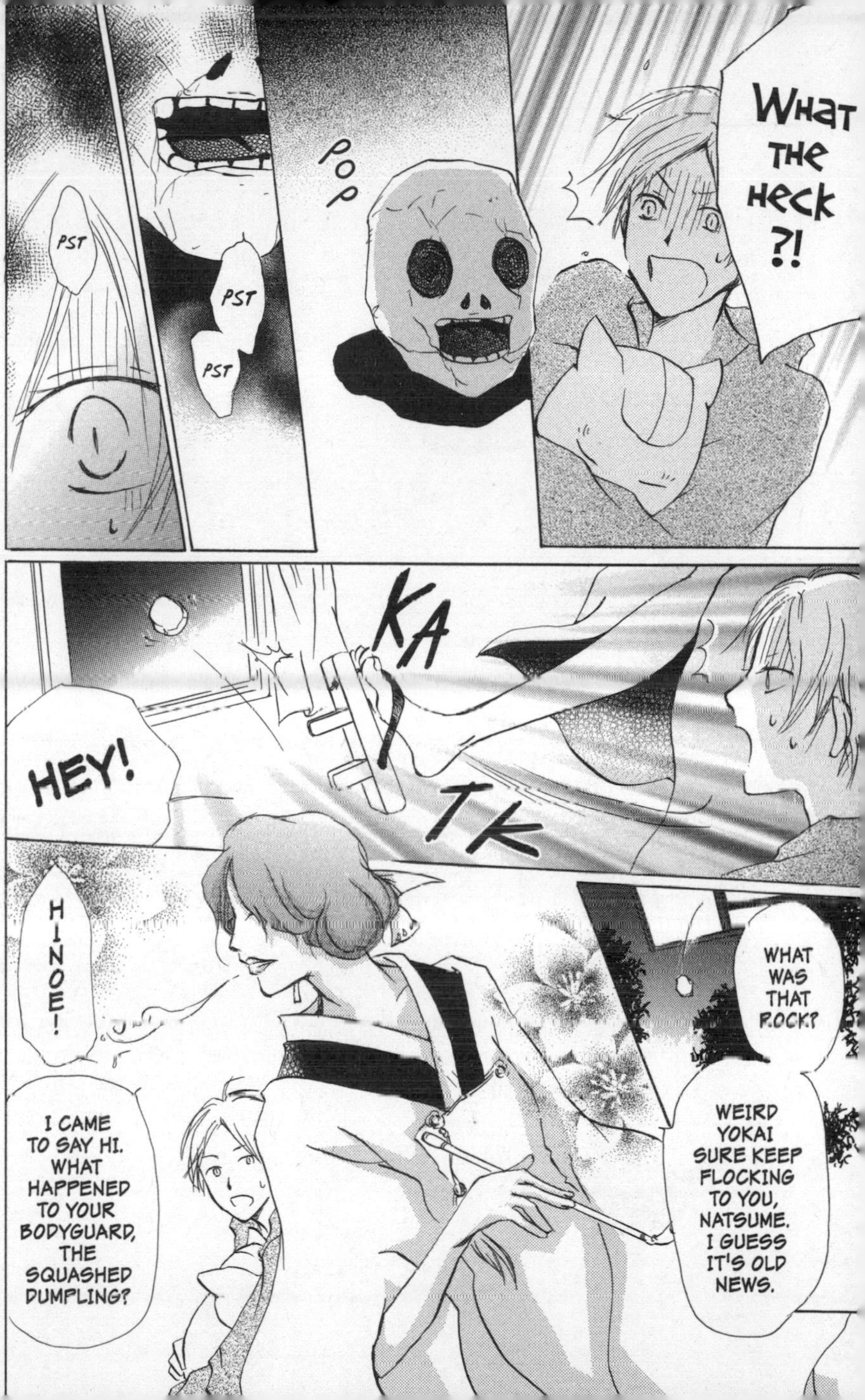
WHAT THE HECK ?!
POP
PST
PST
PST
KA
TK
HEY!
WHAT WAS THAT ROCK?
HINOE!
WEIRD YOKAI SURE KEEP FLOCKING TO YOU, NATSUME. I GUESS IT'S OLD NEWS.
I CAME TO SAY HI. WHAT HAPPENED TO YOUR BODYGUARD, THE SQUASHED DUMPLING?

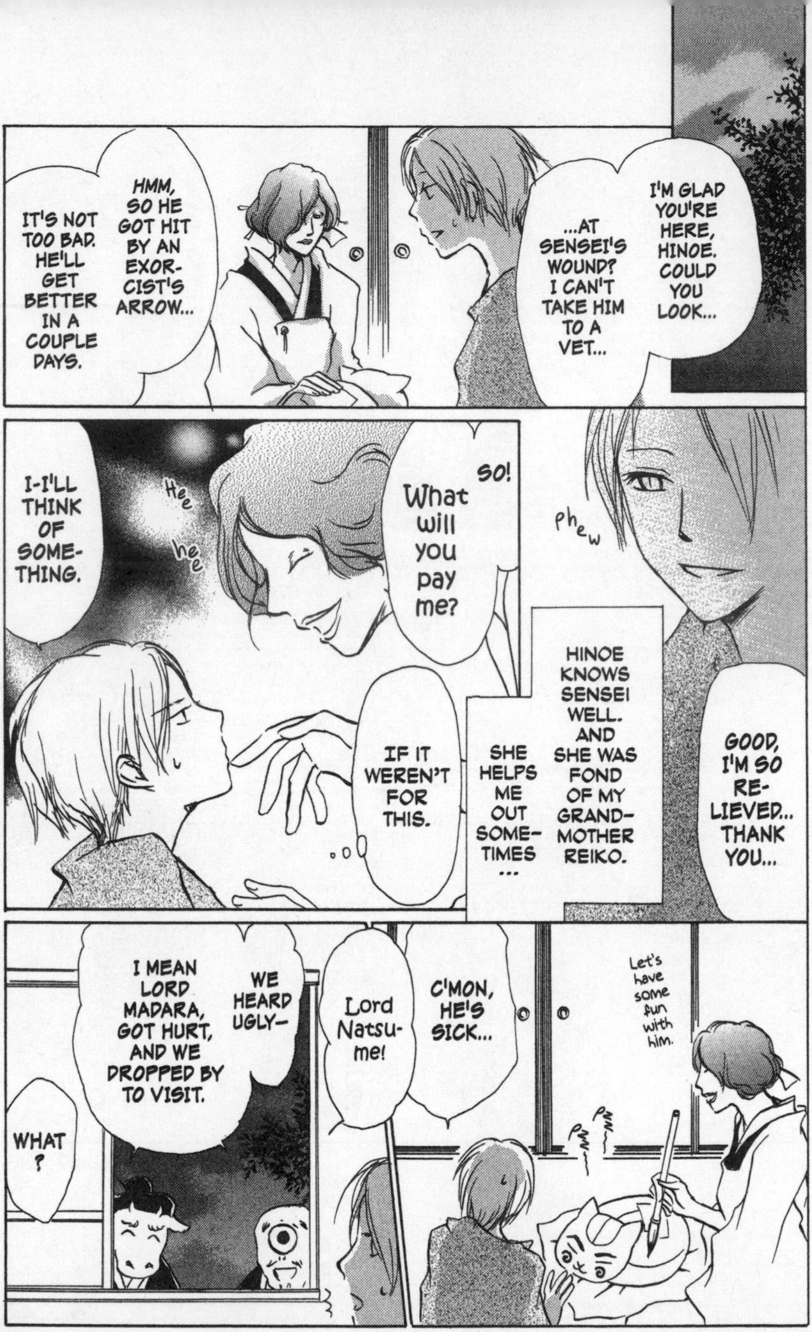
I'M GLAD YOU'RE HERE, HINOE. COULD YOU LOOK...
...AT SENSEI'S WOUND? I CAN'T TAKE HIM TO A VET...
HMM, SO HE GOT HIT BY AN EXOR-CIST'S ARROW...
IT'S NOT TOO BAD. HE'LL GET BETTER IN A COUPLE DAYS.
phew
GOOD, I'M SO RE-LIEVED... THANK YOU...
HINOE KNOWS SENSEI WELL. AND SHE WAS FOND OF MY GRAND-MOTHER REIKO.
SHE HELPS ME OUT SOME-TIMES ...
SO! What will you pay me?
Hee hee
I-I'LL THINK OF SOME-THING.
IF IT WEREN'T FOR THIS.
Let's have some fun with him.
Pzz Pzz
C'MON, HE'S SICK...
Lord Natsu-me!
WE HEARD UGLY—
I MEAN LORD MADARA, GOT HURT, AND WE DROPPED BY TO VISIT.
WHAT?

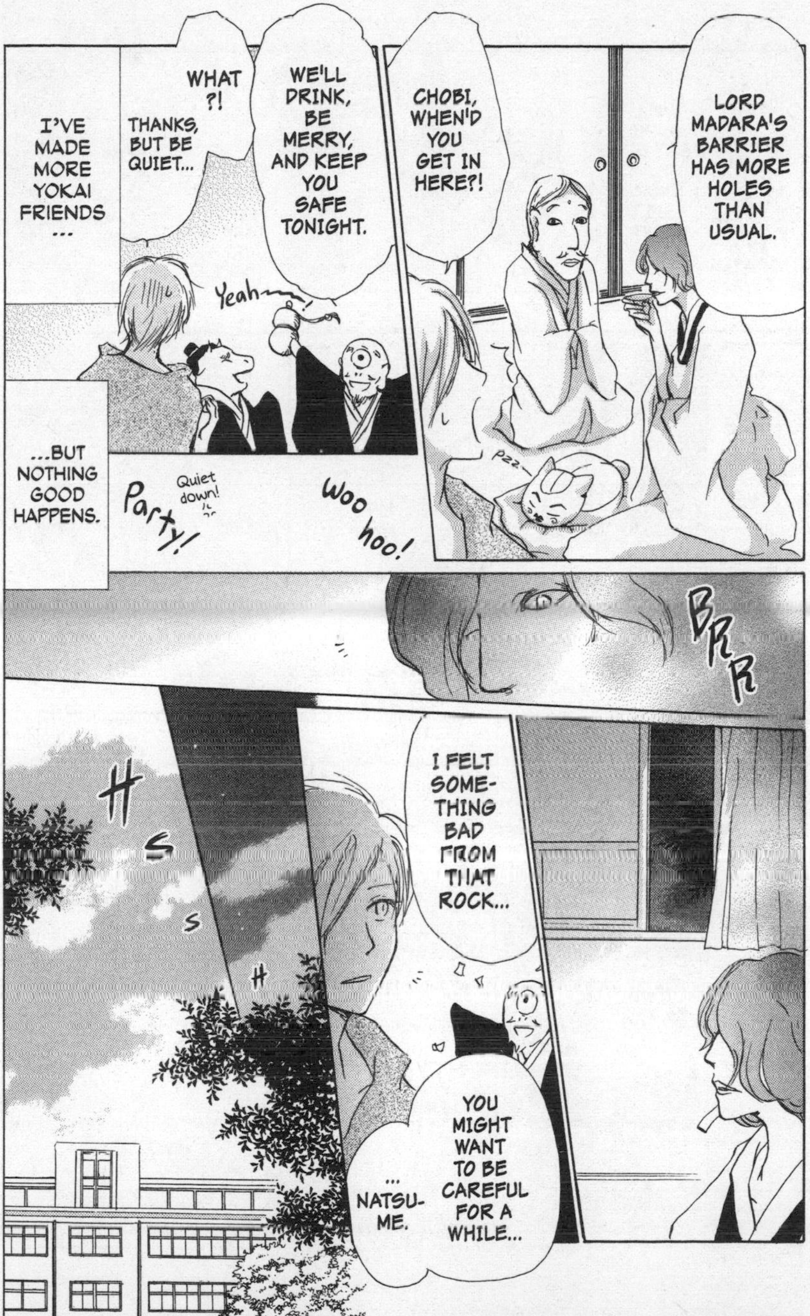

LORD MADARA'S BARRIER HAS MORE HOLES THAN USUAL.
CHOBI, WHEN'D YOU GET IN HERE?!
Pzz
WE'LL DRINK, BE MERRY, AND KEEP YOU SAFE TONIGHT.
WHAT ?!
THANKS, BUT BE QUIET...
I'VE MADE MORE YOKAI FRIENDS ...
Yeah
...BUT NOTHING GOOD HAPPENS.
Woo hoo!
Quiet down!
Party!
BRR
I FELT SOME-THING BAD FROM THAT ROCK...
YOU MIGHT WANT TO BE CAREFUL FOR A WHILE...
... NATSU-ME.
HSSH

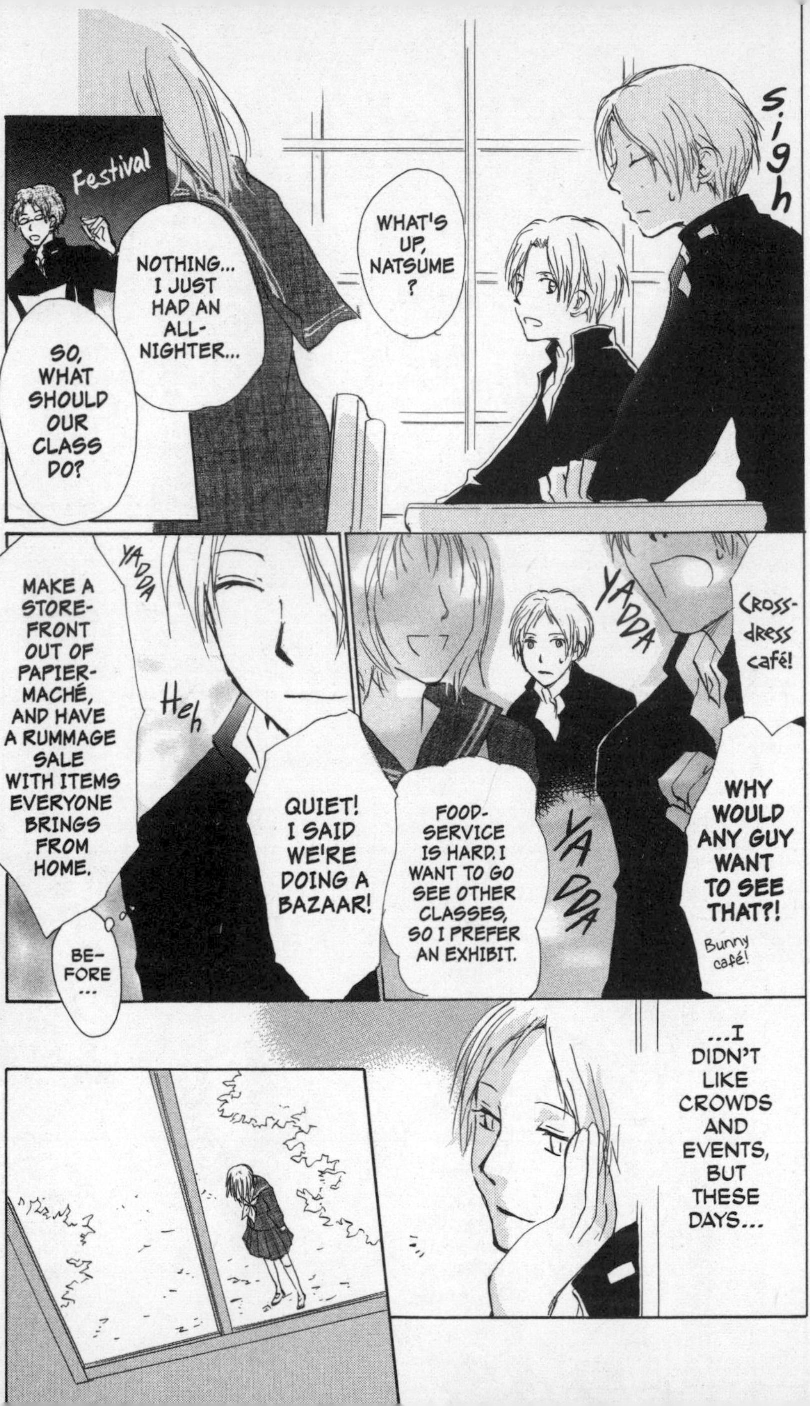

Sigh
WHAT'S UP, NATSUME?
NOTHING... I JUST HAD AN ALL-NIGHTER...
Festival
SO, WHAT SHOULD OUR CLASS DO?
Cross-dress café!
YADDA
WHY WOULD ANY GUY WANT TO SEE THAT?!
Bunny café!
YADDA
FOOD-SERVICE IS HARD. I WANT TO GO SEE OTHER CLASSES, SO I PREFER AN EXHIBIT.
QUIET! I SAID WE'RE DOING A BAZAAR!
YADDA
MAKE A STOREFRONT OUT OF PAPIER-MACHÉ, AND HAVE A RUMMAGE SALE WITH ITEMS EVERYONE BRINGS FROM HOME.
Heh
BEFORE...
...I DIDN'T LIKE CROWDS AND EVENTS, BUT THESE DAYS...

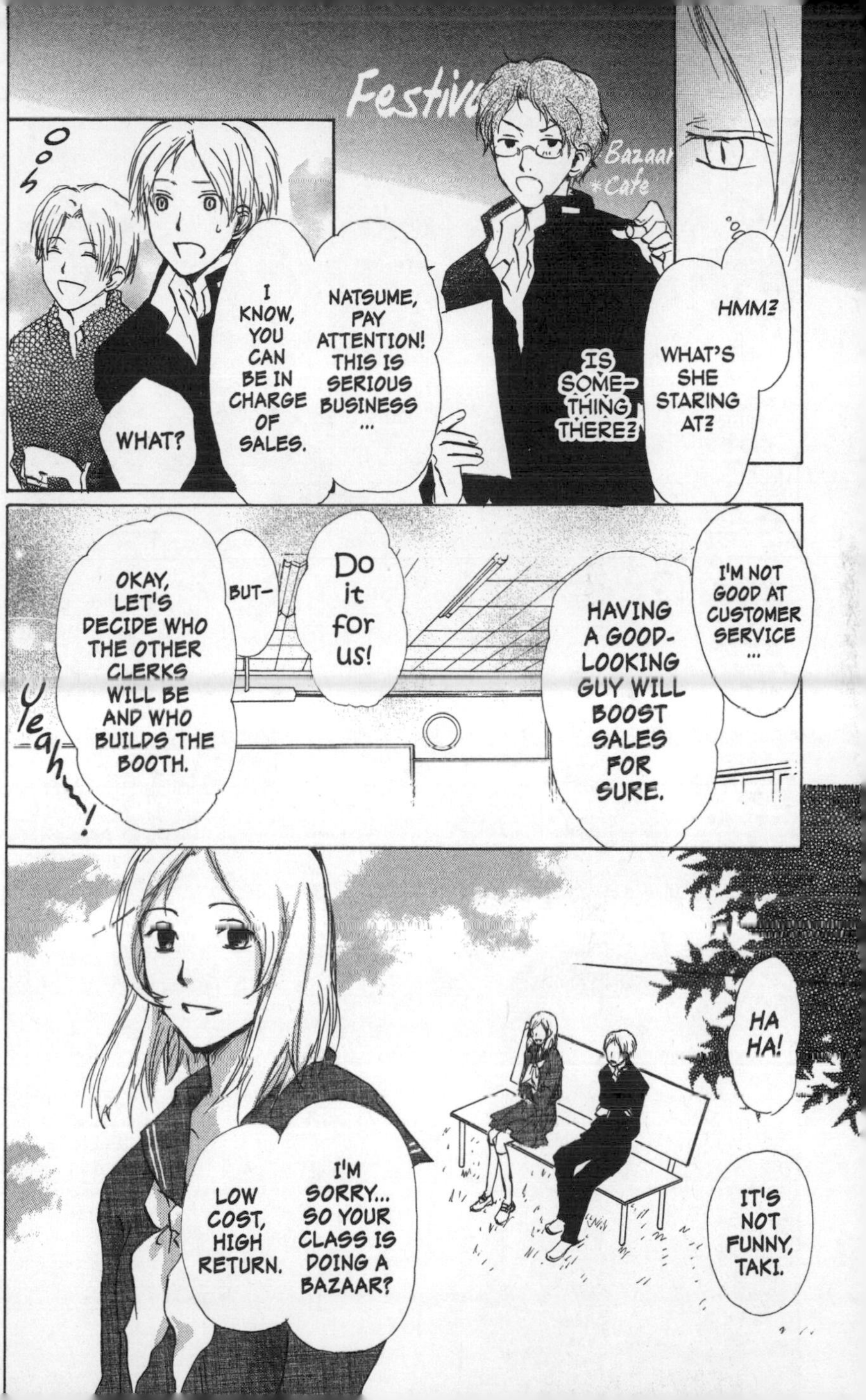
HMM?
WHAT'S SHE STARING AT?
IS SOME-THING THERE?
Festiva
Bazaar
Cafe
NATSUME, PAY ATTENTION! THIS IS SERIOUS BUSINESS...
I KNOW, YOU CAN BE IN CHARGE OF SALES.
WHAT?
Ooh
I'M NOT GOOD AT CUSTOMER SERVICE...
HAVING A GOOD-LOOKING GUY WILL BOOST SALES FOR SURE.
Do it for us!
BUT-
OKAY, LET'S DECIDE WHO THE OTHER CLERKS WILL BE AND WHO BUILDS THE BOOTH.
Yeah~!
HA HA!
IT'S NOT FUNNY, TAKI.
I'M SORRY... SO YOUR CLASS IS DOING A BAZAAR?
LOW COST, HIGH RETURN.

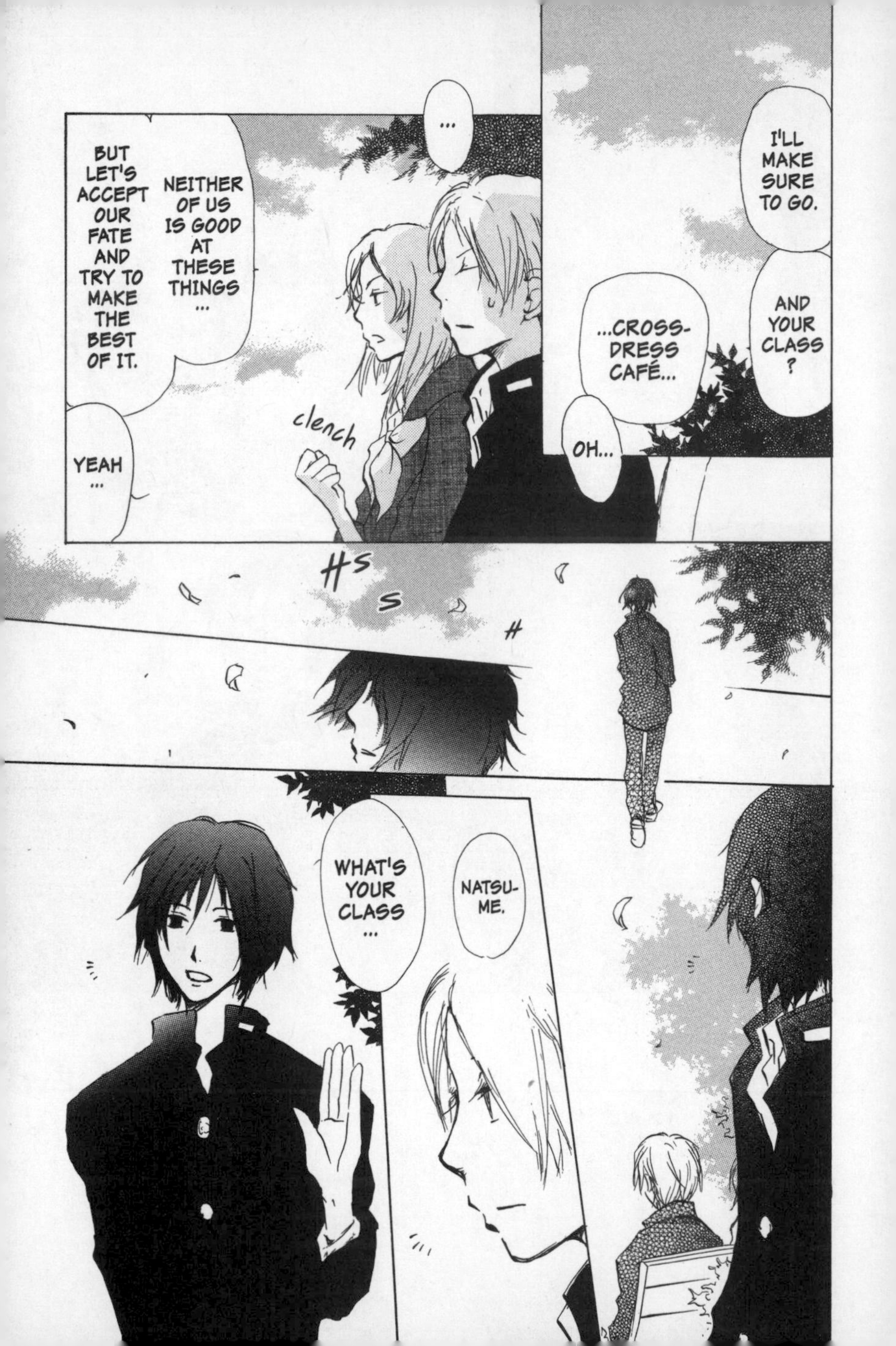
I'LL MAKE SURE TO GO.
AND YOUR CLASS?
...CROSS-DRESS CAFÉ...
OH...
...
NEITHER OF US IS GOOD AT THESE THINGS...
BUT LET'S ACCEPT OUR FATE AND TRY TO MAKE THE BEST OF IT.
clench
YEAH...
NATSU-ME.
WHAT'S YOUR CLASS...

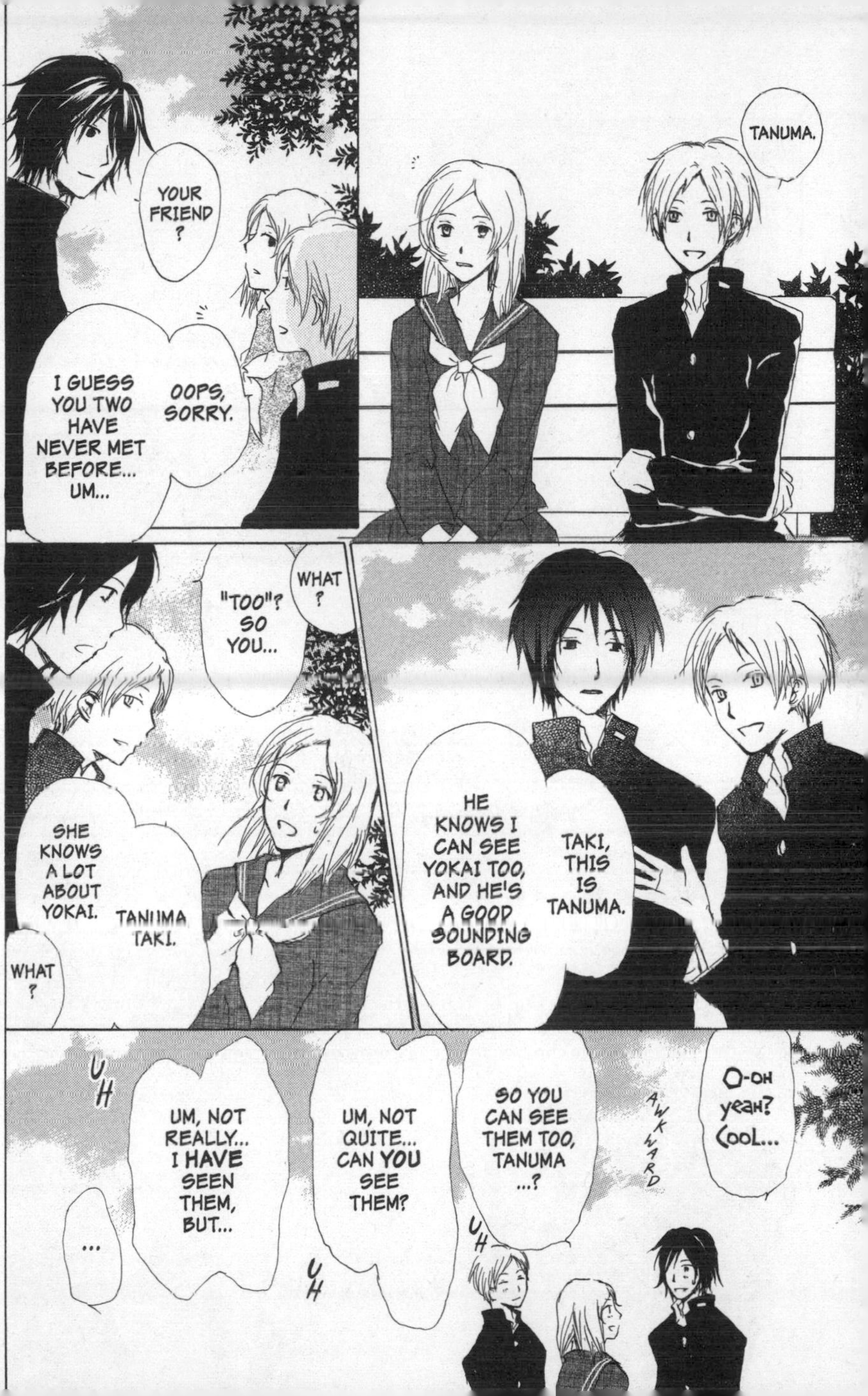
TANUMA.
YOUR FRIEND ?
OOPS, SORRY.
I GUESS YOU TWO HAVE NEVER MET BEFORE... UM...
TAKI, THIS IS TANUMA.
HE KNOWS I CAN SEE YOKAI TOO, AND HE'S A GOOD SOUNDING BOARD.
WHAT ?
"TOO"? SO YOU...
TANUMA TAKI.
SHE KNOWS A LOT ABOUT YOKAI.
WHAT ?
O-OH yeah? COOL...
AWKWARD
SO YOU CAN SEE THEM TOO, TANUMA ...?
UH
UM, NOT QUITE... CAN YOU SEE THEM?
UH
UM, NOT REALLY... I HAVE SEEN THEM, BUT...
UH
...

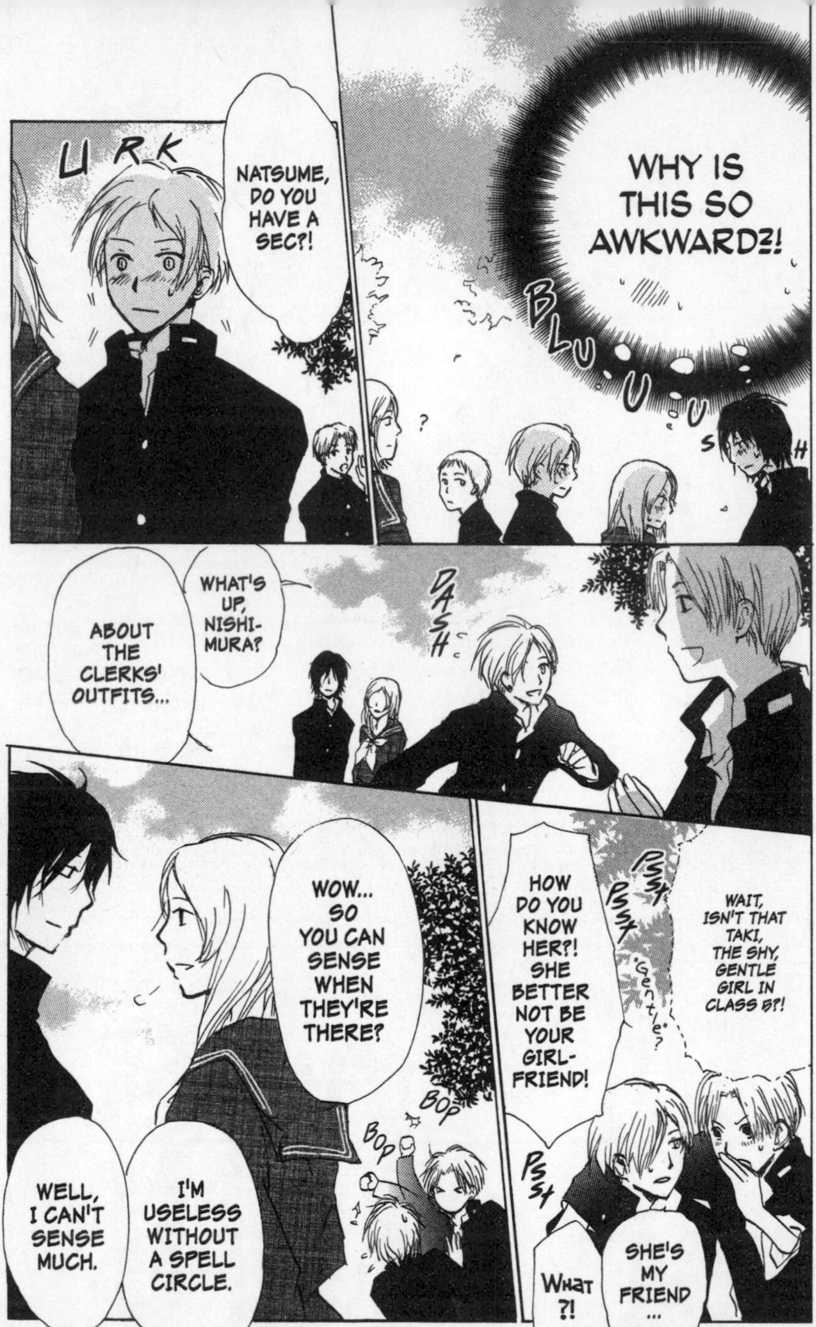
WHY IS THIS SO AWKWARD?!
BLUUUU
SH
URK
NATSUME, DO YOU HAVE A SEC?!
WHAT'S UP, NISHIMURA?
DASH
ABOUT THE CLERKS' OUTFITS...
WAIT, ISN'T THAT TAKI, THE SHY, GENTLE GIRL IN CLASS 5?!
PSST
PSST
"Gentle"?
HOW DO YOU KNOW HER?! SHE BETTER NOT BE YOUR GIRLFRIEND!
PSST
SHE'S MY FRIEND...
WHAT?!
WOW... SO YOU CAN SENSE WHEN THEY'RE THERE?
BOP
BOP
I'M USELESS WITHOUT A SPELL CIRCLE.
WELL, I CAN'T SENSE MUCH.

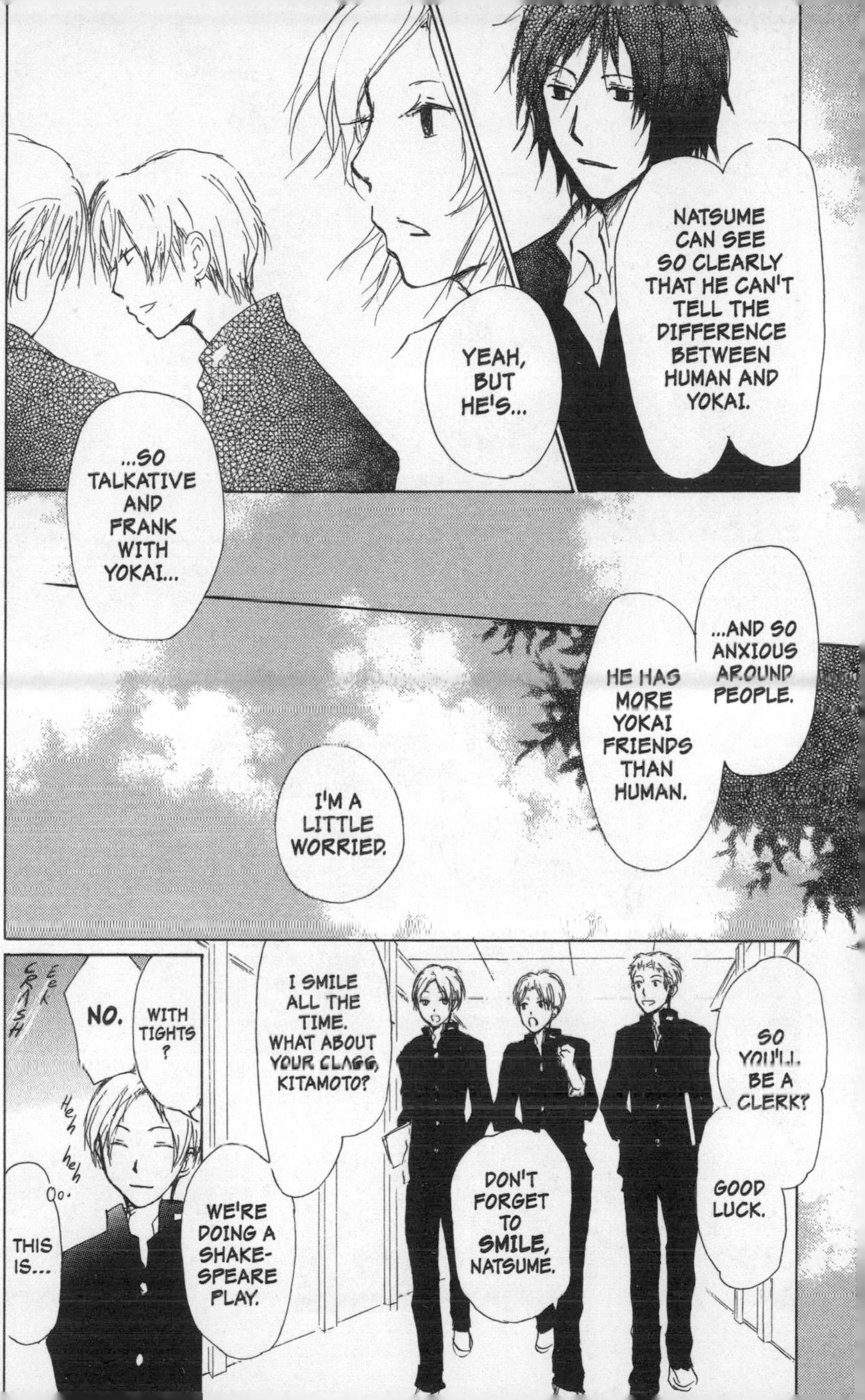
NATSUME CAN SEE SO CLEARLY THAT HE CAN'T TELL THE DIFFERENCE BETWEEN HUMAN AND YOKAI.
YEAH, BUT HE'S...
...SO TALKATIVE AND FRANK WITH YOKAI...
...AND SO ANXIOUS AROUND PEOPLE.
HE HAS MORE YOKAI FRIENDS THAN HUMAN.
I'M A LITTLE WORRIED.
SO YOU'LL BE A CLERK?
GOOD LUCK.
DON'T FORGET TO SMILE, NATSUME.
I SMILE ALL THE TIME. WHAT ABOUT YOUR CLASS, KITAMOTO?
WE'RE DOING A SHAKE-SPEARE PLAY.
WITH TIGHTS?
NO.
Eek
CRASH
Heh heh
Oo.
THIS IS...

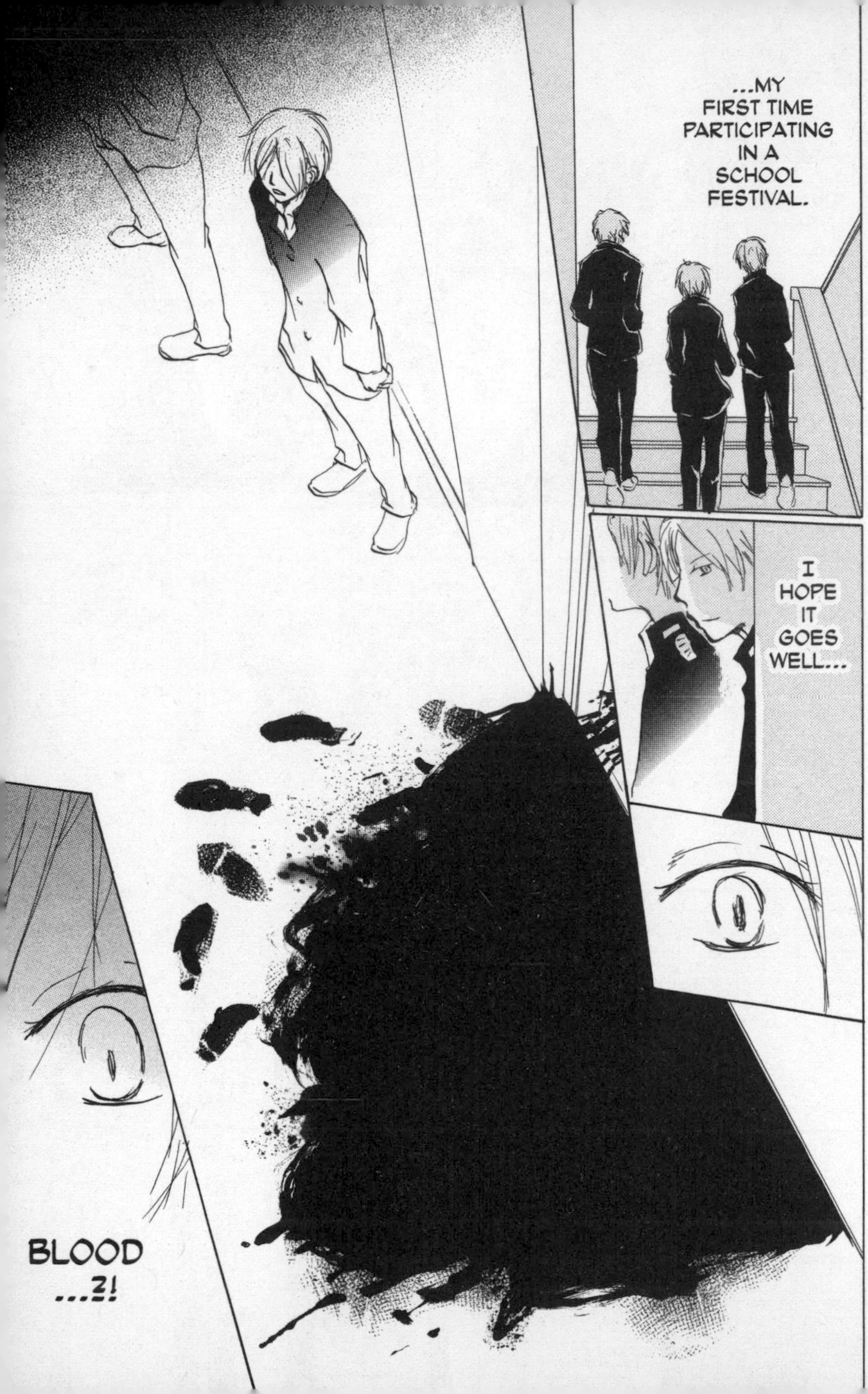
...MY FIRST TIME PARTICIPATING IN A SCHOOL FESTIVAL.
I HOPE IT GOES WELL...
BLOOD ...?!

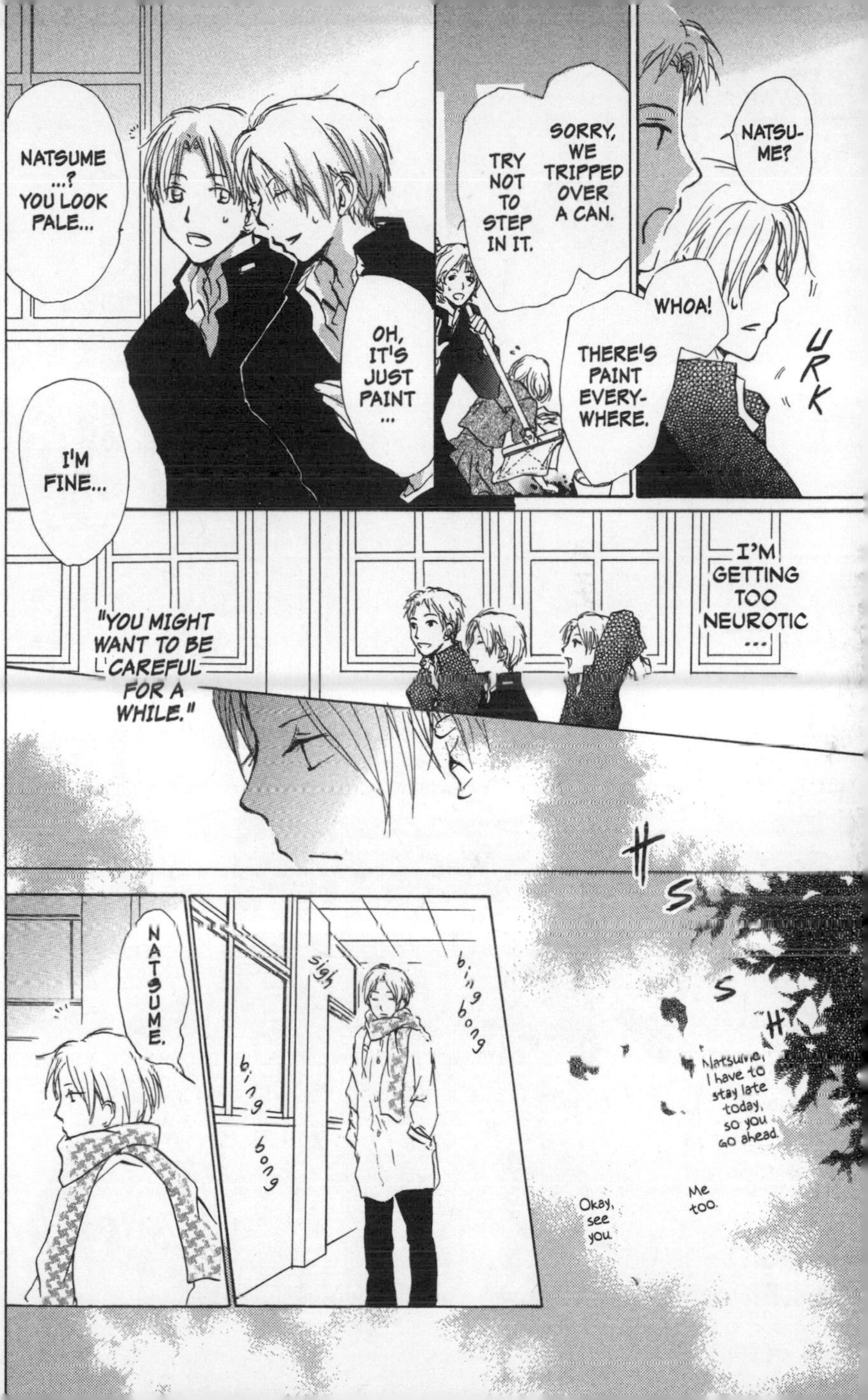
NATSU-ME?
URK
WHOA!
THERE'S PAINT EVERY-WHERE.
SORRY, WE TRIPPED OVER A CAN.
TRY NOT TO STEP IN IT.
NATSUME ...? YOU LOOK PALE...
OH, IT'S JUST PAINT ...
I'M FINE...
I'M GETTING TOO NEUROTIC ...
"YOU MIGHT WANT TO BE CAREFUL FOR A WHILE."
HSSH
Natsume, I have to stay late today, so you GO ahead.
Me too.
Okay, see you.
bing bong
sigh
bing bong
NATSUME.

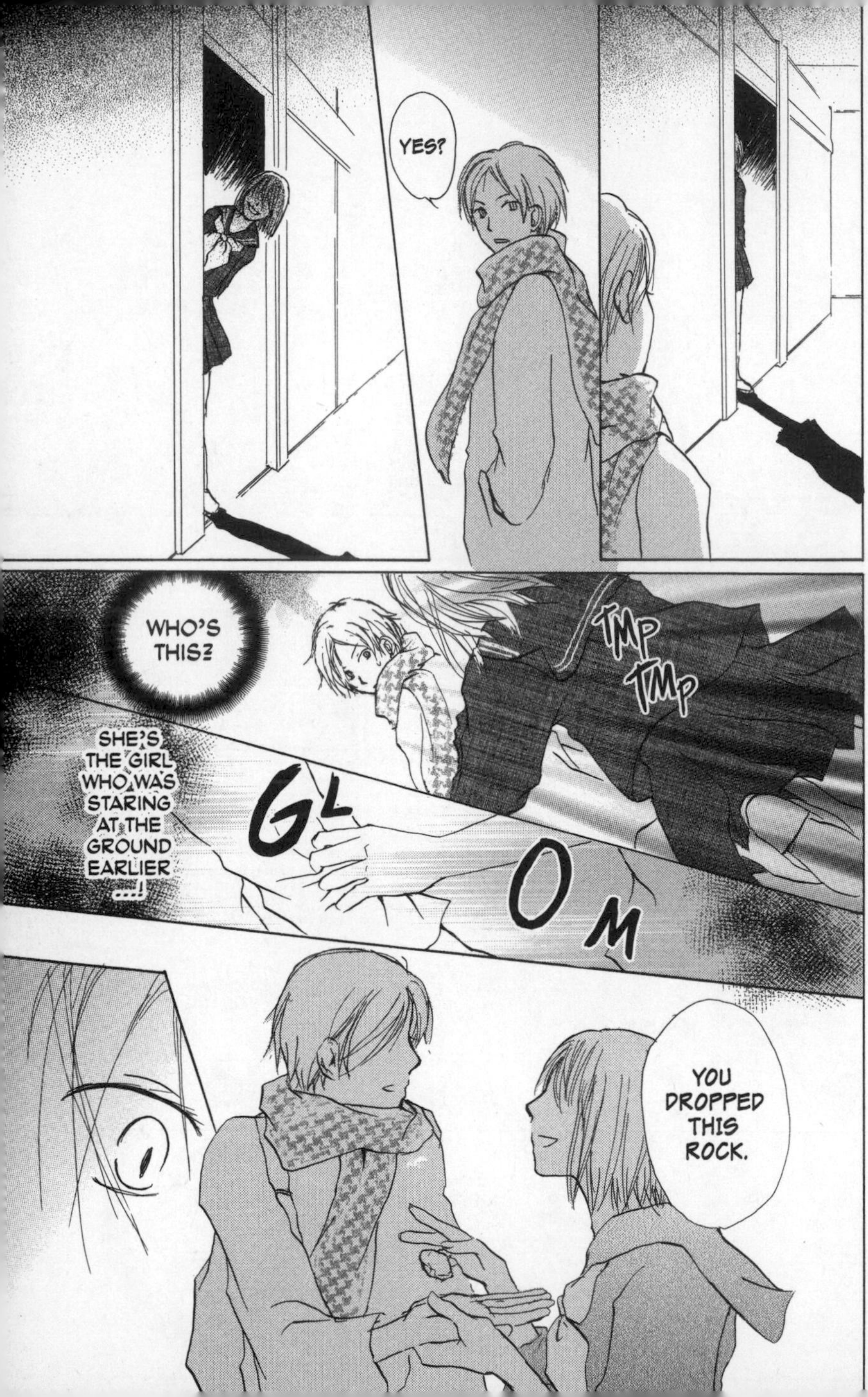
YES?
TMP TMP
WHO'S THIS?
SHE'S THE GIRL WHO WAS STARING AT THE GROUND EARLIER ...!
GLOOM
YOU DROPPED THIS ROCK.

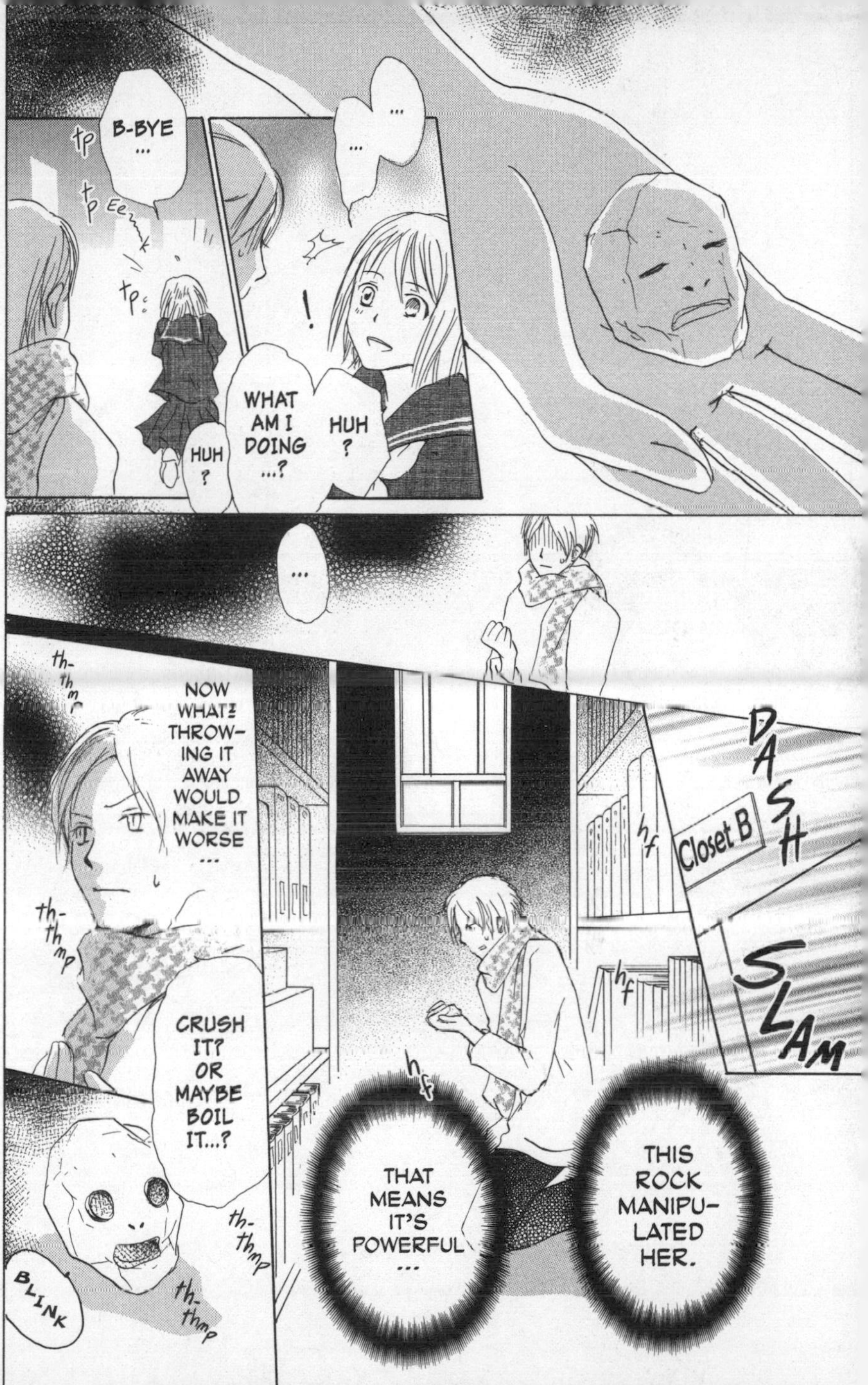
...
...
!
HUH ?
WHAT AM I DOING ...?
HUH ?
B-BYE ...
tp
tp Eeek
tp
...
DASH
Closet B
SLAM
hf
hf
THIS ROCK MANIPULATED HER.
THAT MEANS IT'S POWERFUL ...
hf
NOW WHAT? THROWING IT AWAY WOULD MAKE IT WORSE ...
th-thmp
th-thmp
CRUSH IT? OR MAYBE BOIL IT...?
th-thmp
th-thmp
BLINK

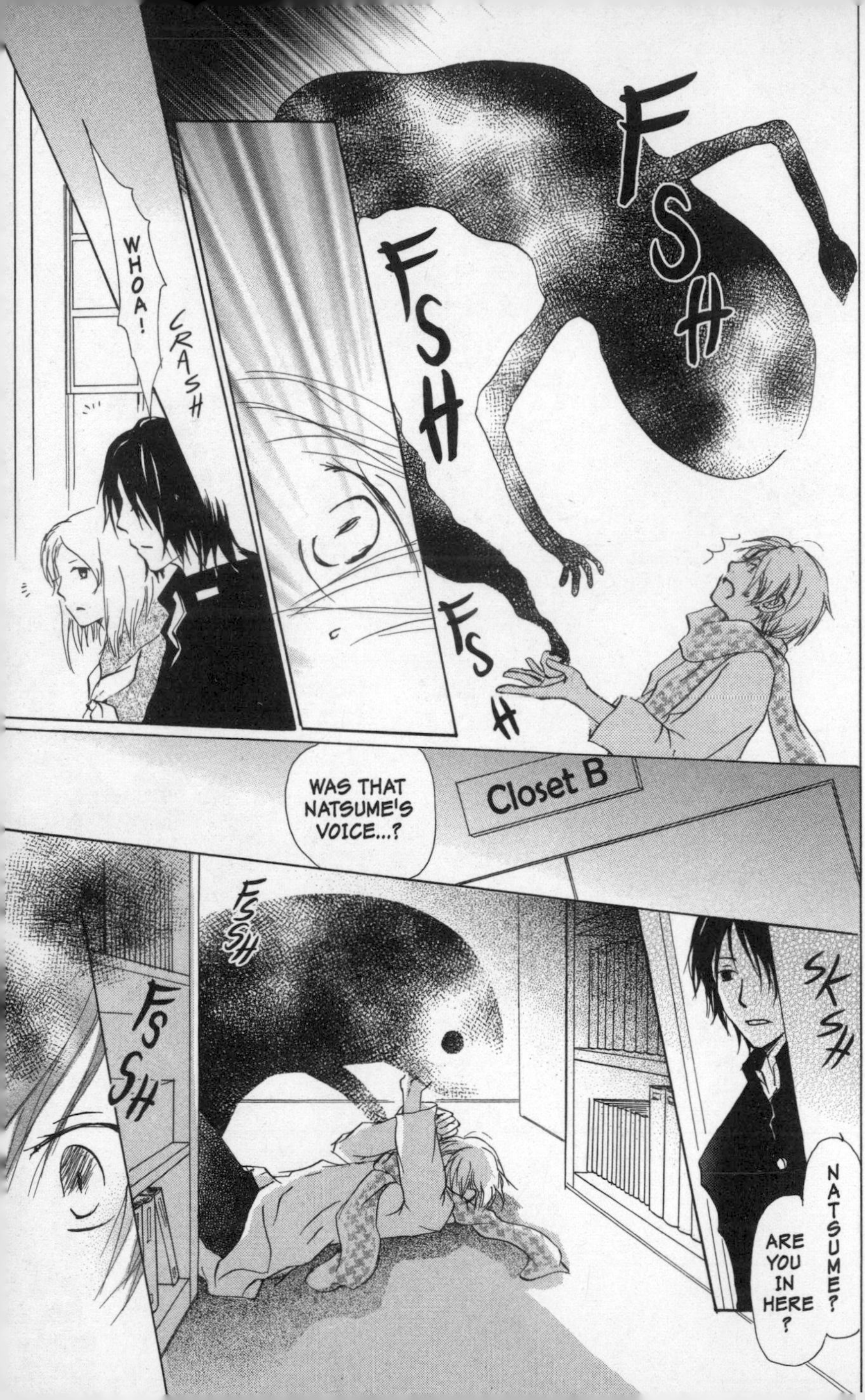
FSH
FSH
FSH
WHOA!
CRASH
Closet B
WAS THAT NATSUME'S VOICE...?
SKSH
NATSUME?
ARE YOU IN HERE?
FSSH
FSSH

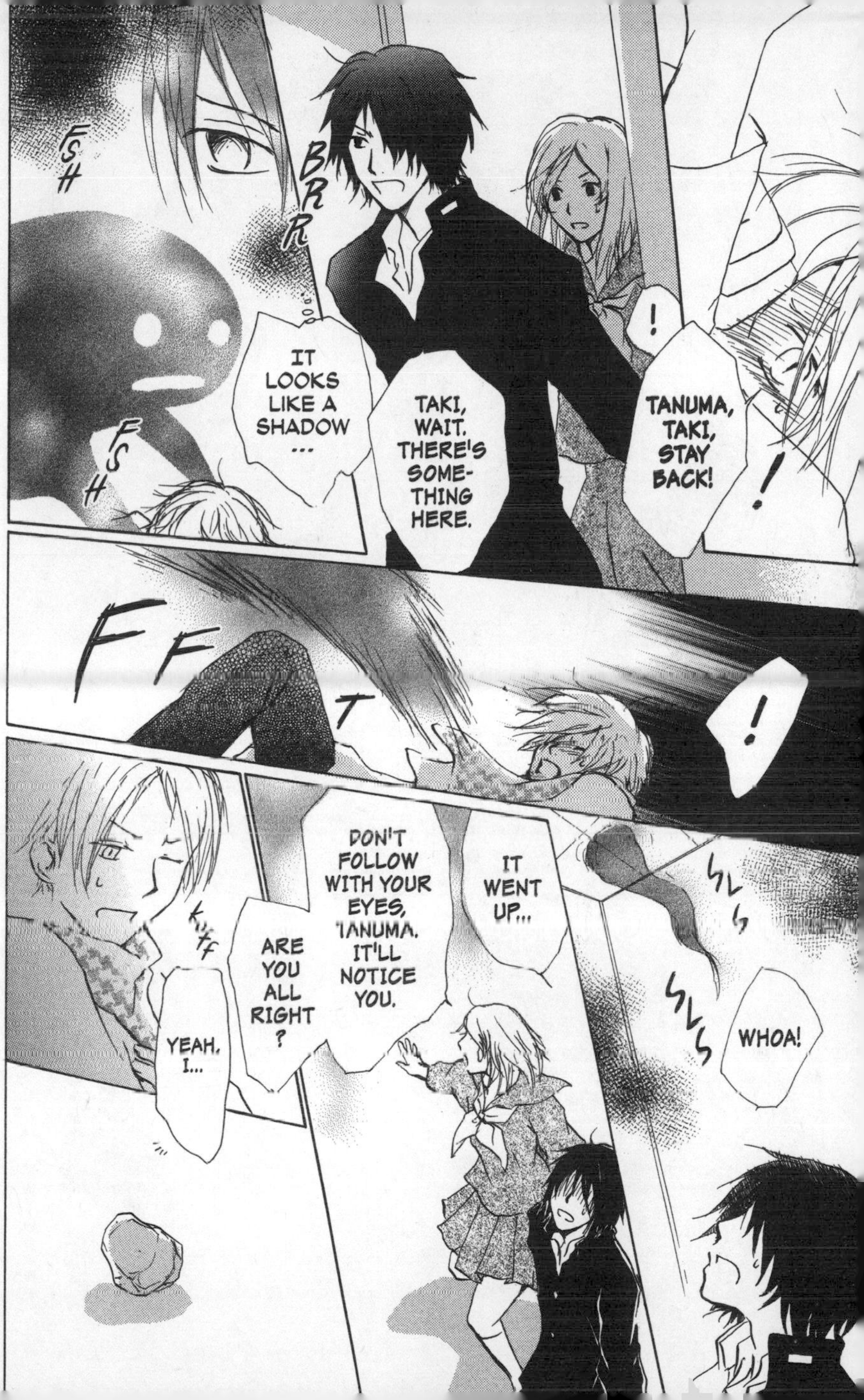
!
TANUMA, TAKI, STAY BACK!
!
TAKI, WAIT. THERE'S SOME-THING HERE.
IT LOOKS LIKE A SHADOW ...
BRR
FSH
FSH
!
T
FFF
WHOA!
SLS
SLS
IT WENT UP...
DON'T FOLLOW WITH YOUR EYES, TANUMA. IT'LL NOTICE YOU.
ARE YOU ALL RIGHT ?
KOFF
YEAH, I...

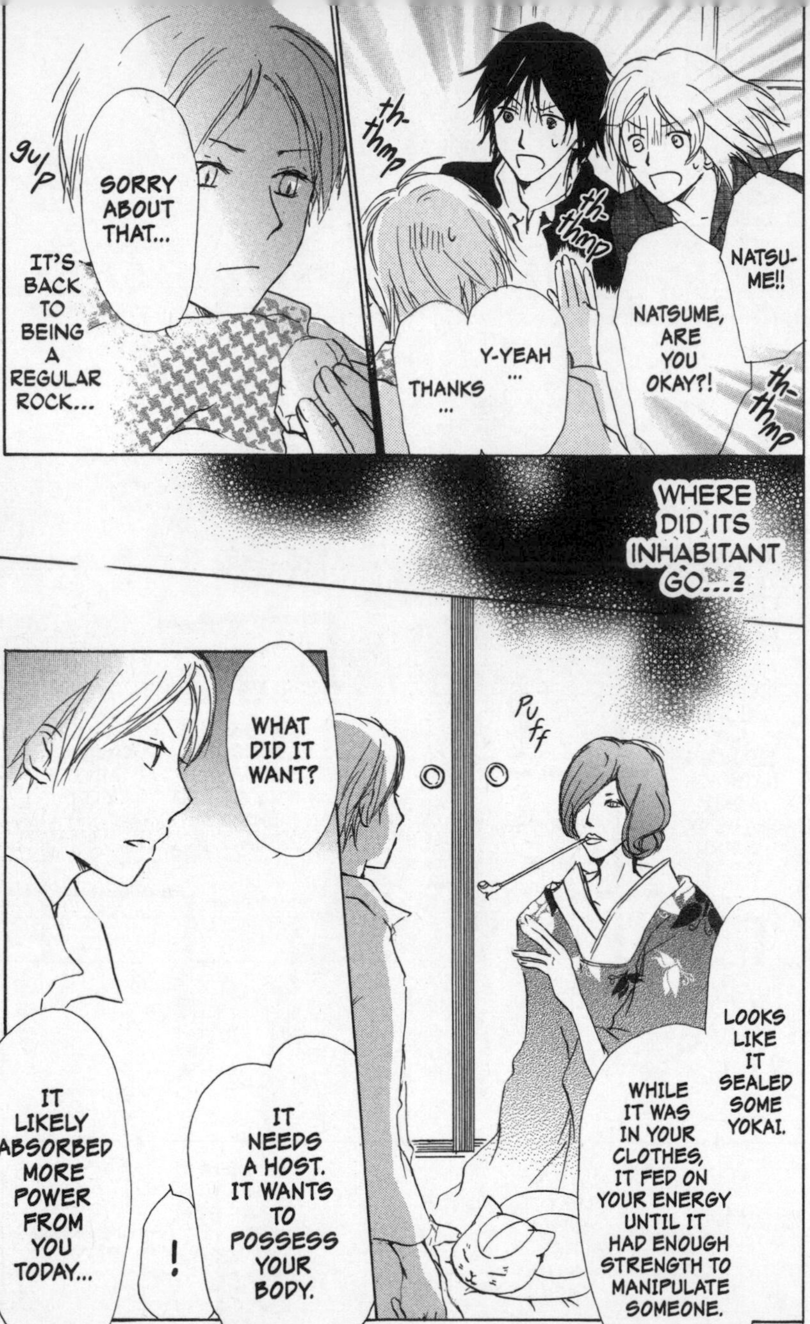
th-thmp
NATSUME!!
NATSUME, ARE YOU OKAY?!
th-thmp
th-thmp
Y-YEAH ...
THANKS ...
gulp
SORRY ABOUT THAT...
IT'S BACK TO BEING A REGULAR ROCK...
WHERE DID ITS INHABITANT GO...?
WHAT DID IT WANT?
Puff
LOOKS LIKE IT SEALED SOME YOKAI.
WHILE IT WAS IN YOUR CLOTHES, IT FED ON YOUR ENERGY UNTIL IT HAD ENOUGH STRENGTH TO MANIPULATE SOMEONE.
IT NEEDS A HOST. IT WANTS TO POSSESS YOUR BODY.
!
IT LIKELY ABSORBED MORE POWER FROM YOU TODAY...

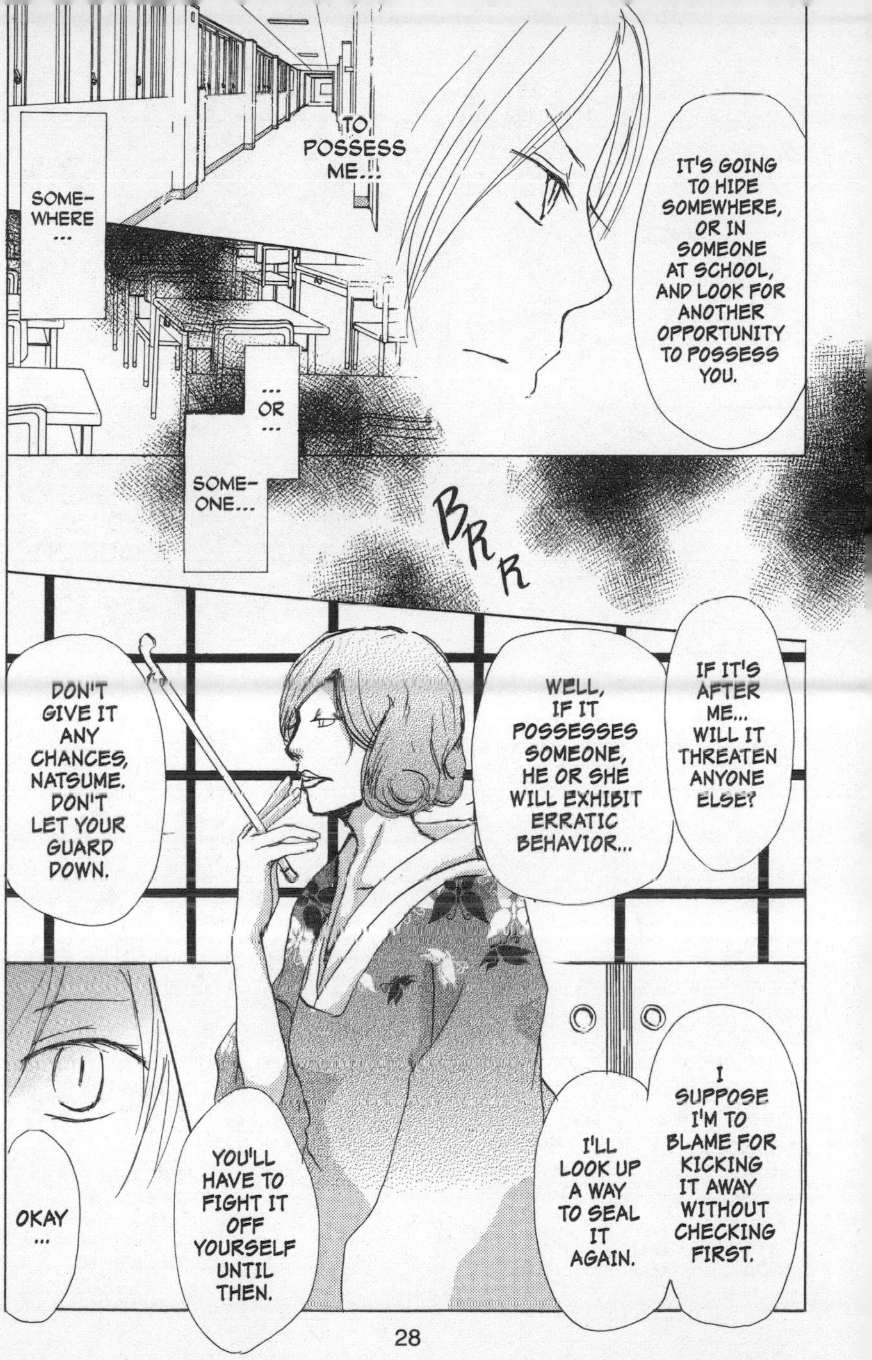
IT'S GOING TO HIDE SOMEWHERE, OR IN SOMEONE AT SCHOOL, AND LOOK FOR ANOTHER OPPORTUNITY TO POSSESS YOU.
TO POSSESS ME...
SOME-WHERE ...
... OR ...
SOME-ONE...
BRR
IF IT'S AFTER ME... WILL IT THREATEN ANYONE ELSE?
WELL, IF IT POSSESSES SOMEONE, HE OR SHE WILL EXHIBIT ERRATIC BEHAVIOR...
DON'T GIVE IT ANY CHANCES, NATSUME. DON'T LET YOUR GUARD DOWN.
I SUPPOSE I'M TO BLAME FOR KICKING IT AWAY WITHOUT CHECKING FIRST.
I'LL LOOK UP A WAY TO SEAL IT AGAIN.
YOU'LL HAVE TO FIGHT IT OFF YOURSELF UNTIL THEN.
OKAY ...

THANKS, HINOE.
Later.
PZZ PZZ
SIGH...
SENSEI.
OUR SCHOOL IS HAVING A CULTURE FESTIVAL.
I'M GOING TO BE A CLERK IN A BAZAAR.
THERE'LL BE A LOT OF SHOWS, BOOTHS AND CAFÉS. I'M SURE IT'LL BE FUN.

01

Hello, I'm Midorikawa. This is my 16th total graphic novel, and the eighth for Natsume.

It was my fervent wish for it to somehow be longer than three volumes. I'm so happy that it's been able to go on for so long.

I'd like to thank all my readers and everyone in the editorial department. I'll continue to craft each episode with care.

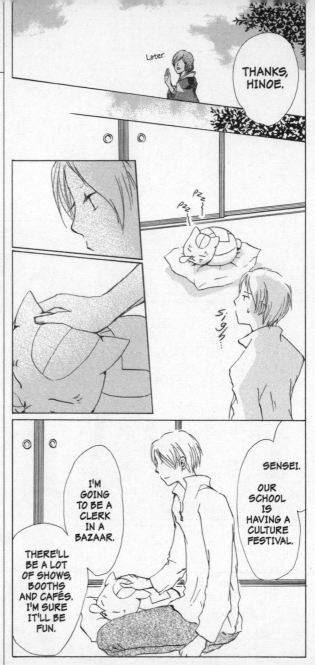

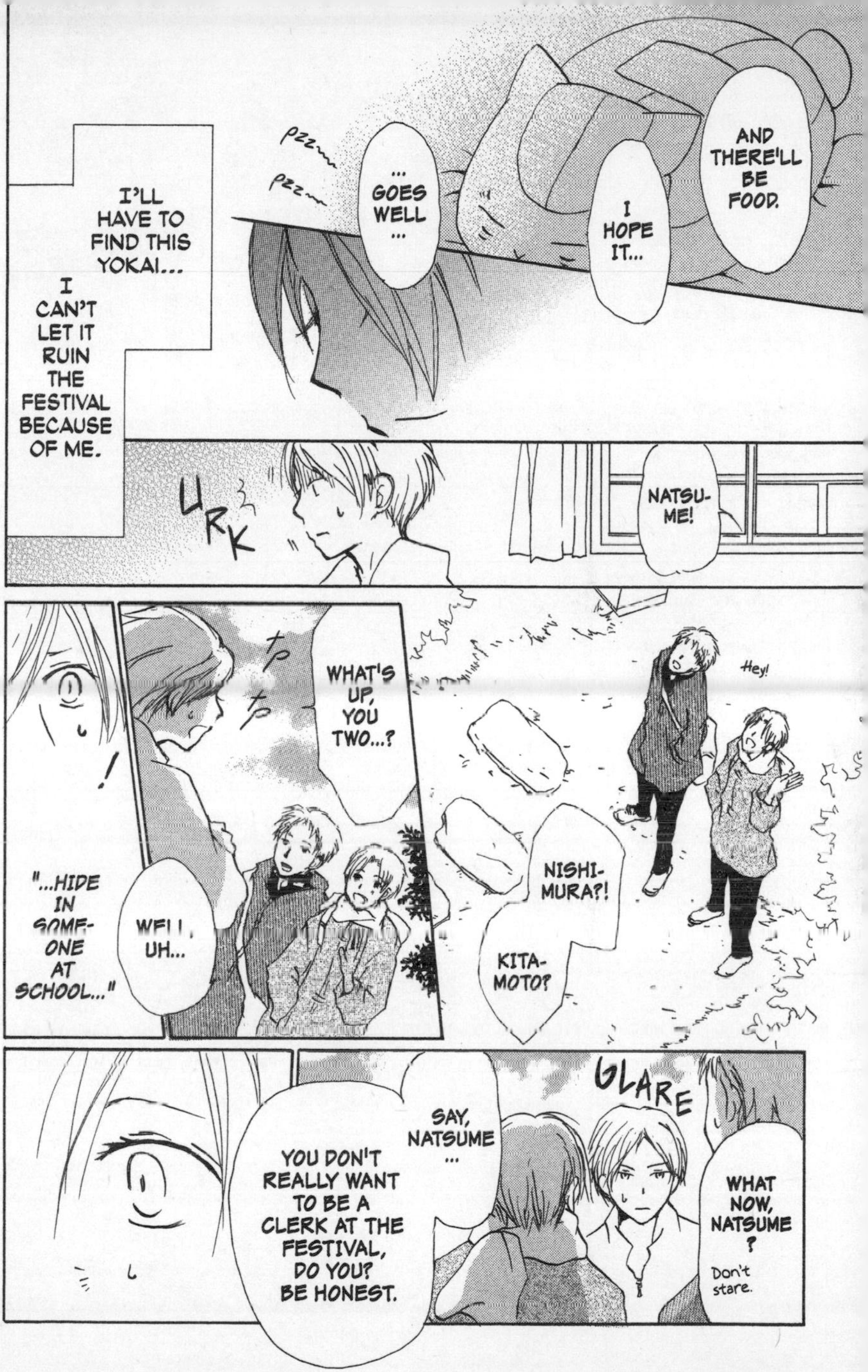
AND THERE'LL BE FOOD.
I HOPE IT...
... GOES WELL ...
pzz~ pzz~
I'LL HAVE TO FIND THIS YOKAI...
I CAN'T LET IT RUIN THE FESTIVAL BECAUSE OF ME.
NATSU-ME!
URK
Hey!
NISHI-MURA?!
KITA-MOTO?
WHAT'S UP, YOU TWO...?
WELL, UH...
"...HIDE IN SOME-ONE AT SCHOOL..."
GLARE
WHAT NOW, NATSUME?
Don't stare.
SAY, NATSUME...
YOU DON'T REALLY WANT TO BE A CLERK AT THE FESTIVAL, DO YOU? BE HONEST.

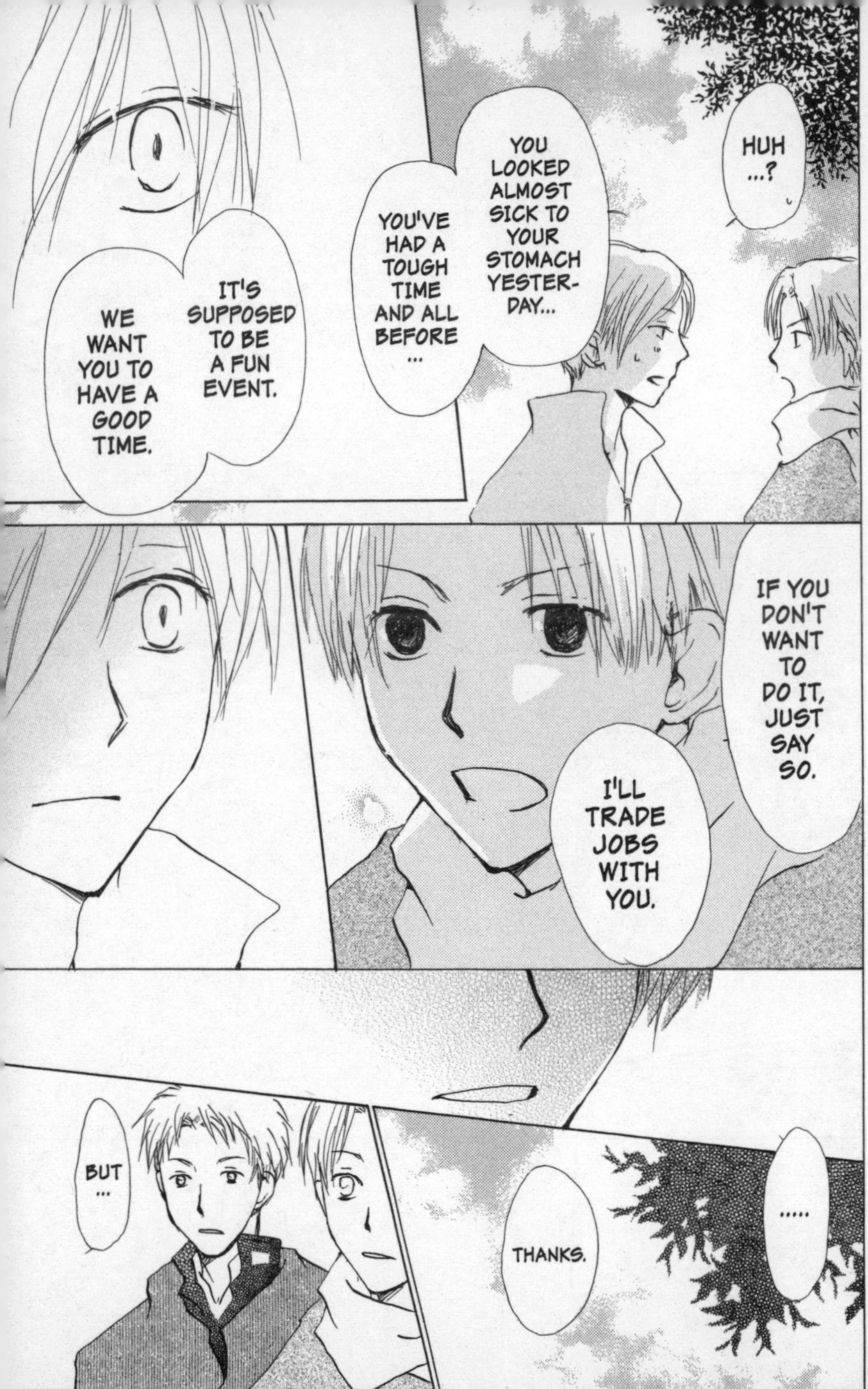
HUH ...?
YOU LOOKED ALMOST SICK TO YOUR STOMACH YESTER-DAY...
YOU'VE HAD A TOUGH TIME AND ALL BEFORE ...
IT'S SUPPOSED TO BE A FUN EVENT.
WE WANT YOU TO HAVE A GOOD TIME.
IF YOU DON'T WANT TO DO IT, JUST SAY SO.
I'LL TRADE JOBS WITH YOU.
.....
THANKS.
BUT ...

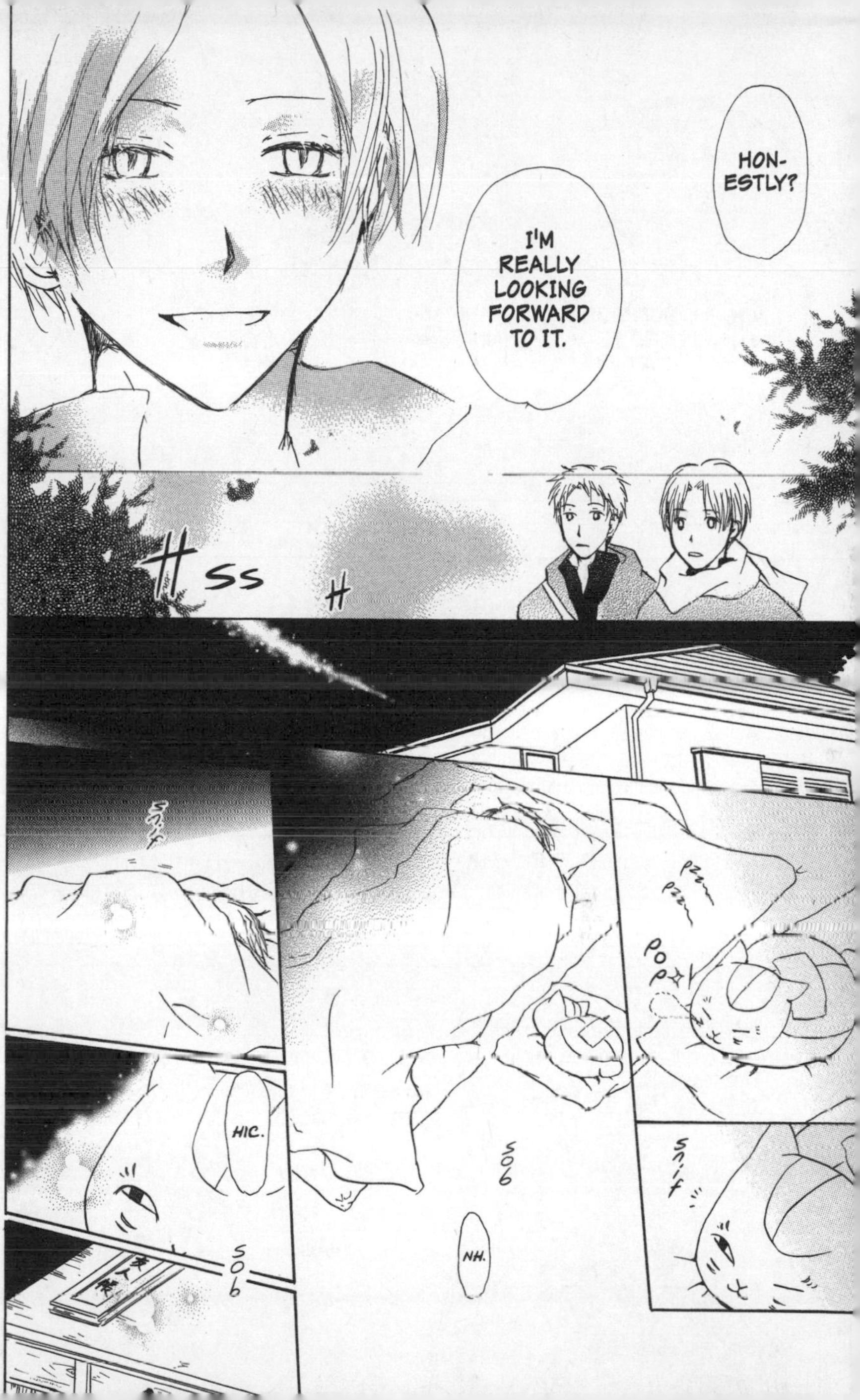
HON-ESTLY?
I'M REALLY LOOKING FORWARD TO IT.
HSS
H
pzz
pzz
POP
sniff
sob
NH.
sniff
HIC.
sob

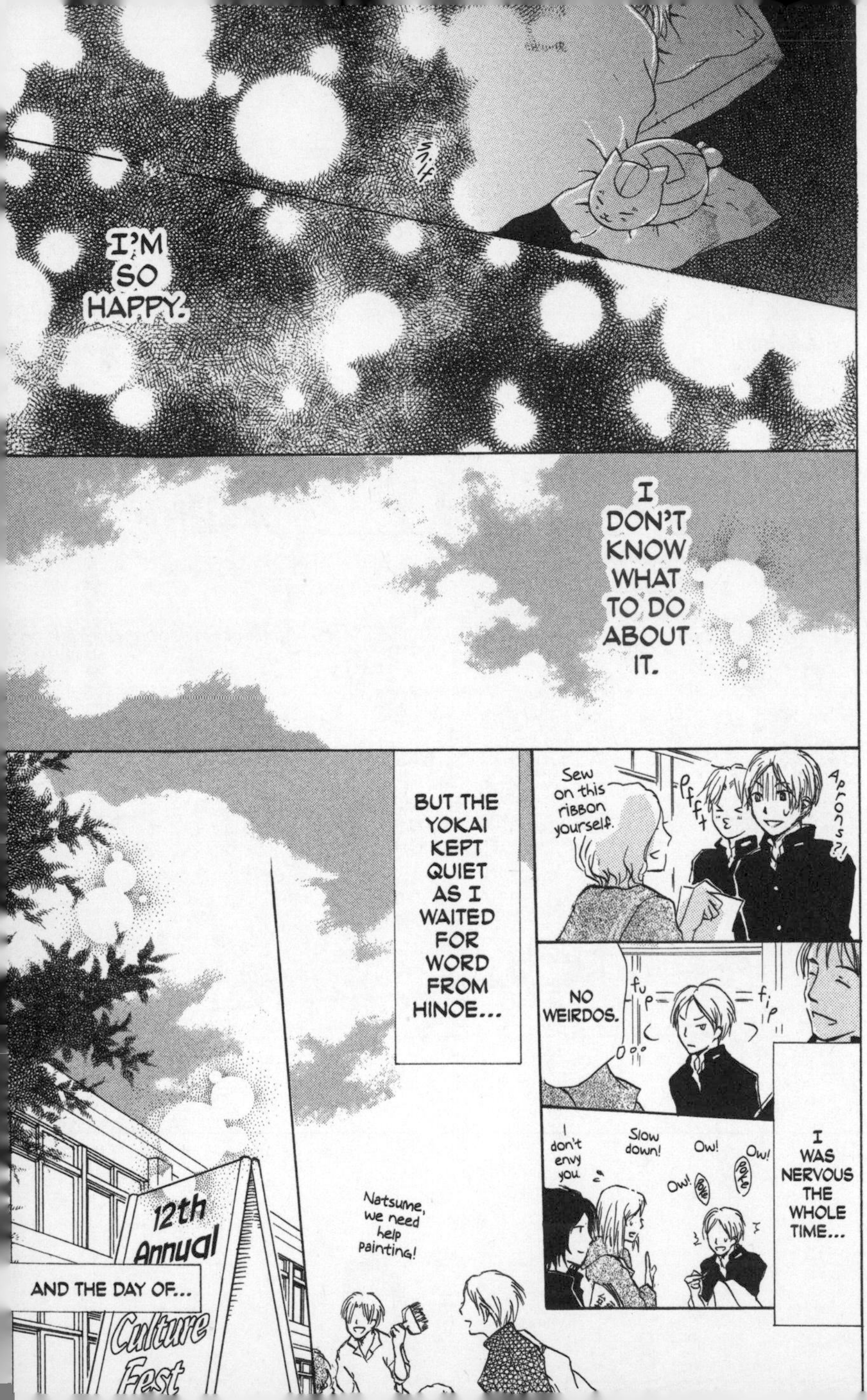
snif
I'M SO HAPPY.
I DON'T KNOW WHAT TO DO ABOUT IT.
Aprons?!
pffft
Sew on this ribbon yourself.
fip
NO WEIRDOS.
fup
I WAS NERVOUS THE WHOLE TIME...
Ow!
Ow!
Slow down!
I don't envy you.
BUT THE YOKAI KEPT QUIET AS I WAITED FOR WORD FROM HINOE...
Natsume, we need help painting!
12th Annual Culture Fest
AND THE DAY OF...

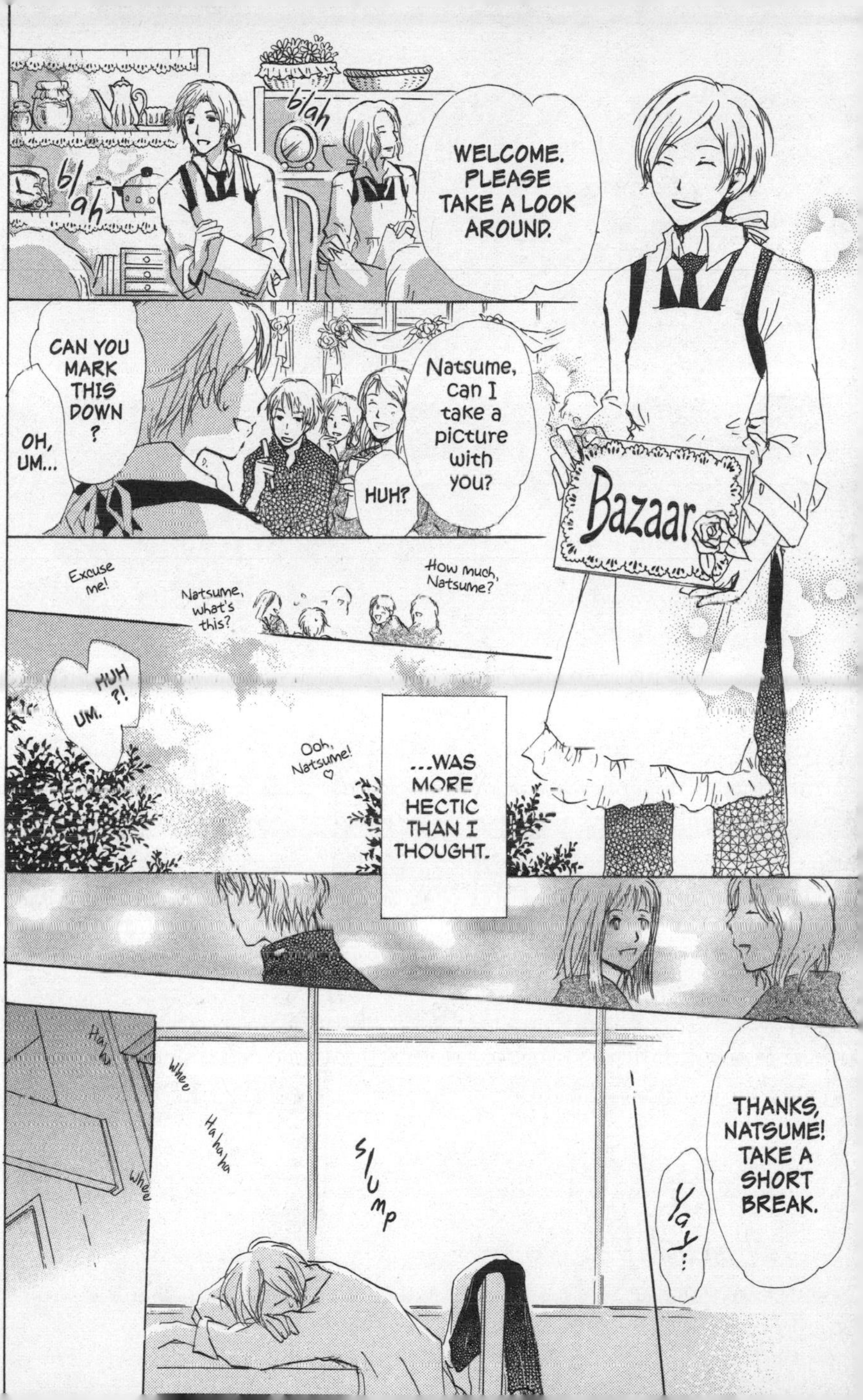
WELCOME. PLEASE TAKE A LOOK AROUND.
Bazaar
blah
blah
Natsume, can I take a picture with you?
HUH?
CAN YOU MARK THIS DOWN?
OH, UM...
How much, Natsume?
Natsume, what's this?
Excuse me!
Ooh, Natsume! ♡
HUH ?!
UM.
...WAS MORE HECTIC THAN I THOUGHT.
THANKS, NATSUME! TAKE A SHORT BREAK.
Yay...
slump
Hahaha
whee
Haha
whee

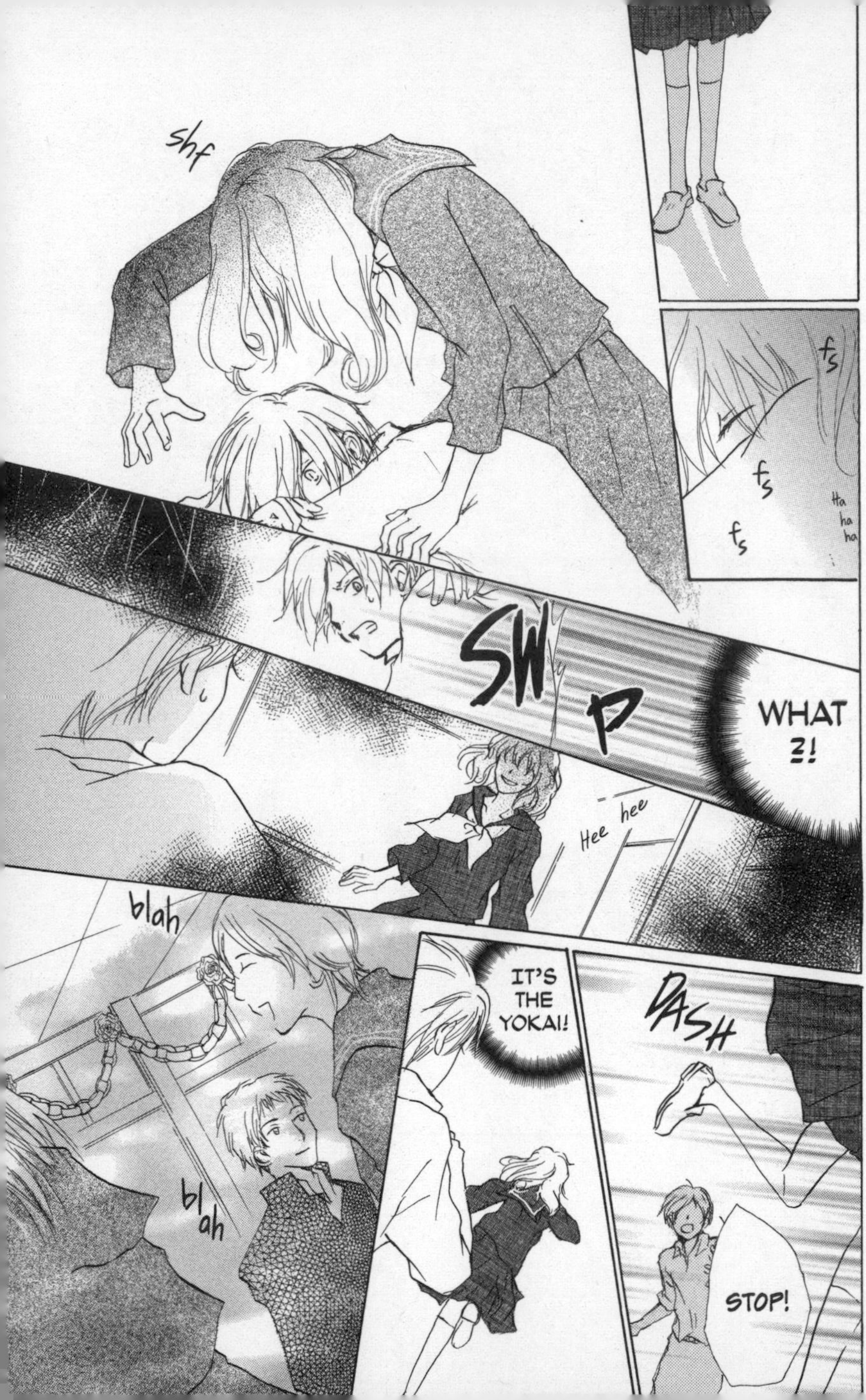
fs
fs
fs
Ha ha ha
shf
SWIP
WHAT?!
Hee hee
DASH
STOP!
IT'S THE YOKAI!
blah
blah

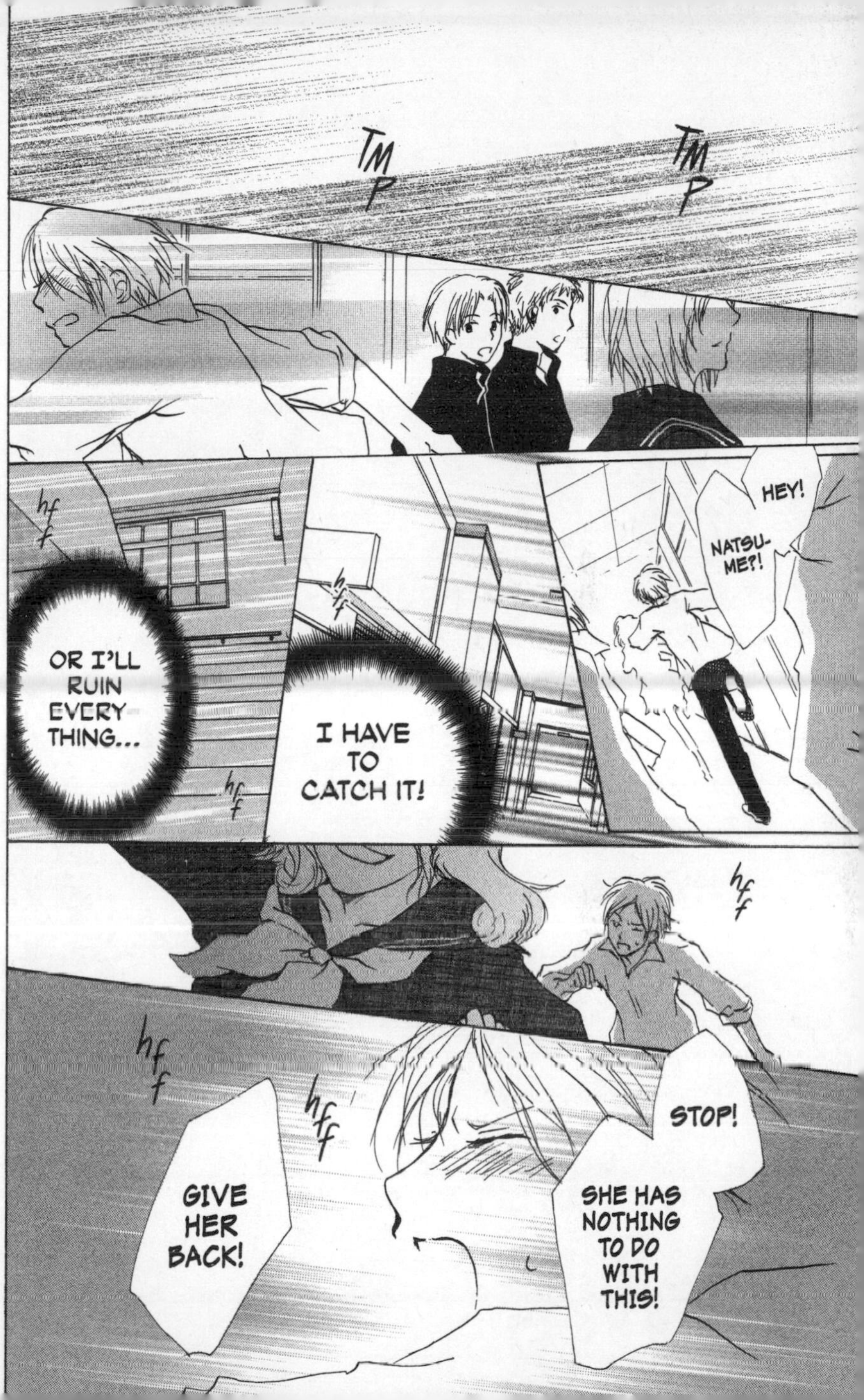
TMP
TMP
HEY!
NATSU-ME?!
hff
I HAVE TO CATCH IT!
hff
OR I'LL RUIN EVERY-THING...
hff
hff
STOP!
SHE HAS NOTHING TO DO WITH THIS!
hff
GIVE HER BACK!
hff

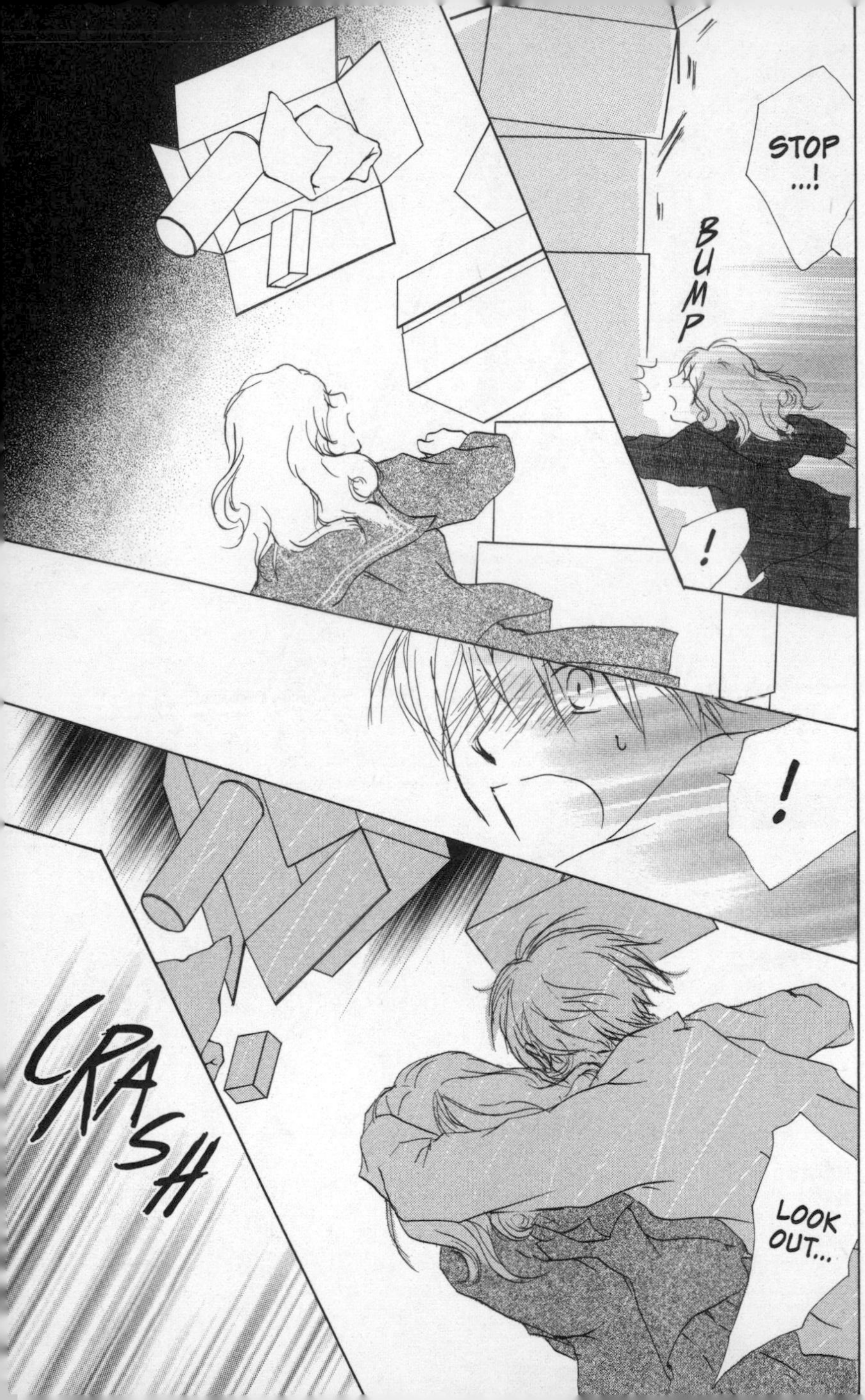
STOP ...!
BUMP
!
!
LOOK OUT...
CRASH

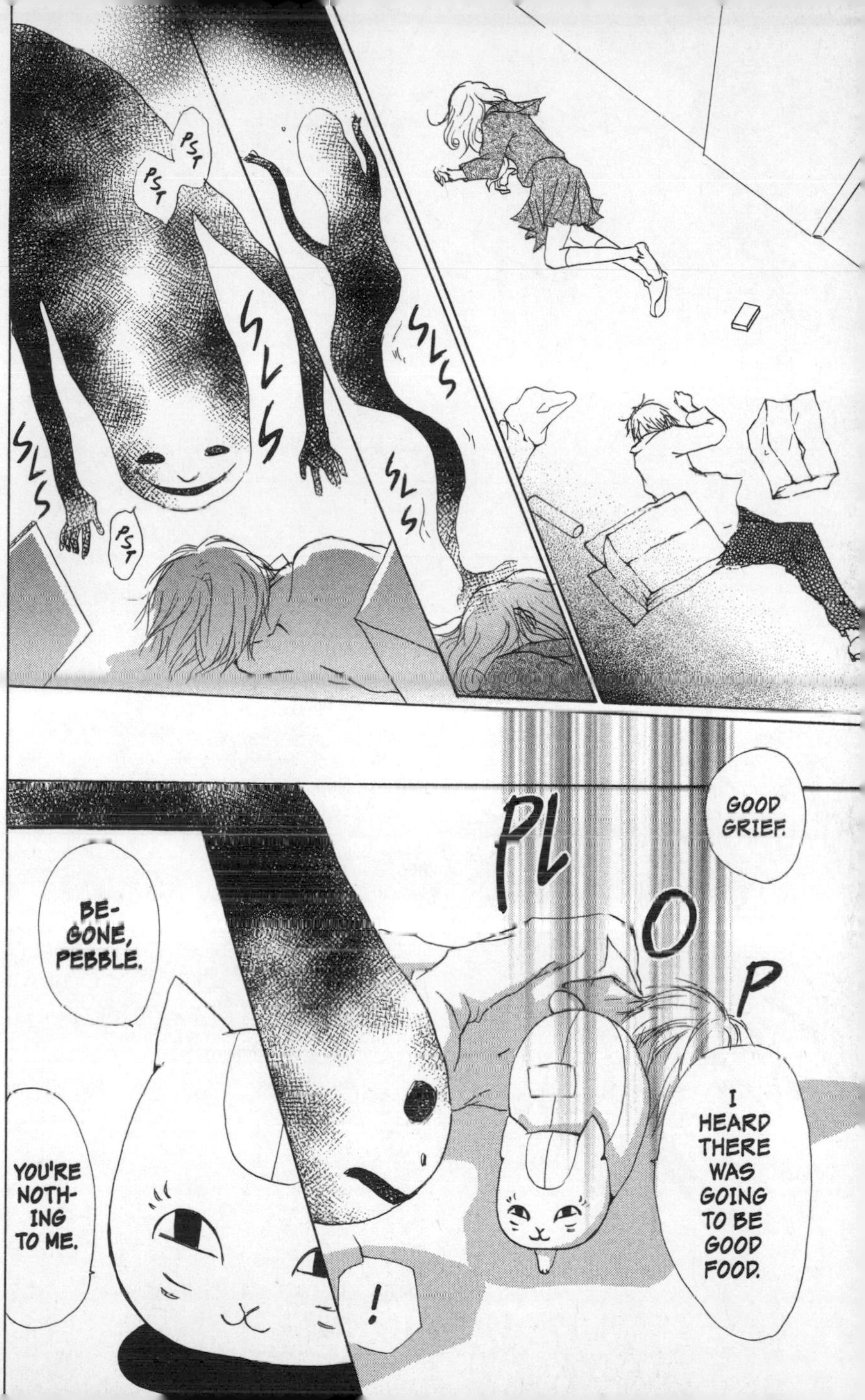

SLS
SLS
PST
PST
SLS
SLS
PST
GOOD GRIEF.
PLOP
I HEARD THERE WAS GOING TO BE GOOD FOOD.
!
BE-GONE, PEBBLE.
YOU'RE NOTHING-ING TO ME.

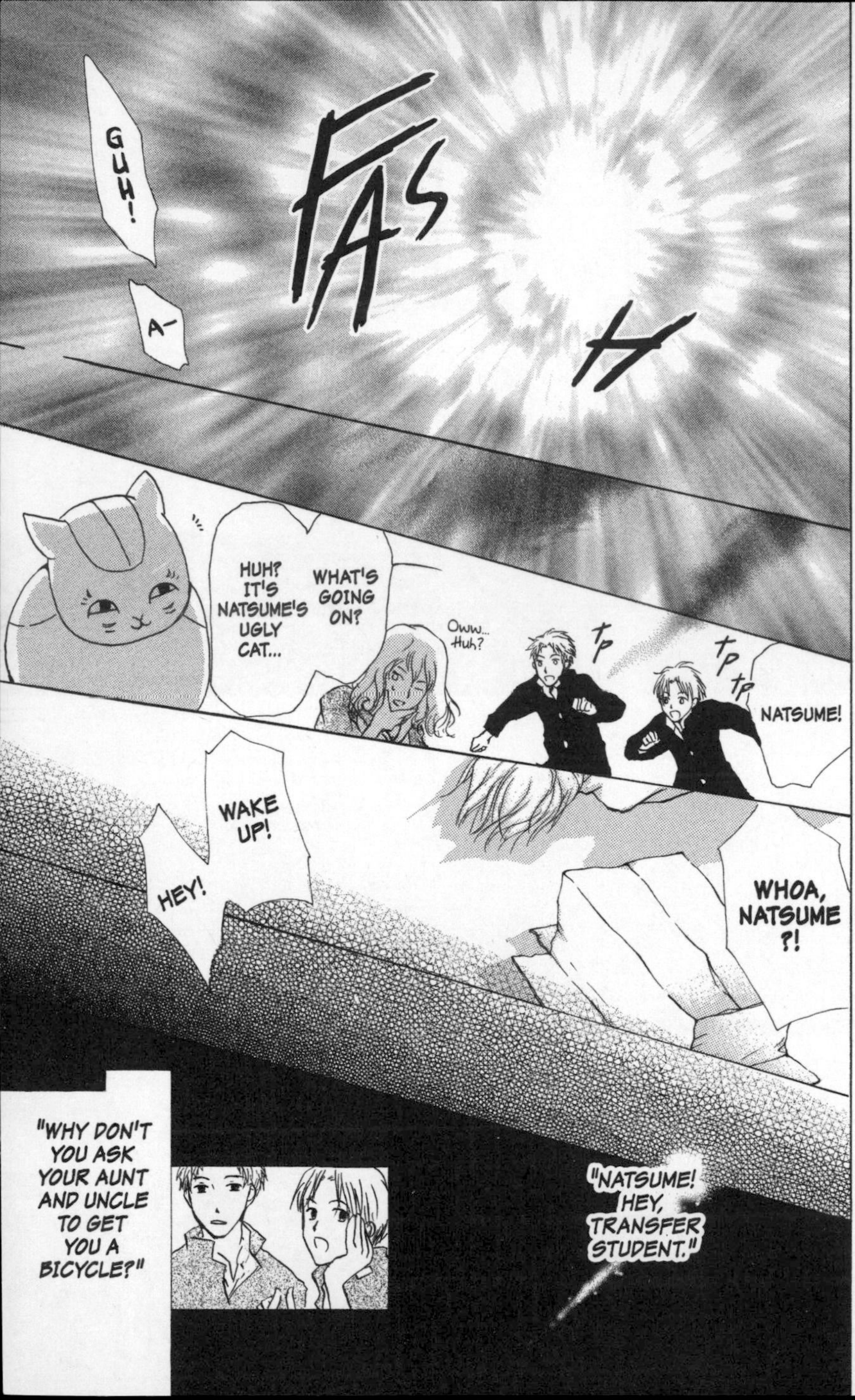
FASH
GUH!
A-
NATSUME!
TP TP
TP
Oww... Huh?
WHAT'S GOING ON?
HUH? IT'S NATSUME'S UGLY CAT...
WHOA, NATSUME?!
WAKE UP!
HEY!
"NATSUME! HEY, TRANSFER STUDENT."
"WHY DON'T YOU ASK YOUR AUNT AND UNCLE TO GET YOU A BICYCLE?"

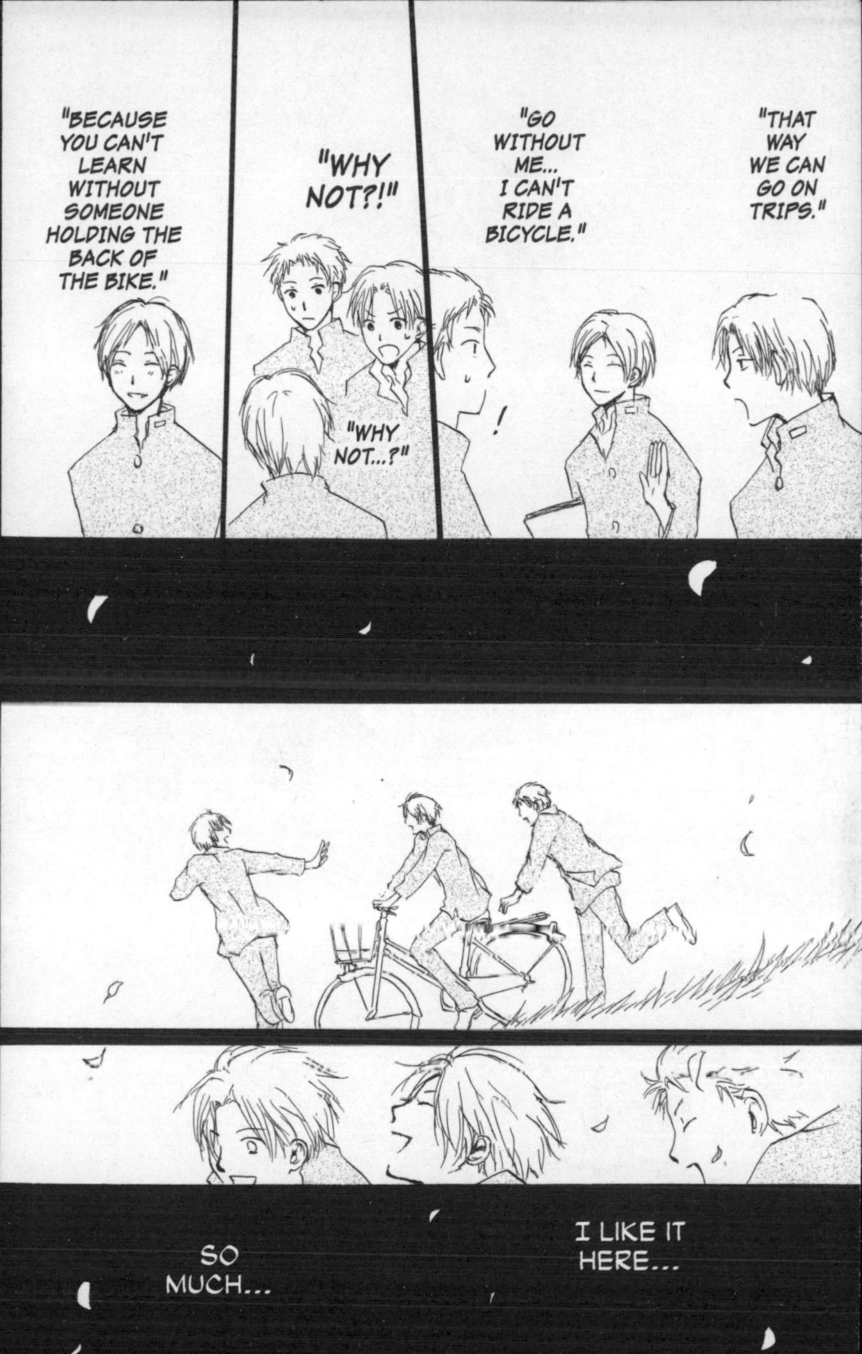
"THAT WAY WE CAN GO ON TRIPS."
"GO WITHOUT ME... I CAN'T RIDE A BICYCLE."
"WHY NOT?!"
"WHY NOT...?"
"BECAUSE YOU CAN'T LEARN WITHOUT SOMEONE HOLDING THE BACK OF THE BIKE."
I LIKE IT HERE...
SO MUCH...

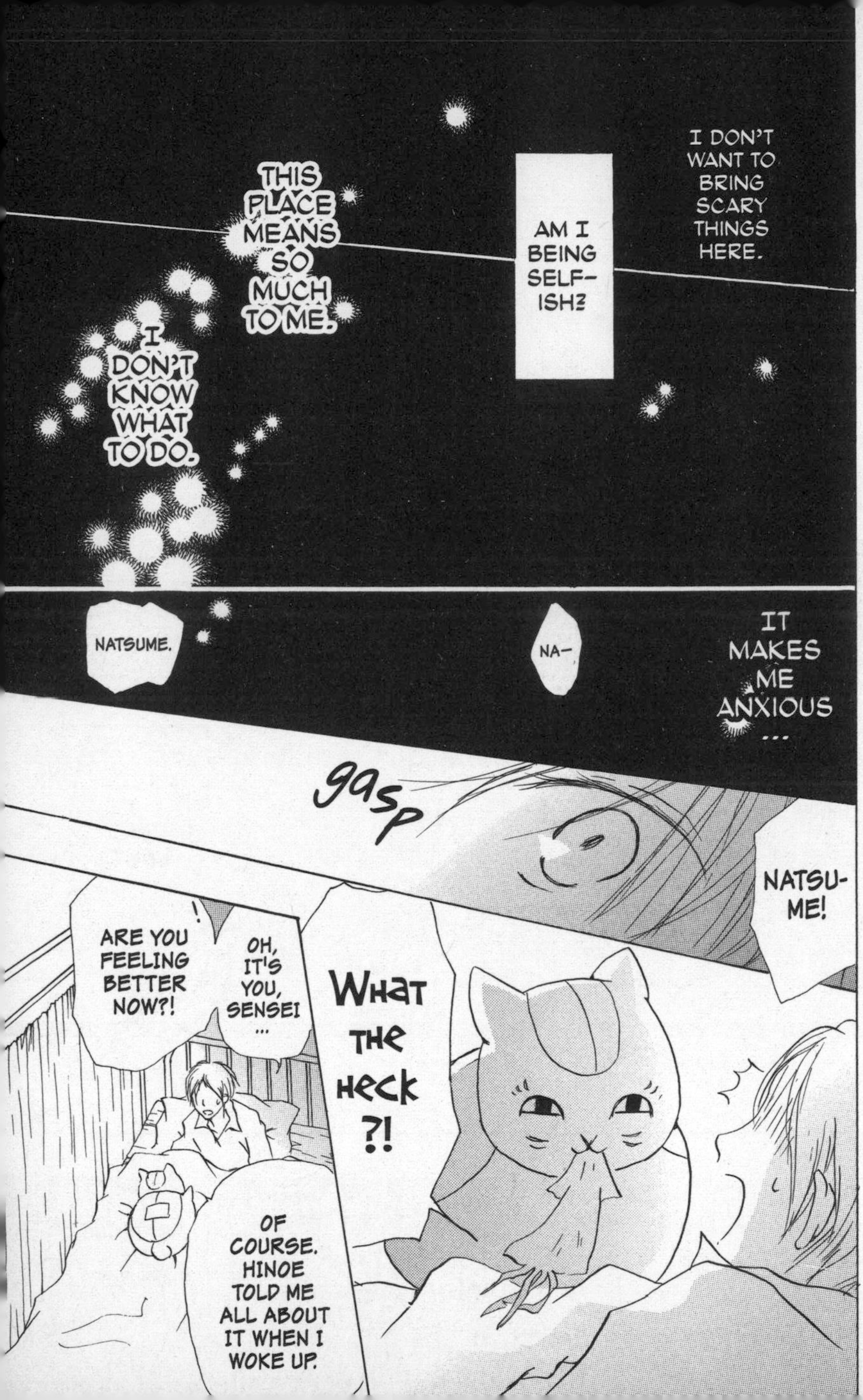
I DON'T WANT TO BRING SCARY THINGS HERE.
AM I BEING SELF-ISH?
THIS PLACE MEANS SO MUCH TO ME.
I DON'T KNOW WHAT TO DO.
IT MAKES ME ANXIOUS...
NA-
NATSUME.
gasp
NATSU-ME!
WHAT THE HECK?!
OH, IT'S YOU, SENSEI...
!
ARE YOU FEELING BETTER NOW?!
OF COURSE. HINOE TOLD ME ALL ABOUT IT WHEN I WOKE UP.

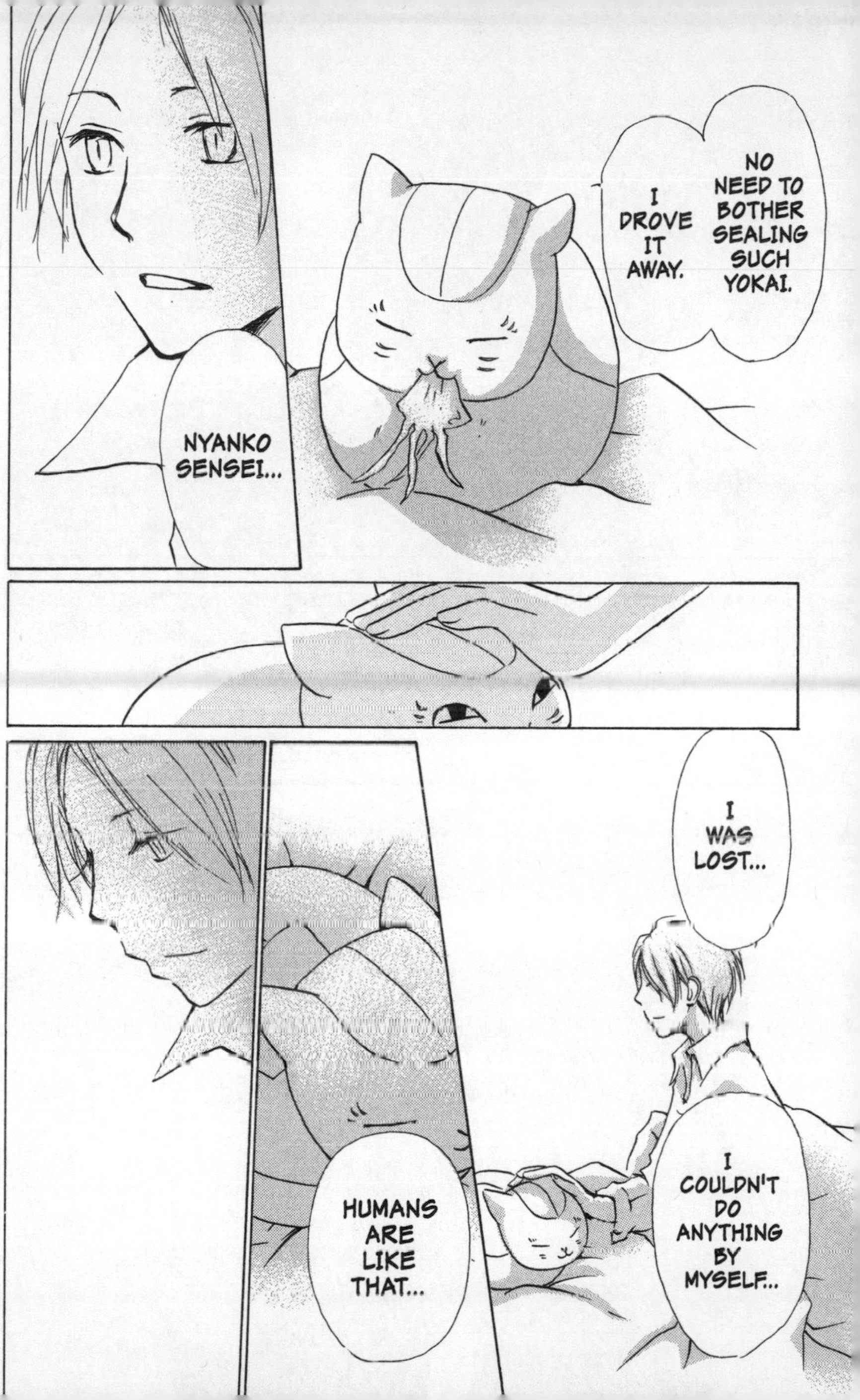
I DROVE IT AWAY. NO NEED TO BOTHER SEALING SUCH YOKAI.
NYANKO SENSEI...
I WAS LOST...
I COULDN'T DO ANYTHING BY MYSELF...
HUMANS ARE LIKE THAT...

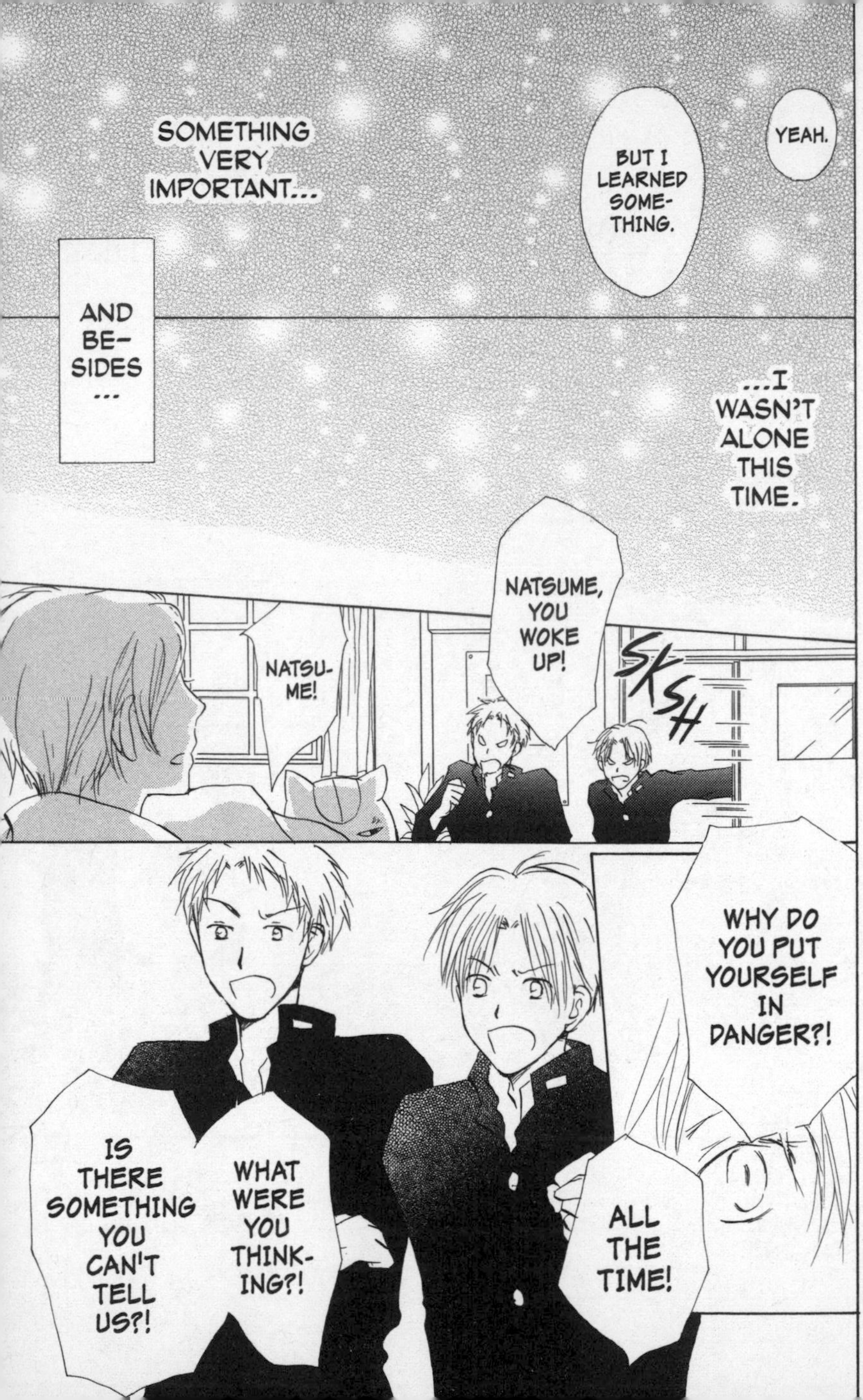
YEAH.
BUT I LEARNED SOME-THING.
SOMETHING VERY IMPORTANT...
AND BE-SIDES...
...I WASN'T ALONE THIS TIME.
SKSH
NATSUME, YOU WOKE UP!
NATSU-ME!
WHY DO YOU PUT YOURSELF IN DANGER?!
ALL THE TIME!
WHAT WERE YOU THINKING?!
IS THERE SOMETHING YOU CAN'T TELL US?!

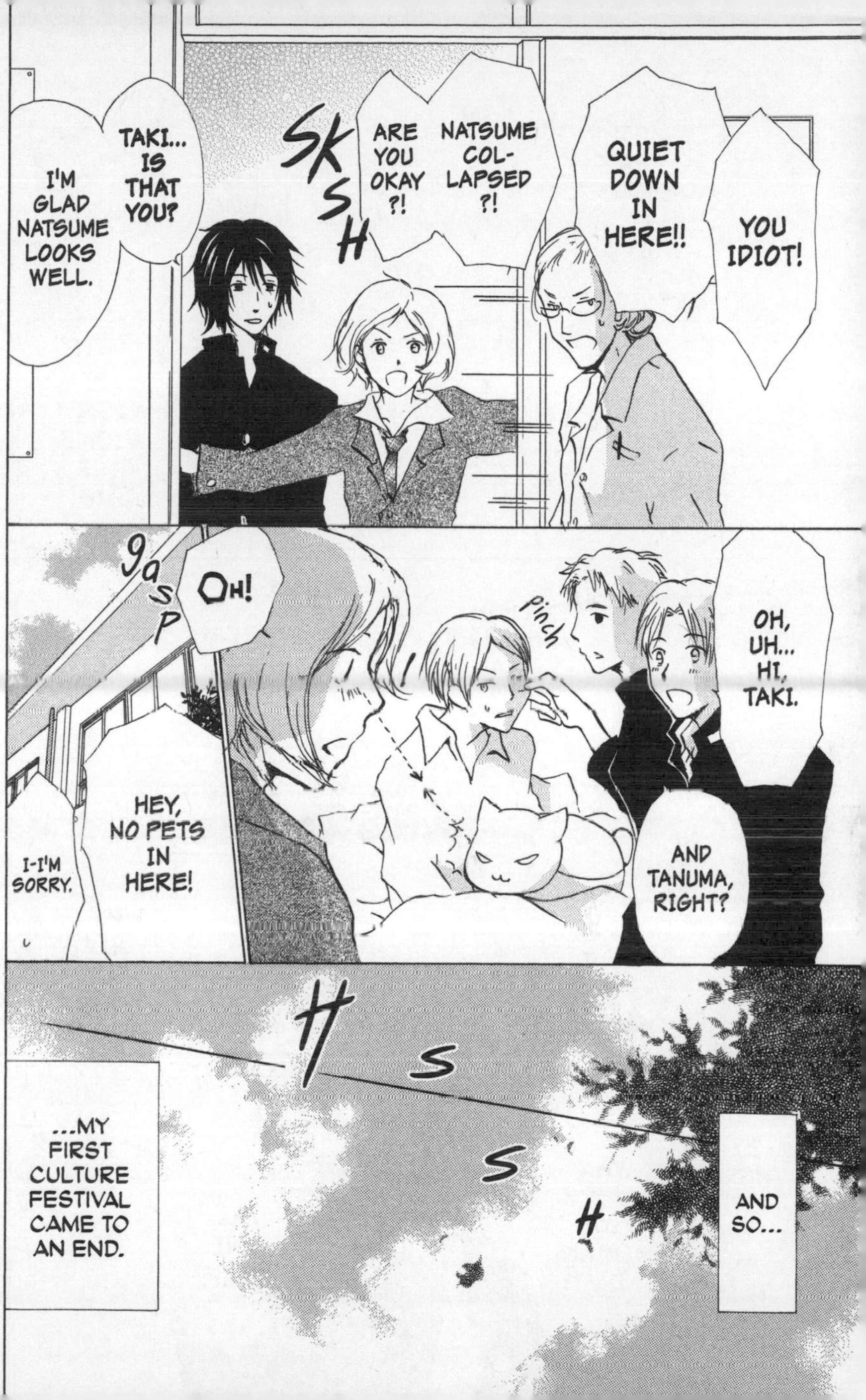
YOU IDIOT!
QUIET DOWN IN HERE!!
NATSUME COL-LAPSED ?!
ARE YOU OKAY ?!
SKSH
TAKI... IS THAT YOU?
I'M GLAD NATSUME LOOKS WELL.
OH, UH... HI, TAKI.
AND TANUMA, RIGHT?
pinch
OH!
gasp
HEY, NO PETS IN HERE!
I-I'M SORRY.
AND SO...
HSSH
...MY FIRST CULTURE FESTIVAL CAME TO AN END.

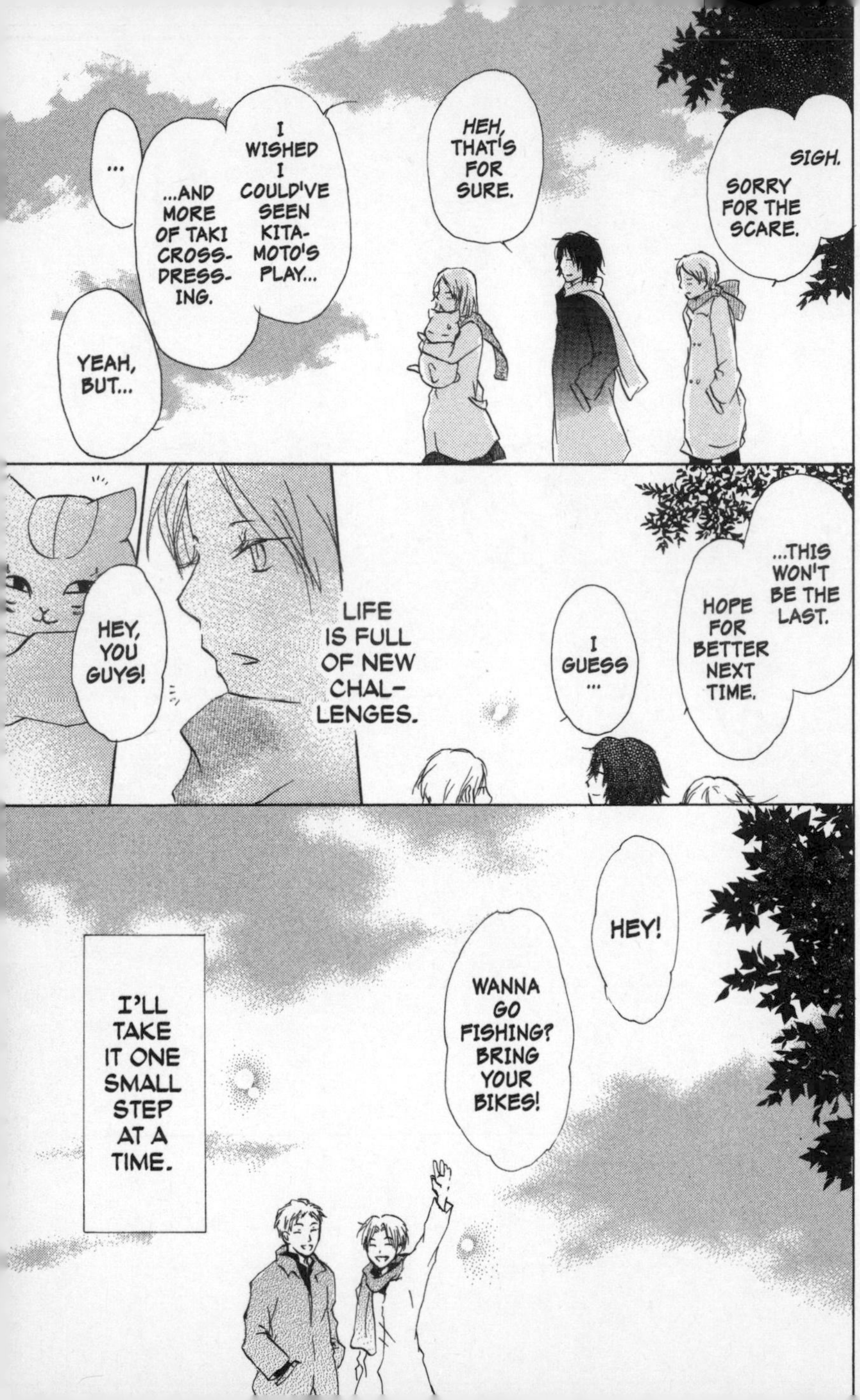
SIGH.
SORRY FOR THE SCARE.
HEH, THAT'S FOR SURE.
I WISHED I COULD'VE SEEN KITA-MOTO'S PLAY...
...AND MORE OF TAKI CROSS-DRESS-ING.
...
YEAH, BUT...
...THIS WON'T BE THE LAST.
HOPE FOR BETTER NEXT TIME.
I GUESS...
LIFE IS FULL OF NEW CHAL-LENGES.
HEY, YOU GUYS!
HEY!
WANNA GO FISHING? BRING YOUR BIKES!
I'LL TAKE IT ONE SMALL STEP AT A TIME.

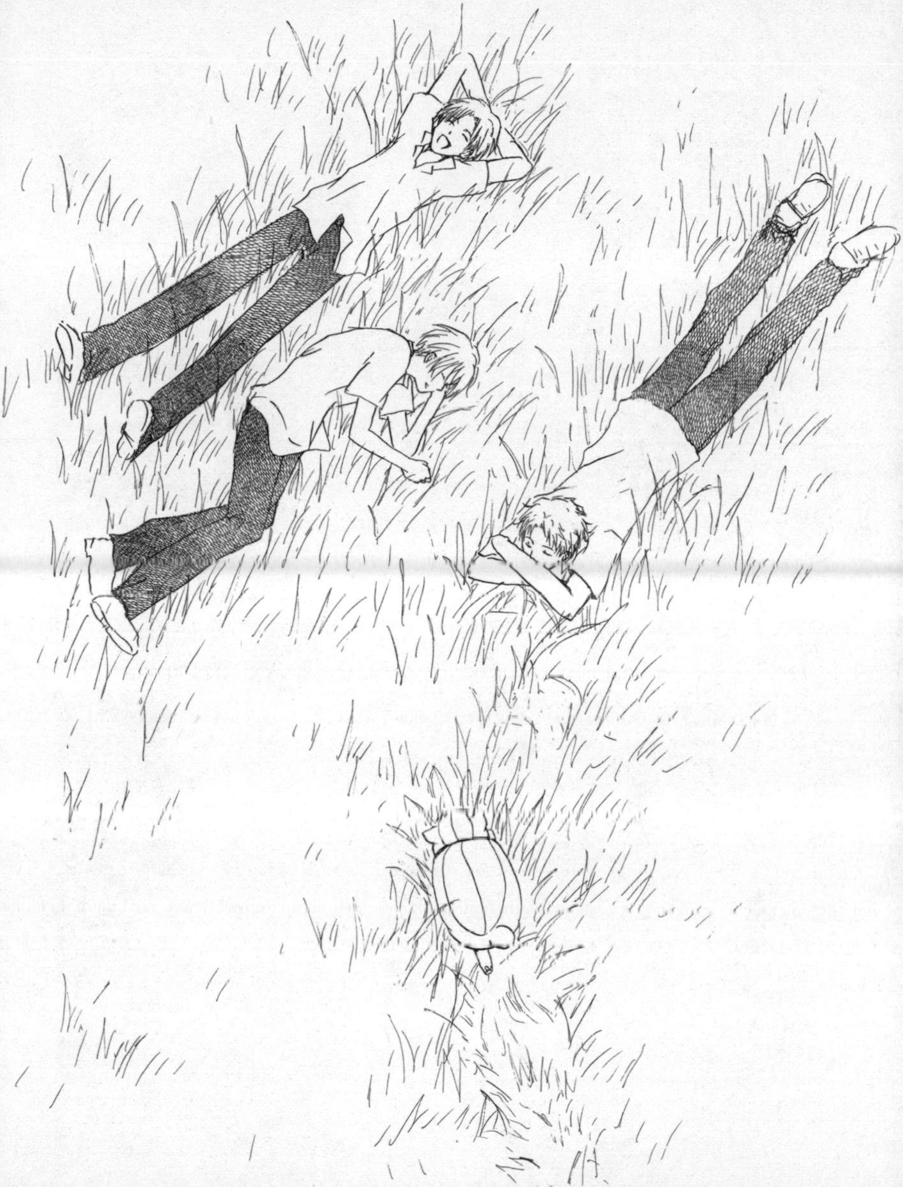

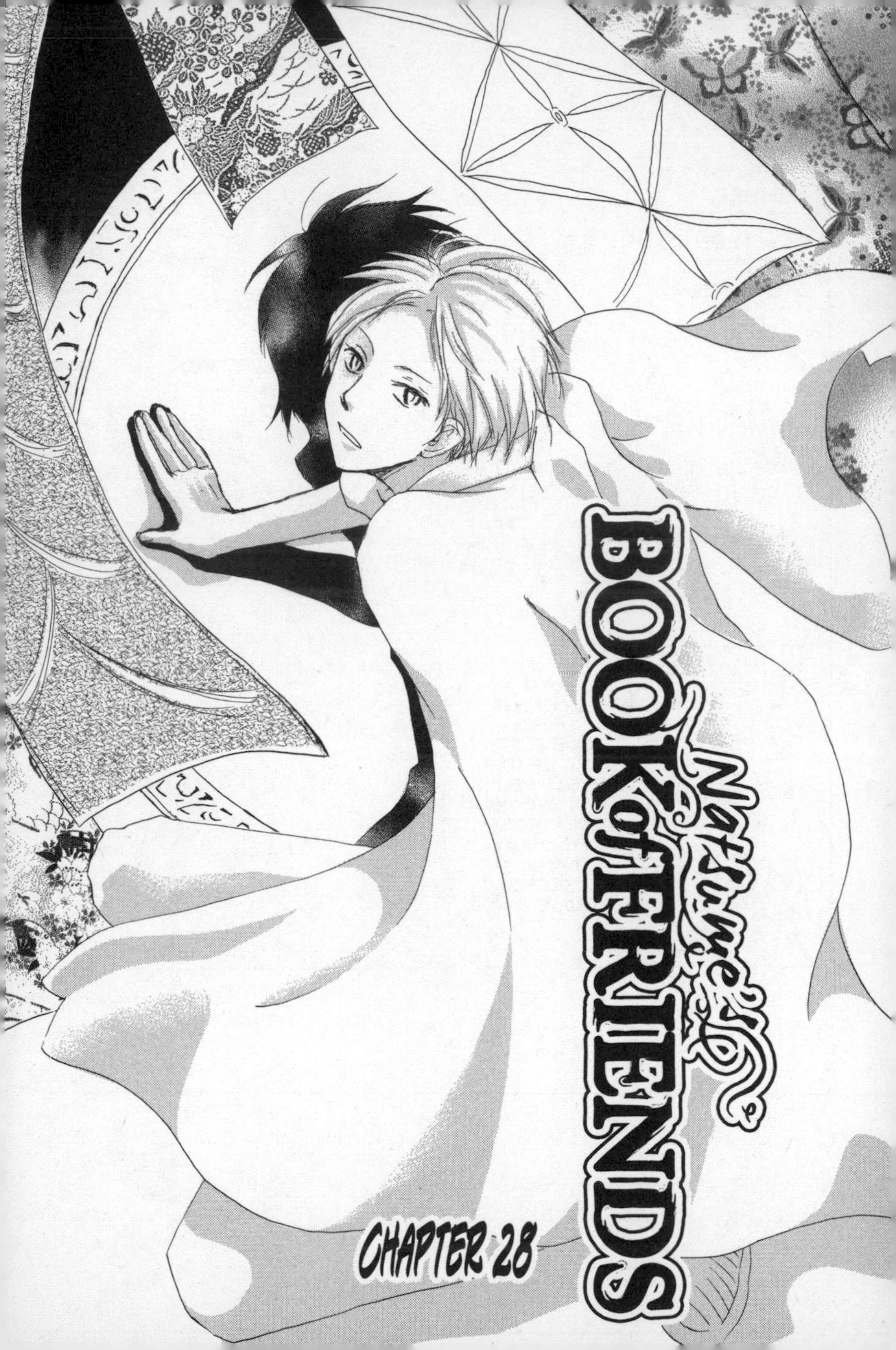
Natsume's
BOOK of FRIENDS
CHAPTER 28

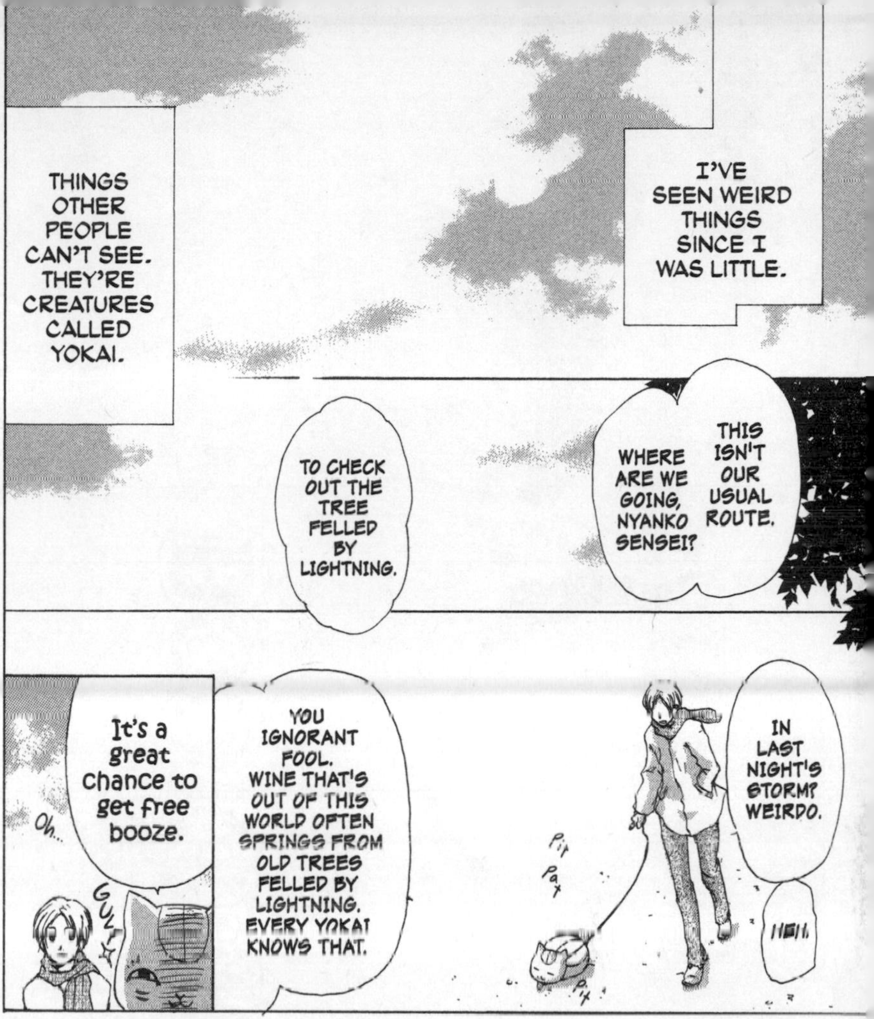
I'VE SEEN WEIRD THINGS SINCE I WAS LITTLE.
THINGS OTHER PEOPLE CAN'T SEE. THEY'RE CREATURES CALLED YOKAI.
THIS ISN'T OUR USUAL ROUTE.
WHERE ARE WE GOING, NYANKO SENSEI?
TO CHECK OUT THE TREE FELLED BY LIGHTNING.
IN LAST NIGHT'S STORM? WEIRDO.
HEH.
Pit
Pat
Pit
YOU IGNORANT FOOL. WINE THAT'S OUT OF THIS WORLD OFTEN SPRINGS FROM OLD TREES FELLED BY LIGHTNING. EVERY YOKAI KNOWS THAT.
It's a great chance to get free booze.
Oh...

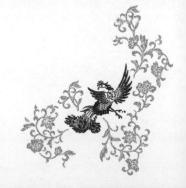

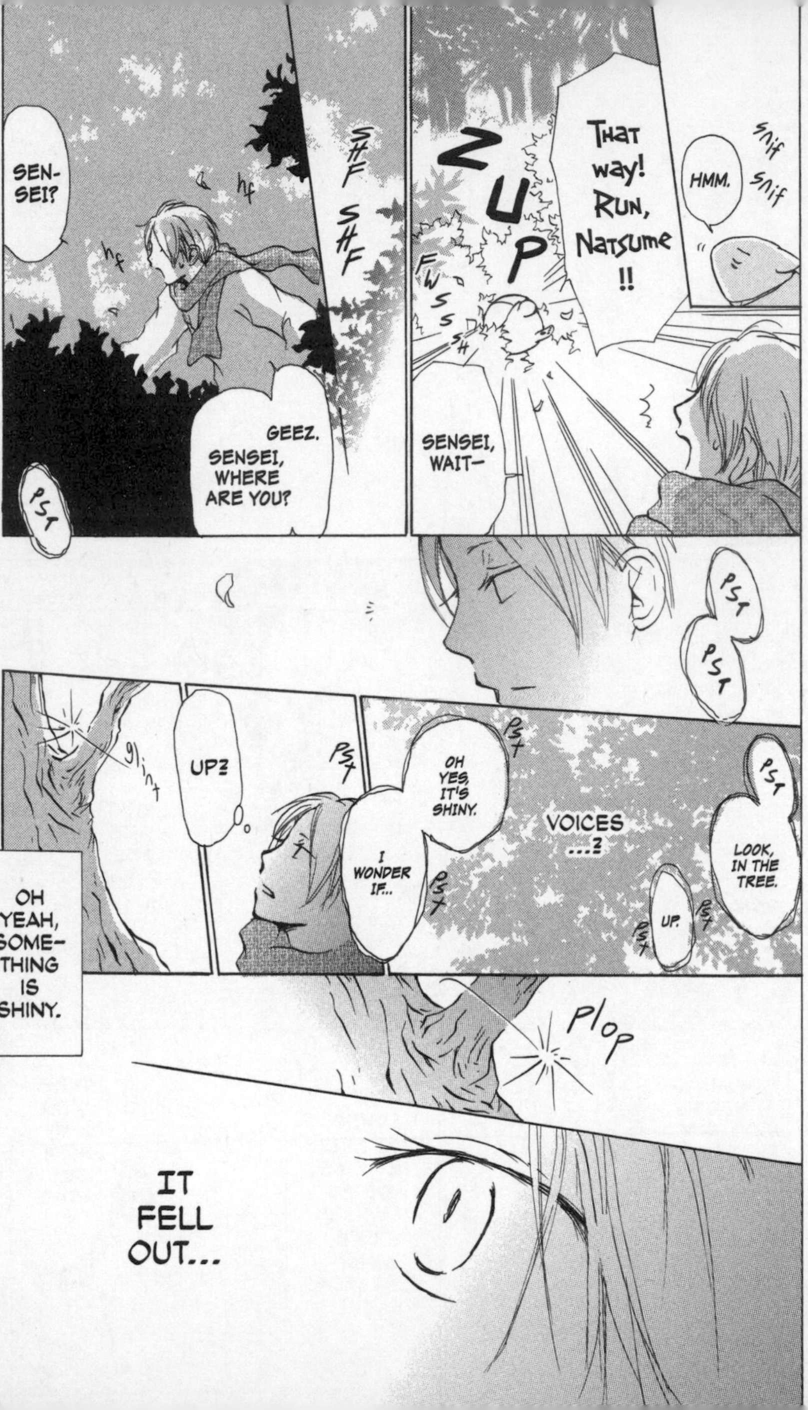

snif snif
HMM.
That way! RUN, Natsume !!
ZUP
FWSSSH
SENSEI, WAIT—
SHF SHF
SEN-SEI?
hf
hf
GEEZ. SENSEI, WHERE ARE YOU?
PST
PST
PST
PST
LOOK, IN THE TREE.
PST
UP.
PST
VOICES ...?
PST
OH YES, IT'S SHINY.
I WONDER IF...
PST
UP?
glint
OH YEAH, SOME-THING IS SHINY.
plop
IT FELL OUT...

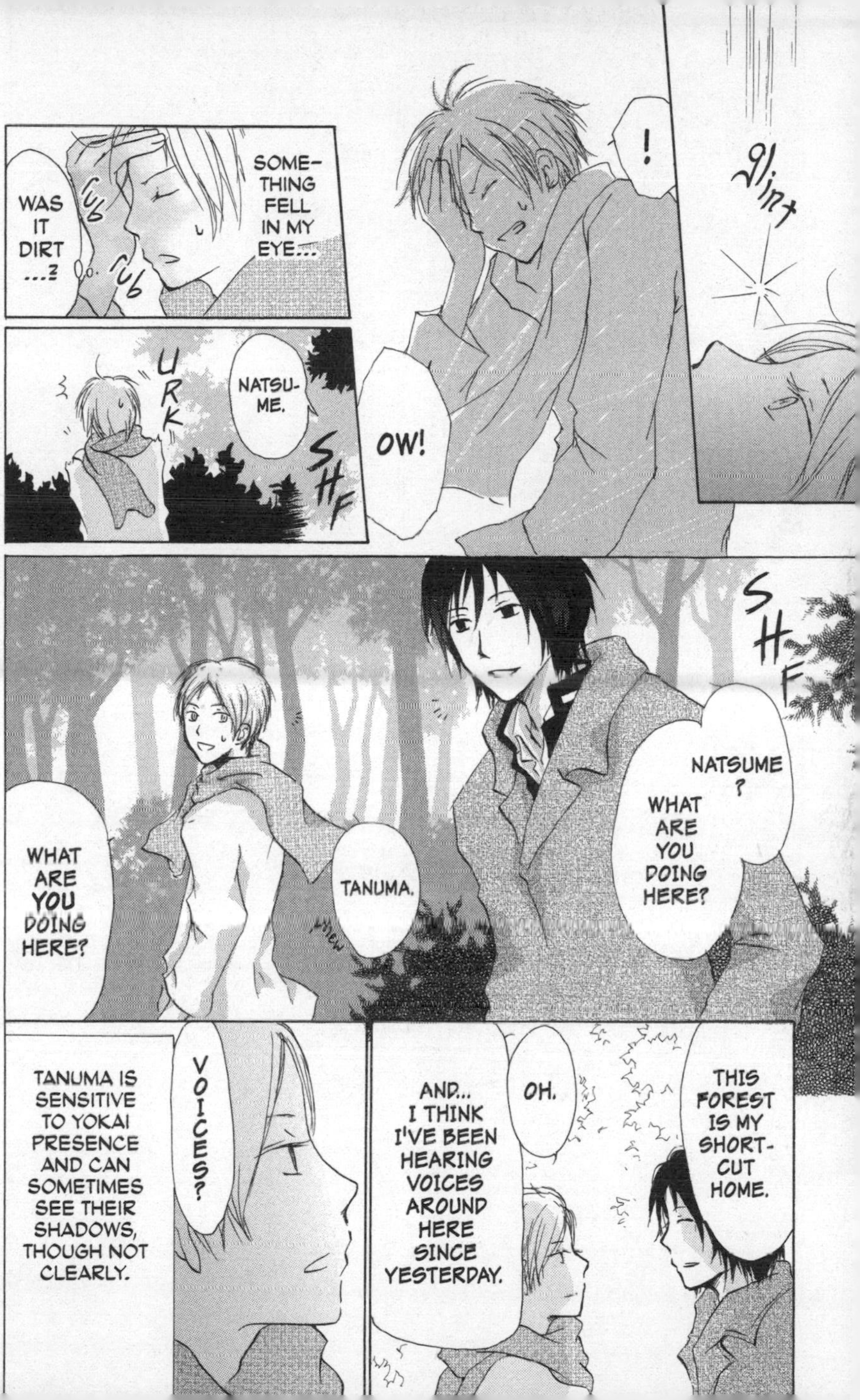
glint
!
OW!
SOME-THING FELL IN MY EYE...
WAS IT DIRT...?
rub rub
SHF
NATSU-ME.
URK
SHF
NATSUME? WHAT ARE YOU DOING HERE?
TANUMA.
WHAT ARE YOU DOING HERE?
THIS FOREST IS MY SHORT-CUT HOME.
OH.
AND... I THINK I'VE BEEN HEARING VOICES AROUND HERE SINCE YESTERDAY.
VOICES?
TANUMA IS SENSITIVE TO YOKAI PRESENCE AND CAN SOMETIMES SEE THEIR SHADOWS, THOUGH NOT CLEARLY.

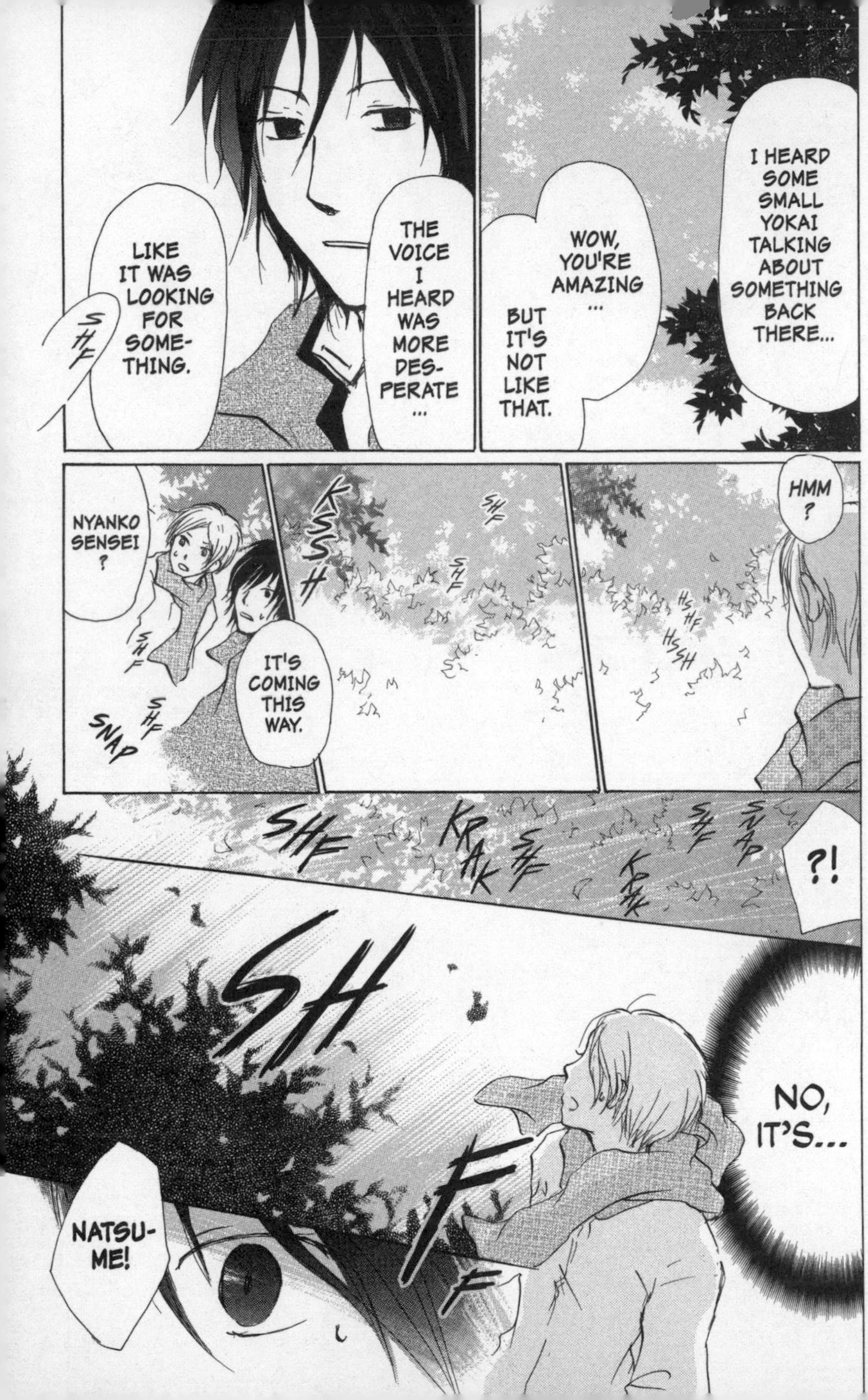
I HEARD SOME SMALL YOKAI TALKING ABOUT SOMETHING BACK THERE...
WOW, YOU'RE AMAZING...
BUT IT'S NOT LIKE THAT.
THE VOICE I HEARD WAS MORE DES-PERATE...
LIKE IT WAS LOOKING FOR SOME-THING.
SHF
HMM?
HSHF
HSSH
KSSH
SHF
SHF
NYANKO SENSEI?
IT'S COMING THIS WAY.
SHF
SHF
SNAP
?!
SNAP
SHF
KRAK
SHF
KRAK
SHF
NO, IT'S...
SH
F
F
NATSU-ME!

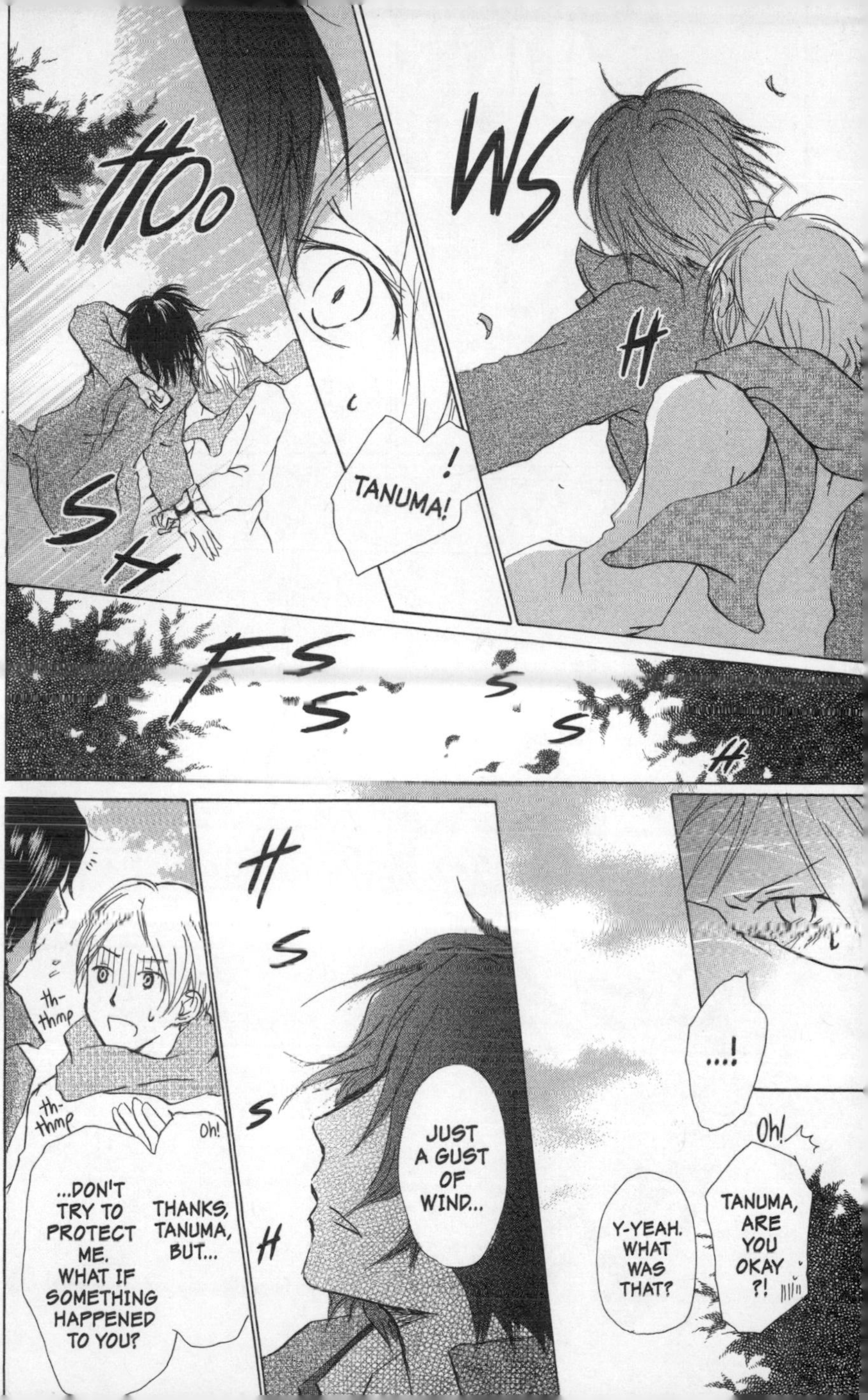
WS
H
!
TANUMA!
HOo
SH
FSSSSSH
...!
Oh!
TANUMA, ARE YOU OKAY?!
Y-YEAH. WHAT WAS THAT?
HSSH
JUST A GUST OF WIND...
th-thmp
th-thmp
Oh!
THANKS, TANUMA, BUT...
...DON'T TRY TO PROTECT ME. WHAT IF SOMETHING HAPPENED TO YOU?

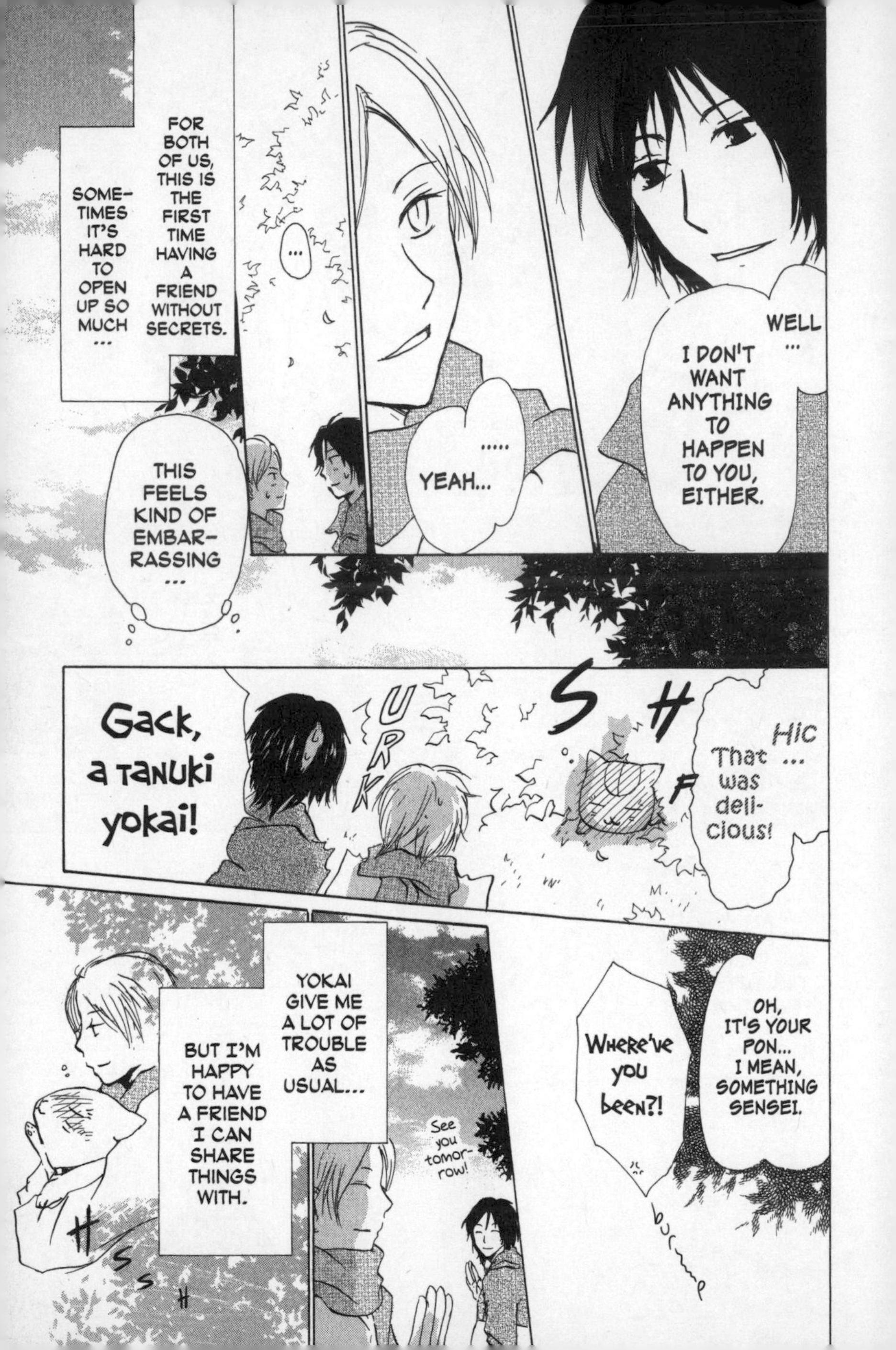
WELL ... I DON'T WANT ANYTHING TO HAPPEN TO YOU, EITHER.
...
..... YEAH...
FOR BOTH OF US, THIS IS THE FIRST TIME HAVING A FRIEND WITHOUT SECRETS.
SOMETIMES IT'S HARD TO OPEN UP SO MUCH ...
THIS FEELS KIND OF EMBARRASSING ...
Hic That ... was delicious!
SHF
URK
Gack, a tanuki yokai!
OH, IT'S YOUR PON... I MEAN, SOMETHING SENSEI.
Where've you been?!
burp
YOKAI GIVE ME A LOT OF TROUBLE AS USUAL...
BUT I'M HAPPY TO HAVE A FRIEND I CAN SHARE THINGS WITH.
See you tomorrow!
HSSH

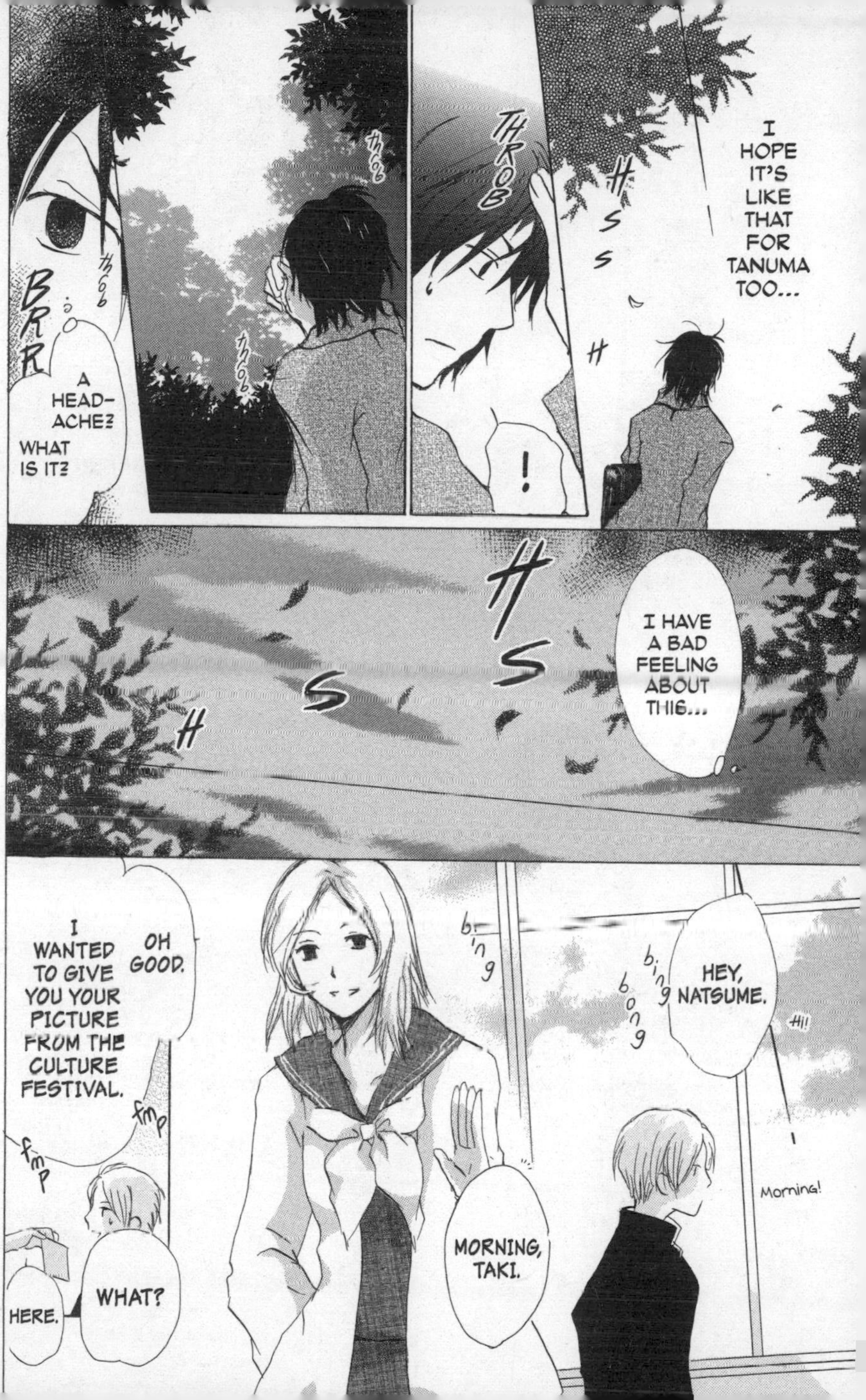
I HOPE IT'S LIKE THAT FOR TANUMA TOO...
HSSH
!
THROB
throb
throb
BRR
A HEAD-ACHE? WHAT IS IT?
throb
HSSH
I HAVE A BAD FEELING ABOUT THIS...
HEY, NATSUME.
Hi!
bing bong
bing
Morning!
MORNING, TAKI.
OH GOOD.
I WANTED TO GIVE YOU YOUR PICTURE FROM THE CULTURE FESTIVAL.
fmp
fmp
WHAT?
HERE.

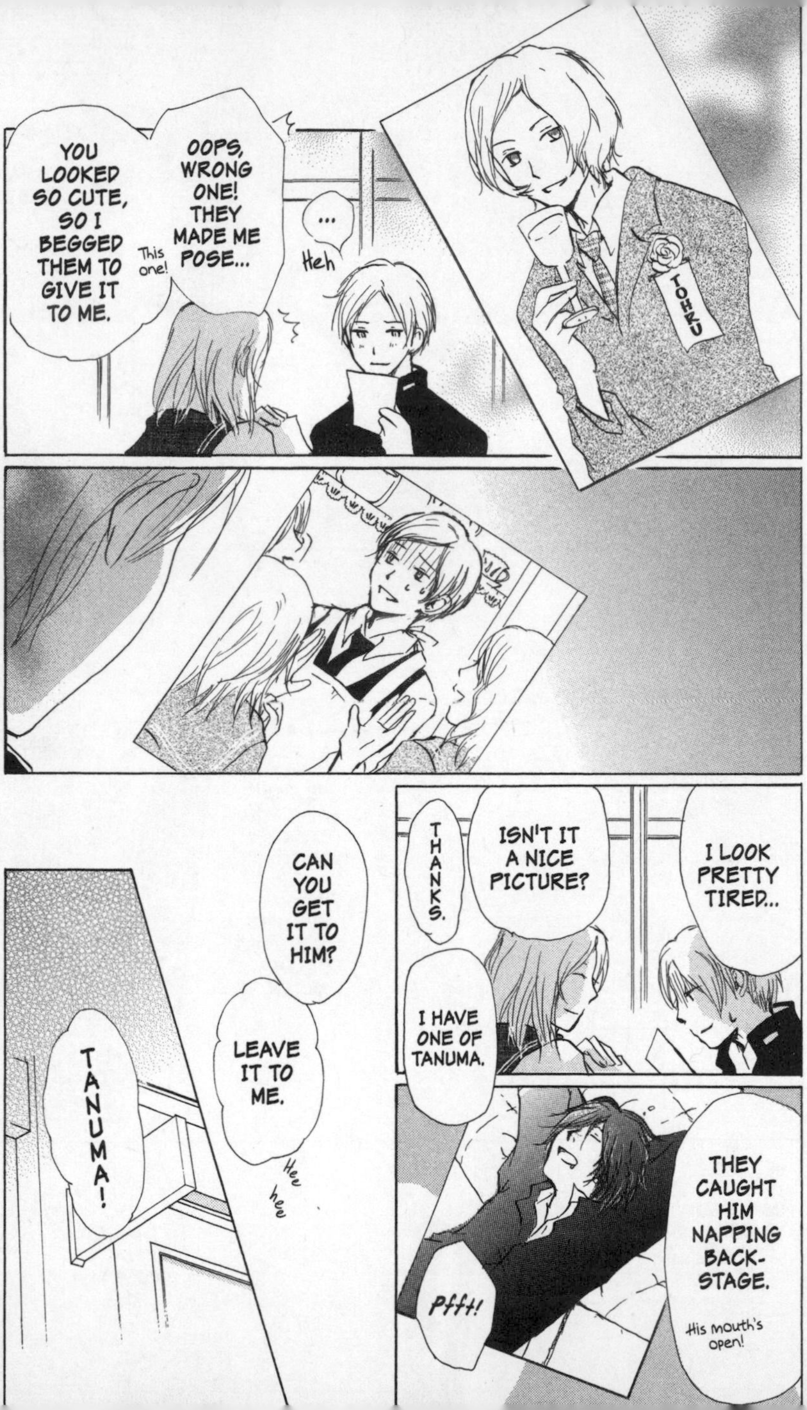
TOHRU
...
Heh
OOPS, WRONG ONE! THEY MADE ME POSE...
This one!
YOU LOOKED SO CUTE, SO I BEGGED THEM TO GIVE IT TO ME.
I LOOK PRETTY TIRED...
ISN'T IT A NICE PICTURE?
THANKS.
I HAVE ONE OF TANUMA.
THEY CAUGHT HIM NAPPING BACK-STAGE.
His mouth's open!
Pfft!
CAN YOU GET IT TO HIM?
LEAVE IT TO ME.
Hee hee
TANUMA!

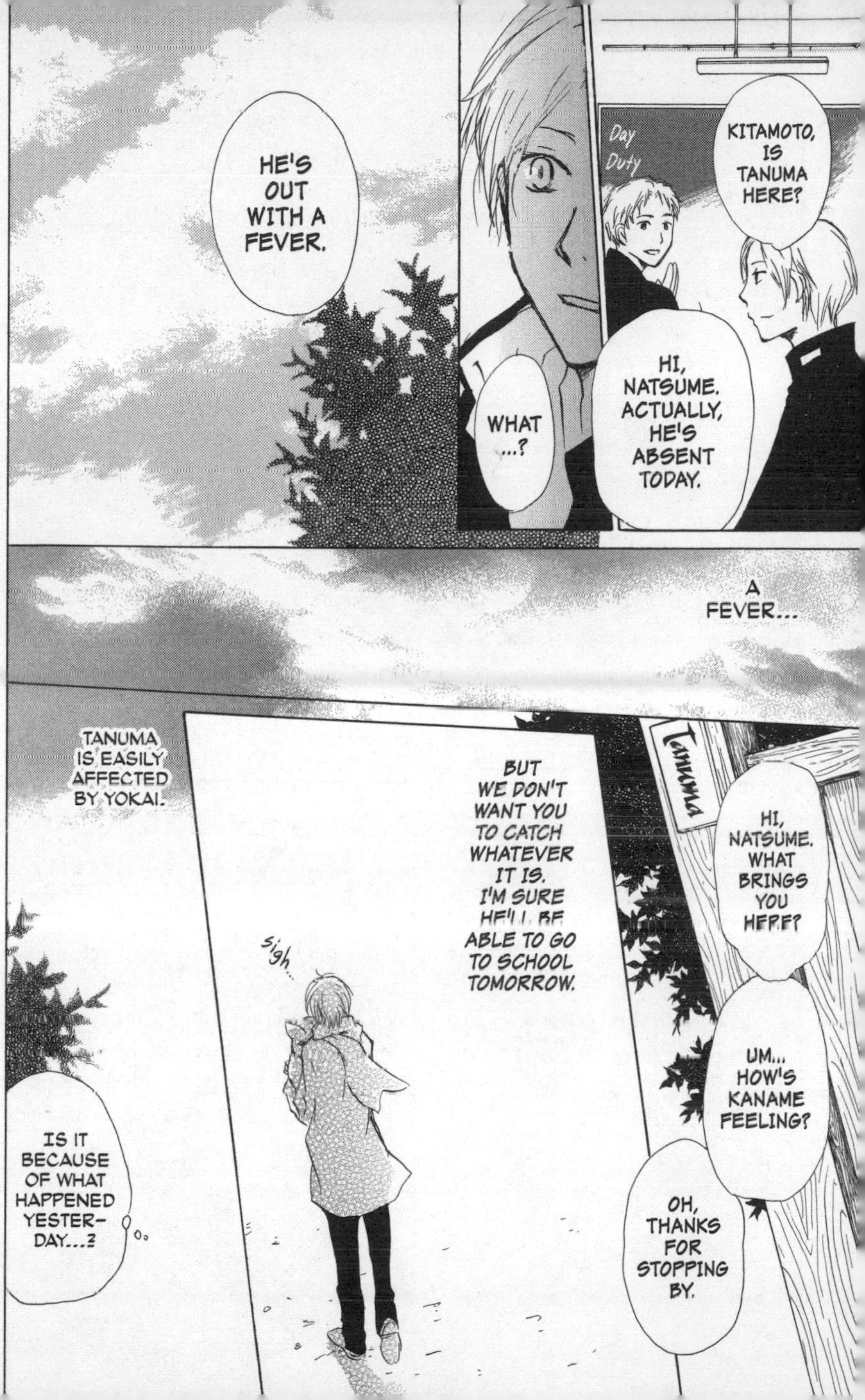
KITAMOTO, IS TANUMA HERE?
Day Duty
HI, NATSUME. ACTUALLY, HE'S ABSENT TODAY.
WHAT ...?
HE'S OUT WITH A FEVER.
A FEVER...
Tanuma
HI, NATSUME. WHAT BRINGS YOU HERE?
UM... HOW'S KANAME FEELING?
OH, THANKS FOR STOPPING BY.
BUT WE DON'T WANT YOU TO CATCH WHATEVER IT IS. I'M SURE HE'LL BE ABLE TO GO TO SCHOOL TOMORROW.
sigh...
TANUMA IS EASILY AFFECTED BY YOKAI.
IS IT BECAUSE OF WHAT HAPPENED YESTER-DAY...?

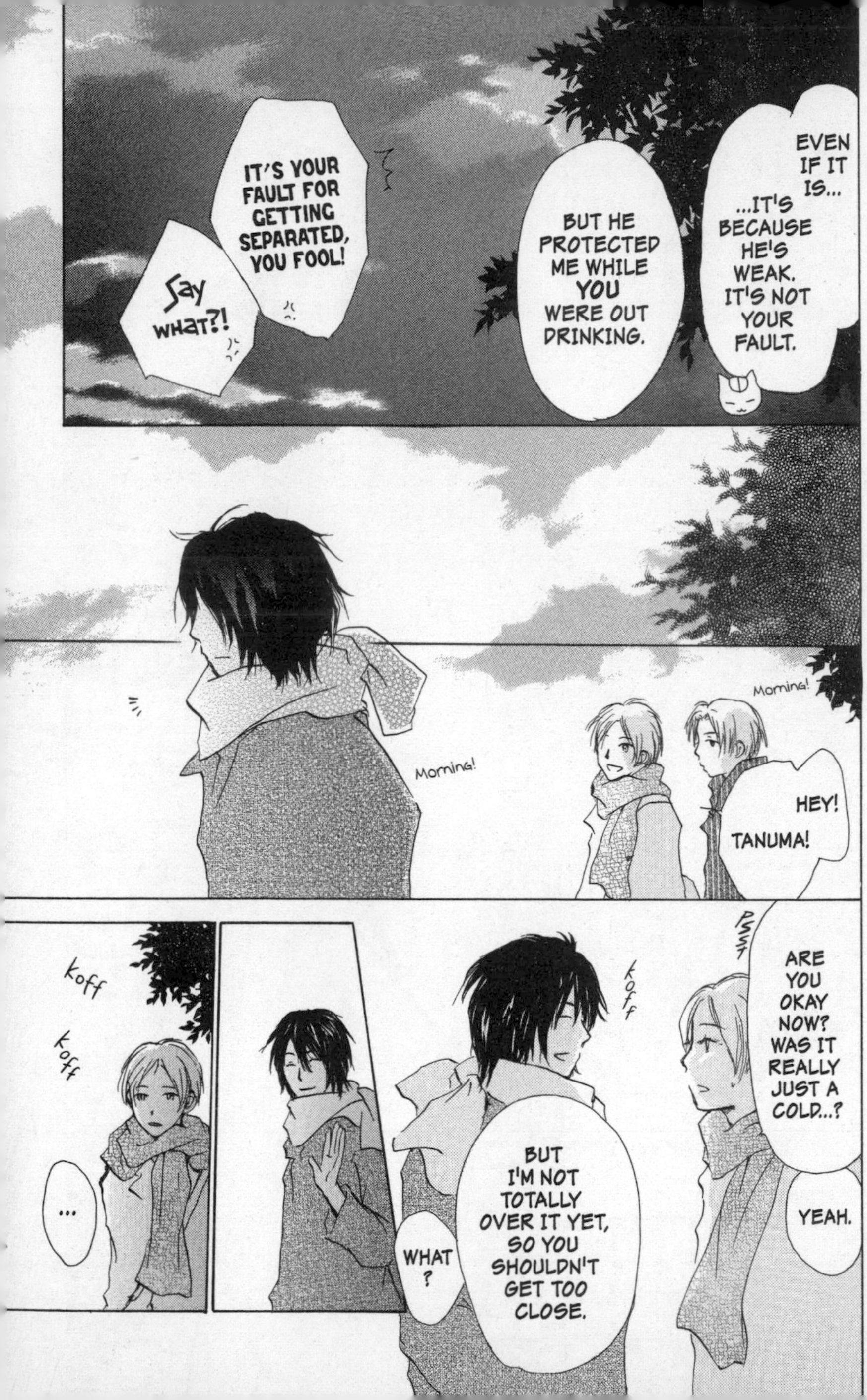
EVEN IF IT IS...
...IT'S BECAUSE HE'S WEAK. IT'S NOT YOUR FAULT.
BUT HE PROTECTED ME WHILE YOU WERE OUT DRINKING.
IT'S YOUR FAULT FOR GETTING SEPARATED, YOU FOOL!
Say WHAT?!
Morning!
HEY! TANUMA!
Morning!
PSST
ARE YOU OKAY NOW? WAS IT REALLY JUST A COLD...?
YEAH.
koff
BUT I'M NOT TOTALLY OVER IT YET, SO YOU SHOULDN'T GET TOO CLOSE.
WHAT?
koff
koff
...

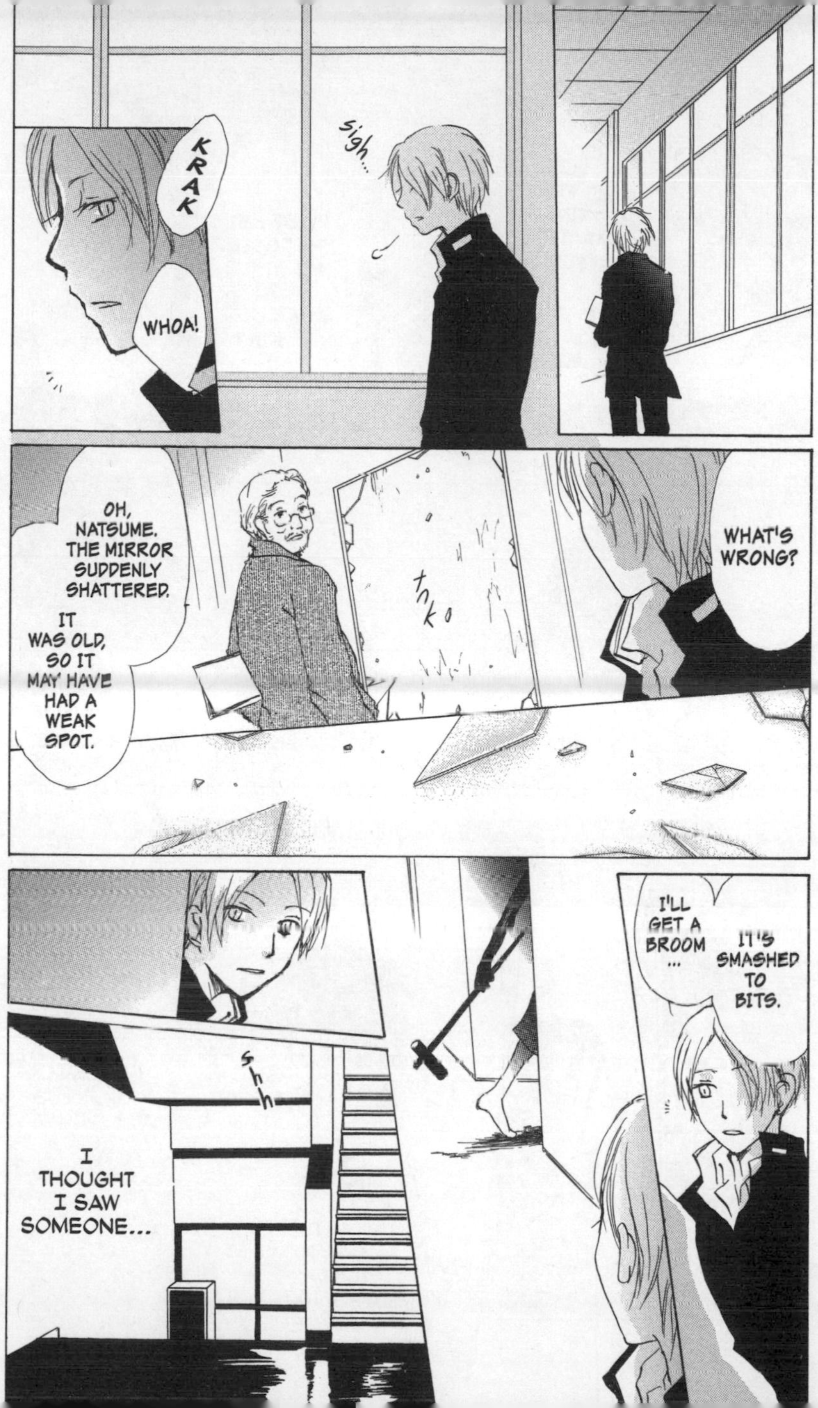
sigh...
KRAK
WHOA!
WHAT'S WRONG?
OH, NATSUME. THE MIRROR SUDDENLY SHATTERED.
IT WAS OLD, SO IT MAY HAVE HAD A WEAK SPOT.
IT'S SMASHED TO BITS.
I'LL GET A BROOM...
shh
I THOUGHT I SAW SOMEONE...

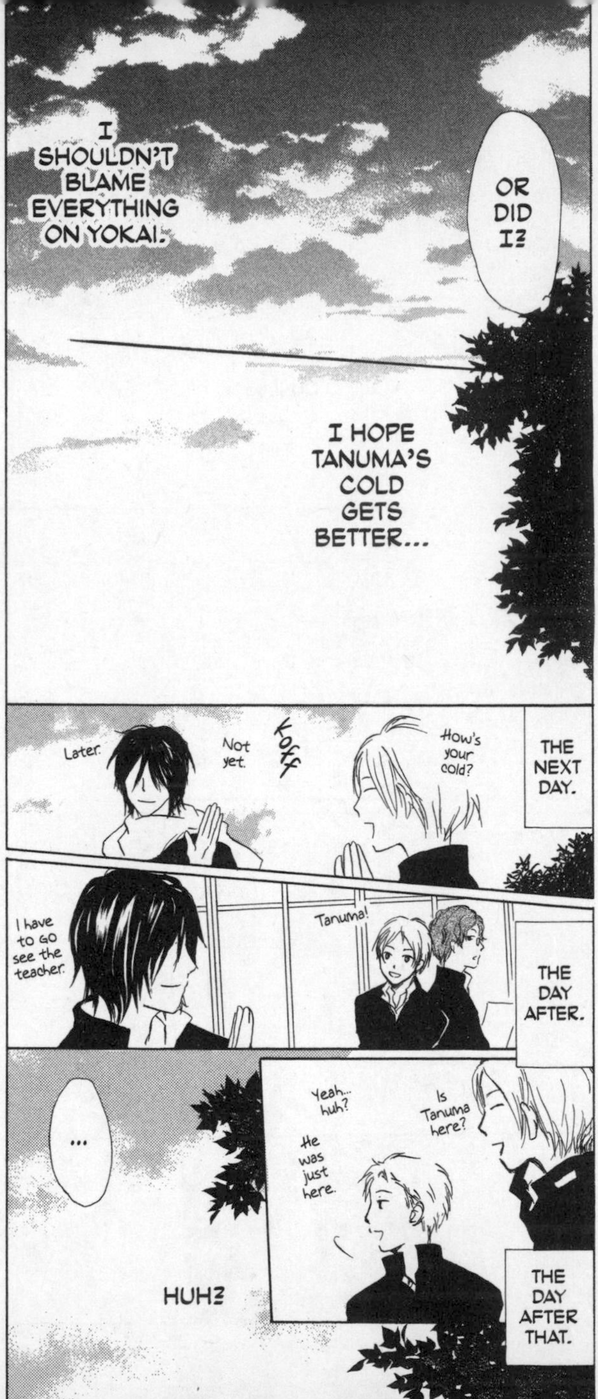

I SHOULDN'T BLAME EVERYTHING ON YOKAI.
OR DID I?
I HOPE TANUMA'S COLD GETS BETTER...
THE NEXT DAY.
How's your cold?
KOFF
Not yet.
Later.
THE DAY AFTER.
Tanuma!
I have to go see the teacher.
THE DAY AFTER THAT.
Is Tanuma here?
Yeah... huh?
He was just here.
...
HUH?

02

❋Nyan Book

Last time, I wrote about how they published a Fan Book to commemorate the anime release. This time, they made something called a Nyan Book. I got a call asking, "May we have permission to make a Nyan Book for Nyanko Sensei?" It sounded so lovely that I approved on the spot. I got a little anxious, wondering if that ugly calico cat could really carry an entire book by himself. But they came up with many cute and fun articles.

It looks like Nyanko Sensei is going on a journey. It's a perfect book for anyone who loves kitty cats, even creepy-looking ones. Please check it out.

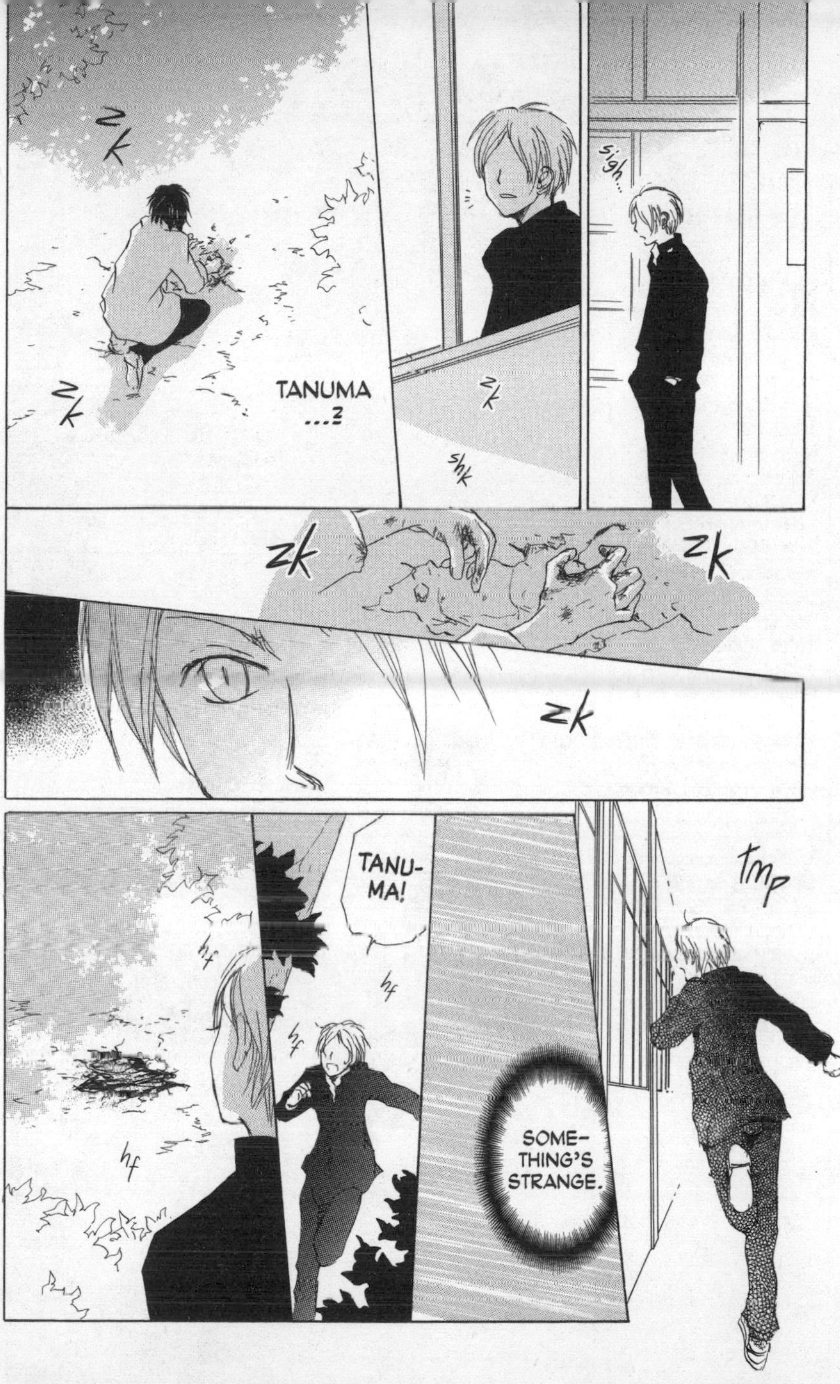
sigh...
zk
shk
zk
TANUMA ...?
zk
zk
zk
zk
tmp
SOME-THING'S STRANGE.
TANU-MA!
hf
hf
hf
hf

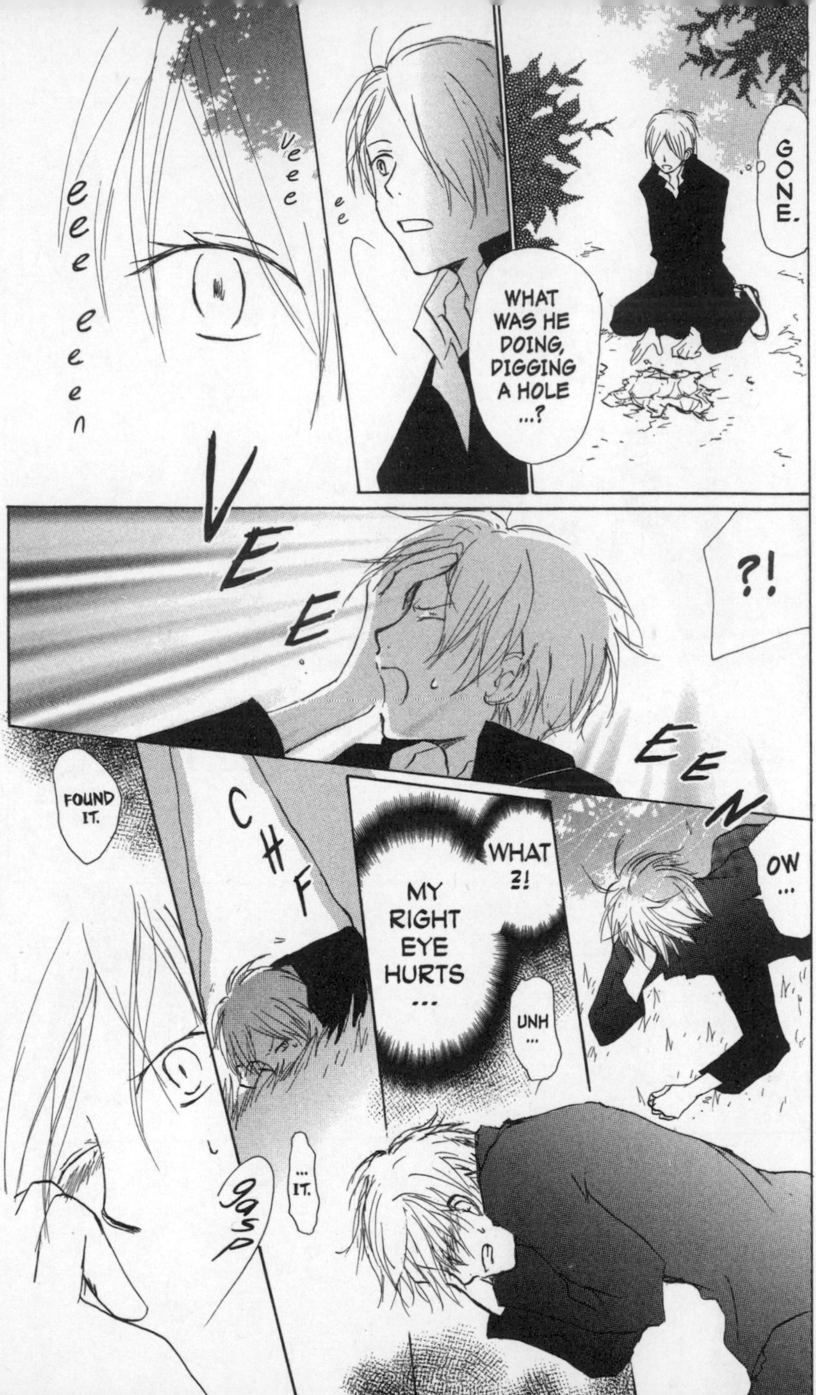
GONE.
WHAT WAS HE DOING, DIGGING A HOLE ...?
Veee ee
eee e e e n
?!
VE E
EEN
OW ...
WHAT?!
MY RIGHT EYE HURTS ...
UNH ...
FOUND IT.
CHF
... IT.
gasp

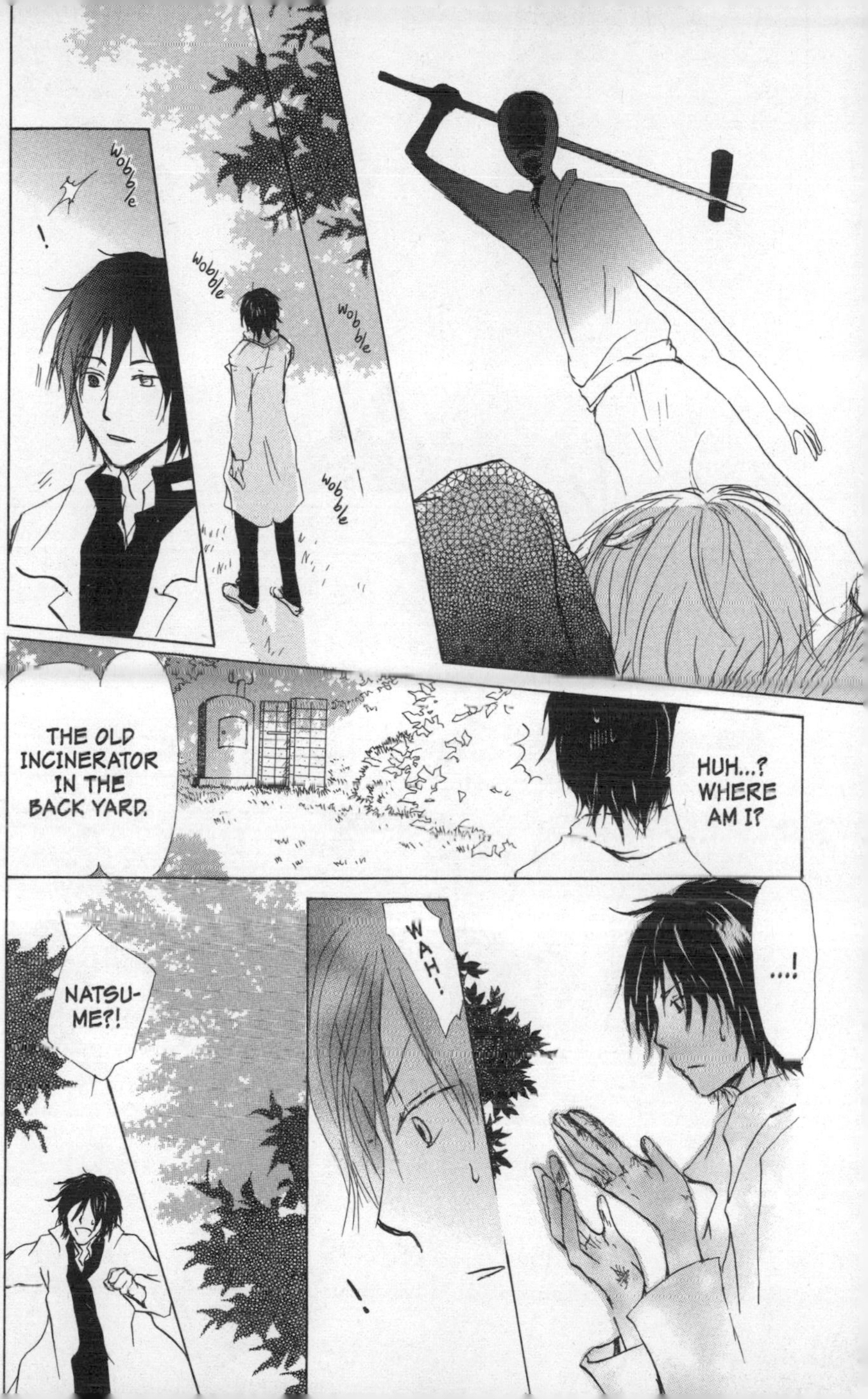
wobble
wobble
wobble
wobble
!
HUH...? WHERE AM I?
THE OLD INCINERATOR IN THE BACK YARD.
...!
WAH!
!
NATSU-ME?!

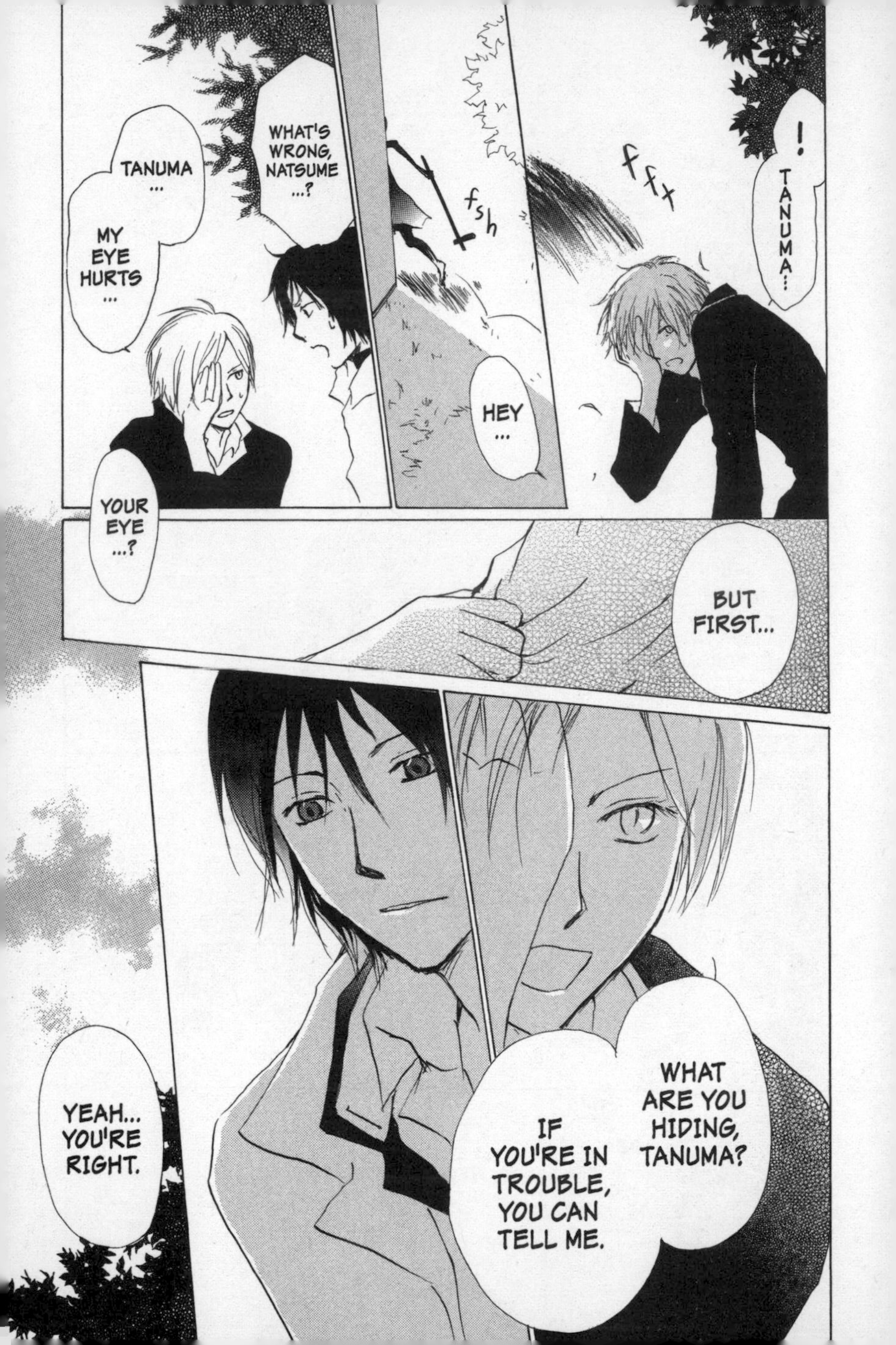
!
TANUMA...!
ffx
fsh
HEY ...
WHAT'S WRONG, NATSUME ...?
TANUMA ...
MY EYE HURTS ...
YOUR EYE ...?
BUT FIRST...
WHAT ARE YOU HIDING, TANUMA?
IF YOU'RE IN TROUBLE, YOU CAN TELL ME.
YEAH... YOU'RE RIGHT.

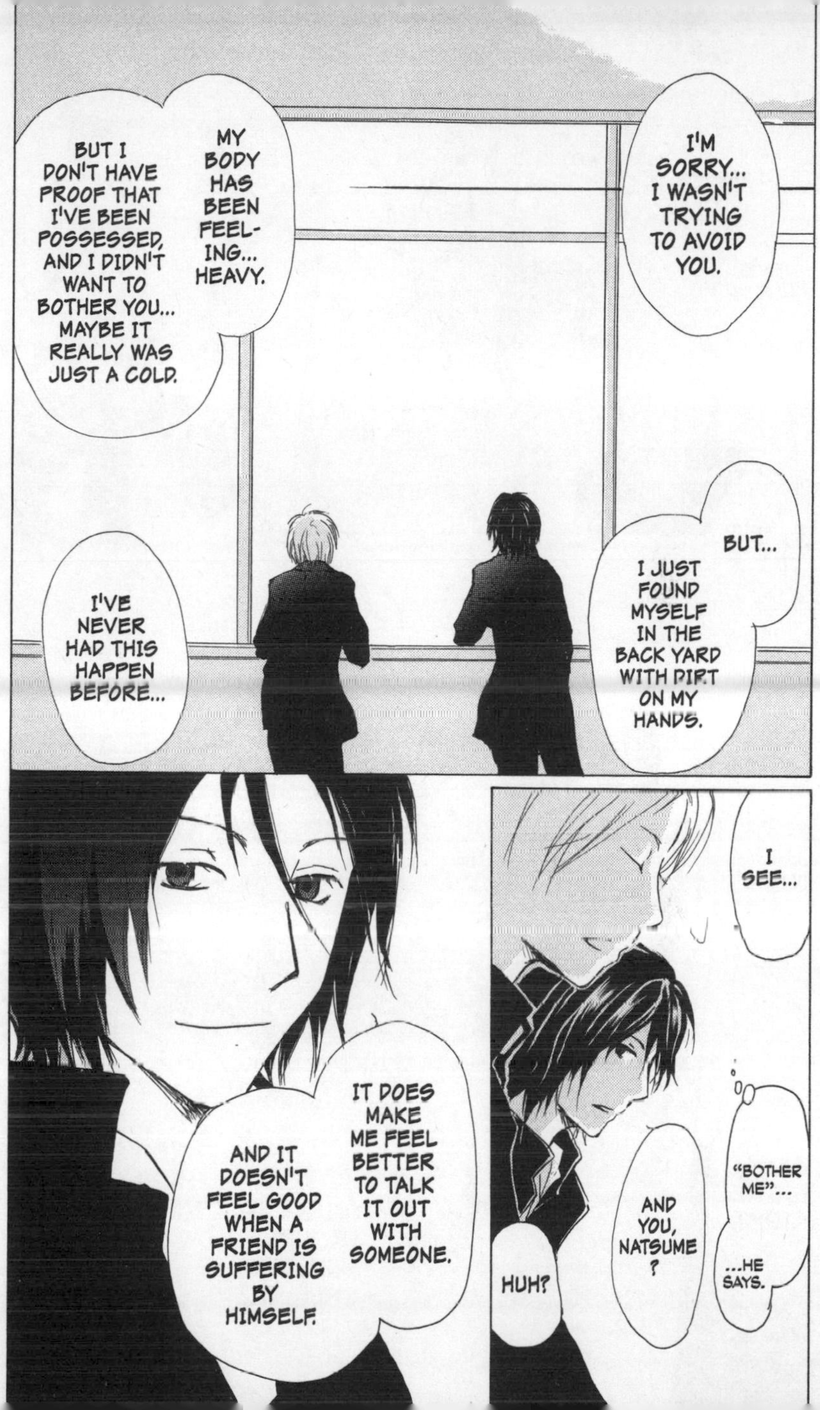
I'M SORRY... I WASN'T TRYING TO AVOID YOU.
MY BODY HAS BEEN FEEL-ING... HEAVY.
BUT I DON'T HAVE PROOF THAT I'VE BEEN POSSESSED, AND I DIDN'T WANT TO BOTHER YOU... MAYBE IT REALLY WAS JUST A COLD.
BUT...
I JUST FOUND MYSELF IN THE BACK YARD WITH DIRT ON MY HANDS.
I'VE NEVER HAD THIS HAPPEN BEFORE...
I SEE...
"BOTHER ME"...
...HE SAYS.
AND YOU, NATSUME?
HUH?
IT DOES MAKE ME FEEL BETTER TO TALK IT OUT WITH SOMEONE.
AND IT DOESN'T FEEL GOOD WHEN A FRIEND IS SUFFERING BY HIMSELF.

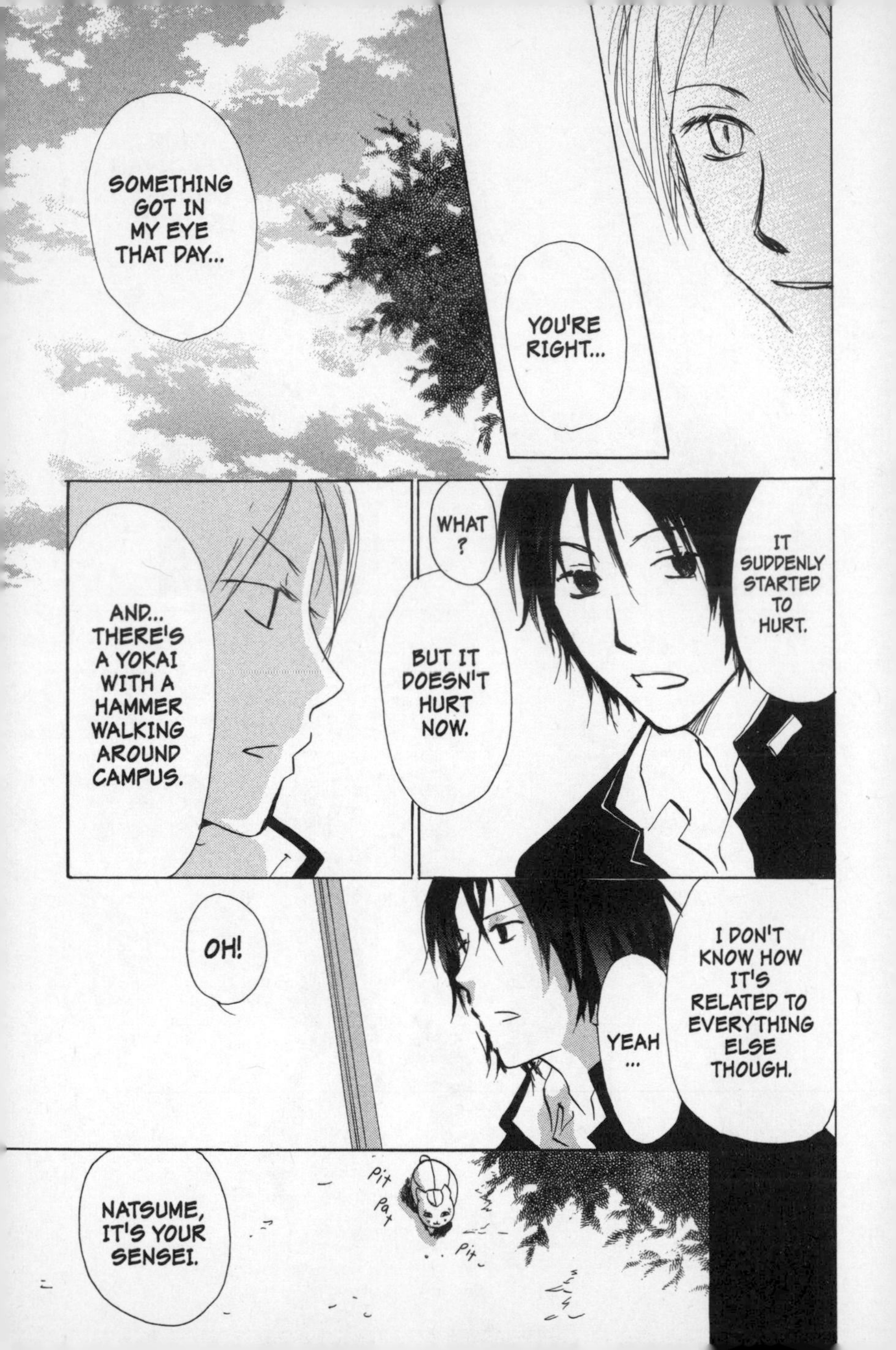

YOU'RE RIGHT...
SOMETHING GOT IN MY EYE THAT DAY...
IT SUDDENLY STARTED TO HURT.
WHAT?
BUT IT DOESN'T HURT NOW.
AND... THERE'S A YOKAI WITH A HAMMER WALKING AROUND CAMPUS.
I DON'T KNOW HOW IT'S RELATED TO EVERYTHING ELSE THOUGH.
YEAH...
OH!
PIT
PAT
PIT
NATSUME, IT'S YOUR SENSEI.

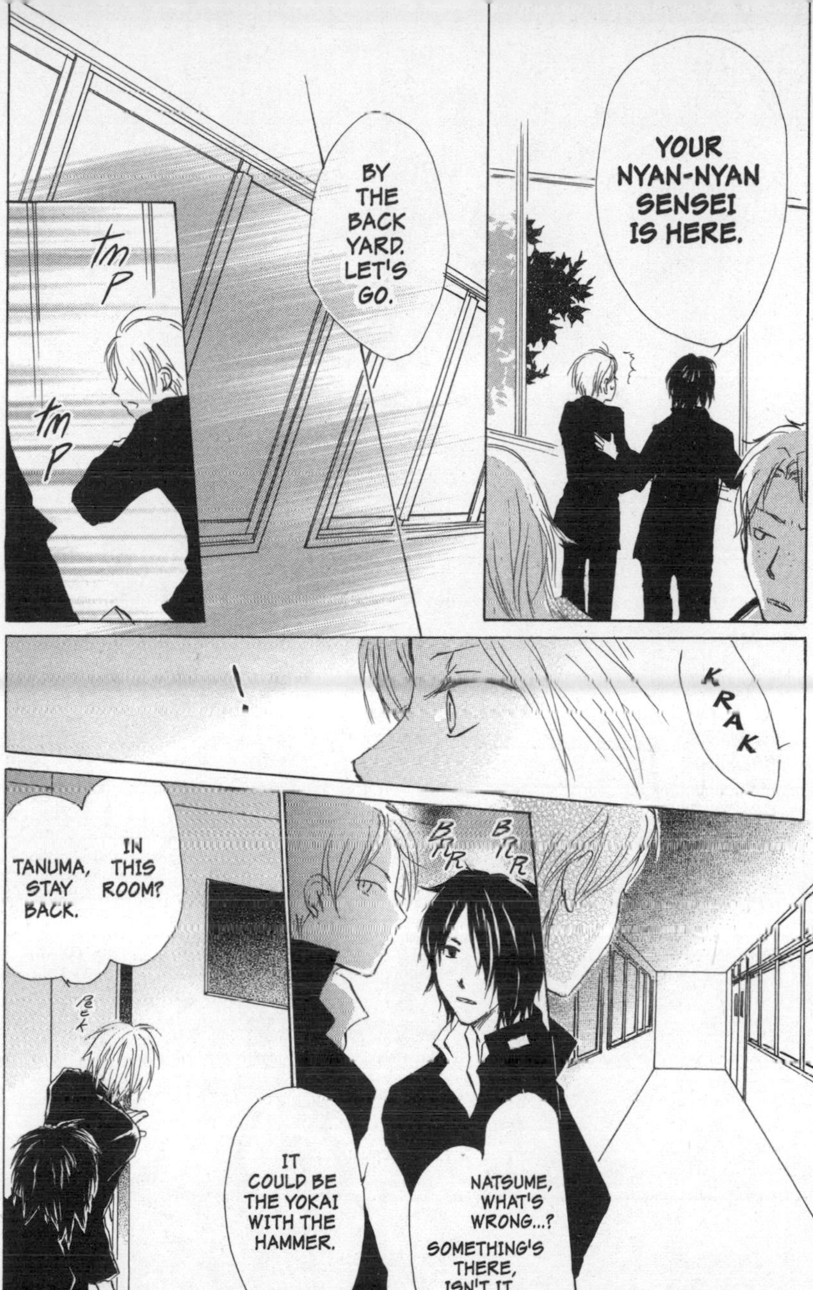
YOUR NYAN-NYAN SENSEI IS HERE.
BY THE BACK YARD. LET'S GO.
tmp
tmp
KRAK
!
BRR
BRR
NATSUME, WHAT'S WRONG...?
SOMETHING'S THERE, ISN'T IT...
IT COULD BE THE YOKAI WITH THE HAMMER.
IN THIS ROOM?
TANUMA, STAY BACK.
PEEK

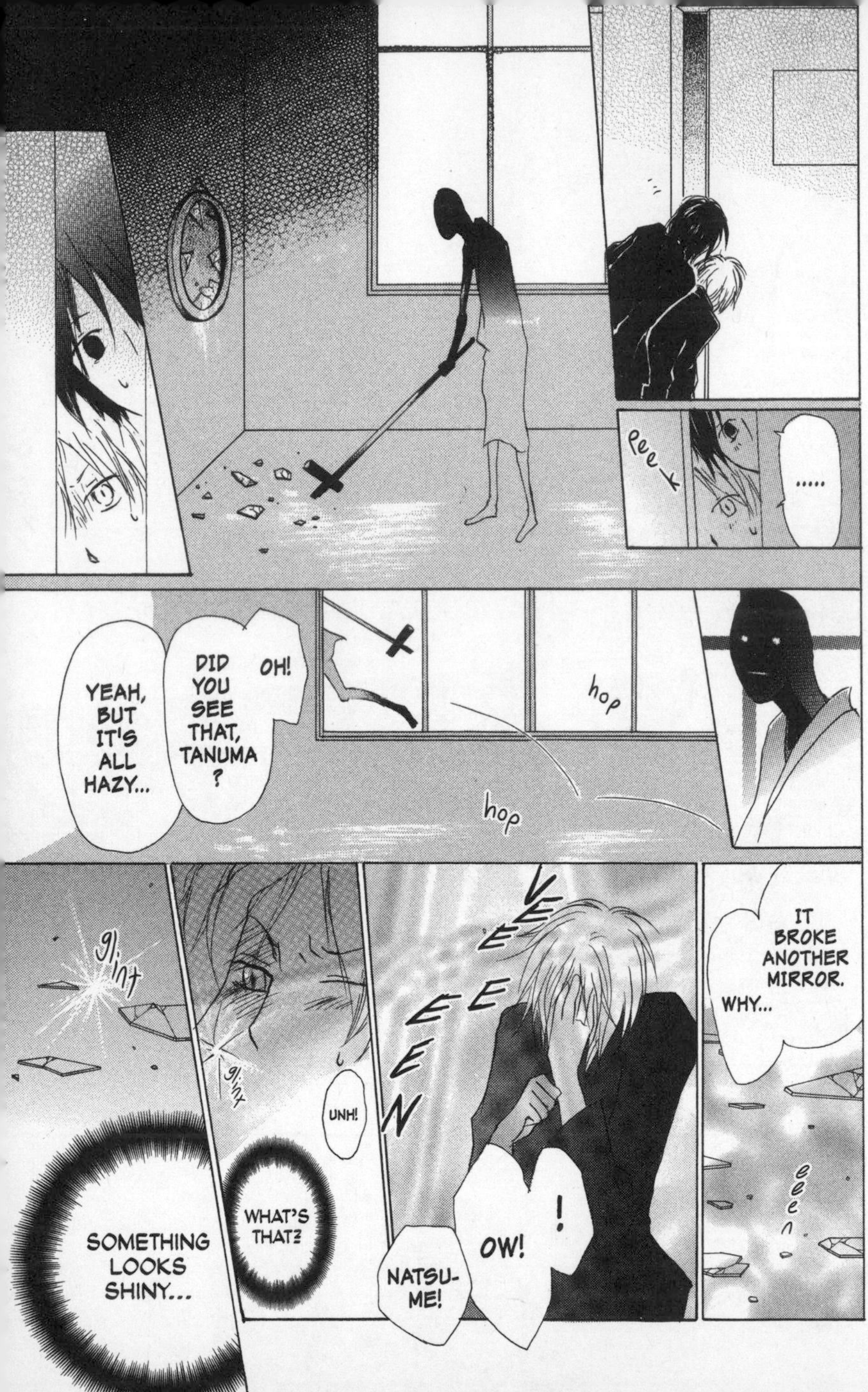

peek
......
hop
hop
OH!
DID YOU SEE THAT, TANUMA?
YEAH, BUT IT'S ALL HAZY...
IT BROKE ANOTHER MIRROR.
WHY...
eeen
VEEEEEEN
!
OW!
NATSU-ME!
UNH!
glint
WHAT'S THAT?
glint
SOMETHING LOOKS SHINY...

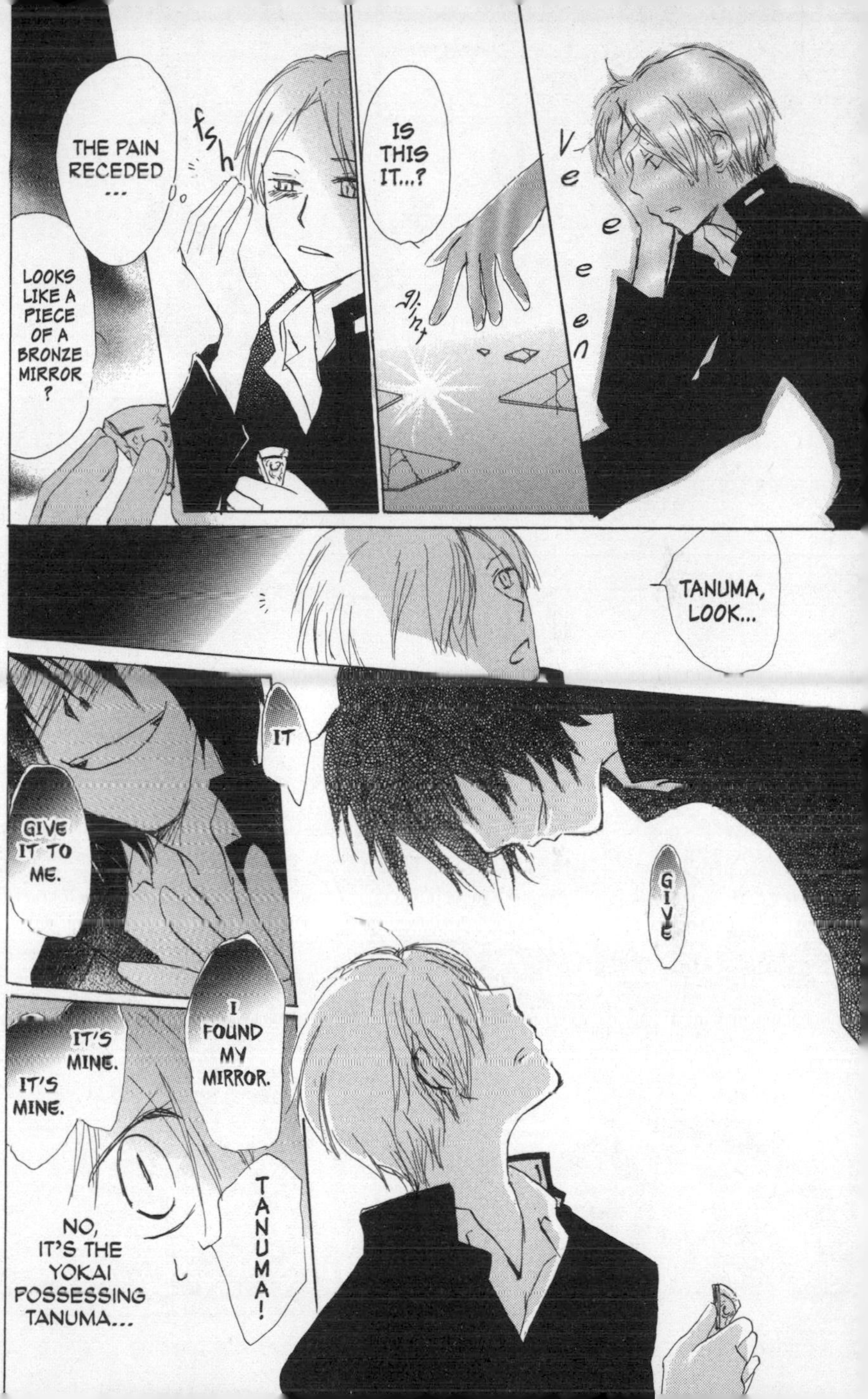
Veeeen
glint
IS THIS IT...?
fsh
THE PAIN RECEDED ...
LOOKS LIKE A PIECE OF A BRONZE MIRROR ?
TANUMA, LOOK...
GIVE
IT
GIVE IT TO ME.
I FOUND MY MIRROR.
IT'S MINE.
IT'S MINE.
TANUMA!
NO, IT'S THE YOKAI POSSESSING TANUMA...

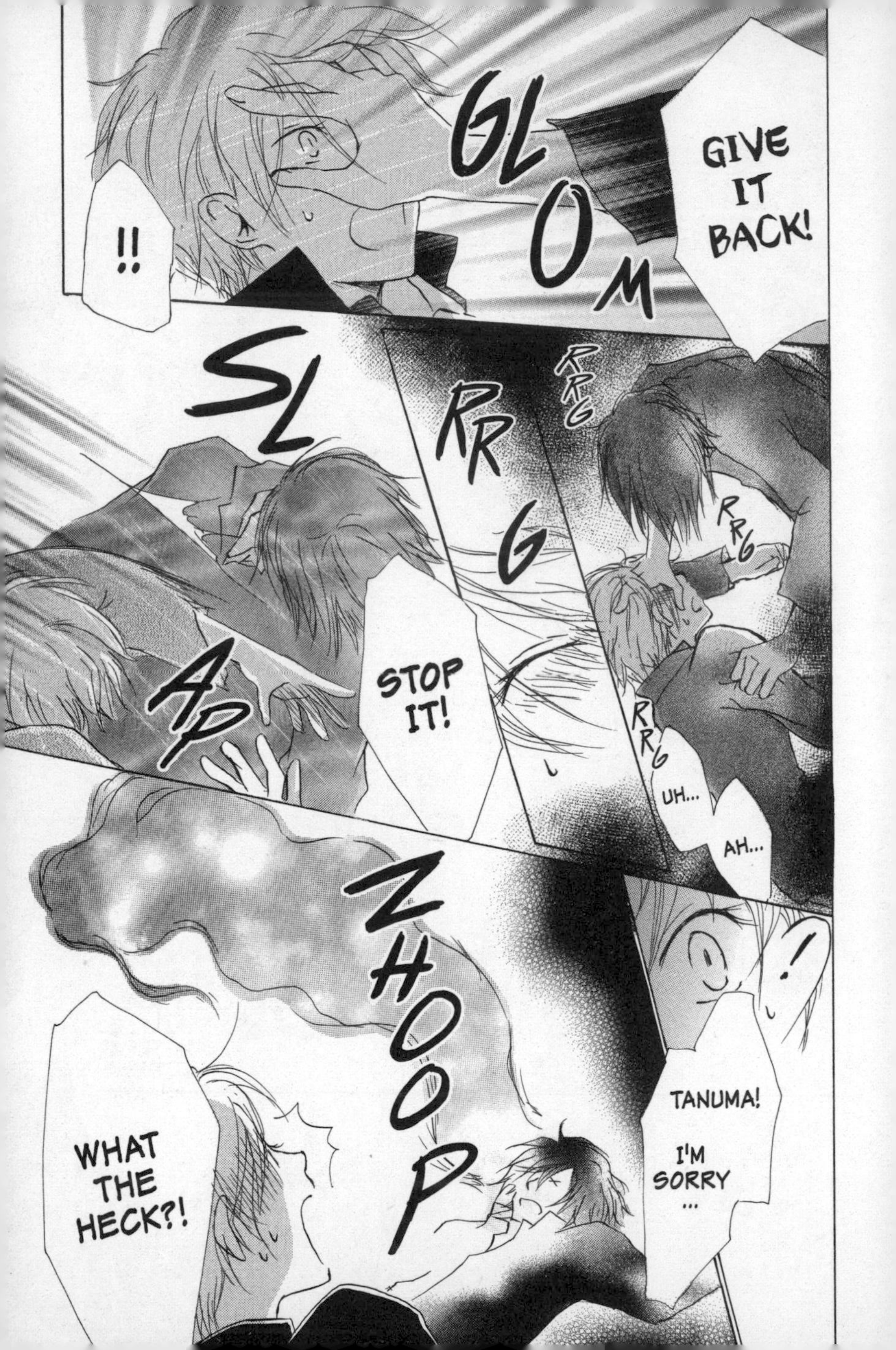
GIVE IT BACK!
GLOM
!!
RRG
RRG
RRG
UH...
AH...
RRG
STOP IT!
SLAP
!
TANUMA!
I'M SORRY ...
ZHOOP
WHAT THE HECK?!

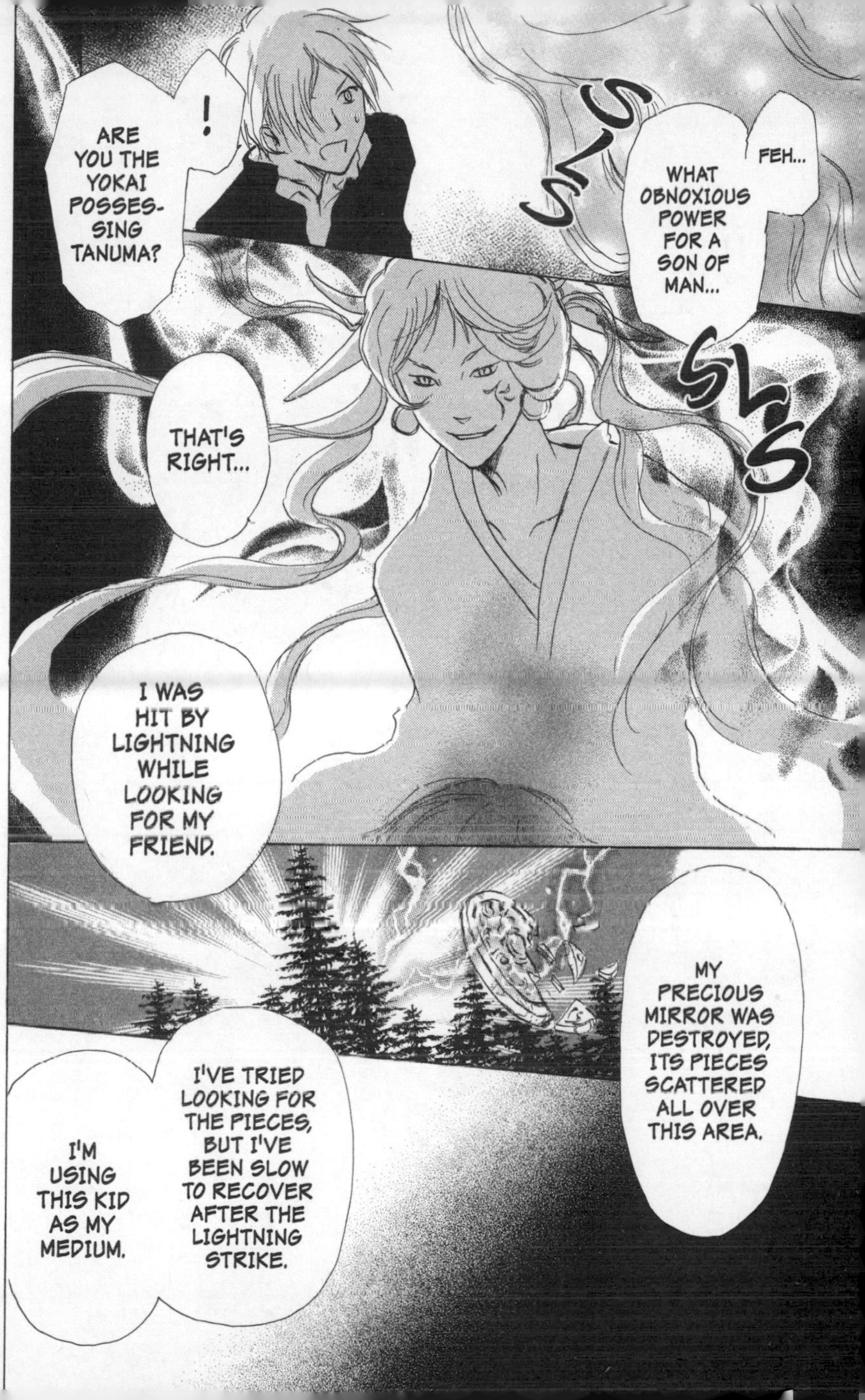
SLS
FEH... WHAT OBNOXIOUS POWER FOR A SON OF MAN...
!
ARE YOU THE YOKAI POSSES-SING TANUMA?
SLS
THAT'S RIGHT...
I WAS HIT BY LIGHTNING WHILE LOOKING FOR MY FRIEND.
MY PRECIOUS MIRROR WAS DESTROYED, ITS PIECES SCATTERED ALL OVER THIS AREA.
I'VE TRIED LOOKING FOR THE PIECES, BUT I'VE BEEN SLOW TO RECOVER AFTER THE LIGHTNING STRIKE.
I'M USING THIS KID AS MY MEDIUM.

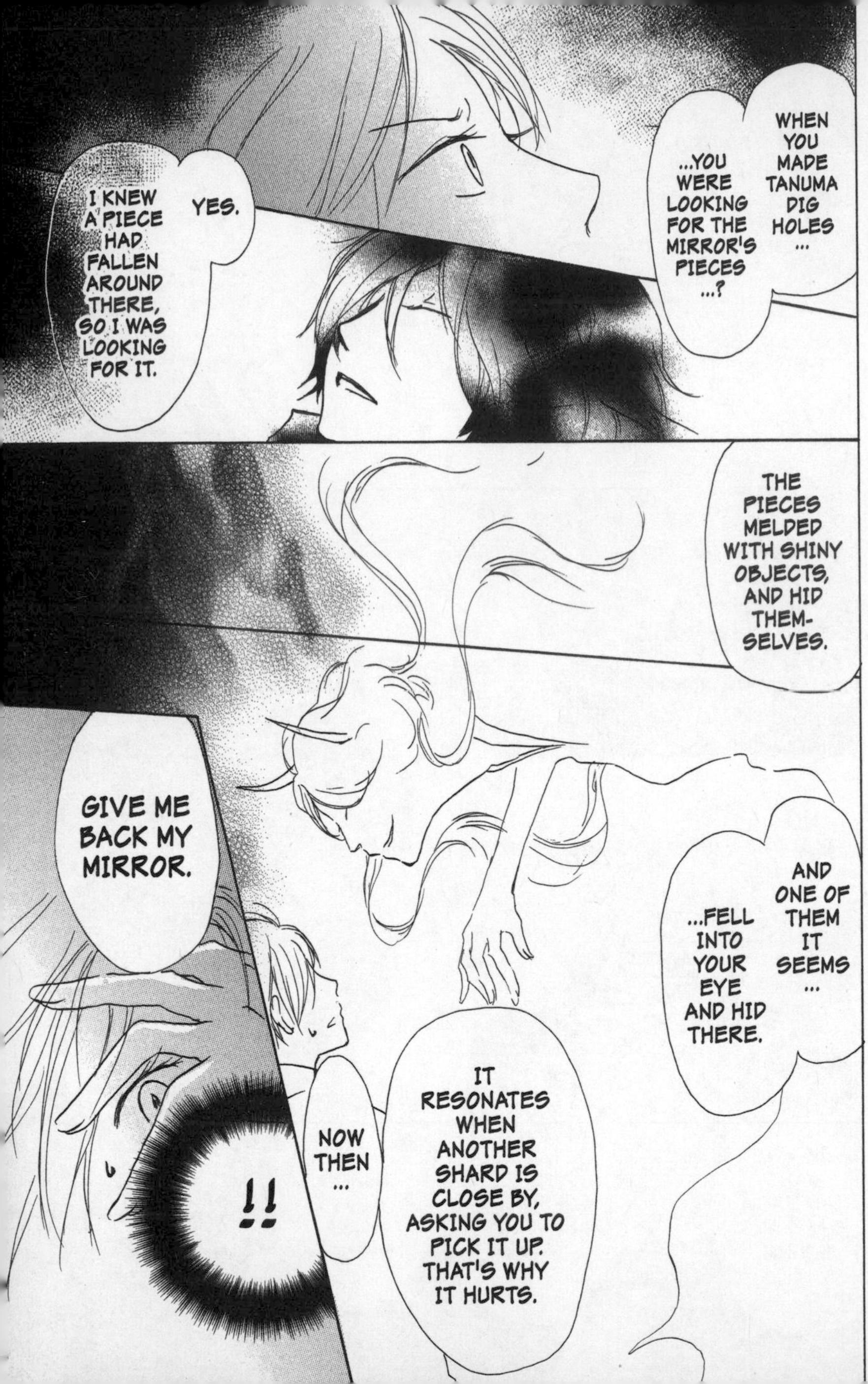

WHEN YOU MADE TANUMA DIG HOLES ...
...YOU WERE LOOKING FOR THE MIRROR'S PIECES ...?
YES.
I KNEW A PIECE HAD FALLEN AROUND THERE, SO I WAS LOOKING FOR IT.
THE PIECES MELDED WITH SHINY OBJECTS, AND HID THEM-SELVES.
AND ONE OF THEM IT SEEMS ...
...FELL INTO YOUR EYE AND HID THERE.
IT RESONATES WHEN ANOTHER SHARD IS CLOSE BY, ASKING YOU TO PICK IT UP. THAT'S WHY IT HURTS.
NOW THEN ...
GIVE ME BACK MY MIRROR.
!!

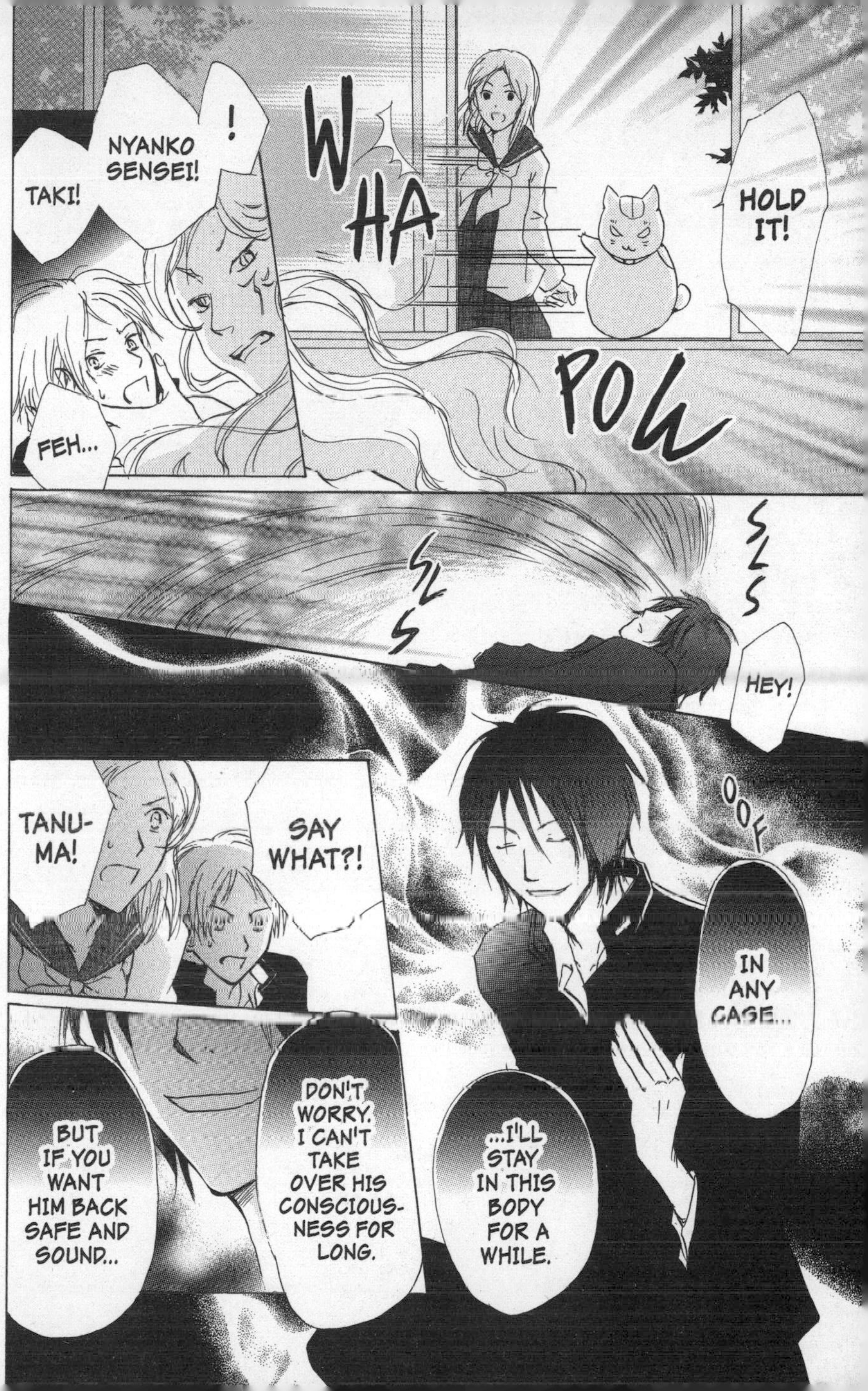
HOLD IT!
POW
WHA
!
NYANKO SENSEI!
TAKI!
FEH...
SLS
SLS
HEY!
OOF
IN ANY CASE...
...I'LL STAY IN THIS BODY FOR A WHILE.
SAY WHAT?!
TANU-MA!
DON'T WORRY. I CAN'T TAKE OVER HIS CONSCIOUS-NESS FOR LONG.
BUT IF YOU WANT HIM BACK SAFE AND SOUND...

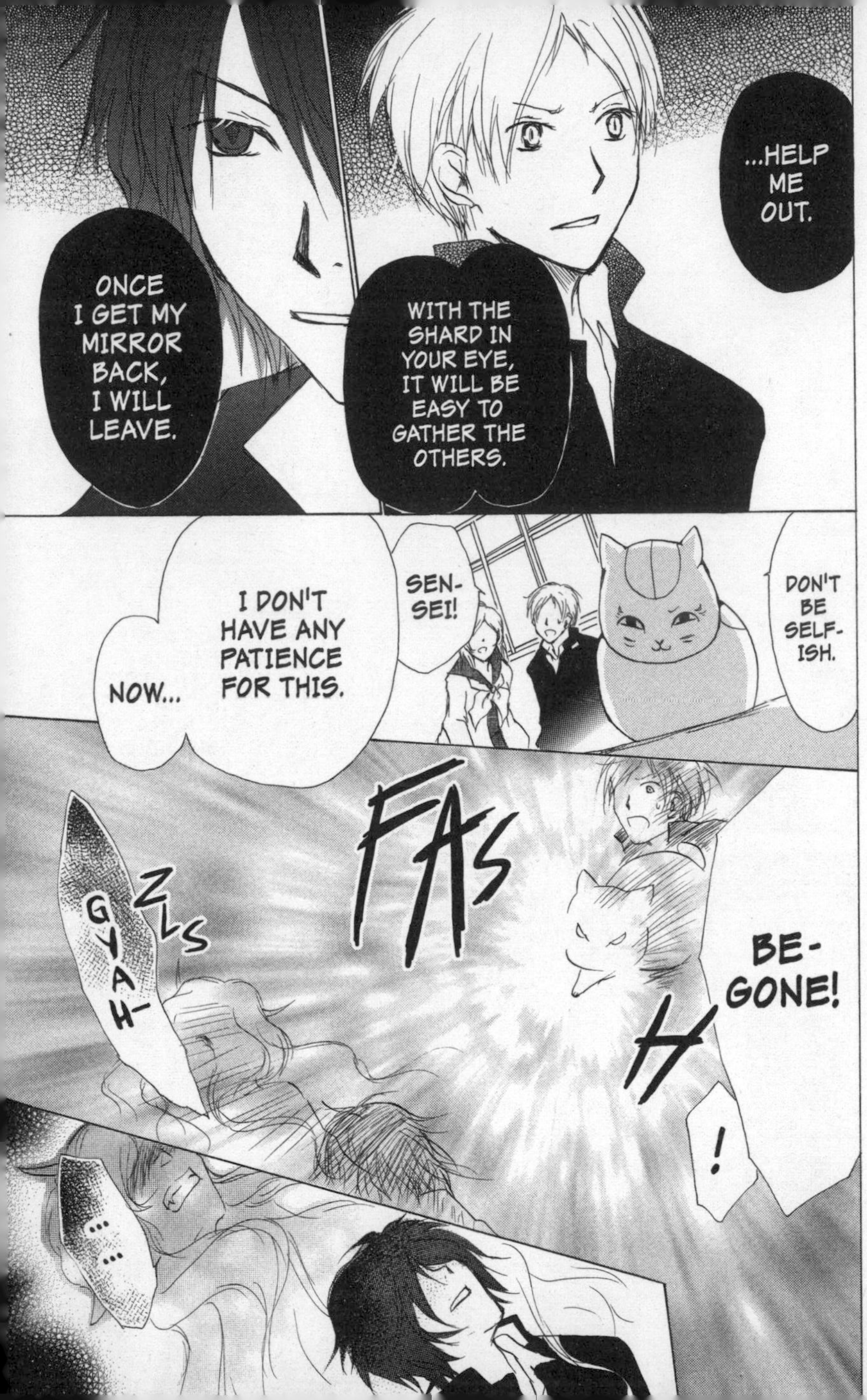
...HELP ME OUT.
WITH THE SHARD IN YOUR EYE, IT WILL BE EASY TO GATHER THE OTHERS.
ONCE I GET MY MIRROR BACK, I WILL LEAVE.
DON'T BE SELF-ISH.
SEN-SEI!
I DON'T HAVE ANY PATIENCE FOR THIS.
NOW...
BE-GONE!
FASH
ZLS
GYAH-
!
......

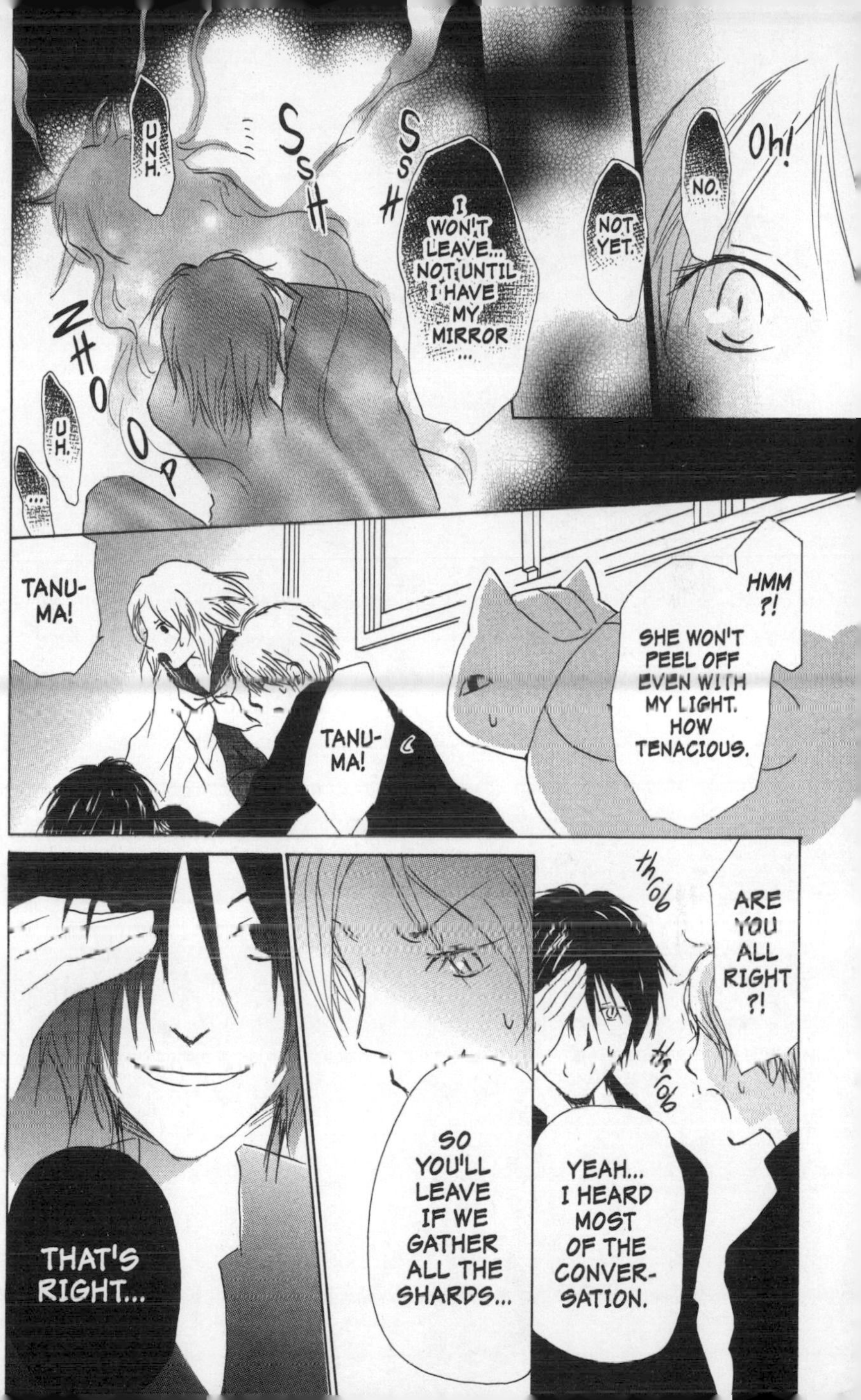
Oh!
NO.
NOT YET.
SSH
SSH
I WON'T LEAVE... NOT UNTIL I HAVE MY MIRROR...
UNH.
ZHOOP
UH.
...
HMM?!
SHE WON'T PEEL OFF EVEN WITH MY LIGHT. HOW TENACIOUS.
TANU-MA!
TANU-MA!
ARE YOU ALL RIGHT?!
throb
throb
YEAH... I HEARD MOST OF THE CONVER-SATION.
SO YOU'LL LEAVE IF WE GATHER ALL THE SHARDS...
THAT'S RIGHT...

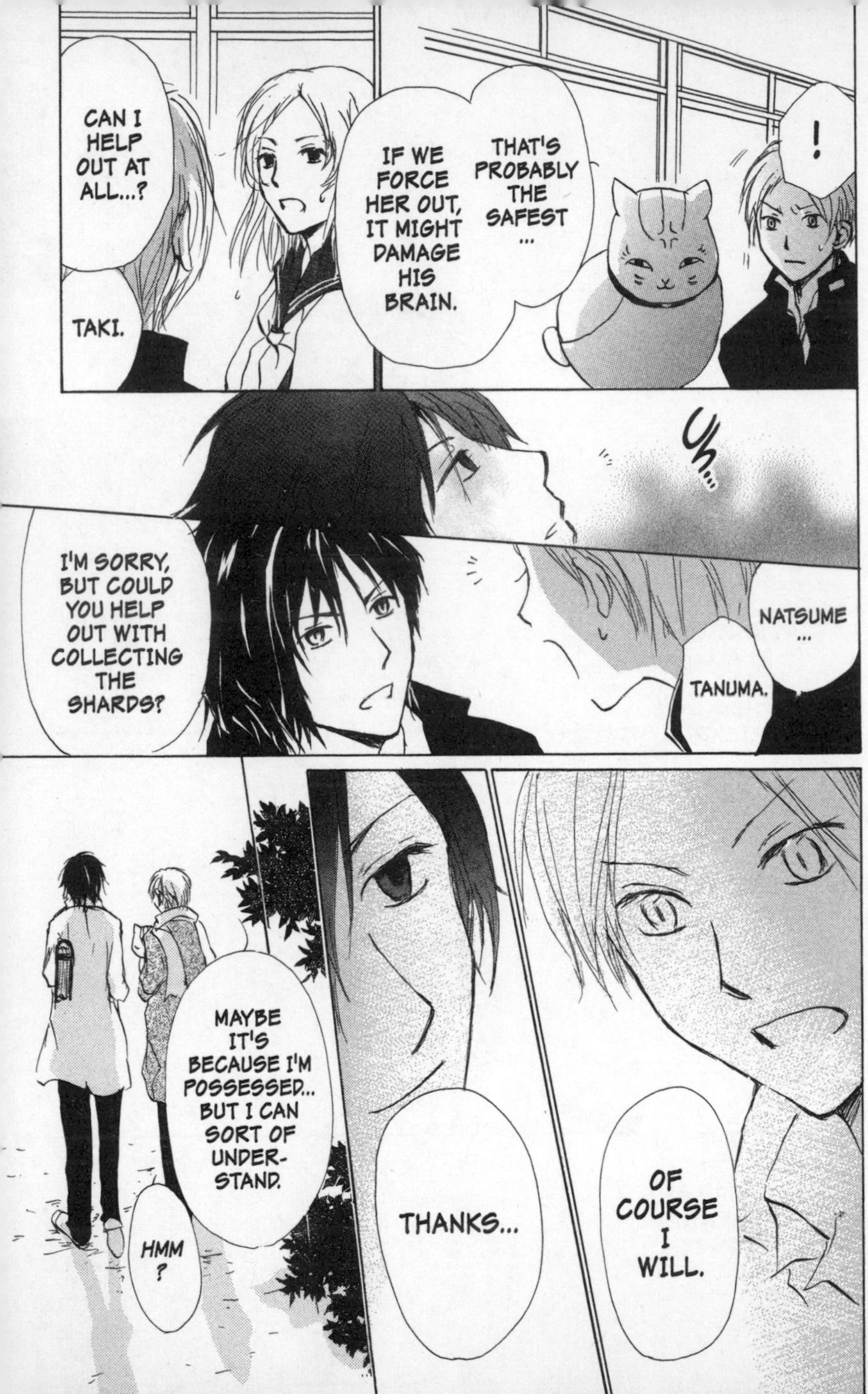
!
THAT'S PROBABLY THE SAFEST ...
IF WE FORCE HER OUT, IT MIGHT DAMAGE HIS BRAIN.
CAN I HELP OUT AT ALL...?
TAKI.
Uh...
NATSUME ...
TANUMA.
I'M SORRY, BUT COULD YOU HELP OUT WITH COLLECTING THE SHARDS?
OF COURSE I WILL.
THANKS...
MAYBE IT'S BECAUSE I'M POSSESSED... BUT I CAN SORT OF UNDER-STAND.
HMM ?

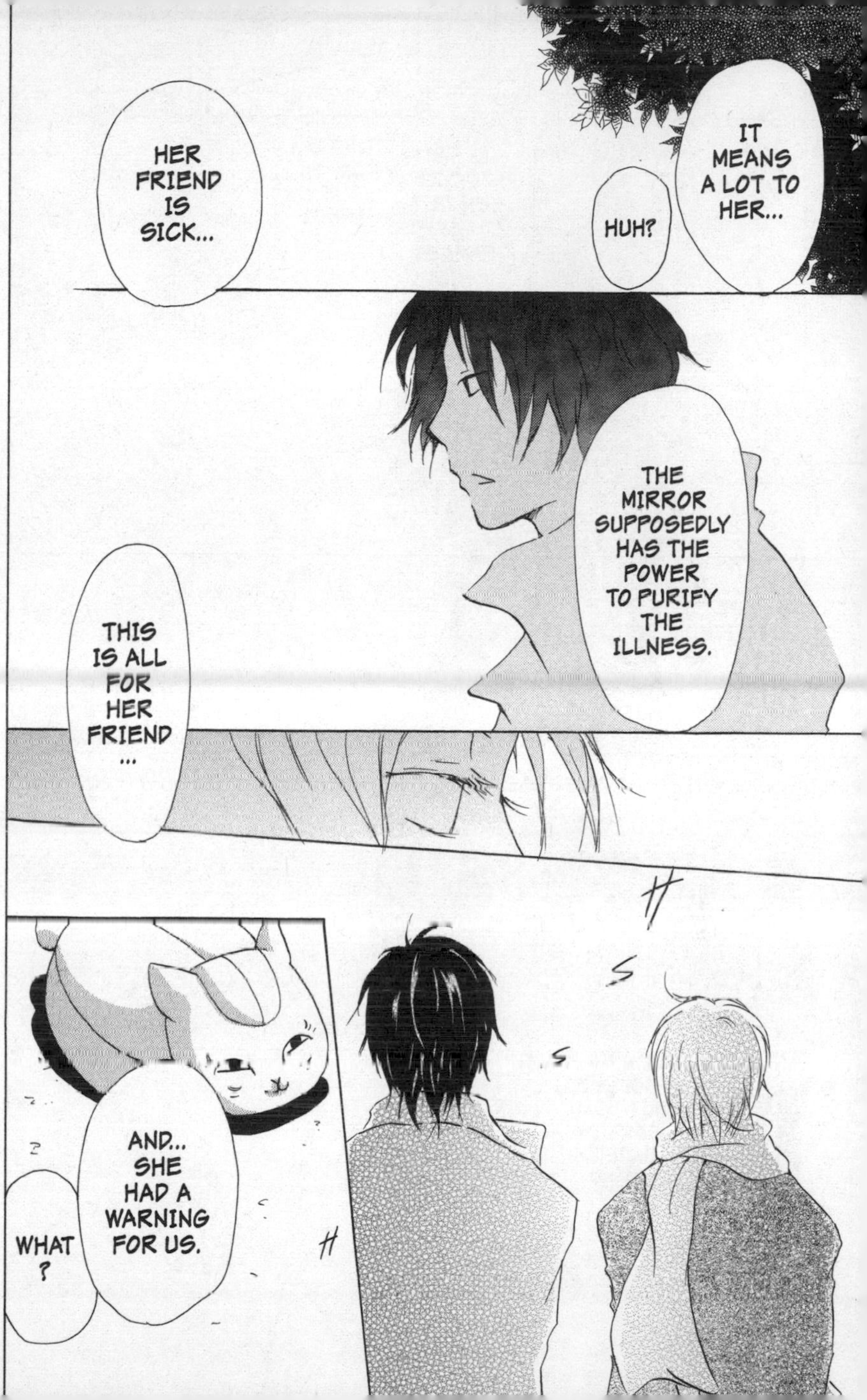
IT MEANS A LOT TO HER...
HUH?
HER FRIEND IS SICK...
THE MIRROR SUPPOSEDLY HAS THE POWER TO PURIFY THE ILLNESS.
THIS IS ALL FOR HER FRIEND...
AND... SHE HAD A WARNING FOR US.
WHAT?

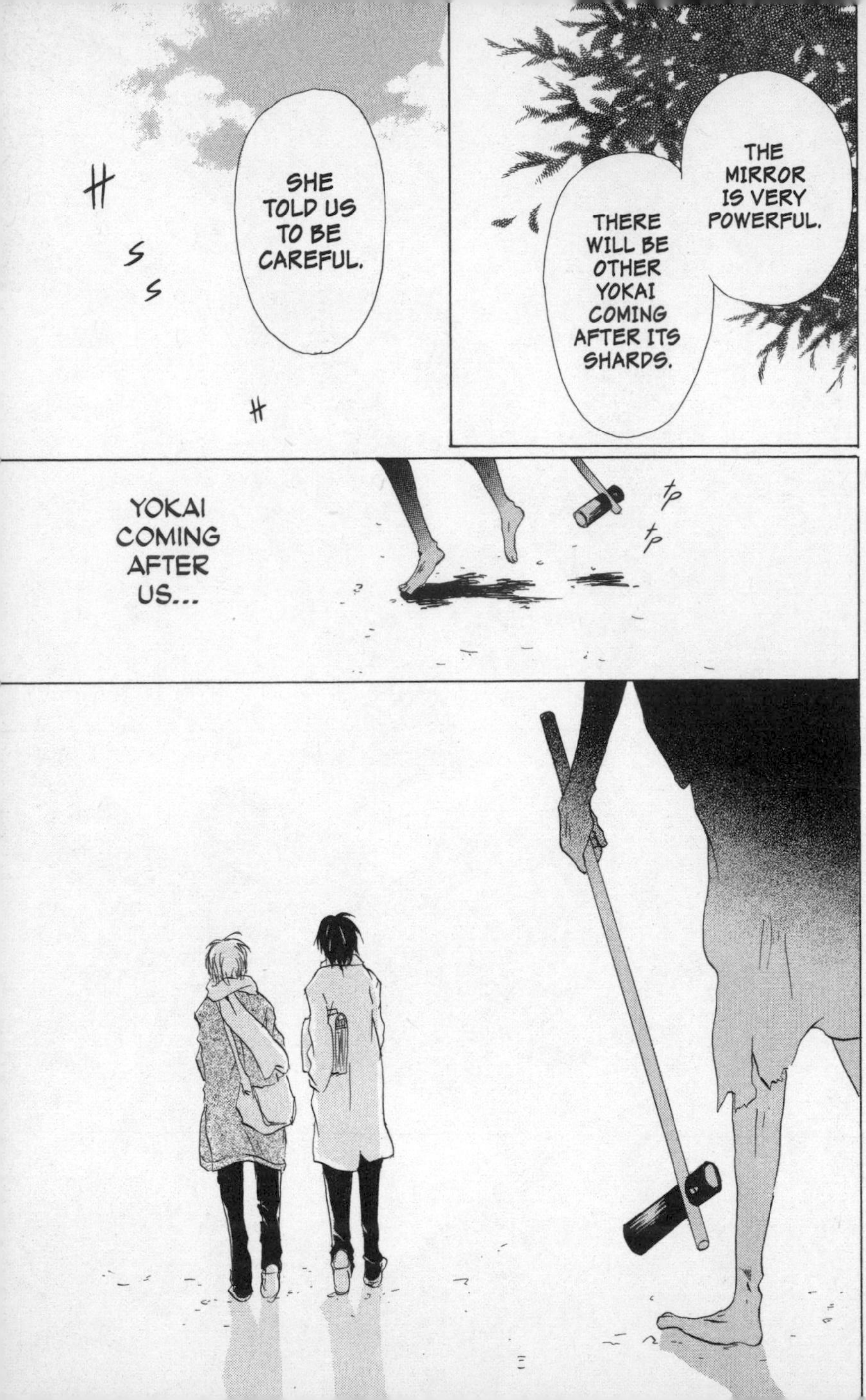
THE MIRROR IS VERY POWERFUL.
THERE WILL BE OTHER YOKAI COMING AFTER ITS SHARDS.
SHE TOLD US TO BE CAREFUL.
TP
TP
YOKAI COMING AFTER US...

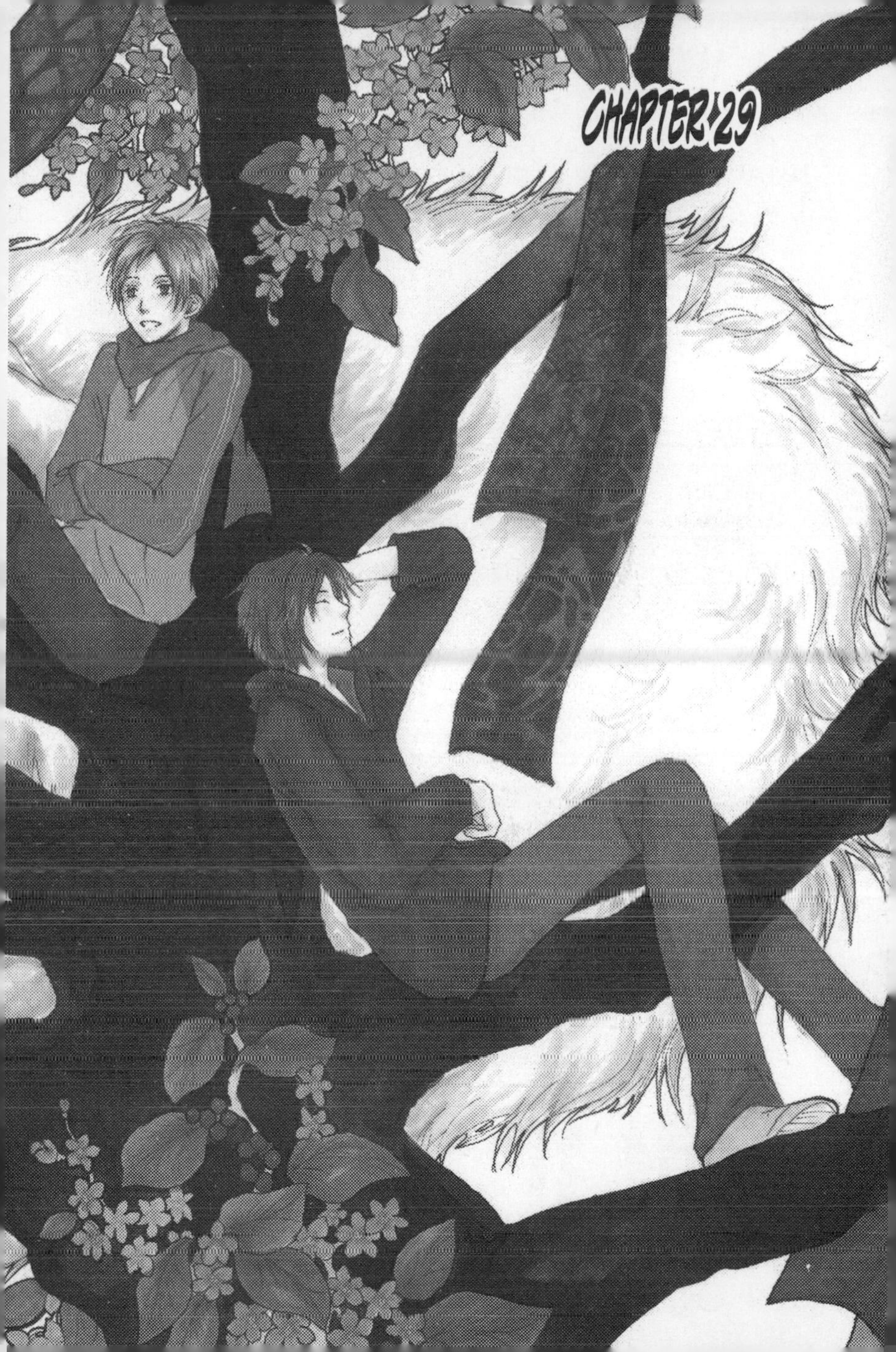
CHAPTER 29

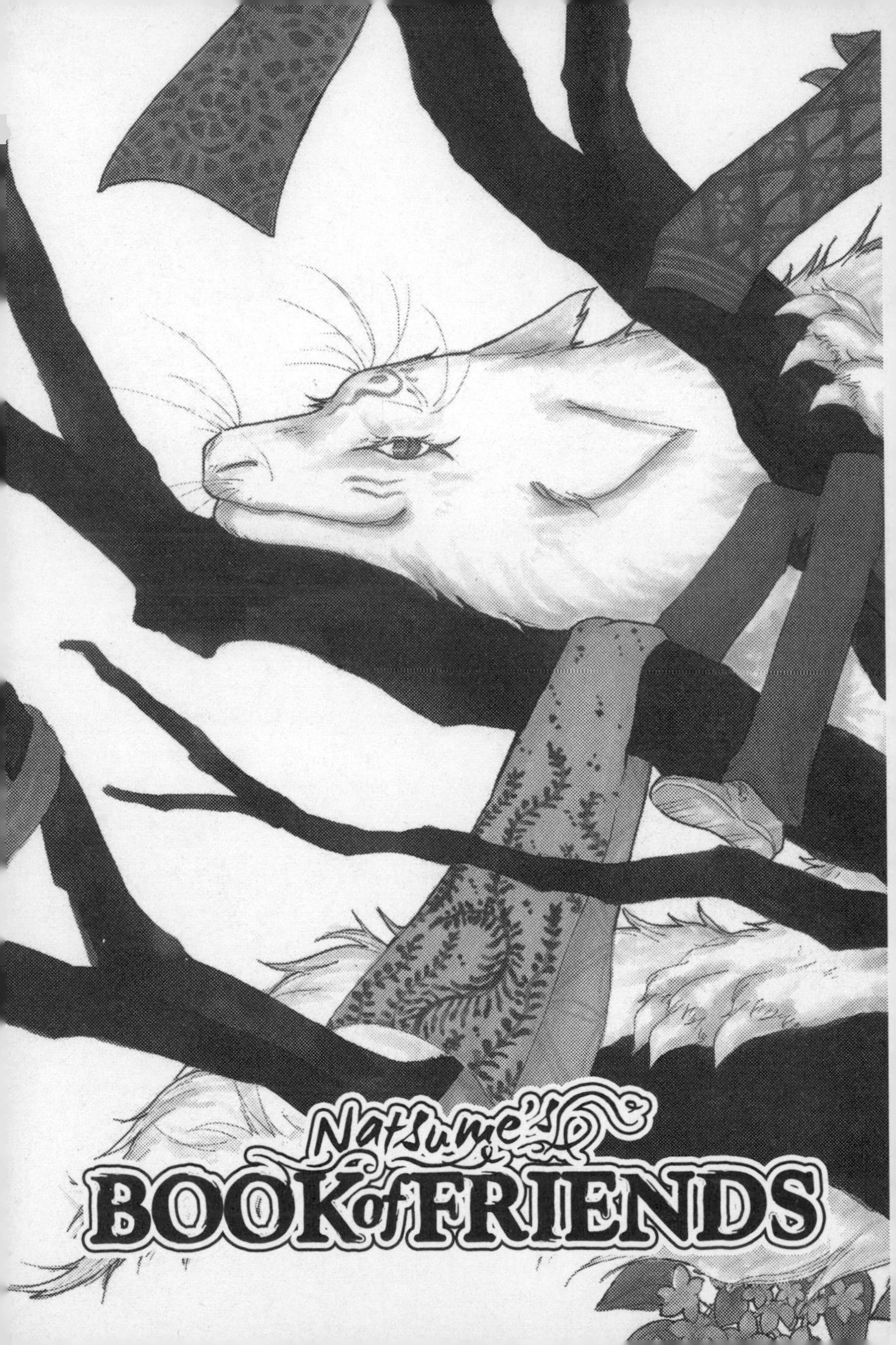
Natsume's
BOOK of FRIENDS

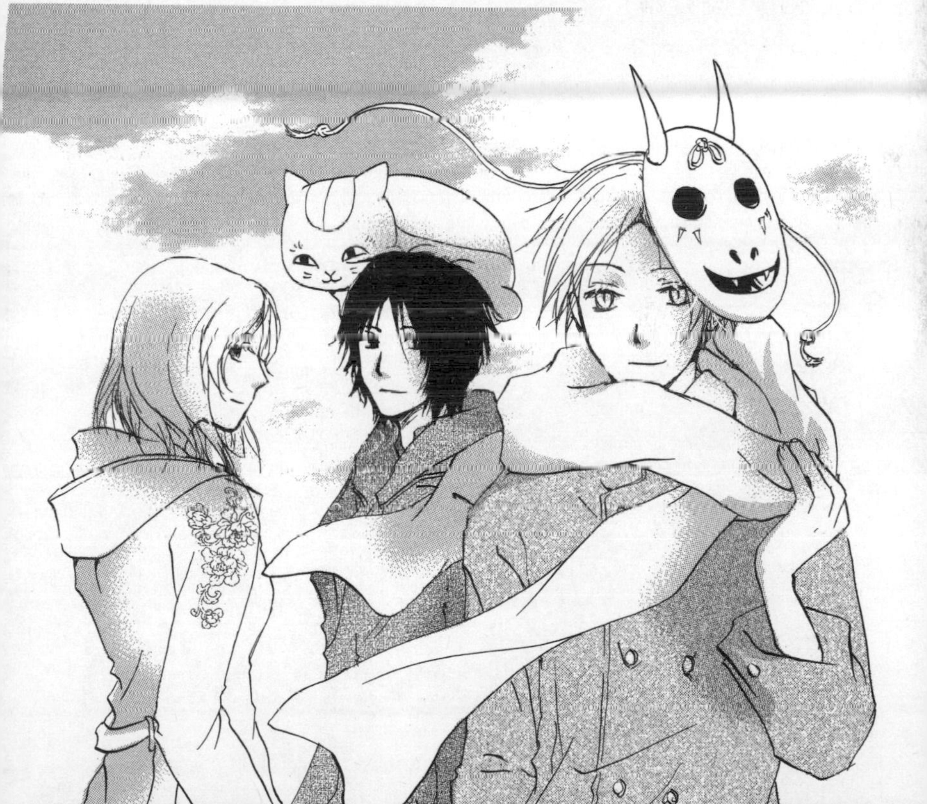

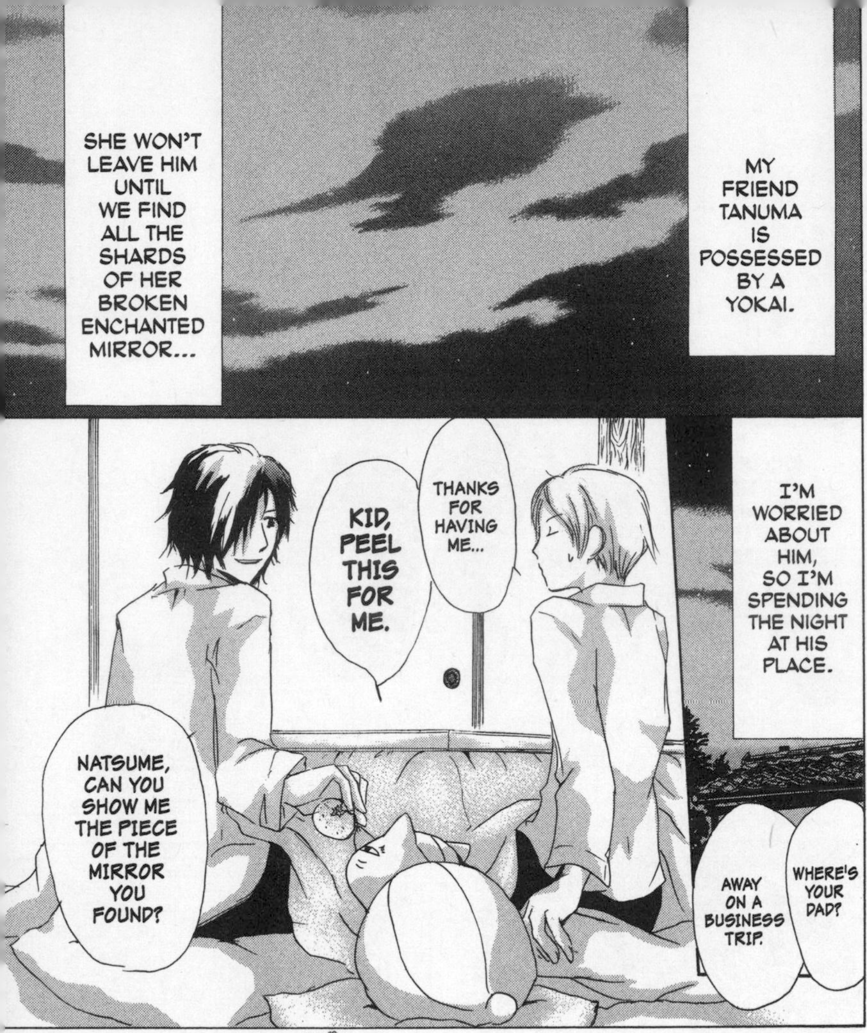
MY FRIEND TANUMA IS POSSESSED BY A YOKAI.
SHE WON'T LEAVE HIM UNTIL WE FIND ALL THE SHARDS OF HER BROKEN ENCHANTED MIRROR...
I'M WORRIED ABOUT HIM, SO I'M SPENDING THE NIGHT AT HIS PLACE.
THANKS FOR HAVING ME...
KID, PEEL THIS FOR ME.
WHERE'S YOUR DAD?
AWAY ON A BUSINESS TRIP.
NATSUME, CAN YOU SHOW ME THE PIECE OF THE MIRROR YOU FOUND?

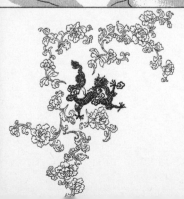

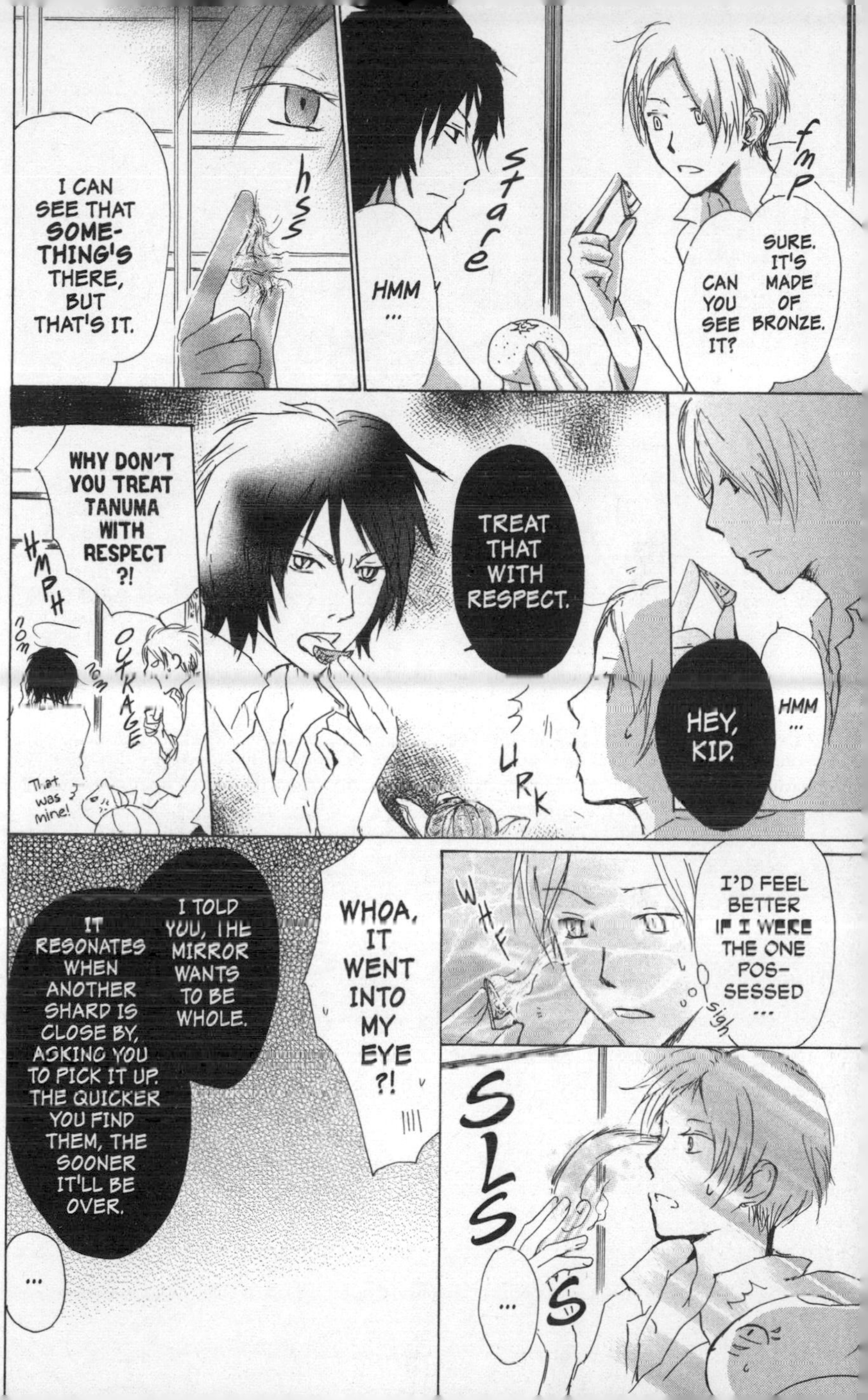
fmp
SURE. IT'S MADE OF BRONZE.
CAN YOU SEE IT?
stare
HMM ...
hss
I CAN SEE THAT SOMETHING'S THERE, BUT THAT'S IT.
HMM ...
HEY, KID.
TREAT THAT WITH RESPECT.
URK
WHY DON'T YOU TREAT TANUMA WITH RESPECT?!
HMPH
OUTRAGE
nom nom
That was mine!
I'D FEEL BETTER IF I WERE THE ONE POS-SESSED ...
WHF
sigh
SLS
S
...
WHOA, IT WENT INTO MY EYE?!
I TOLD YOU, THE MIRROR WANTS TO BE WHOLE.
IT RESONATES WHEN ANOTHER SHARD IS CLOSE BY, ASKING YOU TO PICK IT UP. THE QUICKER YOU FIND THEM, THE SOONER IT'LL BE OVER.
...

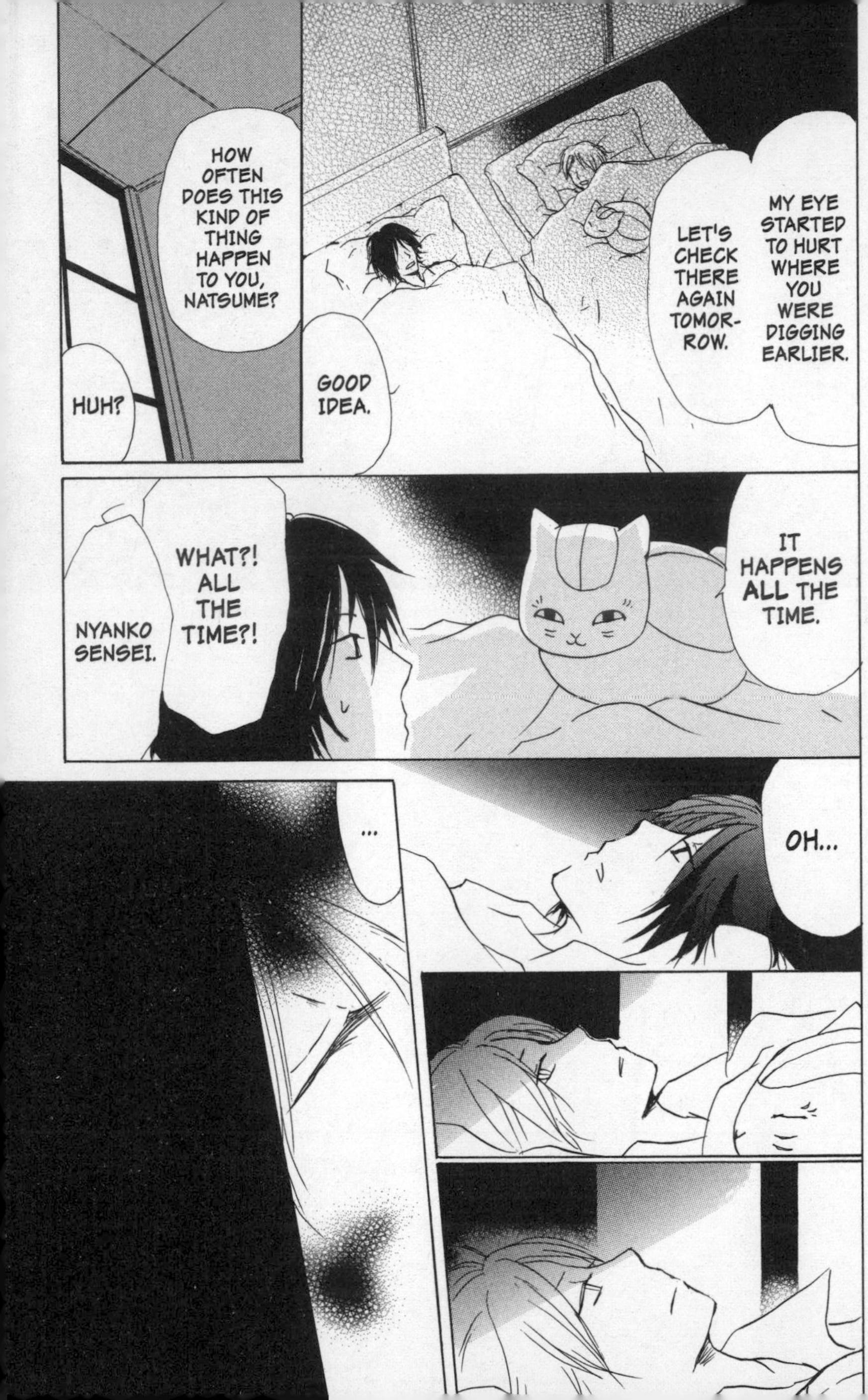

MY EYE STARTED TO HURT WHERE YOU WERE DIGGING EARLIER.
LET'S CHECK THERE AGAIN TOMOR-ROW.
GOOD IDEA.
HOW OFTEN DOES THIS KIND OF THING HAPPEN TO YOU, NATSUME?
HUH?
IT HAPPENS **ALL** THE TIME.
WHAT?! ALL THE TIME?!
NYANKO SENSEI.
OH...
...

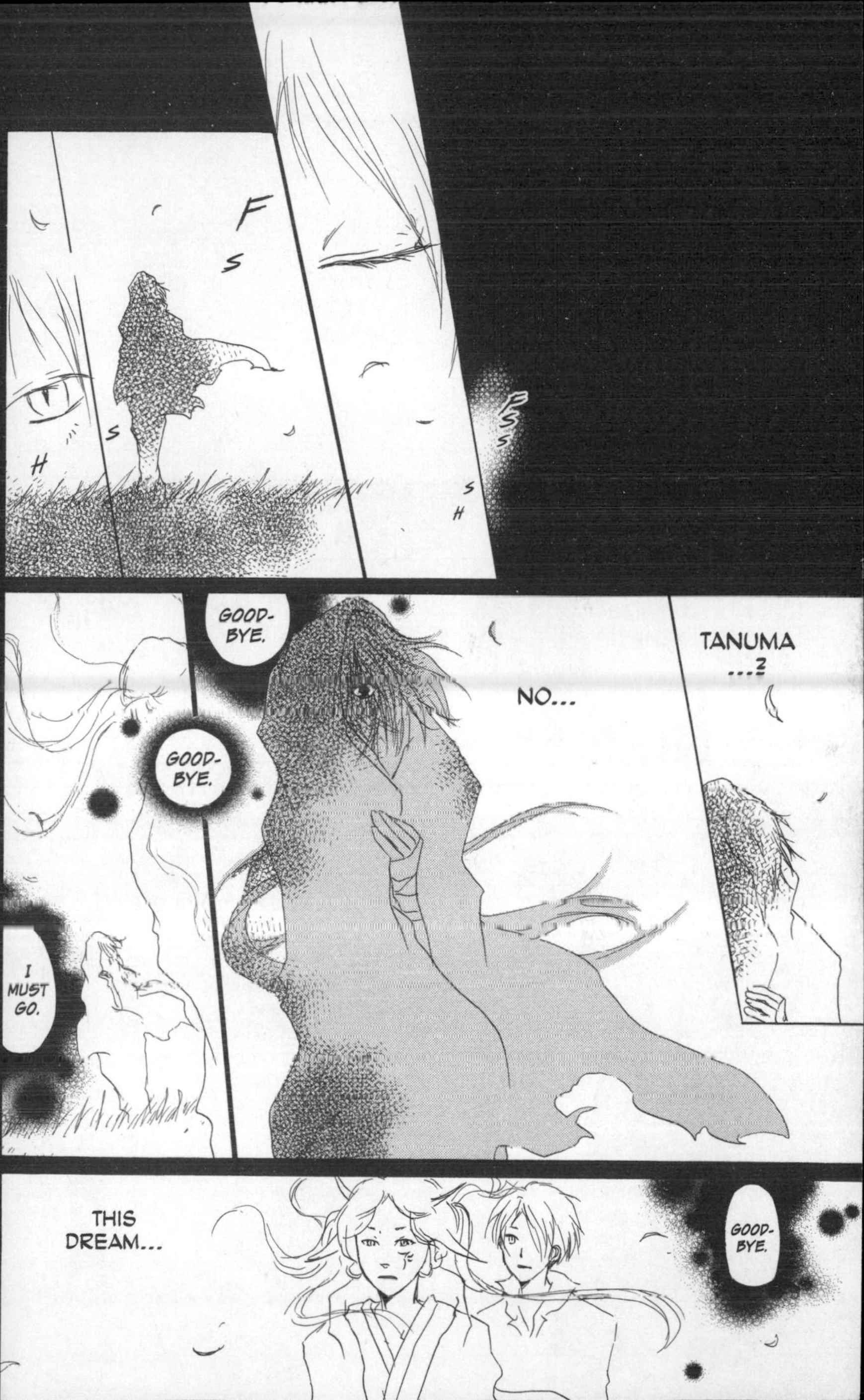
PSSSH
FSSH
SH
TANUMA ...?
NO...
GOOD-BYE.
GOOD-BYE.
I MUST GO.
GOOD-BYE.
THIS DREAM...

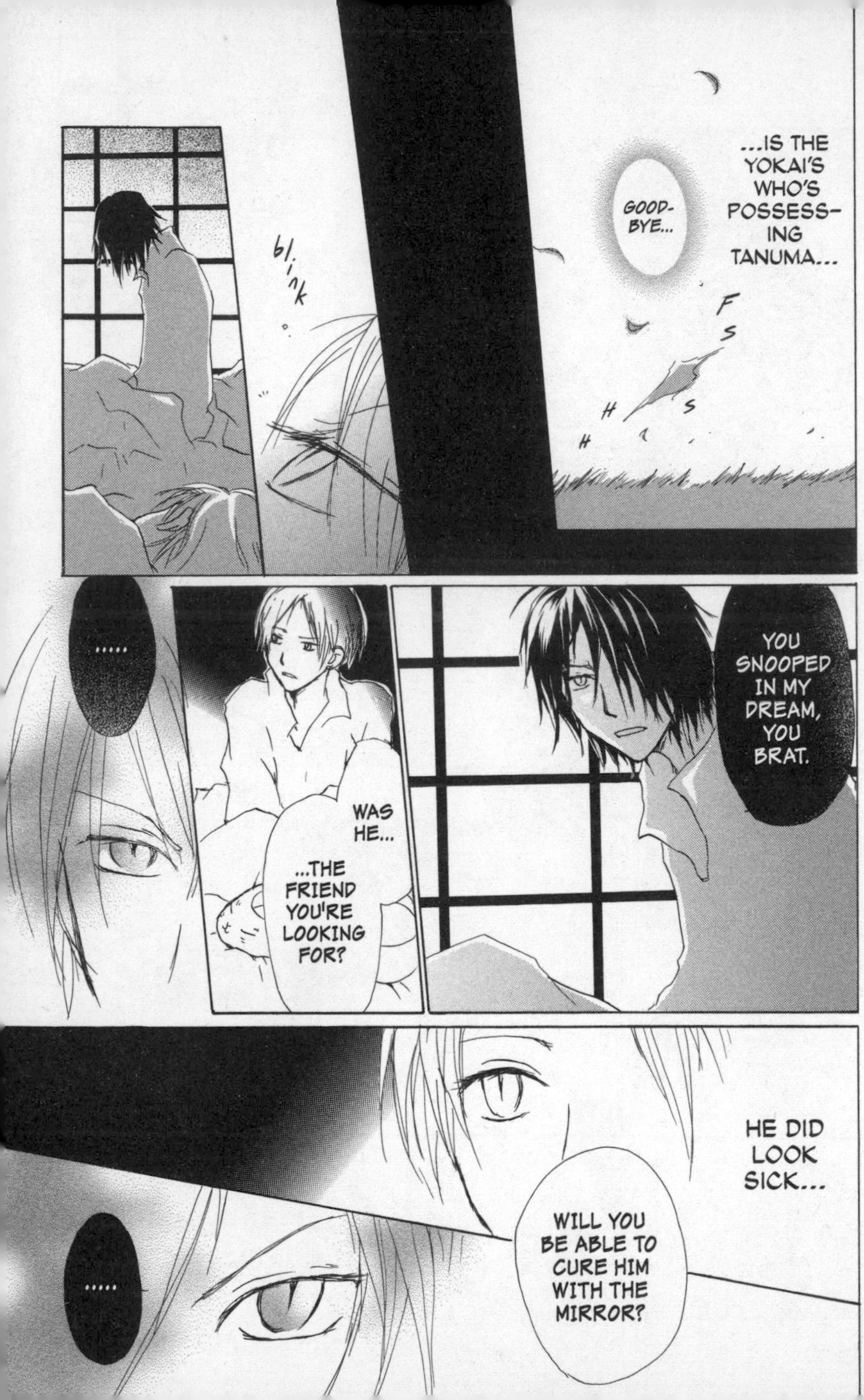
...IS THE YOKAI'S WHO'S POSSESS-ING TANUMA...
GOOD-BYE...
FSSHH
blink
YOU SNOOPED IN MY DREAM, YOU BRAT.
WAS HE...
...THE FRIEND YOU'RE LOOKING FOR?
......
HE DID LOOK SICK...
WILL YOU BE ABLE TO CURE HIM WITH THE MIRROR?
......

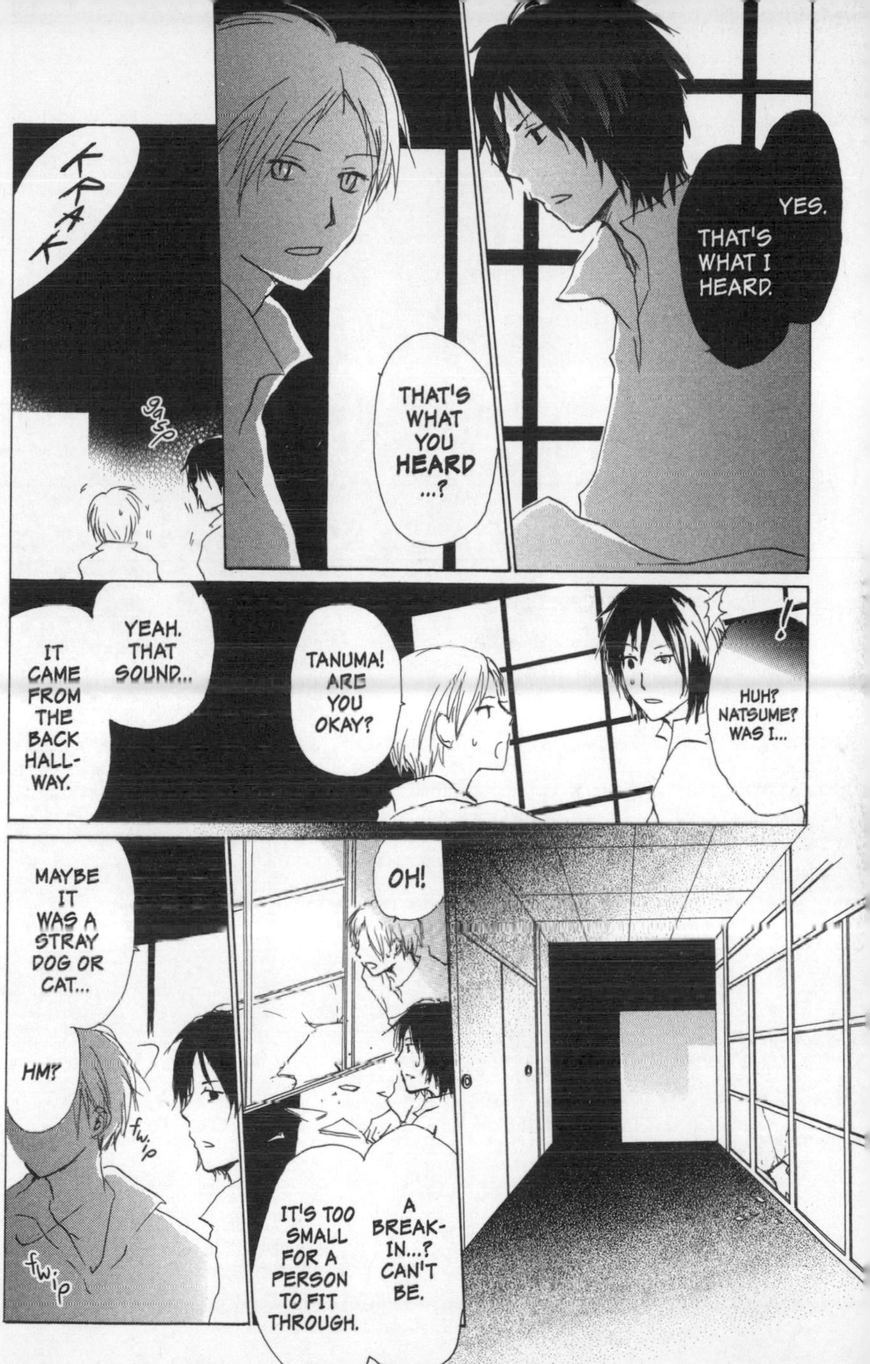
YES.
THAT'S WHAT I HEARD.
THAT'S WHAT YOU HEARD ...?
KRAK
gasp
!
HUH? NATSUME? WAS I...
TANUMA! ARE YOU OKAY?
YEAH. THAT SOUND...
IT CAME FROM THE BACK HALL-WAY.
OH!
A BREAK-IN...? CAN'T BE.
IT'S TOO SMALL FOR A PERSON TO FIT THROUGH.
MAYBE IT WAS A STRAY DOG OR CAT...
HM?
fwip
fwip

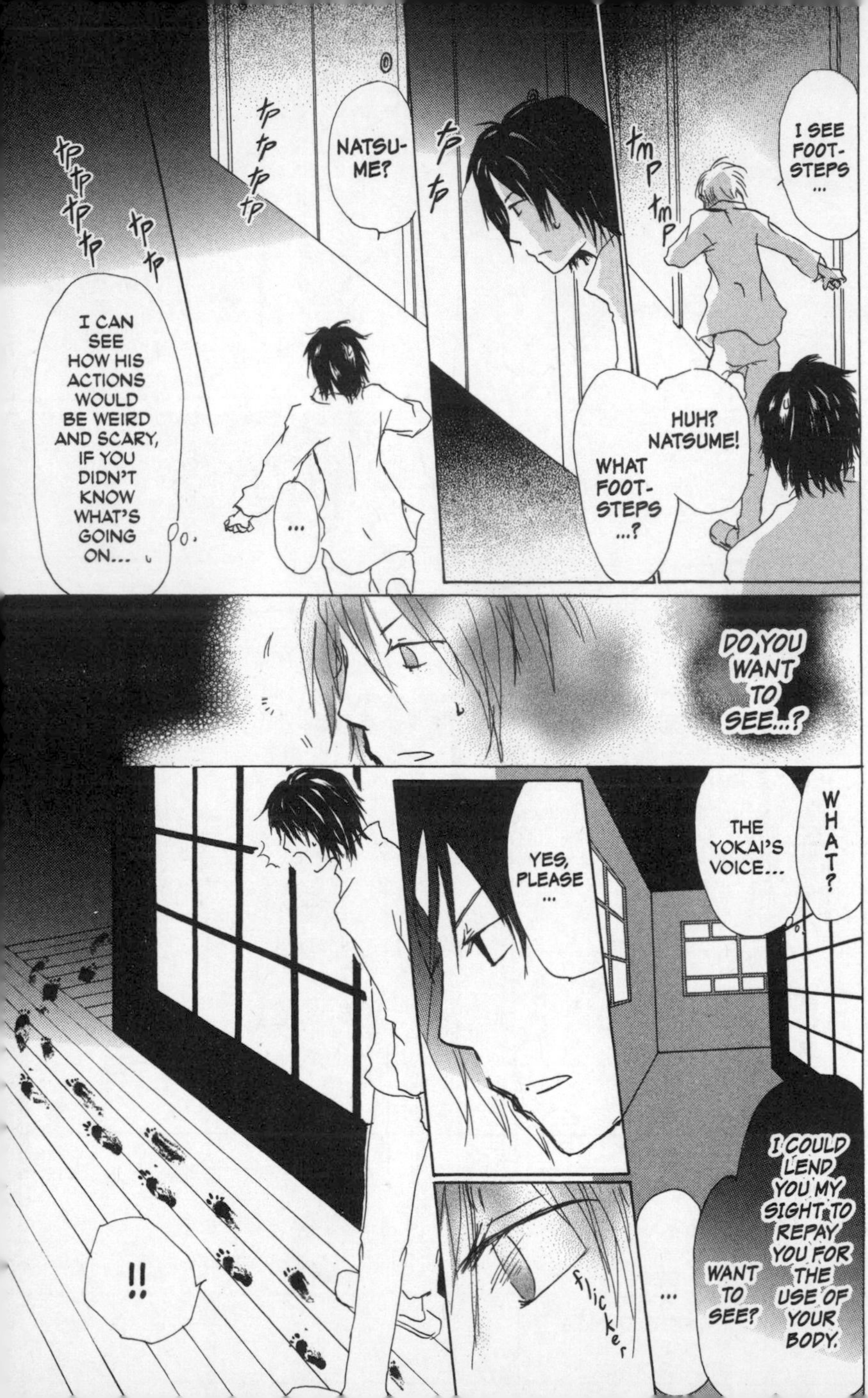
I SEE FOOT-STEPS...
tmp tmp
HUH? NATSUME!
WHAT FOOT-STEPS...?
tp tp
NATSU-ME?
tp tp tp tp
...
tp tp tp tp
tp tp
I CAN SEE HOW HIS ACTIONS WOULD BE WEIRD AND SCARY, IF YOU DIDN'T KNOW WHAT'S GOING ON...
DO YOU WANT TO SEE...?
WHAT?
THE YOKAI'S VOICE...
YES, PLEASE...
I COULD LEND YOU MY SIGHT TO REPAY YOU FOR THE USE OF YOUR BODY.
WANT TO SEE?
...
flicker
!!

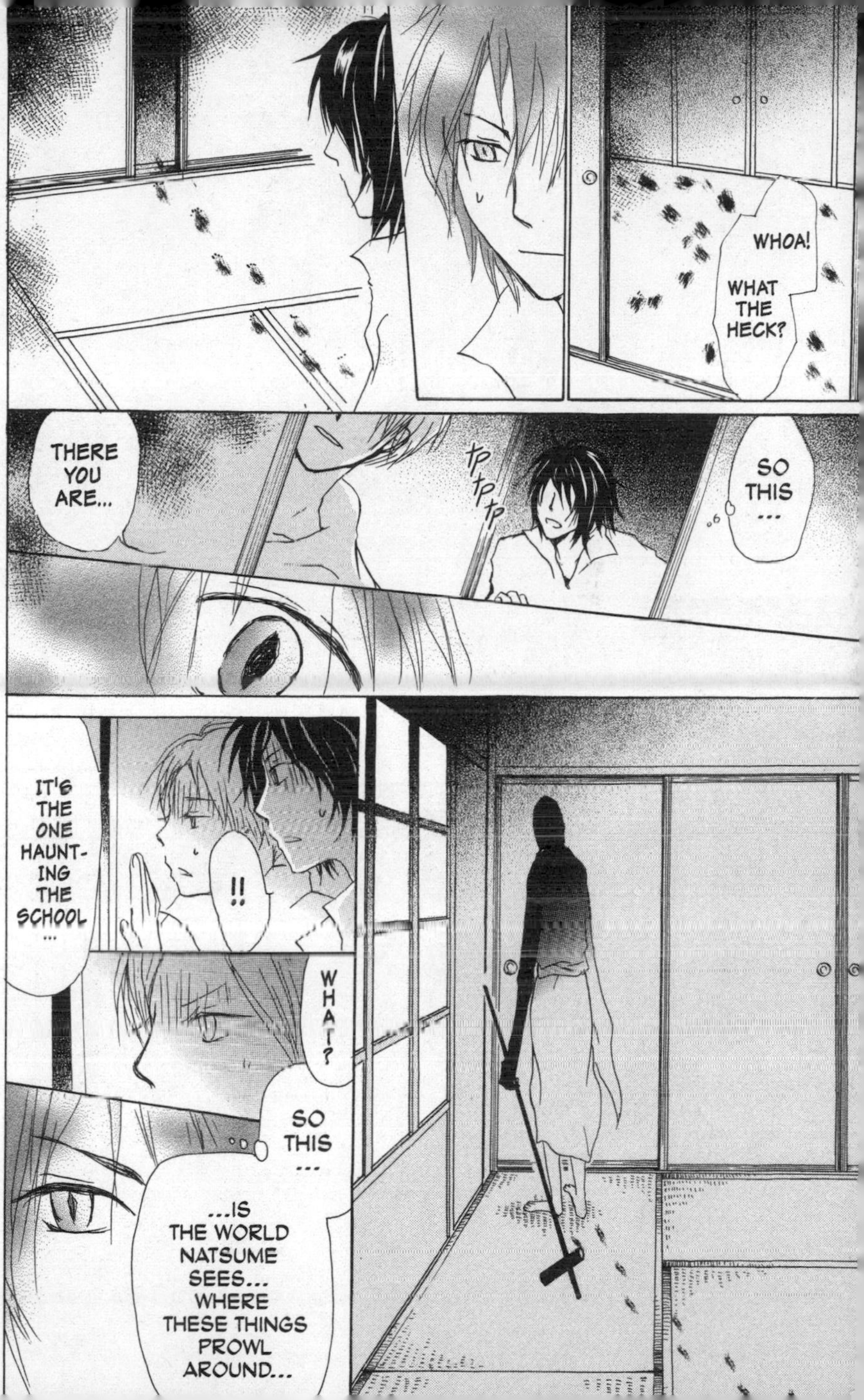
WHOA! WHAT THE HECK?
SO THIS ...
THERE YOU ARE...
!!
IT'S THE ONE HAUNTING THE SCHOOL ...
WHAT?
SO THIS ...
...IS THE WORLD NATSUME SEES... WHERE THESE THINGS PROWL AROUND...

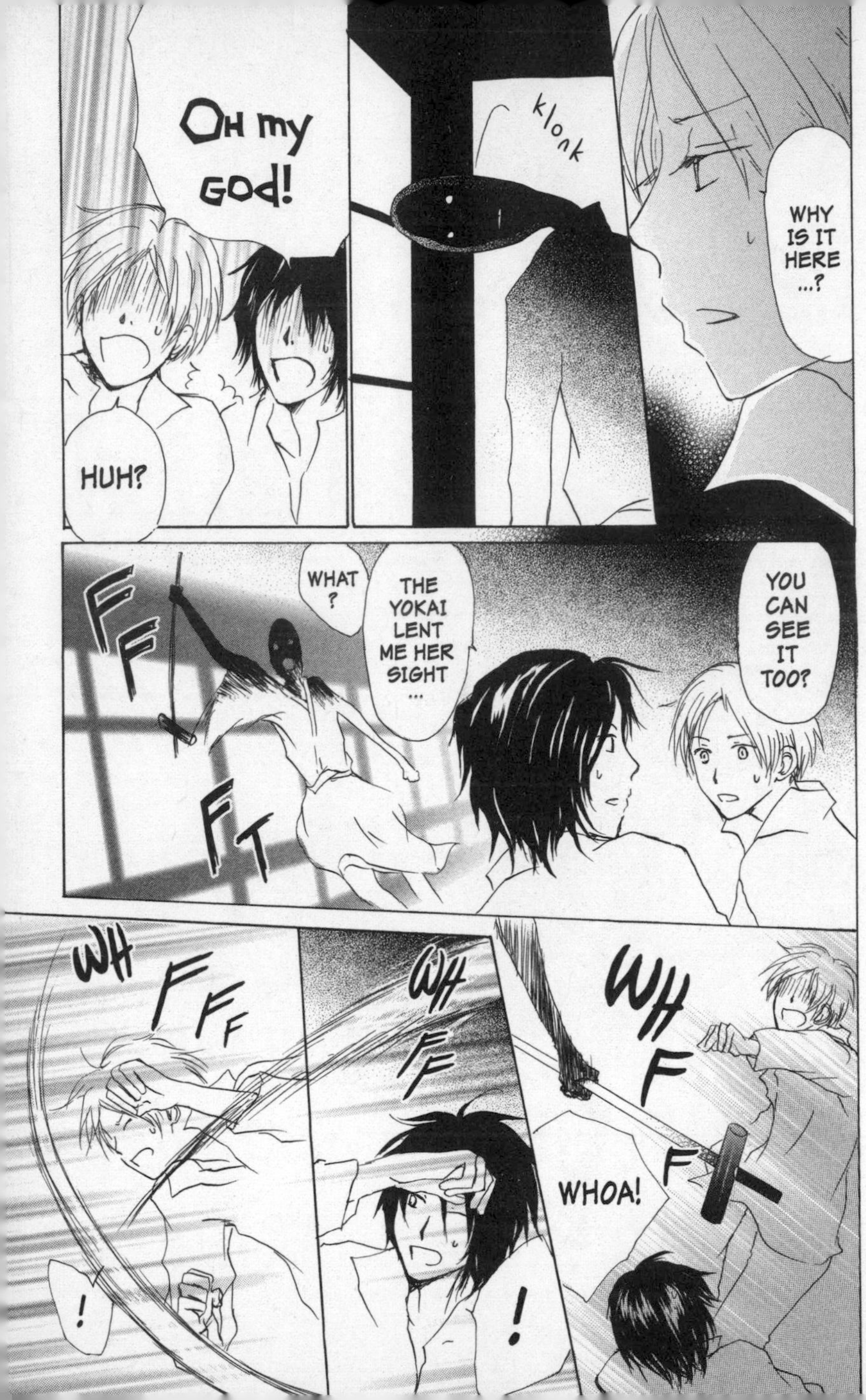
WHY IS IT HERE ...?
klonk
OH my GOD!
HUH?
YOU CAN SEE IT TOO?
THE YOKAI LENT ME HER SIGHT ...
WHAT?
FF
FFT
WHFF
F
WHOA!
WHFF
!
WHFFF
!

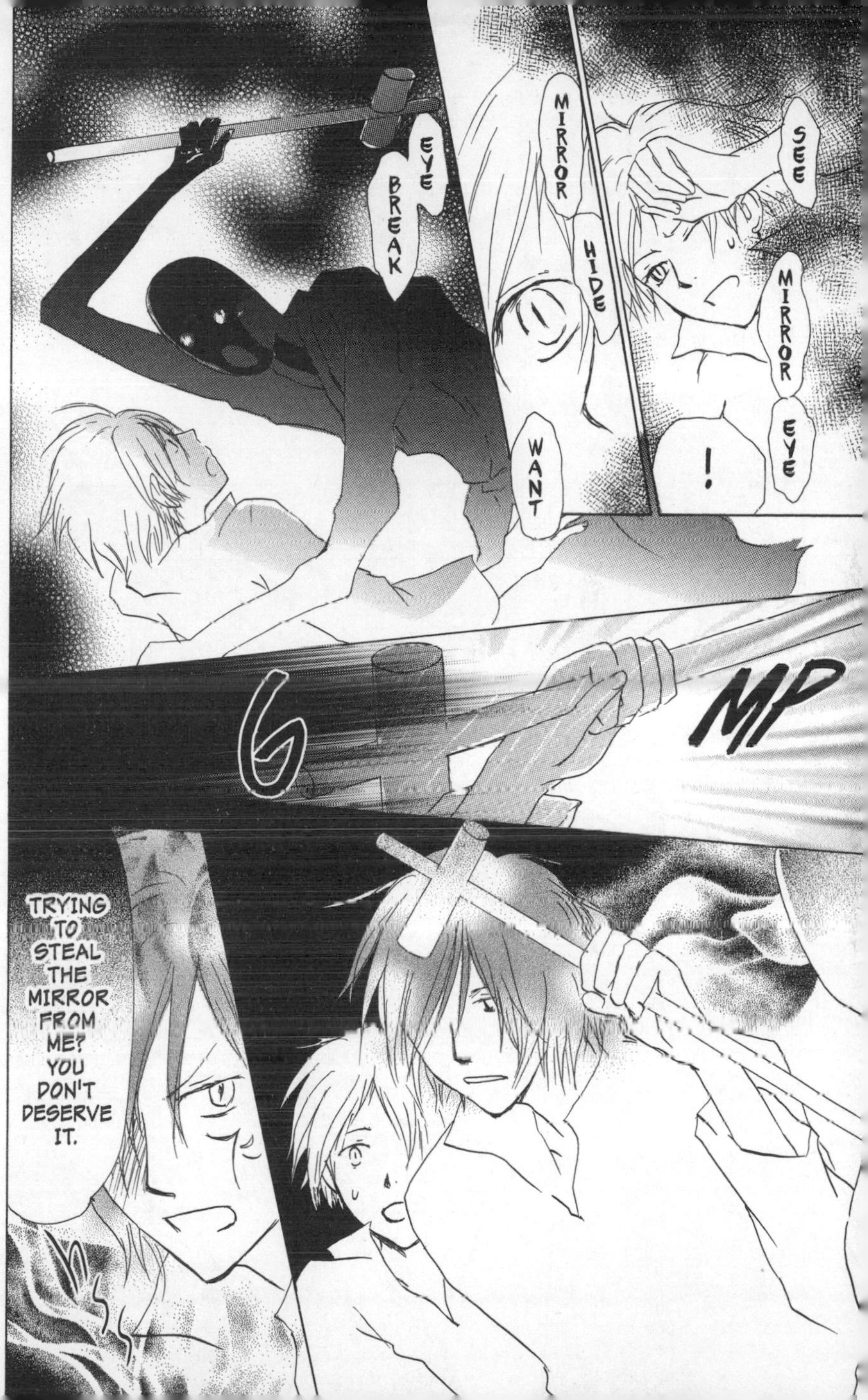
SEE
MIRROR
EYE
!
MIRROR
HIDE
WANT
EYE
BREAK
G
MP
TRYING TO STEAL THE MIRROR FROM ME? YOU DON'T DESERVE IT.

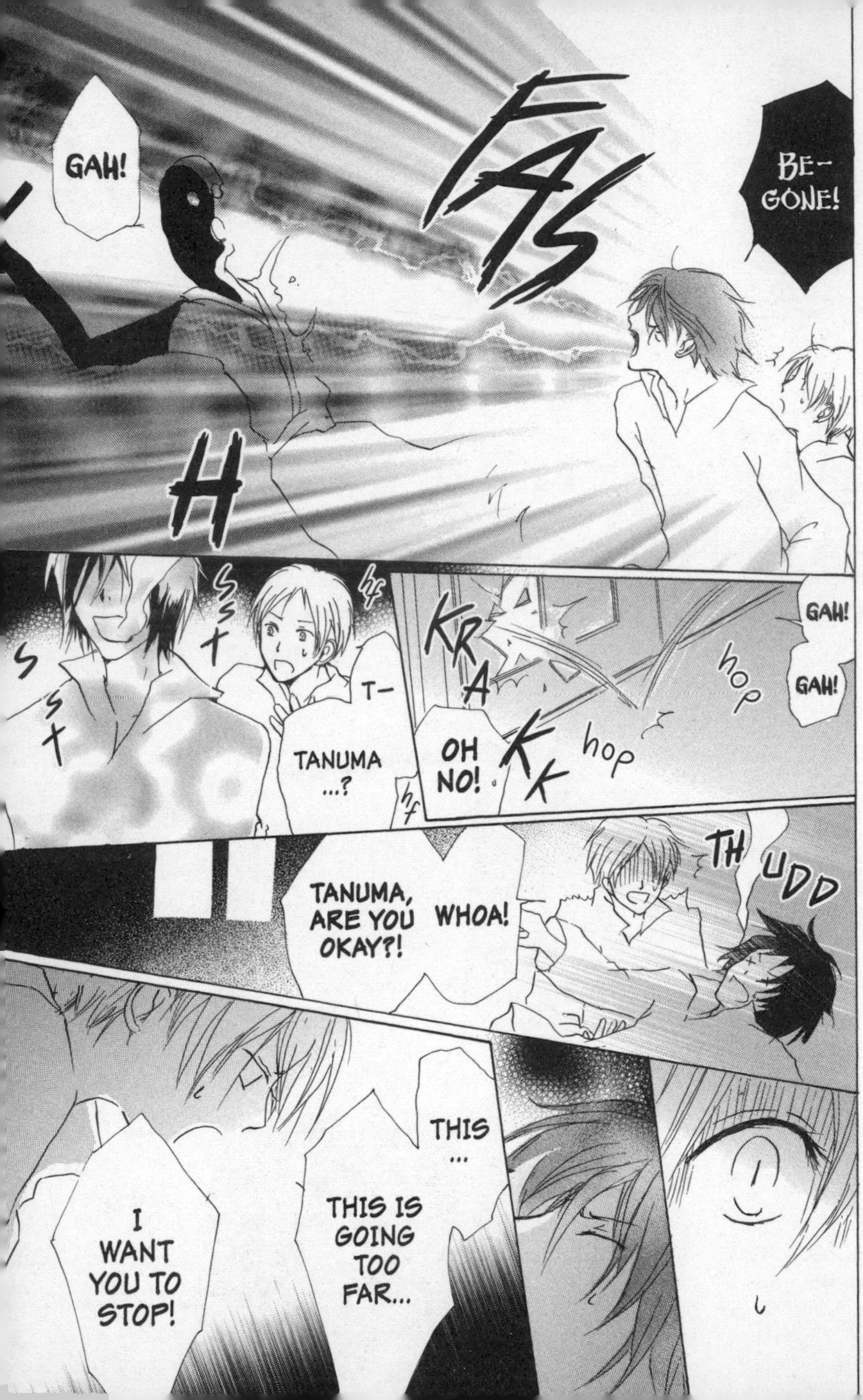
BE-GONE!
FASH
GAH!
GAH!
GAH!
hop hop
KRAKK
OH NO!
hf hf
T-
TANUMA ...?
SSST SSST
THUDD
WHOA!
TANUMA, ARE YOU OKAY?!
THIS ...
THIS IS GOING TOO FAR...
I WANT YOU TO STOP!

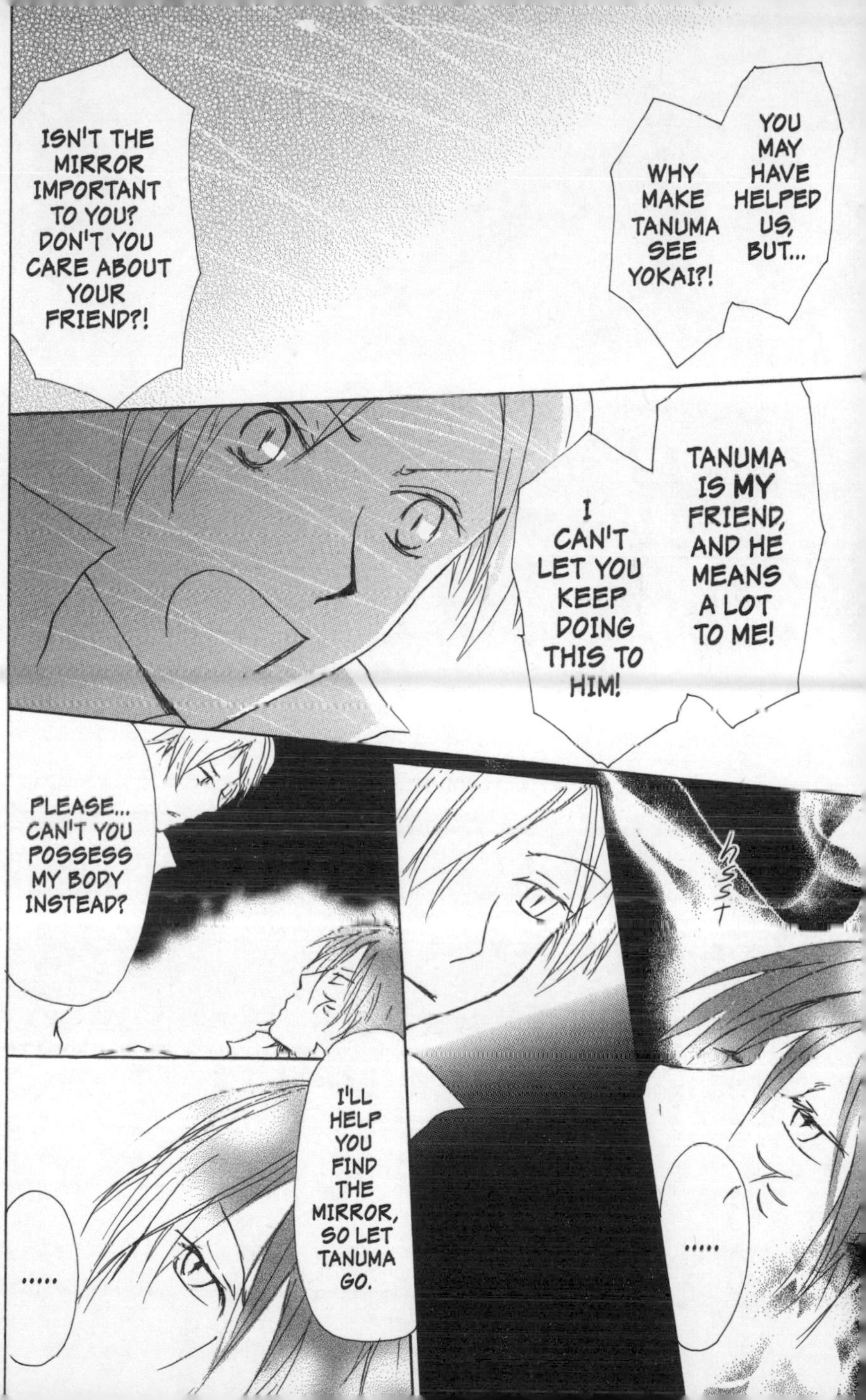
YOU MAY HAVE HELPED US, BUT...
WHY MAKE TANUMA SEE YOKAI?!
ISN'T THE MIRROR IMPORTANT TO YOU? DON'T YOU CARE ABOUT YOUR FRIEND?!
TANUMA IS MY FRIEND, AND HE MEANS A LOT TO ME!
I CAN'T LET YOU KEEP DOING THIS TO HIM!
HSSS
PLEASE... CAN'T YOU POSSESS MY BODY INSTEAD?
.....
I'LL HELP YOU FIND THE MIRROR, SO LET TANUMA GO.
.....

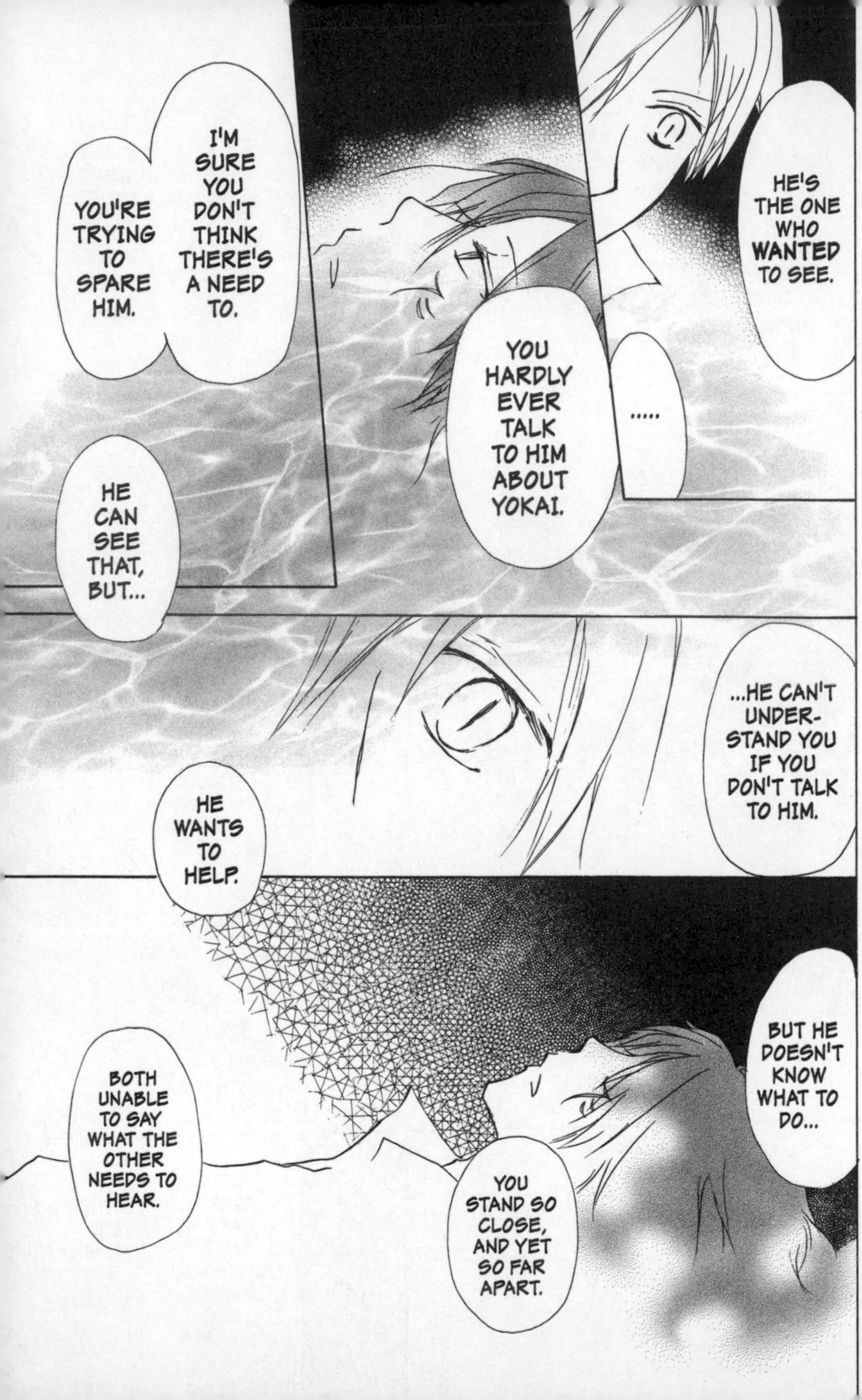
HE'S THE ONE WHO WANTED TO SEE.
.....
YOU HARDLY EVER TALK TO HIM ABOUT YOKAI.
I'M SURE YOU DON'T THINK THERE'S A NEED TO.
YOU'RE TRYING TO SPARE HIM.
HE CAN SEE THAT, BUT...
...HE CAN'T UNDERSTAND YOU IF YOU DON'T TALK TO HIM.
HE WANTS TO HELP.
BUT HE DOESN'T KNOW WHAT TO DO...
YOU STAND SO CLOSE, AND YET SO FAR APART.
BOTH UNABLE TO SAY WHAT THE OTHER NEEDS TO HEAR.

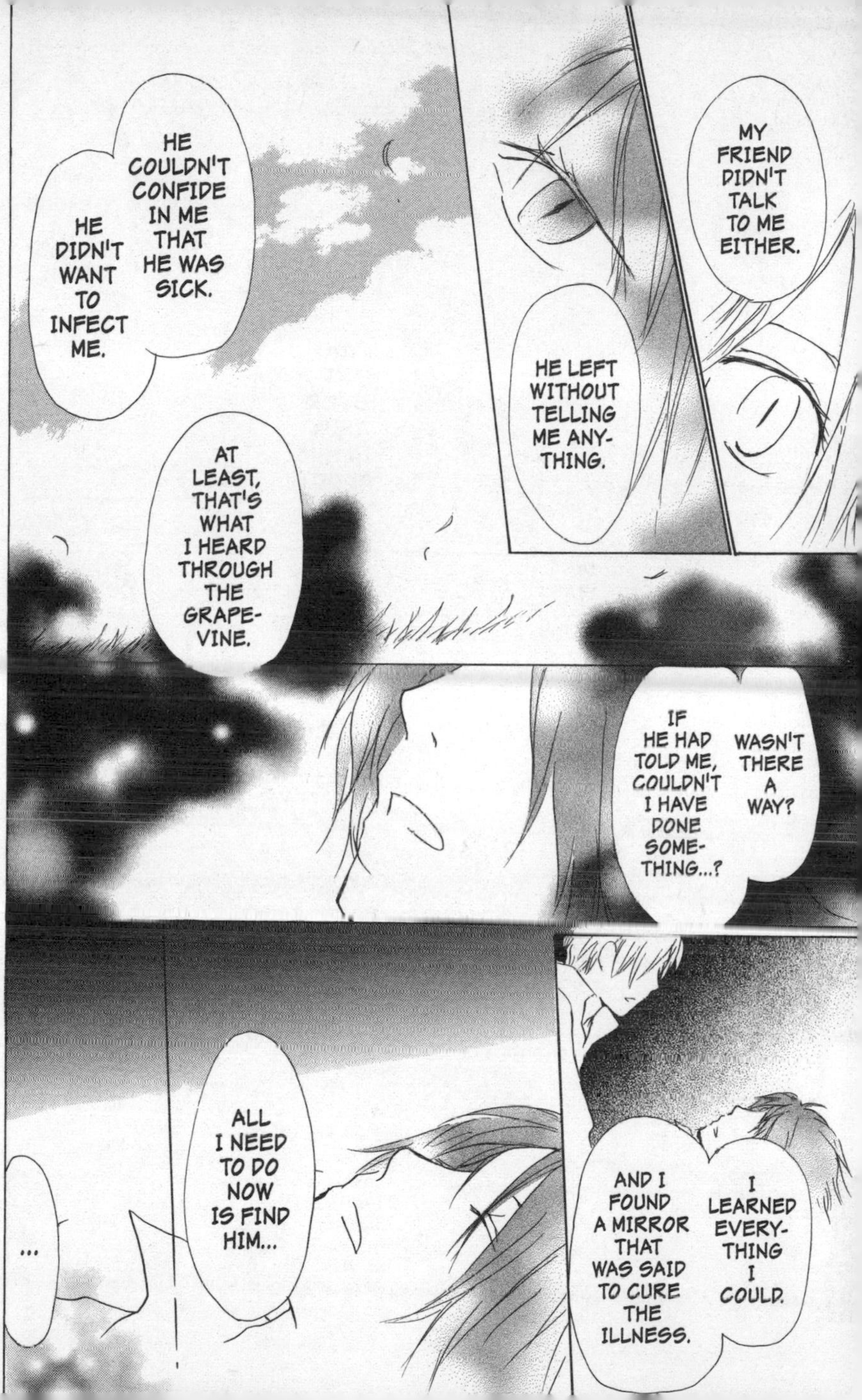
MY FRIEND DIDN'T TALK TO ME EITHER.
HE LEFT WITHOUT TELLING ME ANY-THING.
HE COULDN'T CONFIDE IN ME THAT HE WAS SICK.
HE DIDN'T WANT TO INFECT ME.
AT LEAST, THAT'S WHAT I HEARD THROUGH THE GRAPE-VINE.
WASN'T THERE A WAY?
IF HE HAD TOLD ME, COULDN'T I HAVE DONE SOME-THING...?
I LEARNED EVERY-THING I COULD.
AND I FOUND A MIRROR THAT WAS SAID TO CURE THE ILLNESS.
ALL I NEED TO DO NOW IS FIND HIM...
...

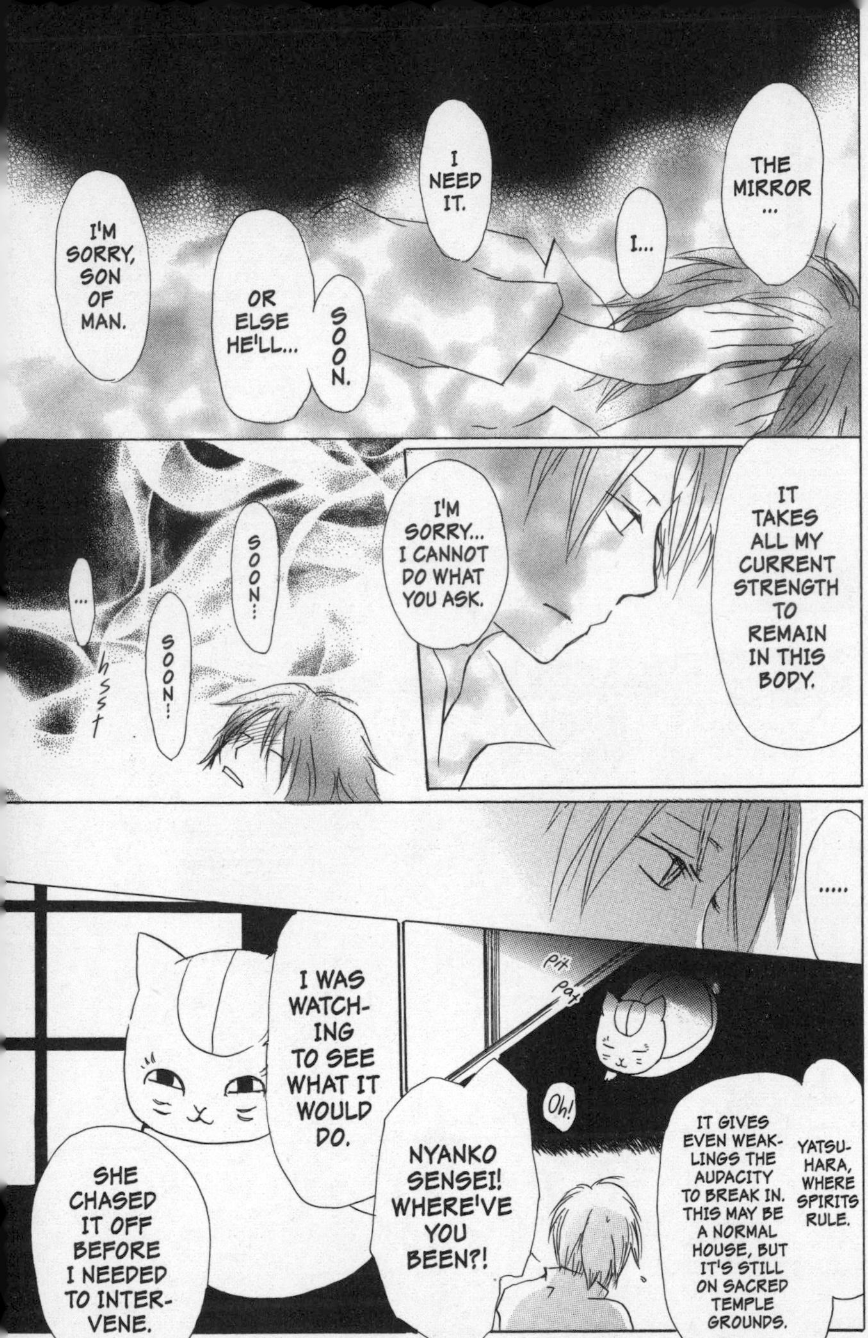
THE MIRROR ...
I...
I NEED IT.
SOON.
OR ELSE HE'LL...
I'M SORRY, SON OF MAN.
IT TAKES ALL MY CURRENT STRENGTH TO REMAIN IN THIS BODY.
I'M SORRY... I CANNOT DO WHAT YOU ASK.
SOOON...
SOOON...
...
hsst
.....
pit
pat
Oh!
YATSUHARA, WHERE SPIRITS RULE.
IT GIVES EVEN WEAKLINGS THE AUDACITY TO BREAK IN. THIS MAY BE A NORMAL HOUSE, BUT IT'S STILL ON SACRED TEMPLE GROUNDS.
NYANKO SENSEI! WHERE'VE YOU BEEN?!
I WAS WATCHING TO SEE WHAT IT WOULD DO.
SHE CHASED IT OFF BEFORE I NEEDED TO INTERVENE.

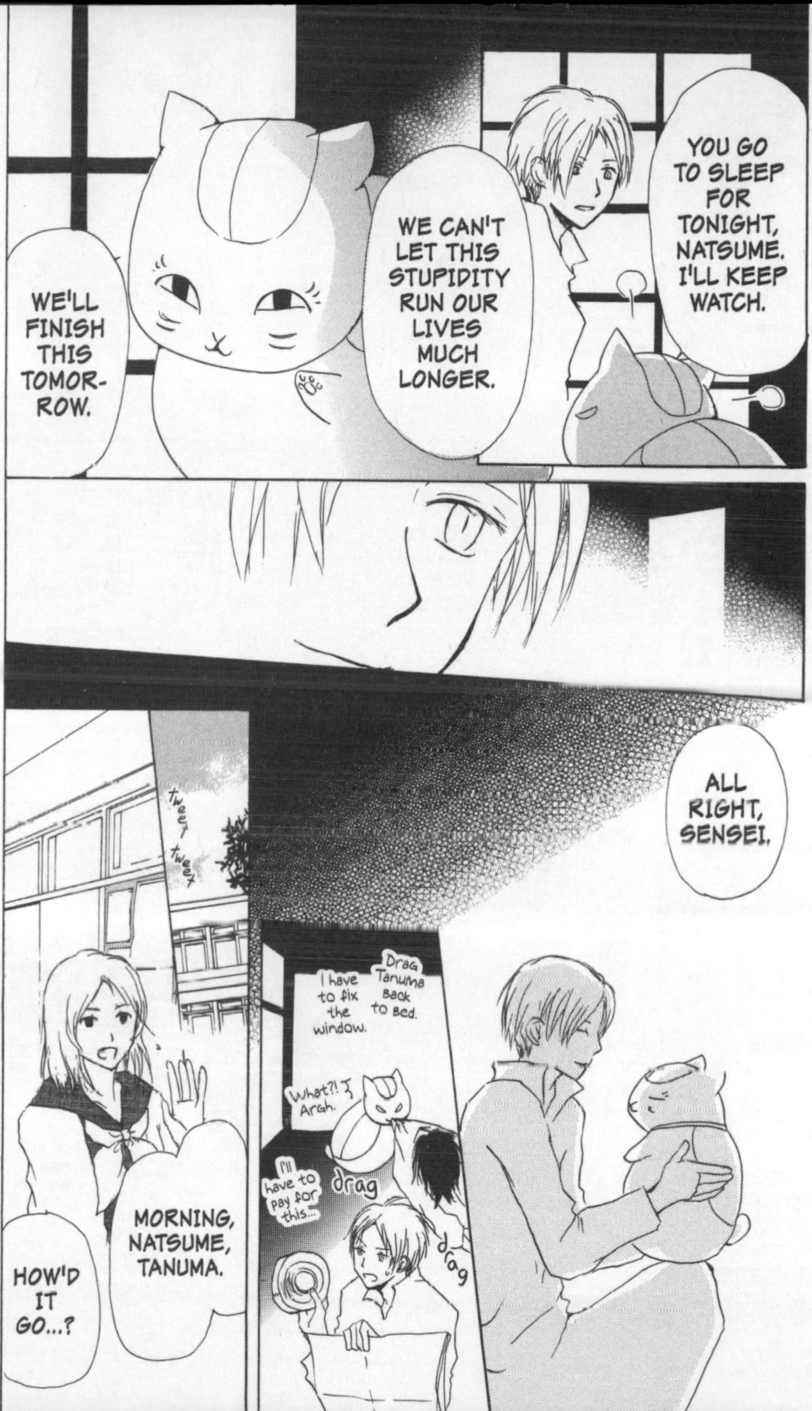
YOU GO TO SLEEP FOR TONIGHT, NATSUME. I'LL KEEP WATCH.
WE CAN'T LET THIS STUPIDITY RUN OUR LIVES MUCH LONGER.
WE'LL FINISH THIS TOMORROW.
ALL RIGHT, SENSEI.
Drag Tanuma back to bed.
I have to fix the window.
What?! Argh.
drag
I'll have to pay for this...
drag
tweet tweet
MORNING, NATSUME, TANUMA.
HOW'D IT GO...?

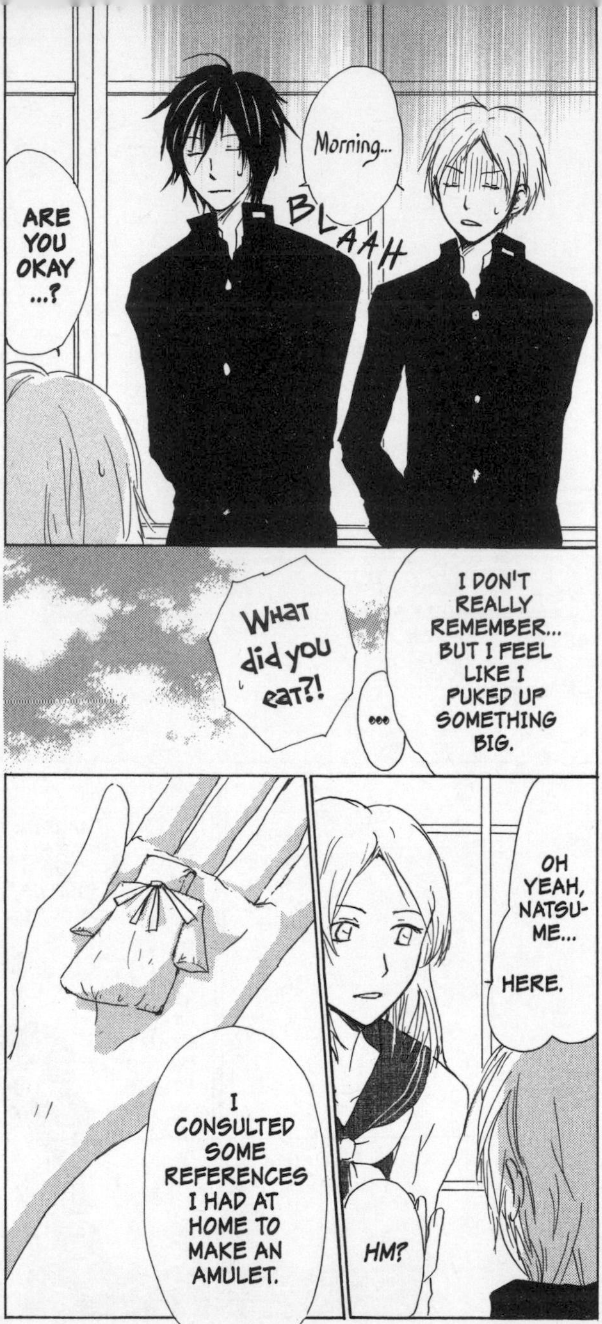
Morning...
BLAAAH
ARE YOU OKAY ...?
I DON'T REALLY REMEMBER... BUT I FEEL LIKE I PUKED UP SOMETHING BIG.
...
What did you eat?!
OH YEAH, NATSU-ME...
HERE.
HM?
I CONSULTED SOME REFERENCES I HAD AT HOME TO MAKE AN AMULET.

03

❀The Culture Festival

I hadn't done any stories yet about participating in a school event, so I picked the Culture Festival.

In the anime, I suggested that Kitamoto be in the same class as Natsume for more of a close-knit feeling. But in the manga, the class assignments are the same as the first episode, and Kitamoto is in the next class over:

Class 1: Kitamoto, Tanuma
Class 2: Nishimura, Natsume, Tsuji
Class 5: Taki

With the school as the stage, I could finally have Tanuma and Taki meet face to face. They would've preferred a more casual introduction, but Natsume doesn't have much experience in this kind of thing, so he made it sound like an introduction in an arranged marriage. I'm sure those two were squirming and wanted to be anywhere but there. I need to let Natsume have these embarrassing experiences from time to time as he grows up.

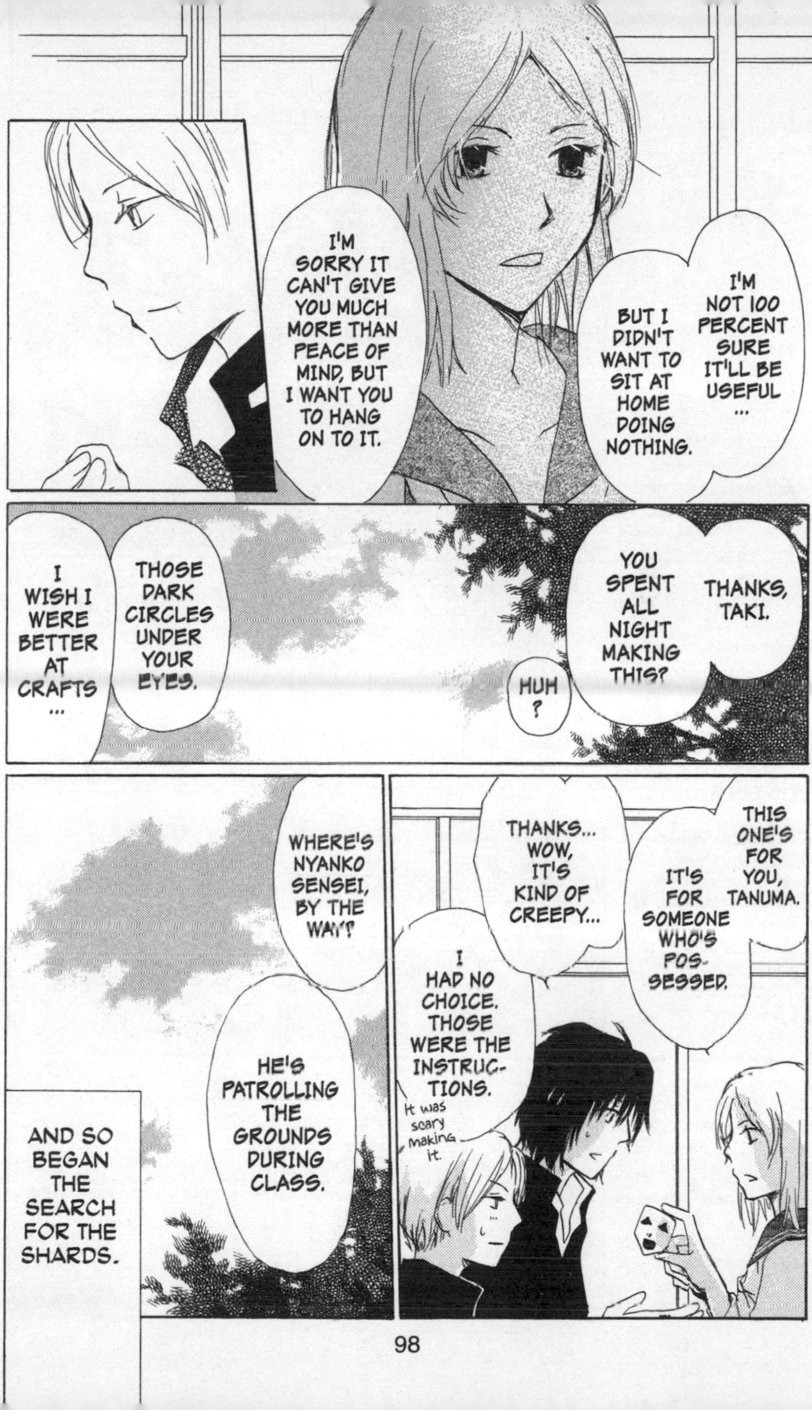
I'M NOT 100 PERCENT SURE IT'LL BE USEFUL ...
BUT I DIDN'T WANT TO SIT AT HOME DOING NOTHING.
I'M SORRY IT CAN'T GIVE YOU MUCH MORE THAN PEACE OF MIND, BUT I WANT YOU TO HANG ON TO IT.
THANKS, TAKI.
YOU SPENT ALL NIGHT MAKING THIS?
HUH?
THOSE DARK CIRCLES UNDER YOUR EYES.
I WISH I WERE BETTER AT CRAFTS ...
THIS ONE'S FOR YOU, TANUMA.
IT'S FOR SOMEONE WHO'S POS-SESSED.
THANKS... WOW, IT'S KIND OF CREEPY...
I HAD NO CHOICE. THOSE WERE THE INSTRUC-TIONS.
It was scary making it.
WHERE'S NYANKO SENSEI, BY THE WAY?
HE'S PATROLLING THE GROUNDS DURING CLASS.
AND SO BEGAN THE SEARCH FOR THE SHARDS.

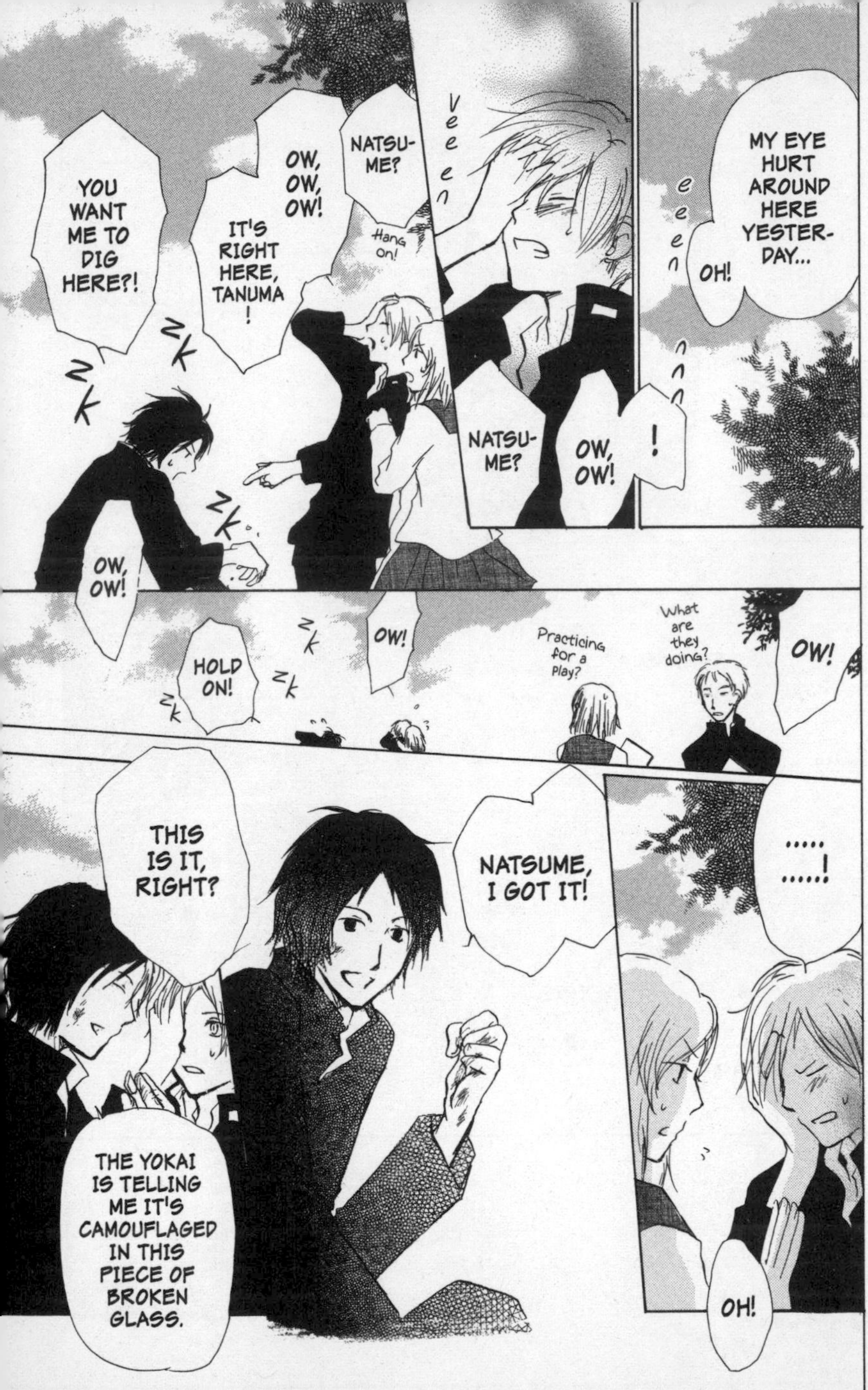
MY EYE HURT AROUND HERE YESTER-DAY...
OH!
eeeen
nnn
Veeen
!
OW, OW!
NATSU-ME?
NATSU-ME?
OW, OW, OW!
Hang on!
IT'S RIGHT HERE, TANUMA!
YOU WANT ME TO DIG HERE?!
ZK
ZK
ZK
OW, OW!
OW!
What are they doing?
Practicing for a play?
OW!
ZK
HOLD ON!
ZK
ZK
.....
.....!
OH!
NATSUME, I GOT IT!
THIS IS IT, RIGHT?
THE YOKAI IS TELLING ME IT'S CAMOUFLAGED IN THIS PIECE OF BROKEN GLASS.

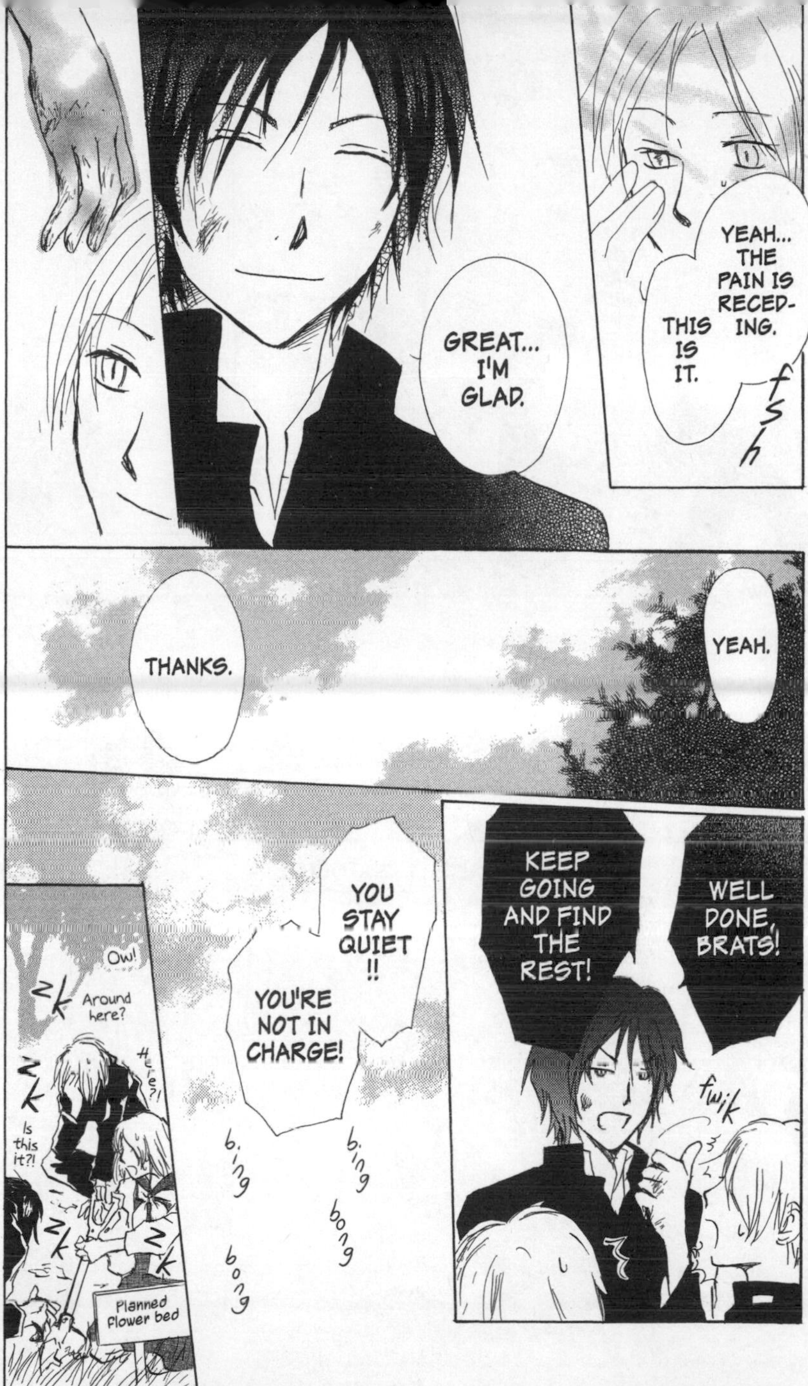
YEAH... THE PAIN IS RECEDING.
THIS IS IT.
fsh
GREAT... I'M GLAD.
YEAH.
THANKS.
WELL DONE, BRATS!
KEEP GOING AND FIND THE REST!
fwik
YOU STAY QUIET!!
YOU'RE NOT IN CHARGE!
bing
bong
bing
bong
Ow!
ZK
Around here?
Here?!
ZK
Is this it?!
ZK
ZK
Planned flower bed

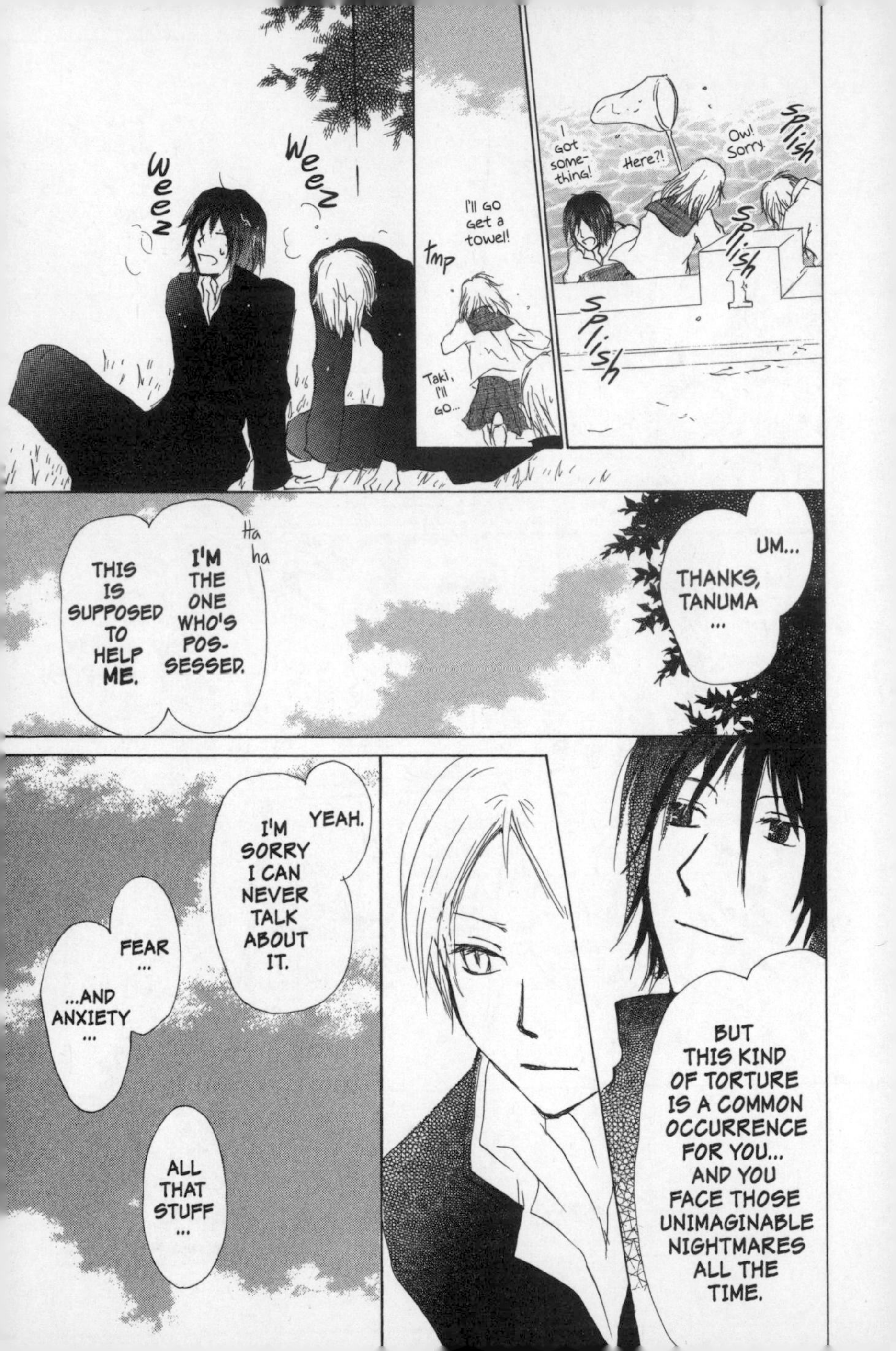
Splish
Ow! Sorry.
Here?!
I got something!
Splish
Splish
I'll go get a towel!
tmp
Taki, I'll go...
Weez
Weez
UM... THANKS, TANUMA...
I'M THE ONE WHO'S POSSESSED.
Ha ha
THIS IS SUPPOSED TO HELP ME.
BUT THIS KIND OF TORTURE IS A COMMON OCCURRENCE FOR YOU... AND YOU FACE THOSE UNIMAGINABLE NIGHTMARES ALL THE TIME.
YEAH.
I'M SORRY I CAN NEVER TALK ABOUT IT.
FEAR...
...AND ANXIETY...
ALL THAT STUFF...

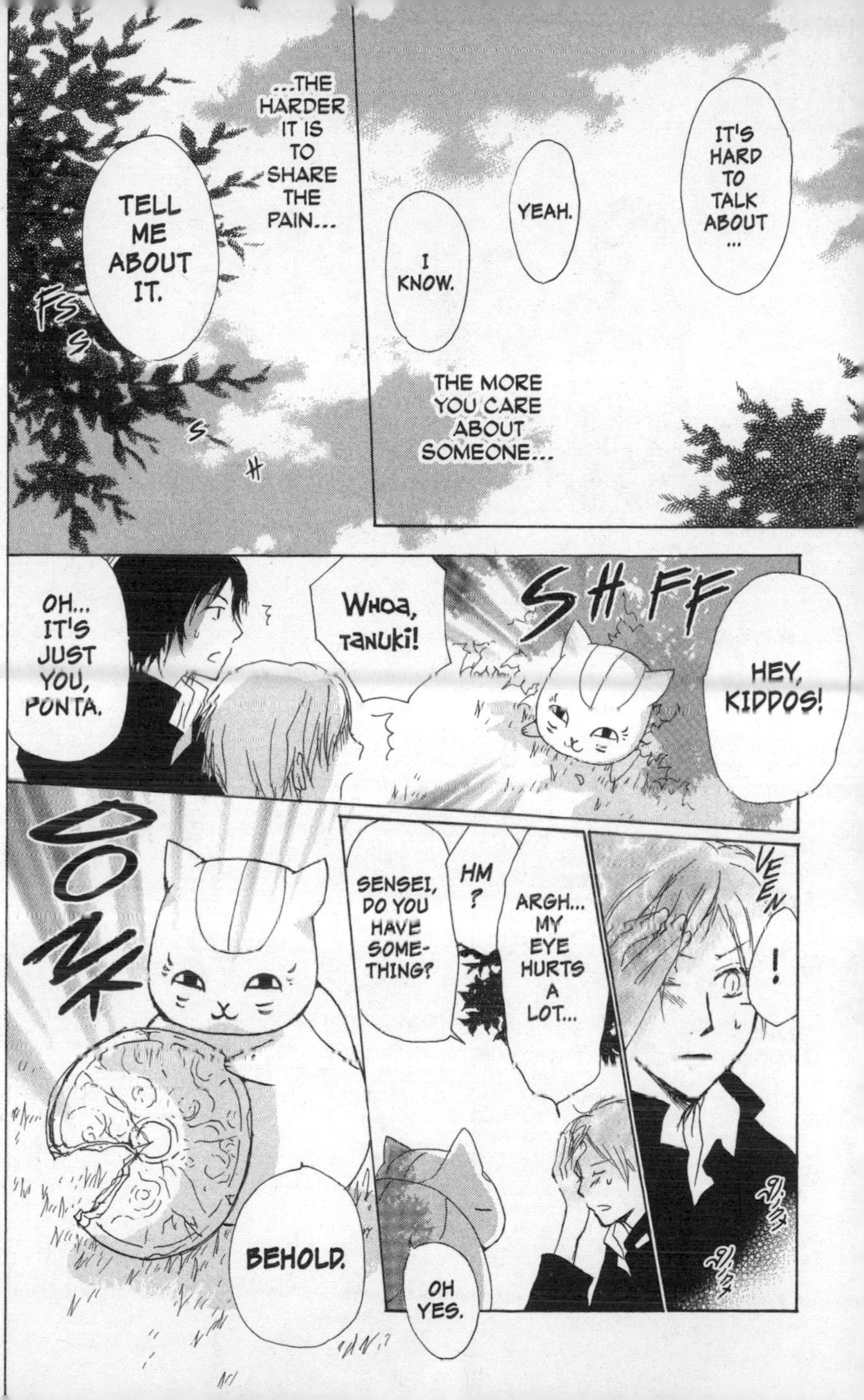
IT'S HARD TO TALK ABOUT ...
YEAH.
I KNOW.
THE MORE YOU CARE ABOUT SOMEONE...
...THE HARDER IT IS TO SHARE THE PAIN...
TELL ME ABOUT IT.
FSSSH
HEY, KIDDOS!
SHFF
Whoa, tanuki!
OH... IT'S JUST YOU, PONTA.
VEEN
!
ARGH... MY EYE HURTS A LOT...
HM?
SENSEI, DO YOU HAVE SOME-THING?
OH YES.
DONK
BEHOLD.

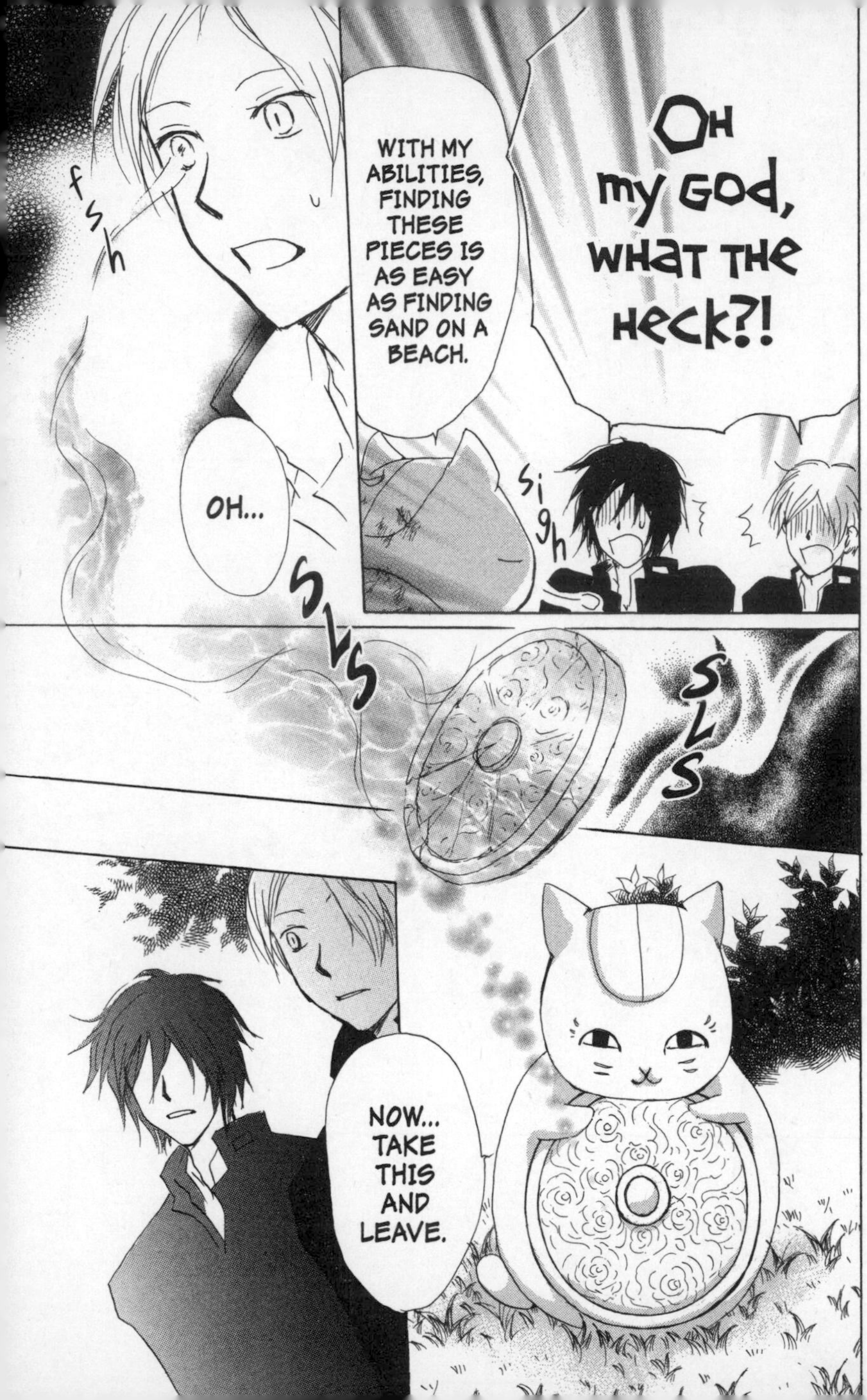
OH my GOD, WHAT THE HECK?!
WITH MY ABILITIES, FINDING THESE PIECES IS AS EASY AS FINDING SAND ON A BEACH.
sigh
fsh
OH...
SLS
SLS
NOW... TAKE THIS AND LEAVE.

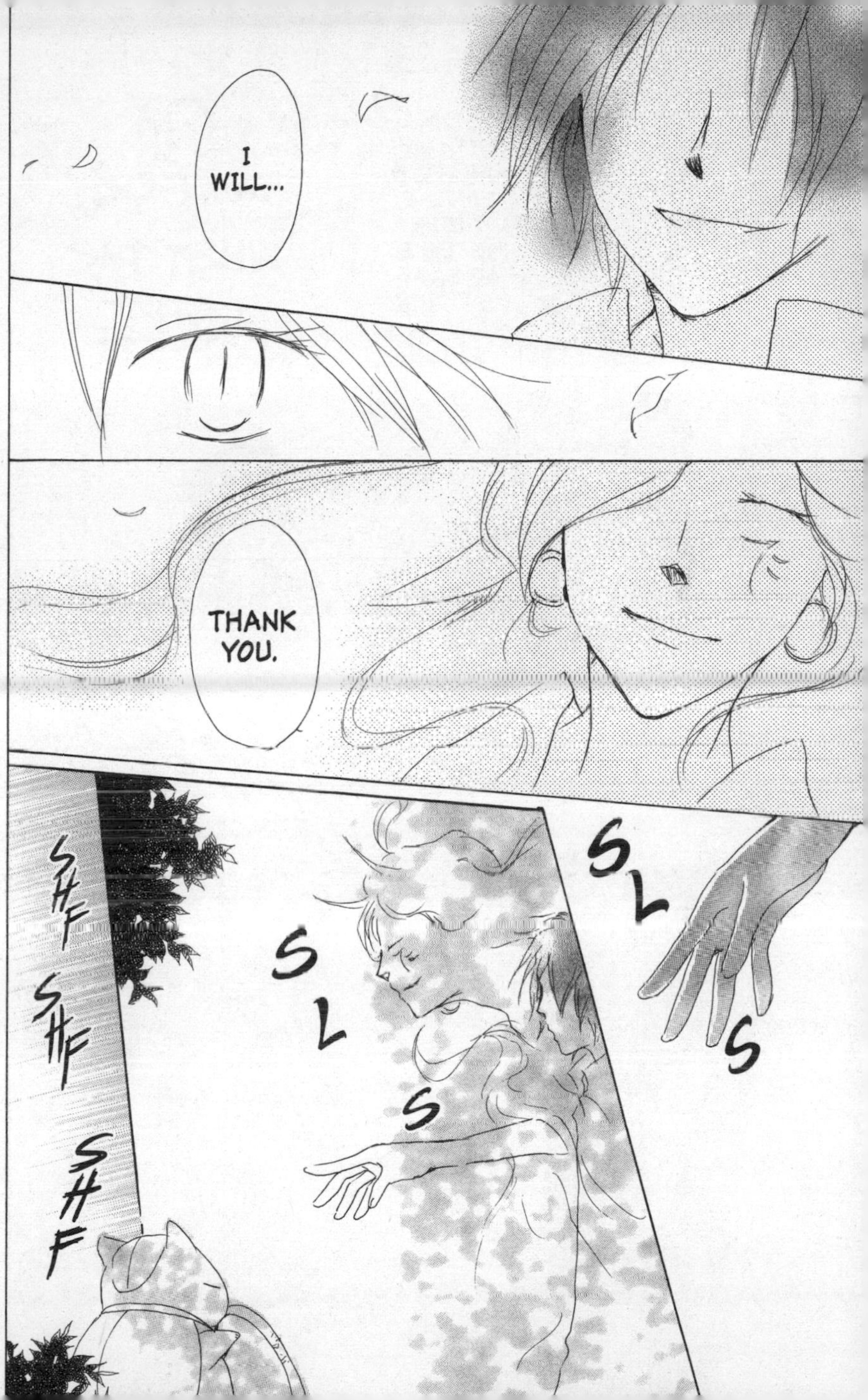
I WILL...
THANK YOU.
S L S
S L S
SHF SHF SHF

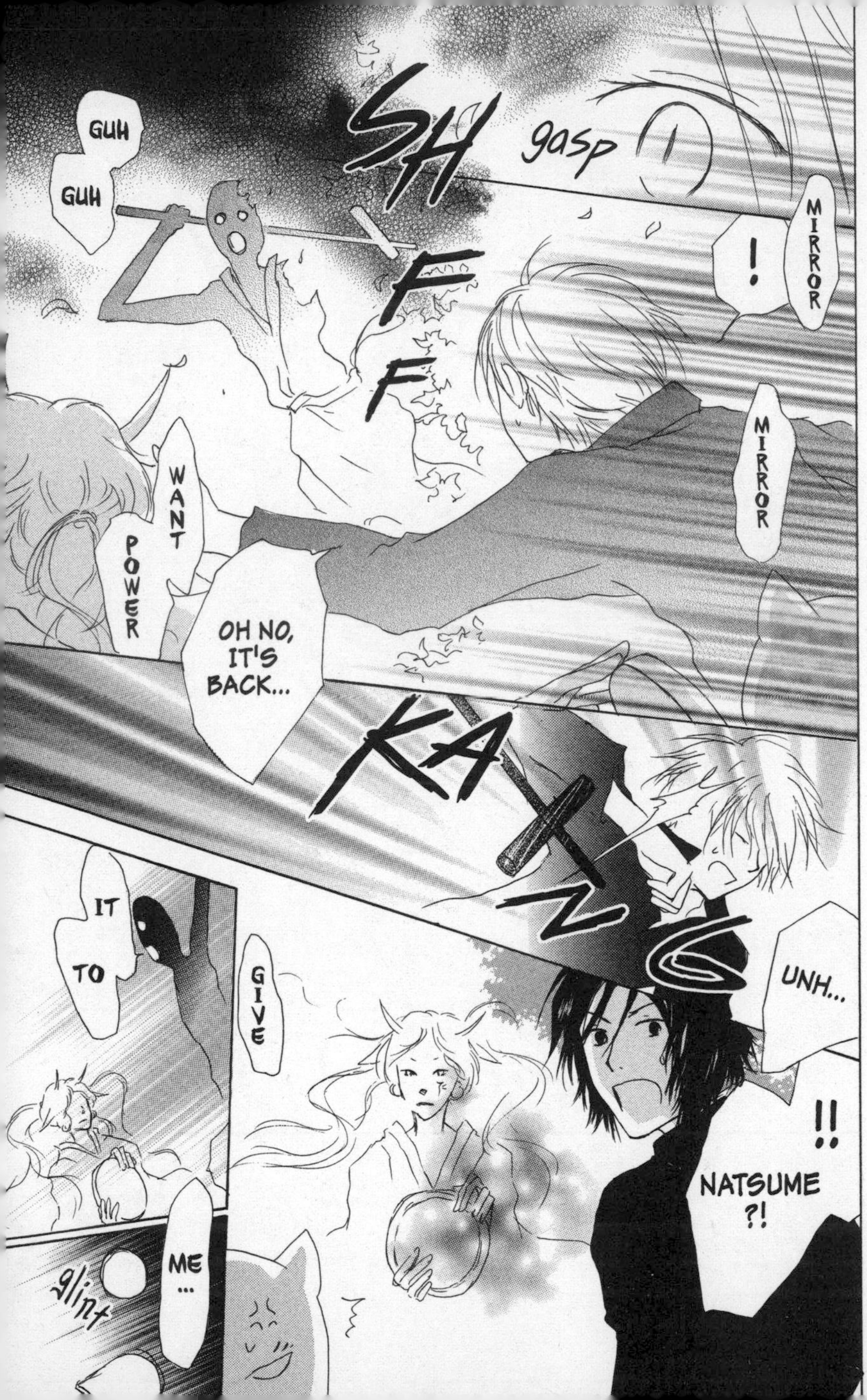
MIRROR
!
gasp
SHFF
GUH GUH
MIRROR
WANT POWER
OH NO, IT'S BACK...
KANG
UNH...
!!
NATSUME ?!
GIVE
IT TO
ME ...
glint

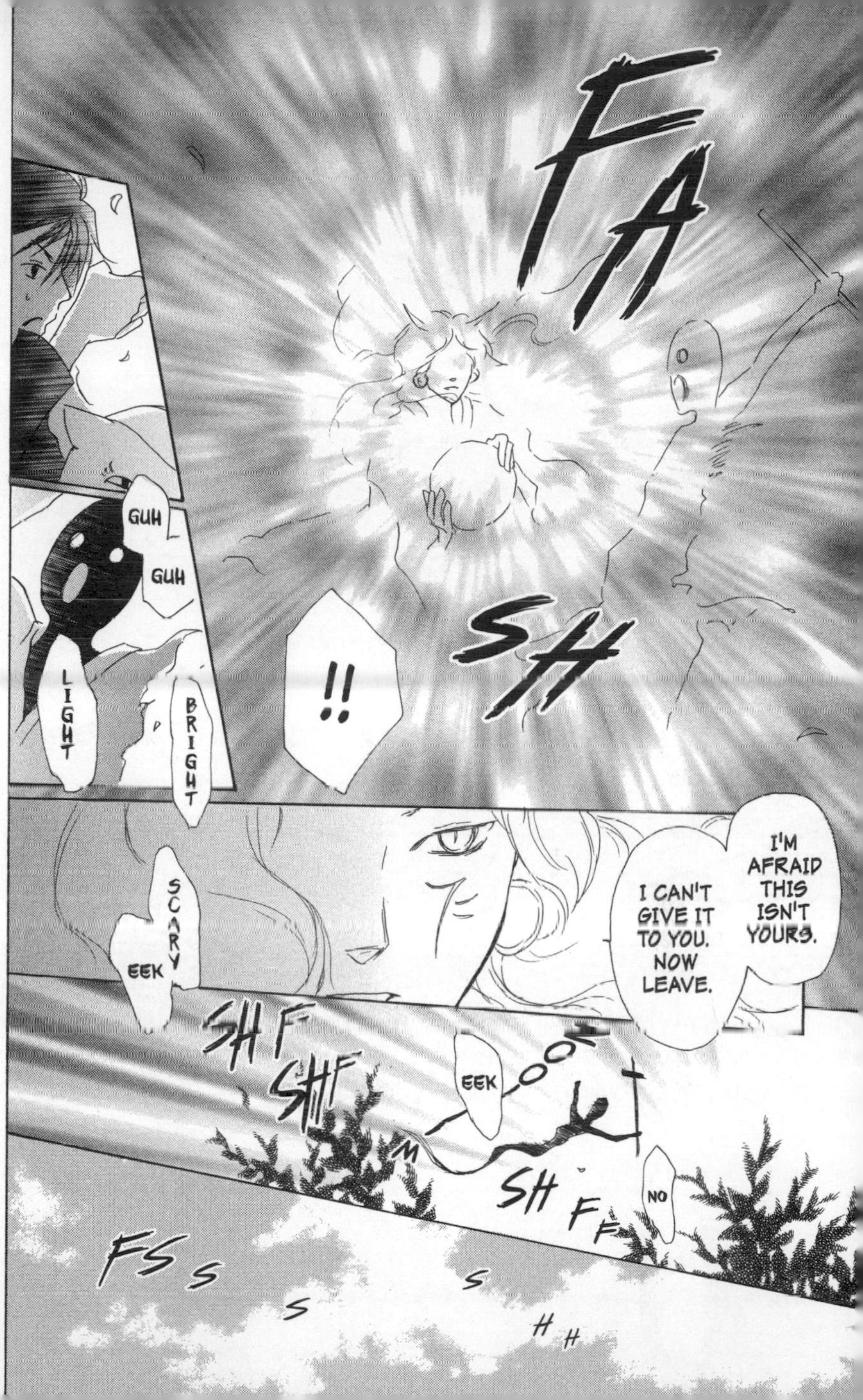
FA
SH
!!
GUH
GUH
BRIGHT
LIGHT
I'M AFRAID THIS ISN'T YOURS.
I CAN'T GIVE IT TO YOU. NOW LEAVE.
SCARY
EEK
SHF
SHF
OOO
EEK
M
NO
SH FF
FSSSSHH

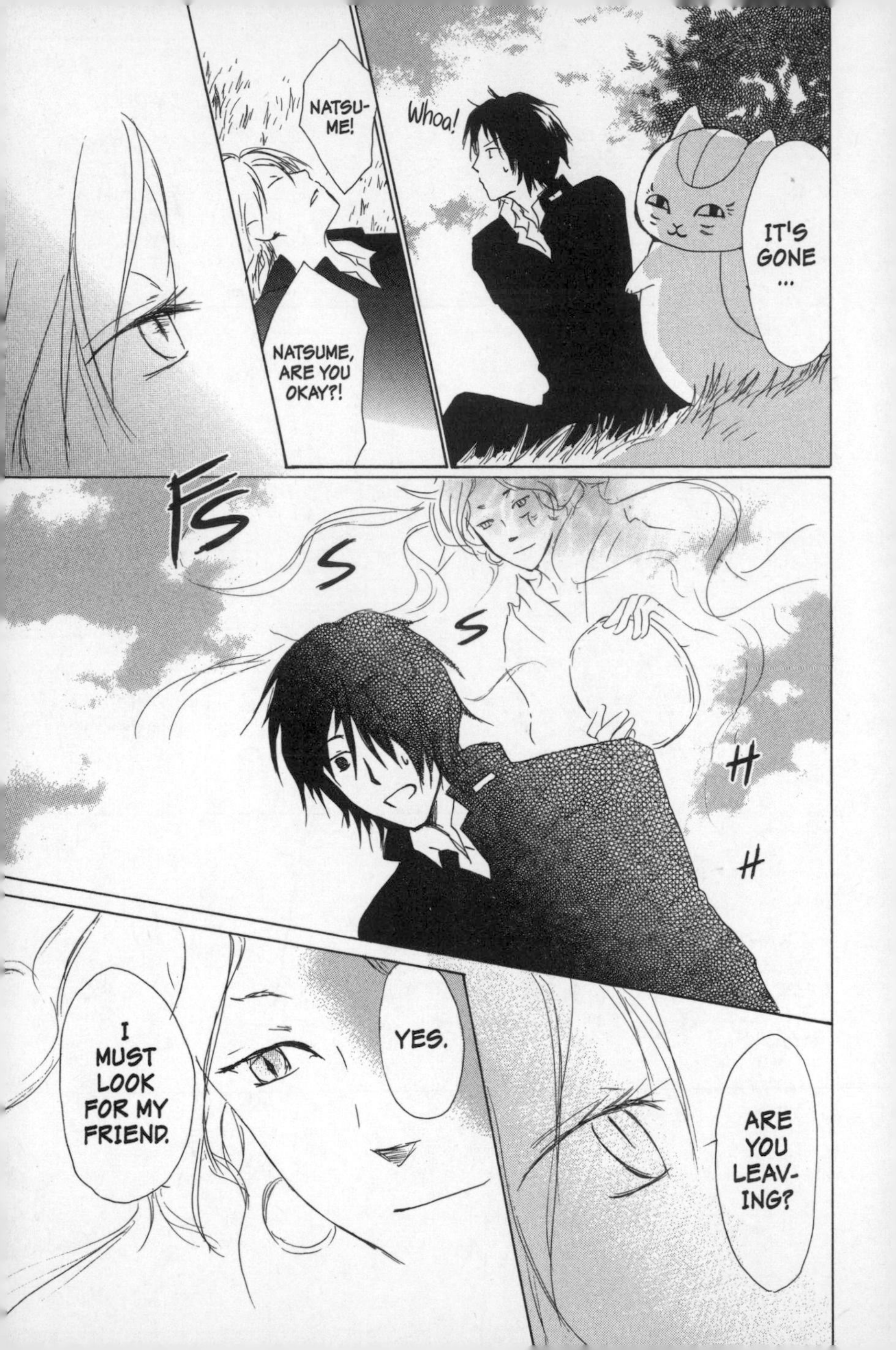
Whoa!
IT'S GONE ...
NATSU-ME!
NATSUME, ARE YOU OKAY?!
FSSS
HH
ARE YOU LEAVING?
YES.
I MUST LOOK FOR MY FRIEND.

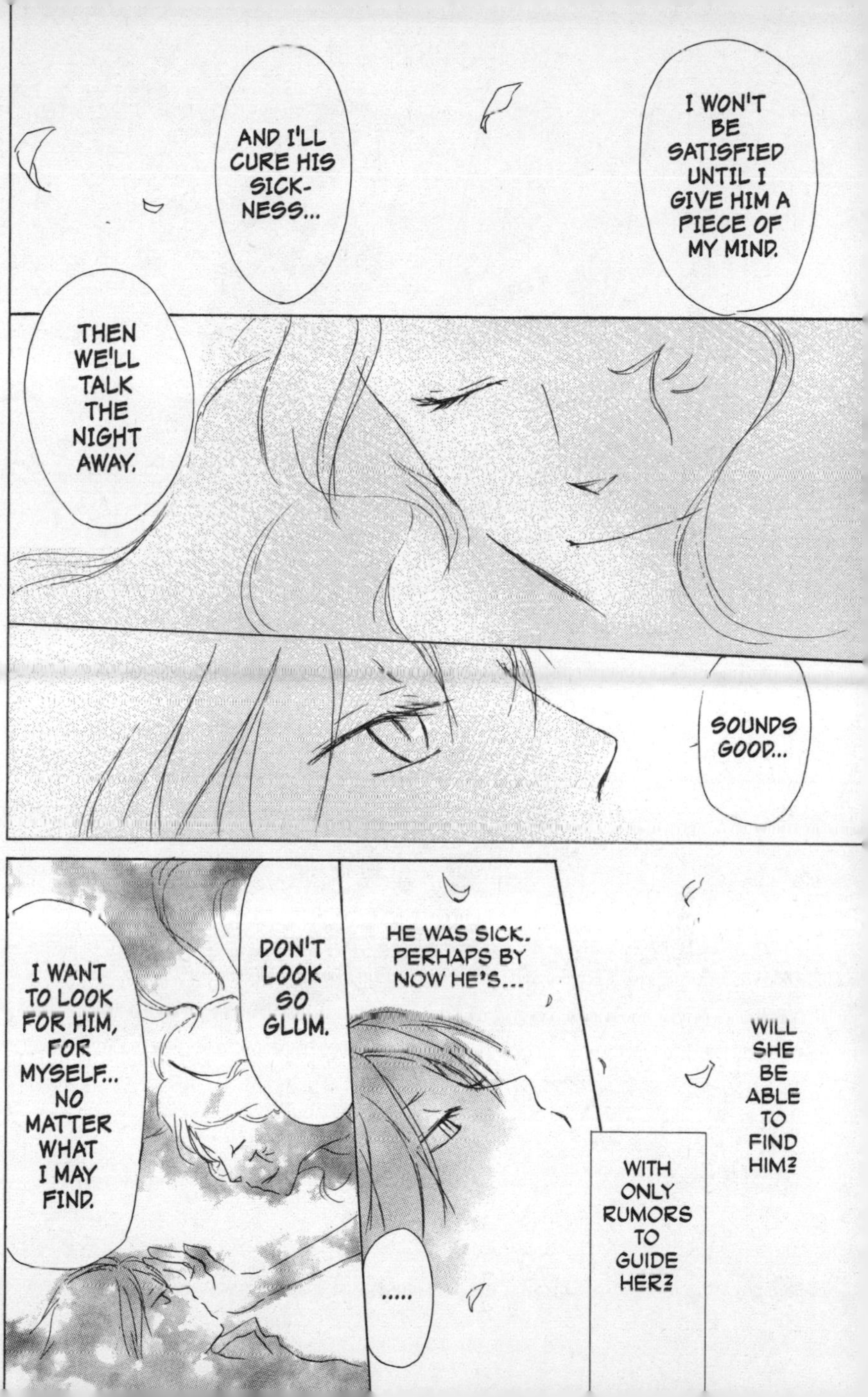
I WON'T BE SATISFIED UNTIL I GIVE HIM A PIECE OF MY MIND.
AND I'LL CURE HIS SICK-NESS...
THEN WE'LL TALK THE NIGHT AWAY.
SOUNDS GOOD...
HE WAS SICK. PERHAPS BY NOW HE'S...
WILL SHE BE ABLE TO FIND HIM?
WITH ONLY RUMORS TO GUIDE HER?
.....
DON'T LOOK SO GLUM.
I WANT TO LOOK FOR HIM, FOR MYSELF... NO MATTER WHAT I MAY FIND.

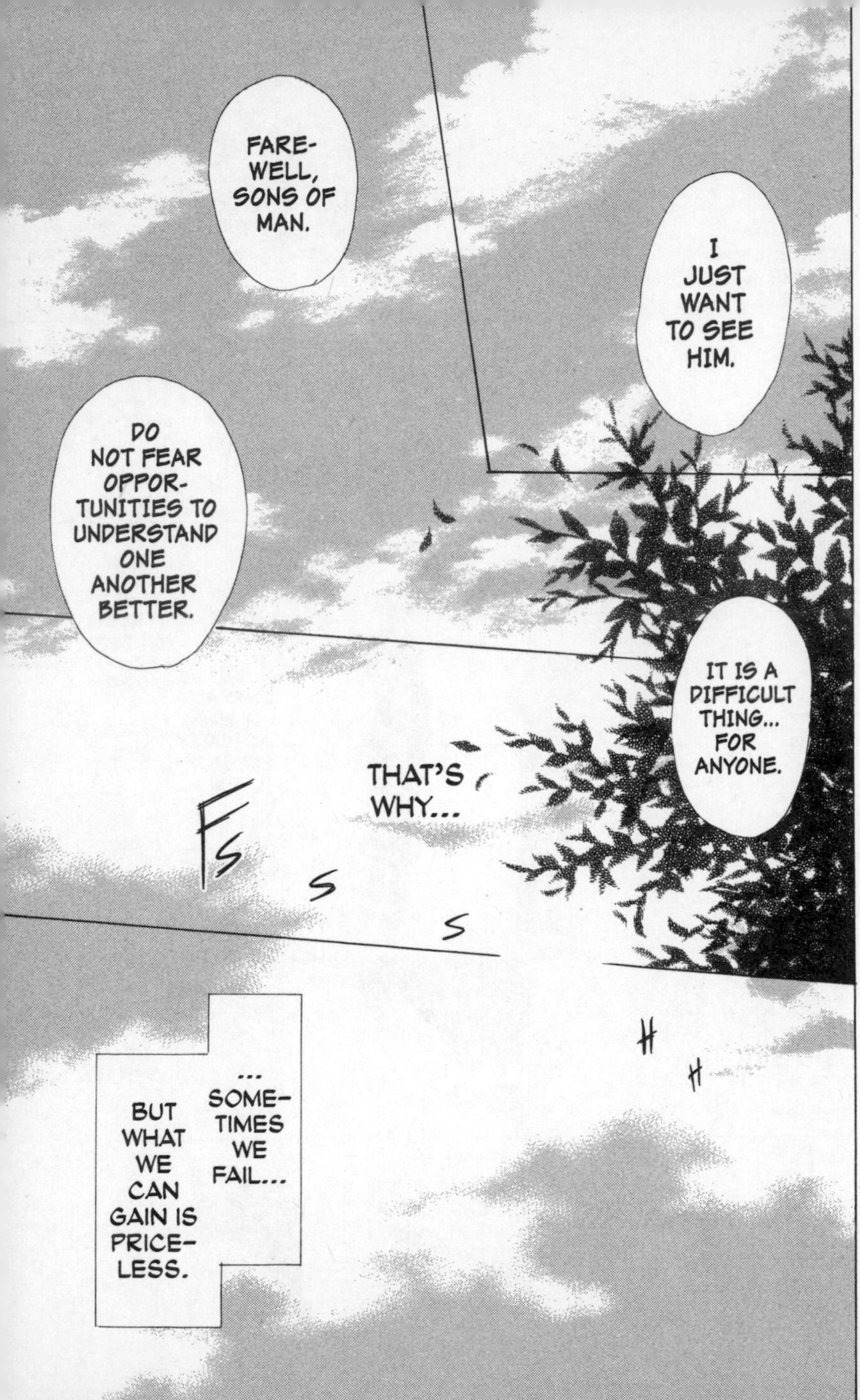
I JUST WANT TO SEE HIM.
FARE-WELL, SONS OF MAN.
DO NOT FEAR OPPOR-TUNITIES TO UNDERSTAND ONE ANOTHER BETTER.
IT IS A DIFFICULT THING... FOR ANYONE.
THAT'S WHY...
FSSS
HH
...SOME-TIMES WE FAIL...
BUT WHAT WE CAN GAIN IS PRICE-LESS.

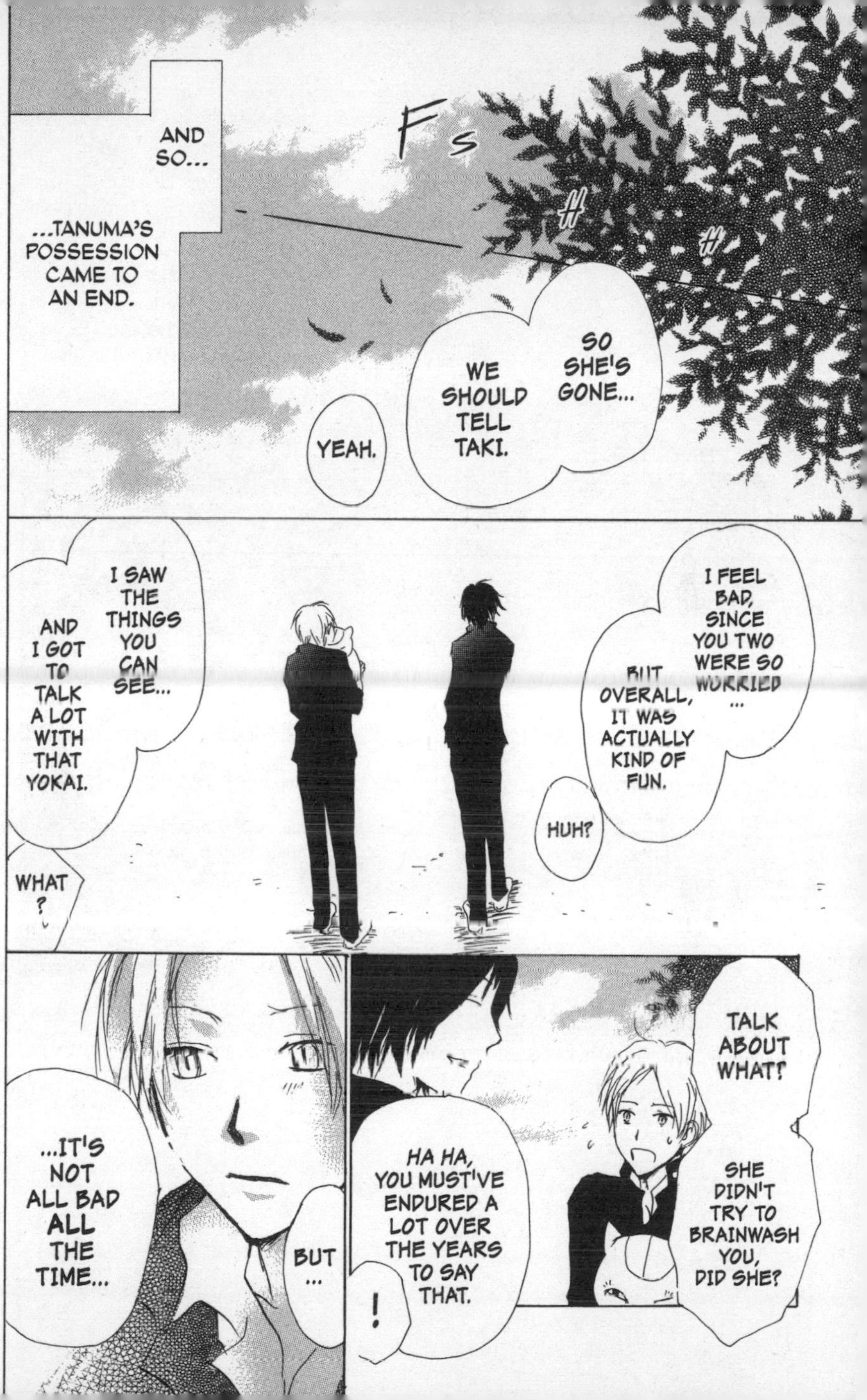
FS
H
H
SO SHE'S GONE...
WE SHOULD TELL TAKI.
YEAH.
AND SO...
...TANUMA'S POSSESSION CAME TO AN END.
I FEEL BAD, SINCE YOU TWO WERE SO WORRIED...
BUT OVERALL, IT WAS ACTUALLY KIND OF FUN.
HUH?
I SAW THE THINGS YOU CAN SEE...
AND I GOT TO TALK A LOT WITH THAT YOKAI.
WHAT?
TALK ABOUT WHAT?
SHE DIDN'T TRY TO BRAINWASH YOU, DID SHE?
HA HA, YOU MUST'VE ENDURED A LOT OVER THE YEARS TO SAY THAT.
!
BUT...
...IT'S NOT ALL BAD ALL THE TIME...

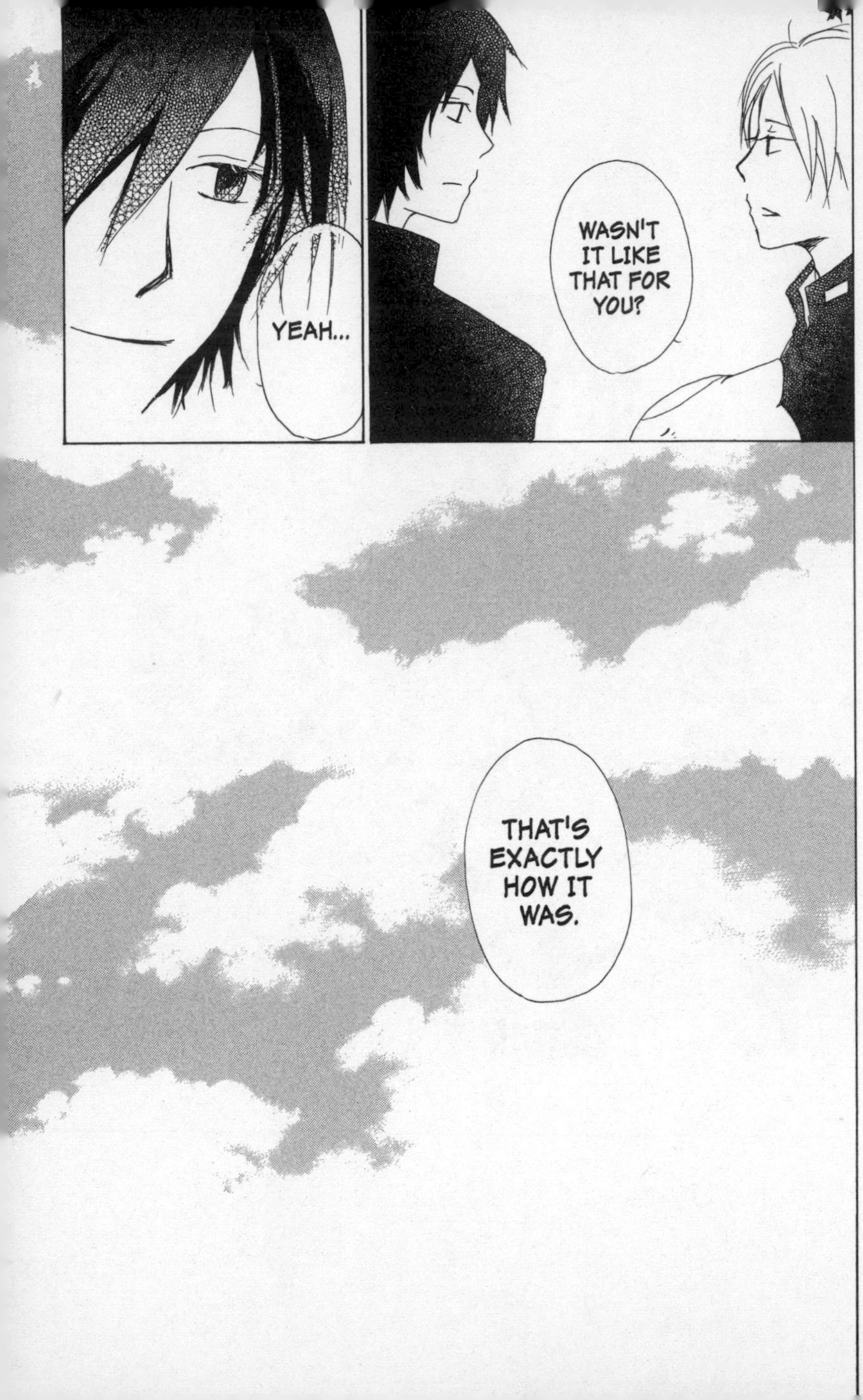
WASN'T IT LIKE THAT FOR YOU?
YEAH...
THAT'S EXACTLY HOW IT WAS.

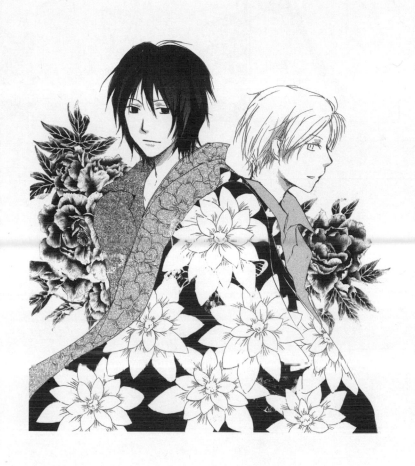

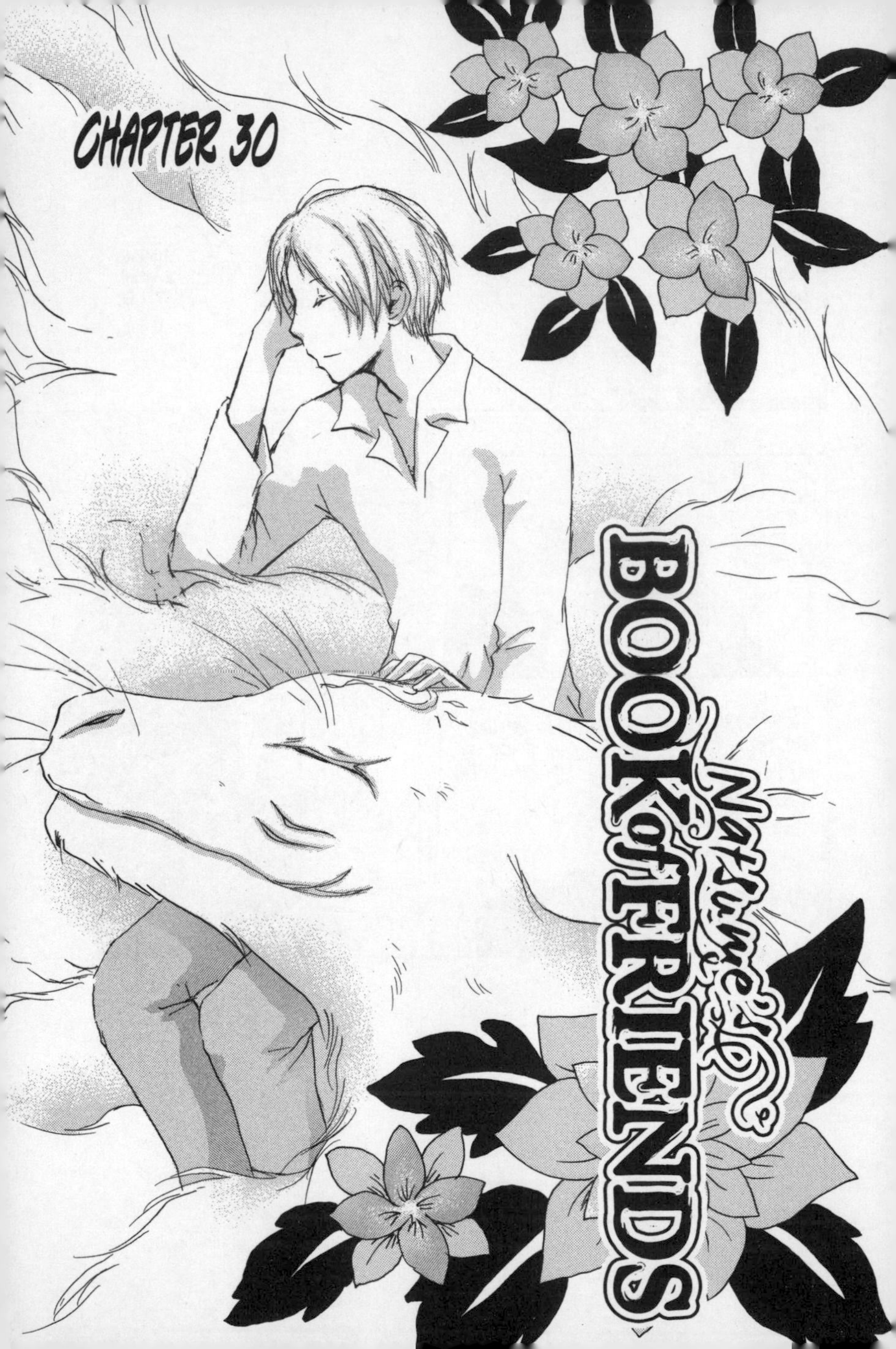
CHAPTER 30
Natsume's
BOOK of FRIENDS

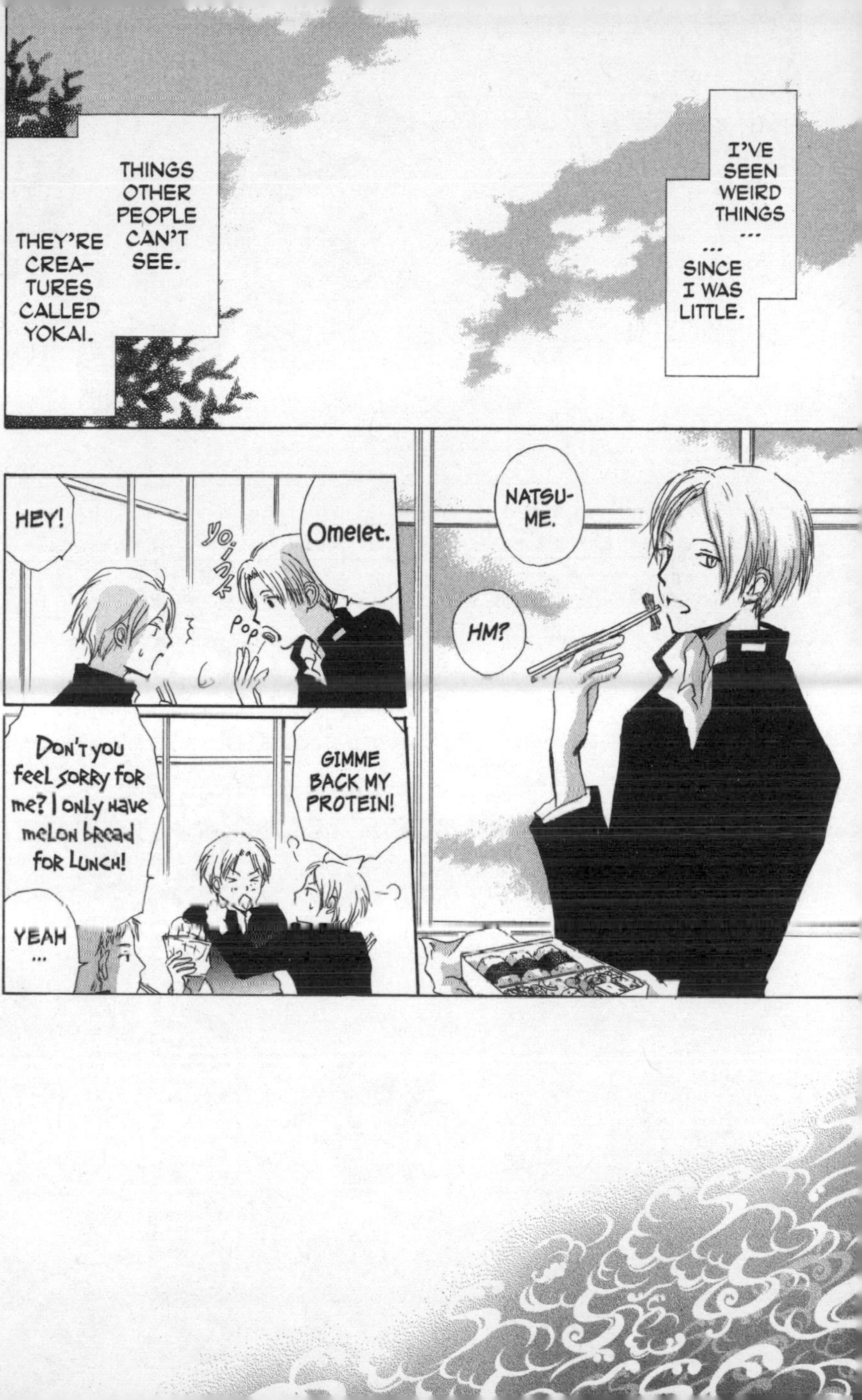
I'VE SEEN WEIRD THINGS... ...SINCE I WAS LITTLE.
THINGS OTHER PEOPLE CAN'T SEE.
THEY'RE CREATURES CALLED YOKAI.
NATSUME.
HM?
Omelet.
yoink
Pop
HEY!
GIMME BACK MY PROTEIN!
Don't you feel sorry for me? I only have melon bread for lunch!
YEAH...

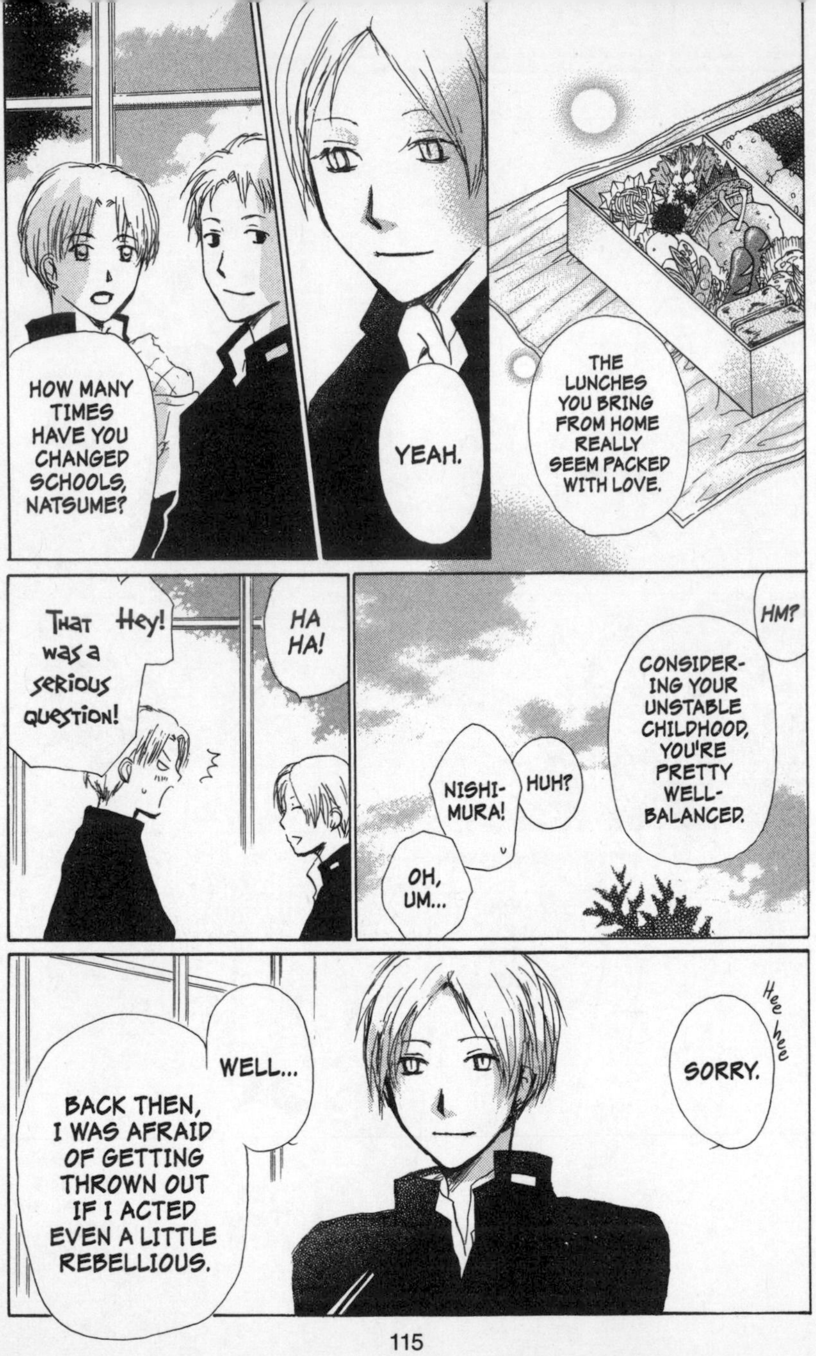
THE LUNCHES YOU BRING FROM HOME REALLY SEEM PACKED WITH LOVE.
YEAH.
HOW MANY TIMES HAVE YOU CHANGED SCHOOLS, NATSUME?
HM?
CONSIDERING YOUR UNSTABLE CHILDHOOD, YOU'RE PRETTY WELL-BALANCED.
HUH?
NISHIMURA!
OH, UM...
HA HA!
Hey!
That was a serious question!
Hee hee
SORRY.
WELL...
BACK THEN, I WAS AFRAID OF GETTING THROWN OUT IF I ACTED EVEN A LITTLE REBELLIOUS.

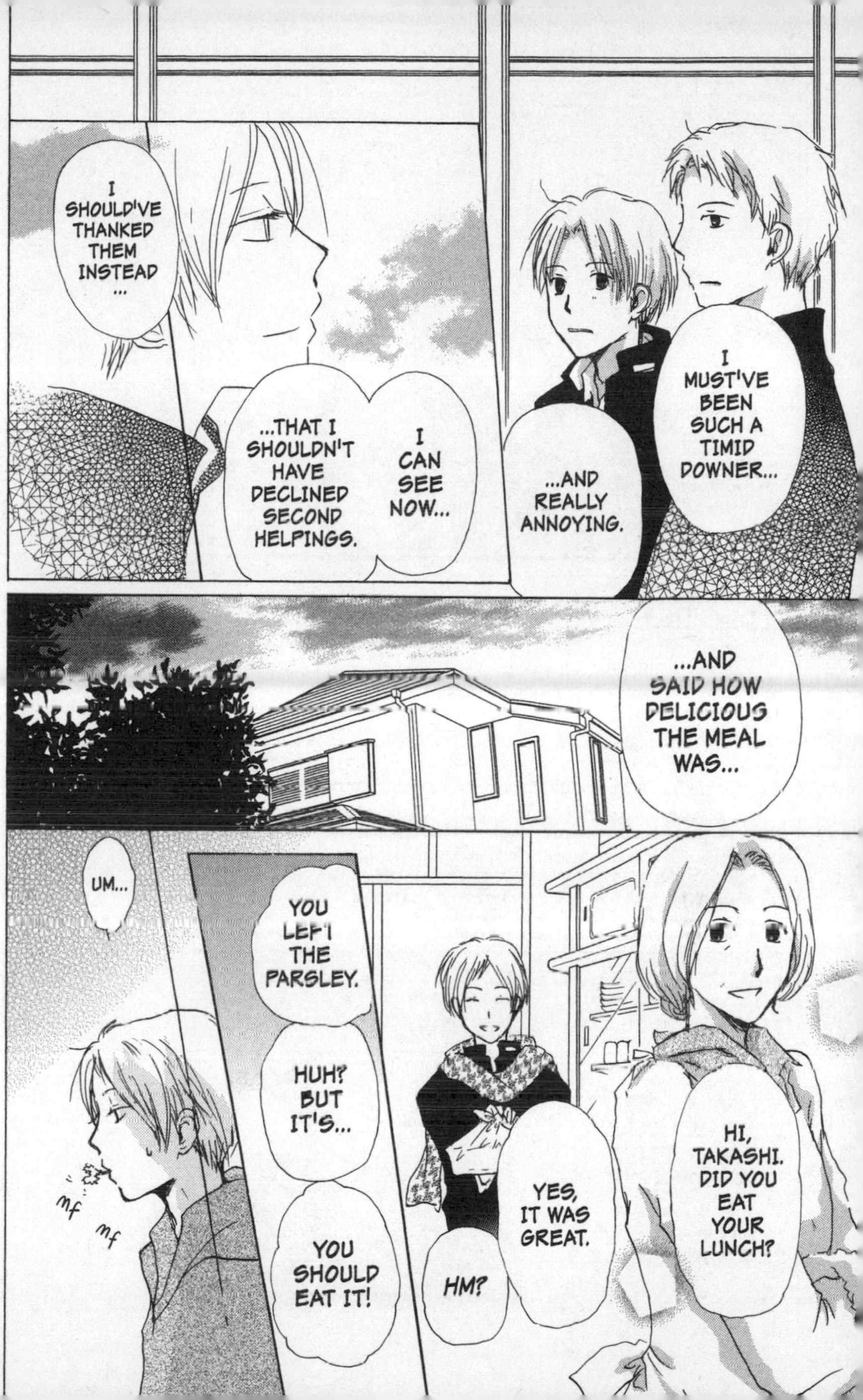

I MUST'VE BEEN SUCH A TIMID DOWNER...
...AND REALLY ANNOYING.
I CAN SEE NOW...
...THAT I SHOULDN'T HAVE DECLINED SECOND HELPINGS.
I SHOULD'VE THANKED THEM INSTEAD ...
...AND SAID HOW DELICIOUS THE MEAL WAS...
HI, TAKASHI. DID YOU EAT YOUR LUNCH?
YES, IT WAS GREAT.
HM?
YOU LEFT THE PARSLEY.
HUH? BUT IT'S...
YOU SHOULD EAT IT!
UM...
mf
mf

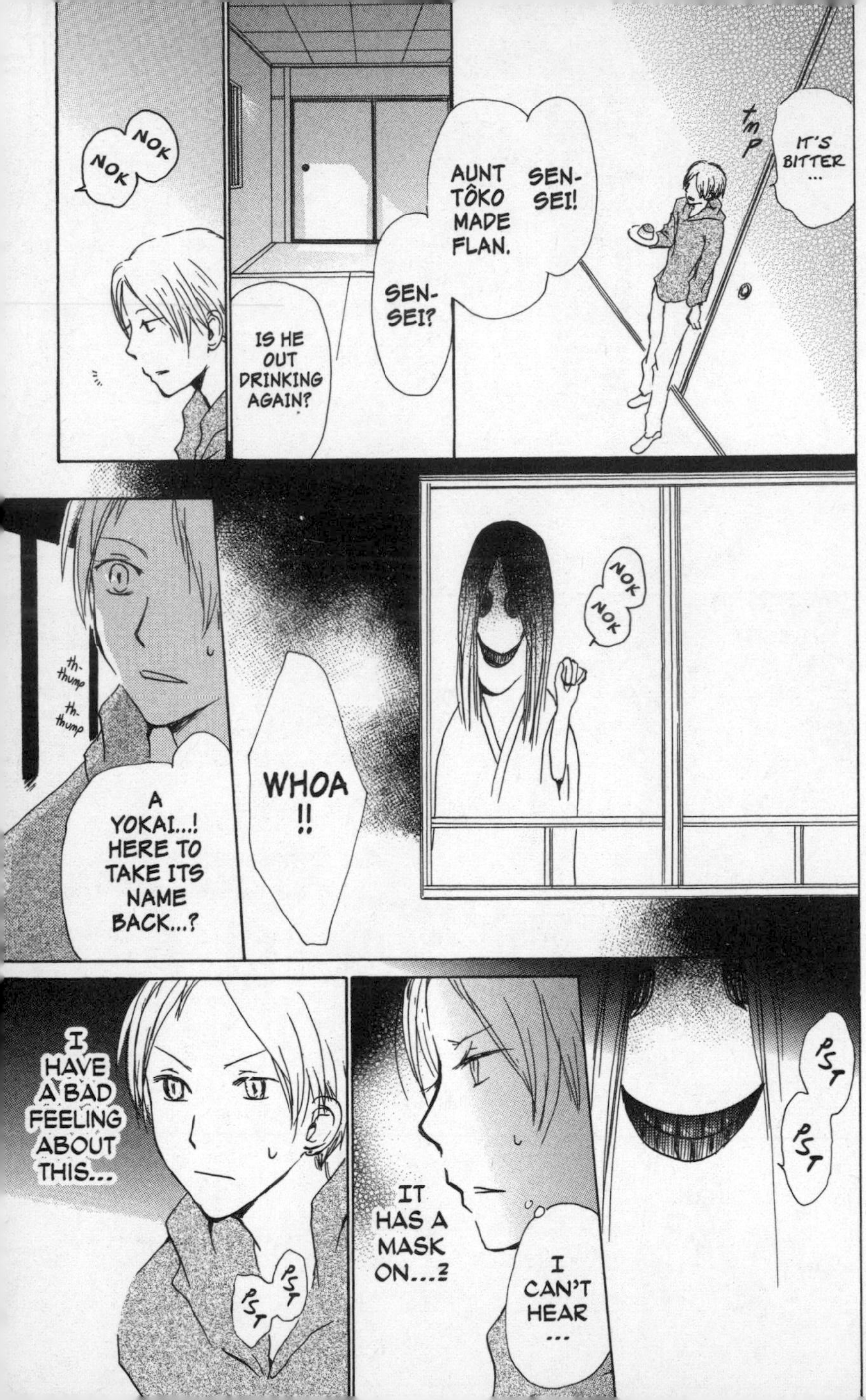

TMP
IT'S BITTER ...
SEN-SEI!
AUNT TÔKO MADE FLAN.
SEN-SEI?
IS HE OUT DRINKING AGAIN?
NOK NOK
NOK NOK
WHOA!!
th-thump th-thump
A YOKAI...! HERE TO TAKE ITS NAME BACK...?
PST PST
I CAN'T HEAR ...
IT HAS A MASK ON...?
I HAVE A BAD FEELING ABOUT THIS...
PST PST

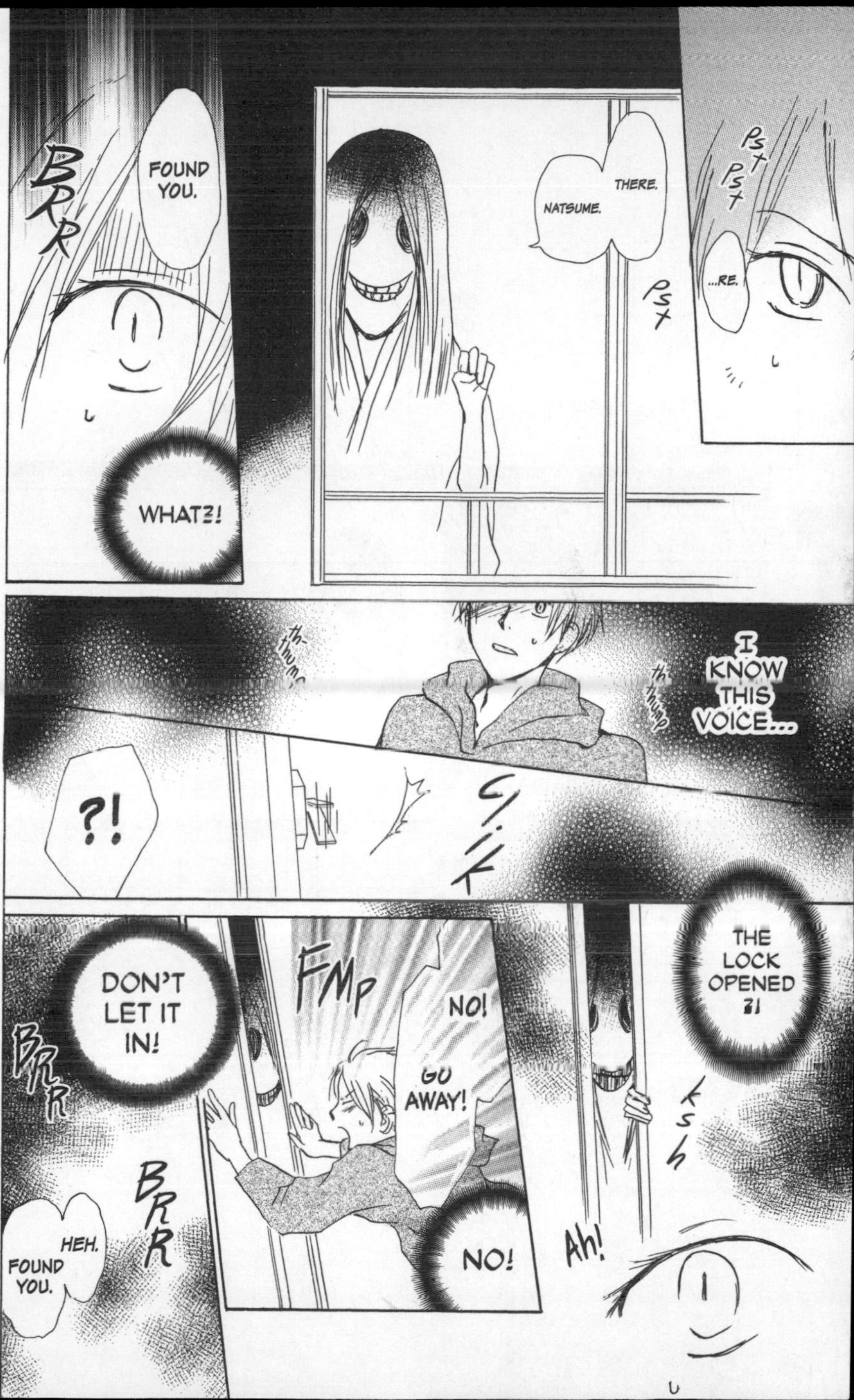

Pst
Pst
...RE.
Pst
THERE.
NATSUME.
FOUND YOU.
BRR
WHAT?!
I KNOW THIS VOICE...
th-thump
th-thump
?!
THE LOCK OPENED?!
ksh
Ah!
FMP
NO!
GO AWAY!
NO!
DON'T LET IT IN!
BRR
BRR
HEH. FOUND YOU.

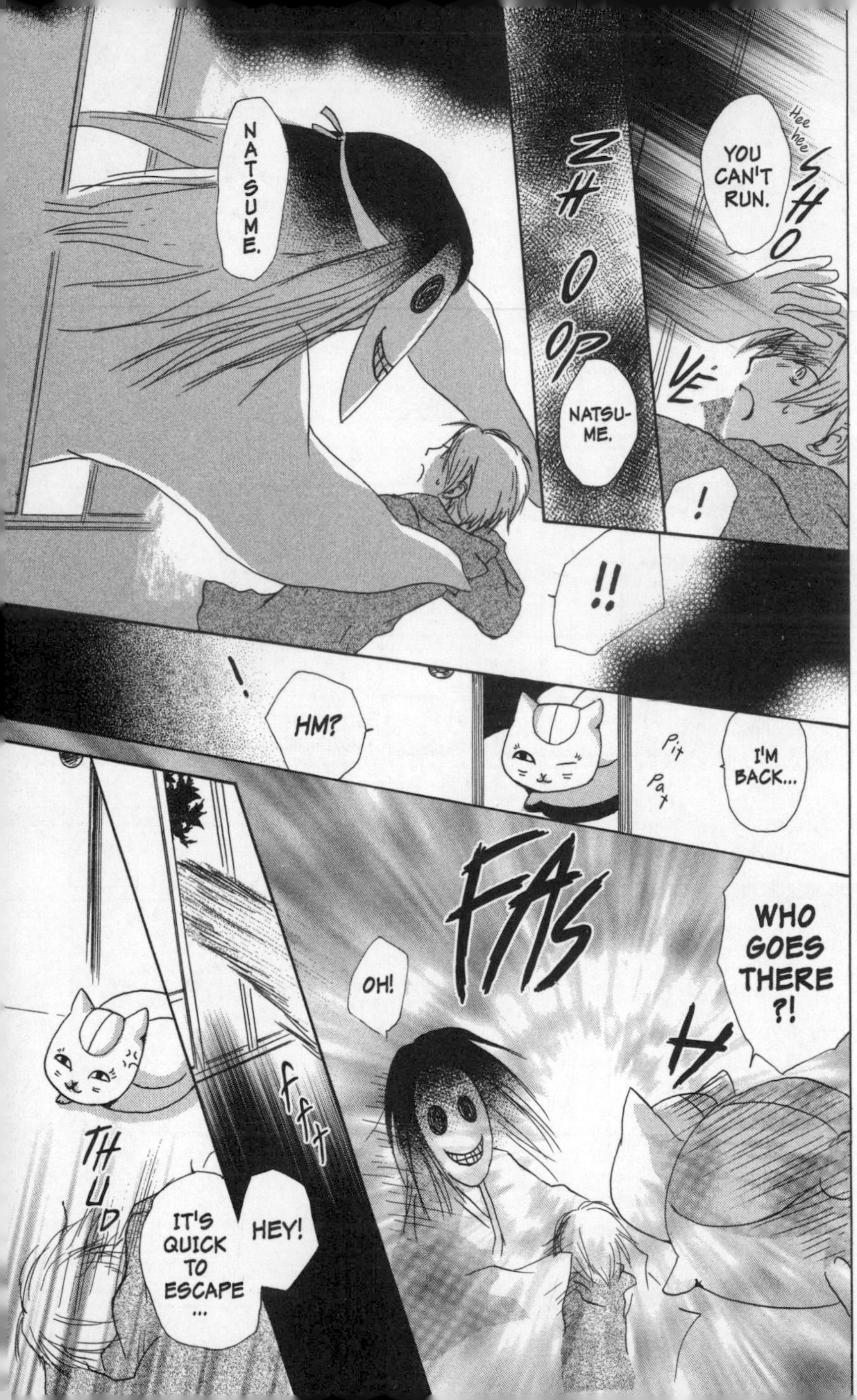
Hee hee
YOU CAN'T RUN.
SHOVE
NATSU-ME.
!
ZHOOP
NATSUME.
!!
I'M BACK...
Pit Pat
HM?
!
WHO GOES THERE?!
FAS
OH!
fft
HEY!
IT'S QUICK TO ESCAPE ...
THUD

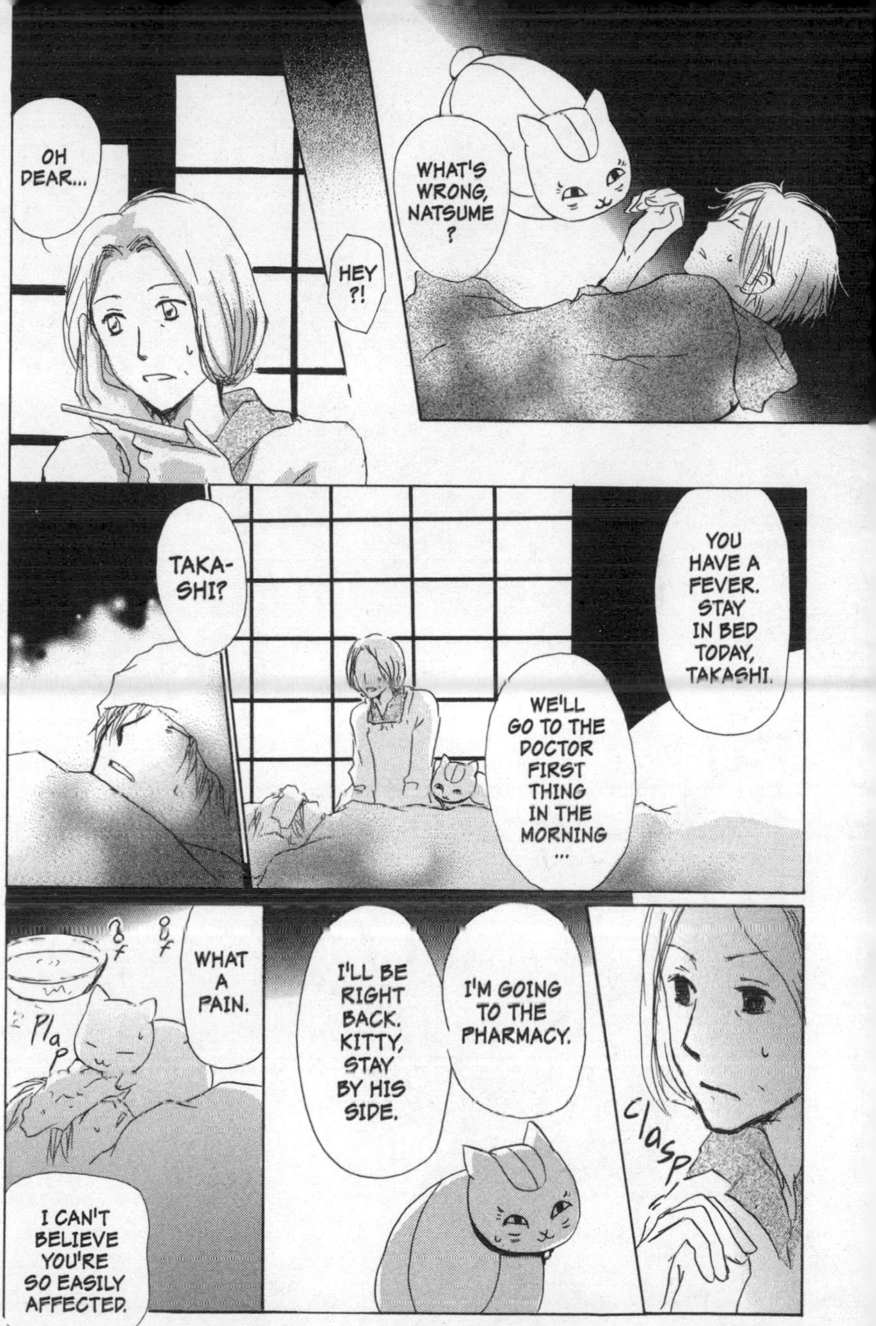
WHAT'S WRONG, NATSUME?
HEY?!
OH DEAR...
YOU HAVE A FEVER. STAY IN BED TODAY, TAKASHI.
WE'LL GO TO THE DOCTOR FIRST THING IN THE MORNING...
TAKA-SHI?
Clasp
I'M GOING TO THE PHARMACY.
I'LL BE RIGHT BACK. KITTY, STAY BY HIS SIDE.
WHAT A PAIN.
Plap
I CAN'T BELIEVE YOU'RE SO EASILY AFFECTED.

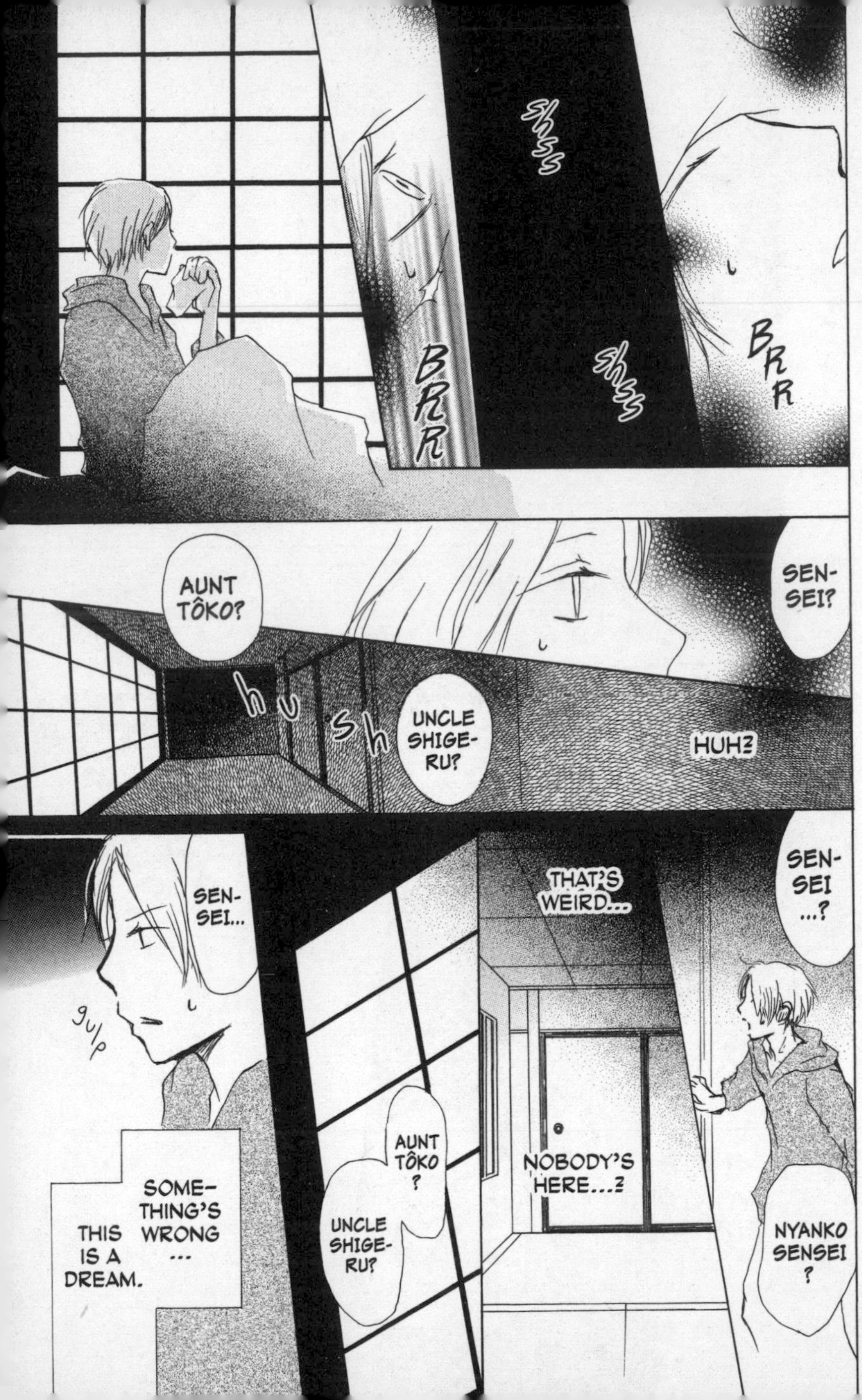
BRR
shss
shss
BRR
SEN-SEI?
AUNT TÔKO?
UNCLE SHIGE-RU?
hush
HUH?
SEN-SEI ...?
THAT'S WEIRD...
NOBODY'S HERE...?
NYANKO SENSEI ?
SEN-SEI...
gulp
AUNT TÔKO ?
UNCLE SHIGE-RU?
SOME-THING'S WRONG ...
THIS IS A DREAM.

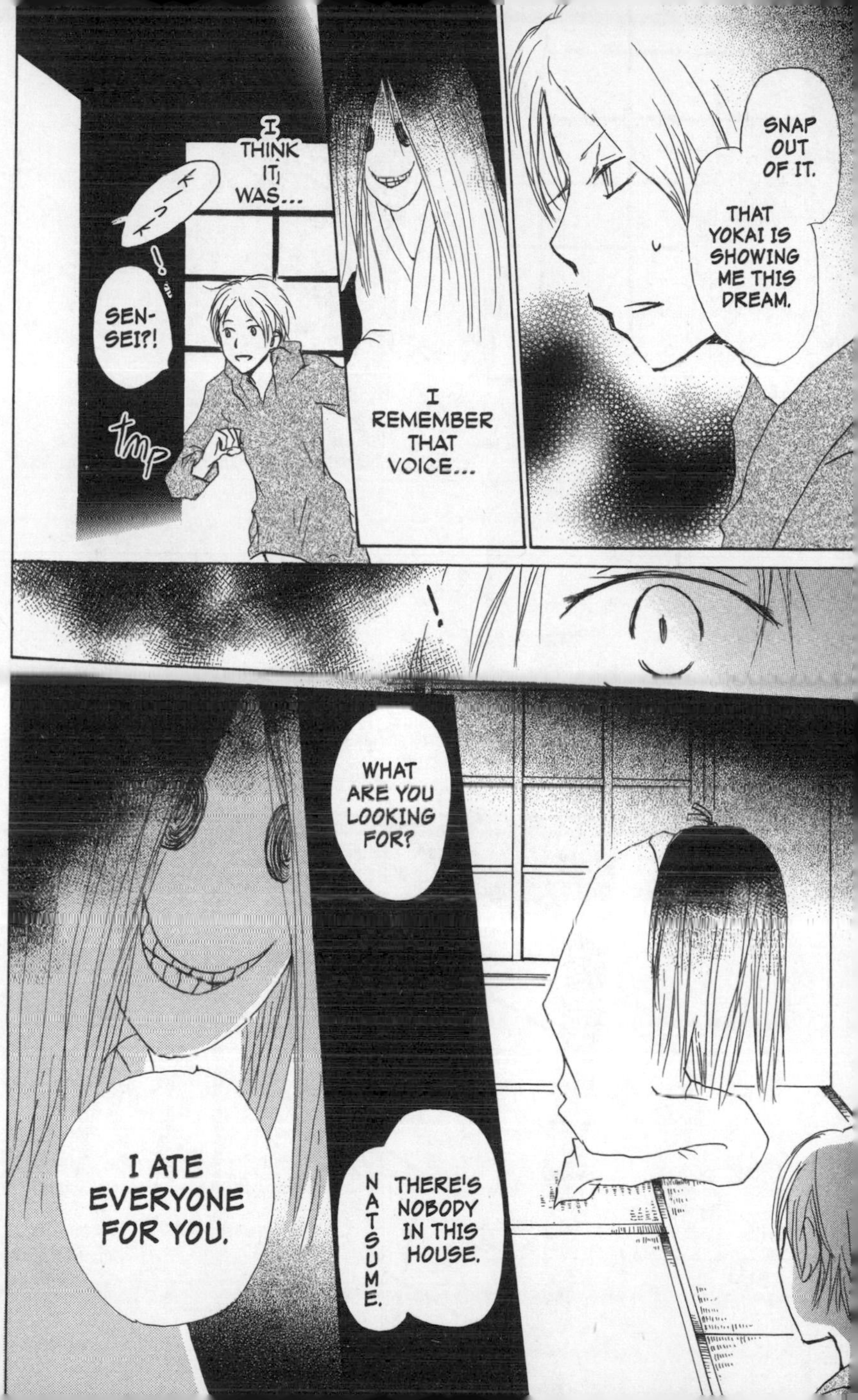
SNAP OUT OF IT.
THAT YOKAI IS SHOWING ME THIS DREAM.
I REMEMBER THAT VOICE...
I THINK IT WAS...
SEN-SEI?!
tmp
!
WHAT ARE YOU LOOKING FOR?
THERE'S NOBODY IN THIS HOUSE.
NATSUME.
I ATE EVERYONE FOR YOU.

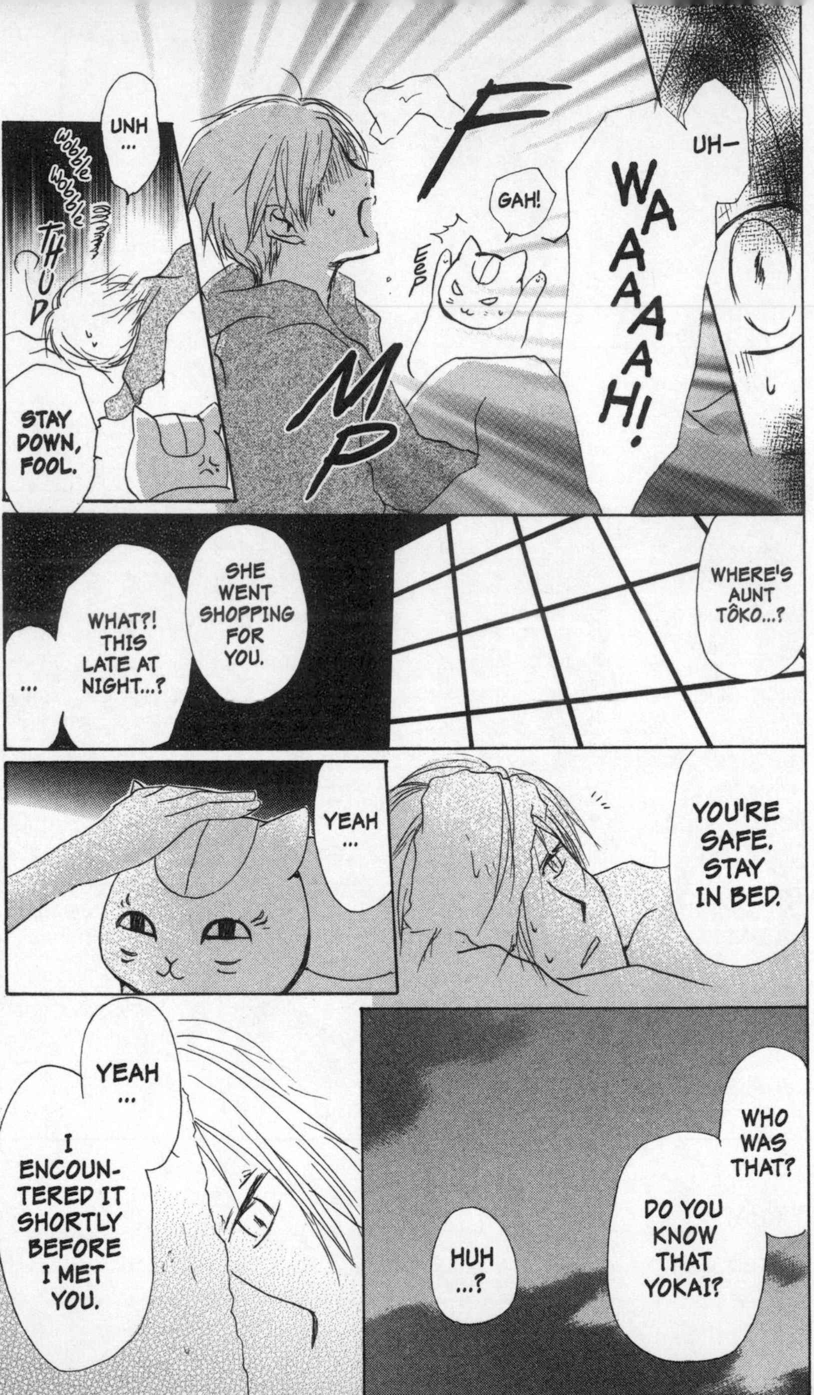
UH— WAAAAAH!
GAH!
EEP
FMP
UNH ...
wobble wobble
THUD
STAY DOWN, FOOL.
WHERE'S AUNT TÔKO...?
SHE WENT SHOPPING FOR YOU.
WHAT?! THIS LATE AT NIGHT...?
...
YOU'RE SAFE. STAY IN BED.
YEAH ...
WHO WAS THAT?
DO YOU KNOW THAT YOKAI?
HUH ...?
YEAH ...
I ENCOUNTERED IT SHORTLY BEFORE I MET YOU.

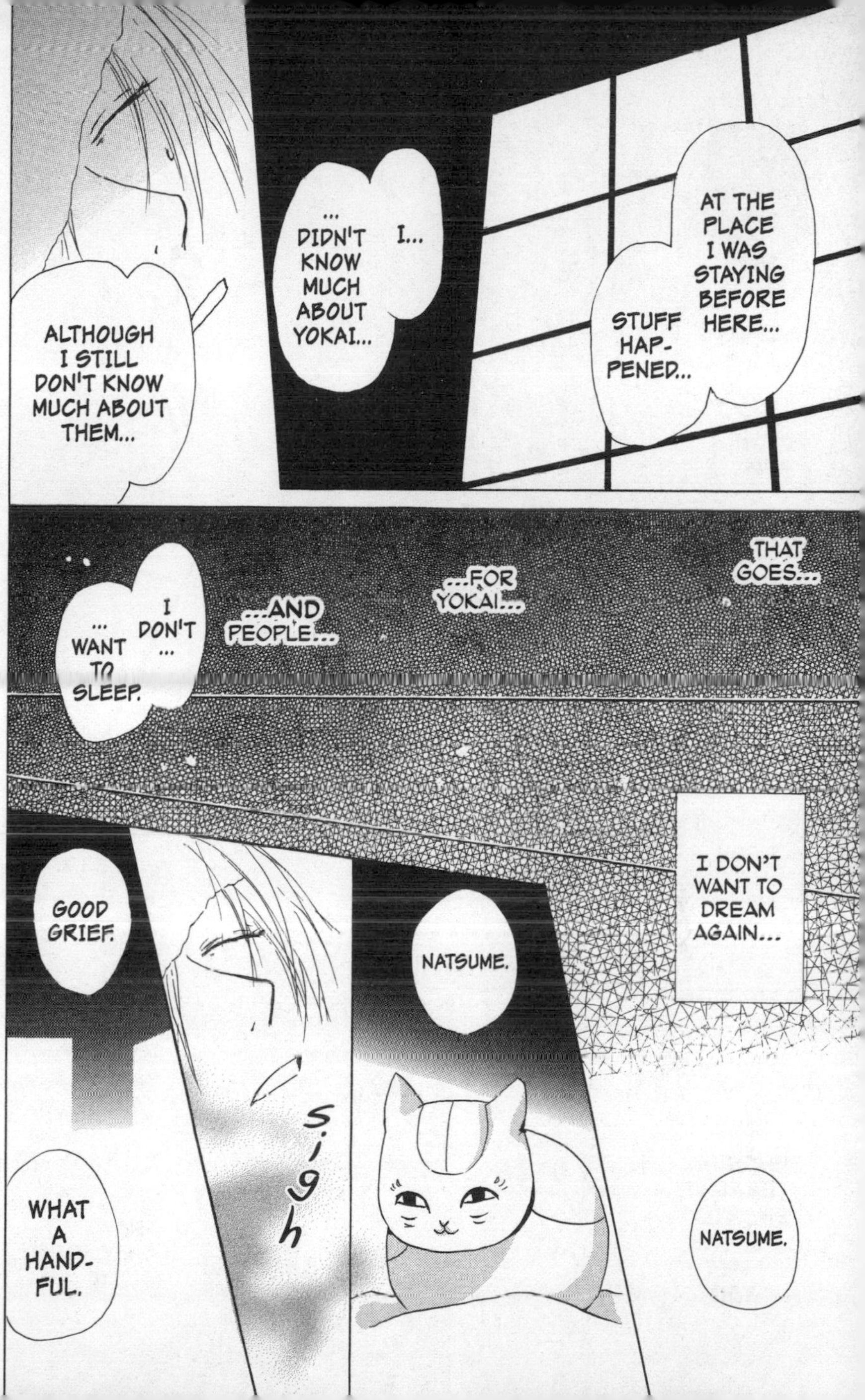
AT THE PLACE I WAS STAYING BEFORE HERE...
STUFF HAP-PENED...
I...
...DIDN'T KNOW MUCH ABOUT YOKAI...
ALTHOUGH I STILL DON'T KNOW MUCH ABOUT THEM...
THAT GOES...
...FOR YOKAI...
...AND PEOPLE...
I DON'T...
...WANT TO SLEEP.
I DON'T WANT TO DREAM AGAIN...
NATSUME.
NATSUME.
Sigh
GOOD GRIEF.
WHAT A HAND-FUL.

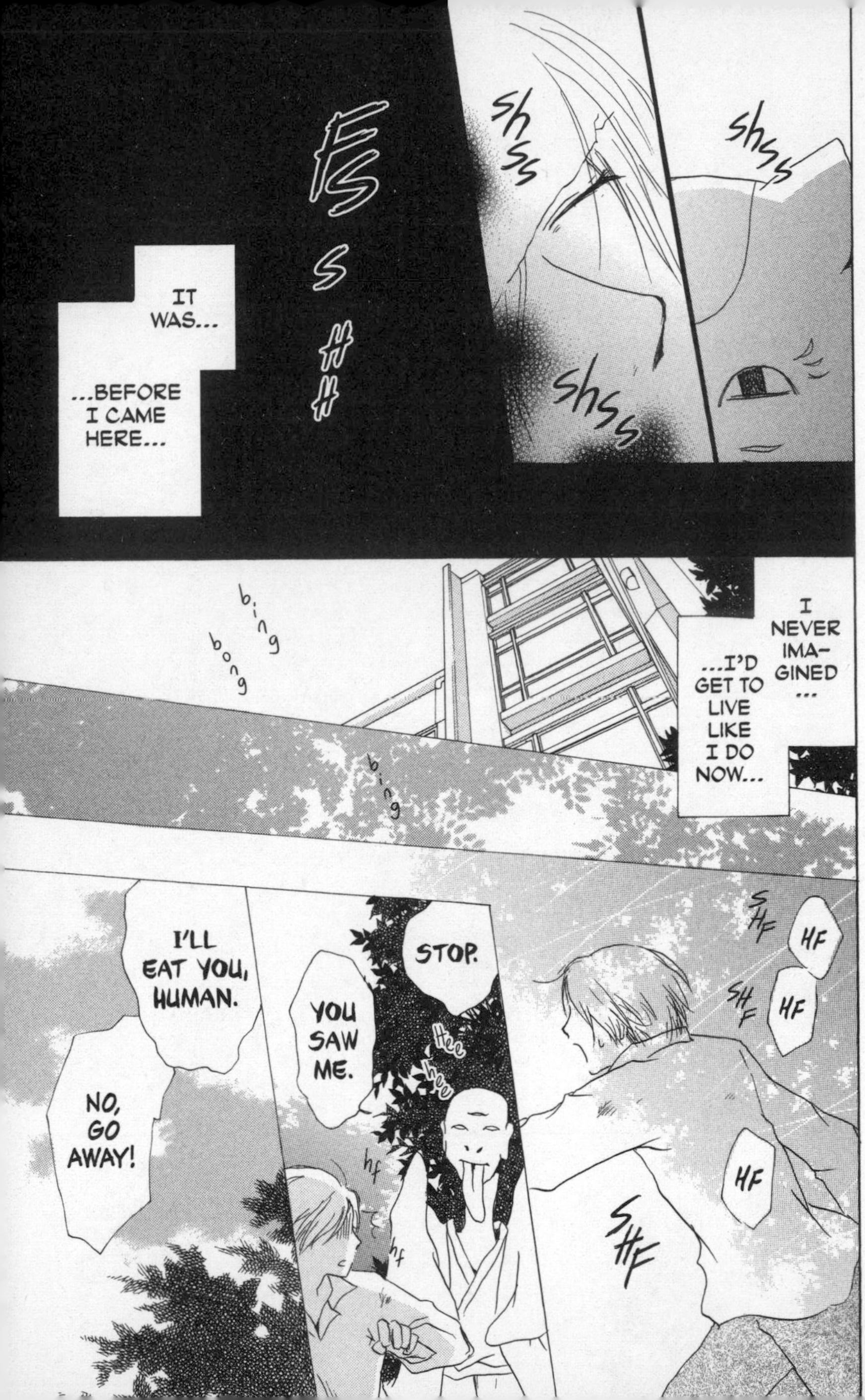
shss
shss
shss
FSSHH
IT WAS...
...BEFORE I CAME HERE...
I NEVER IMAGINED...
...I'D GET TO LIVE LIKE I DO NOW...
bing
bong
bing
SHF
HF
SHF
HF
HF
SHF
STOP.
YOU SAW ME.
hee hee
I'LL EAT YOU, HUMAN.
NO, GO AWAY!
hf
hf

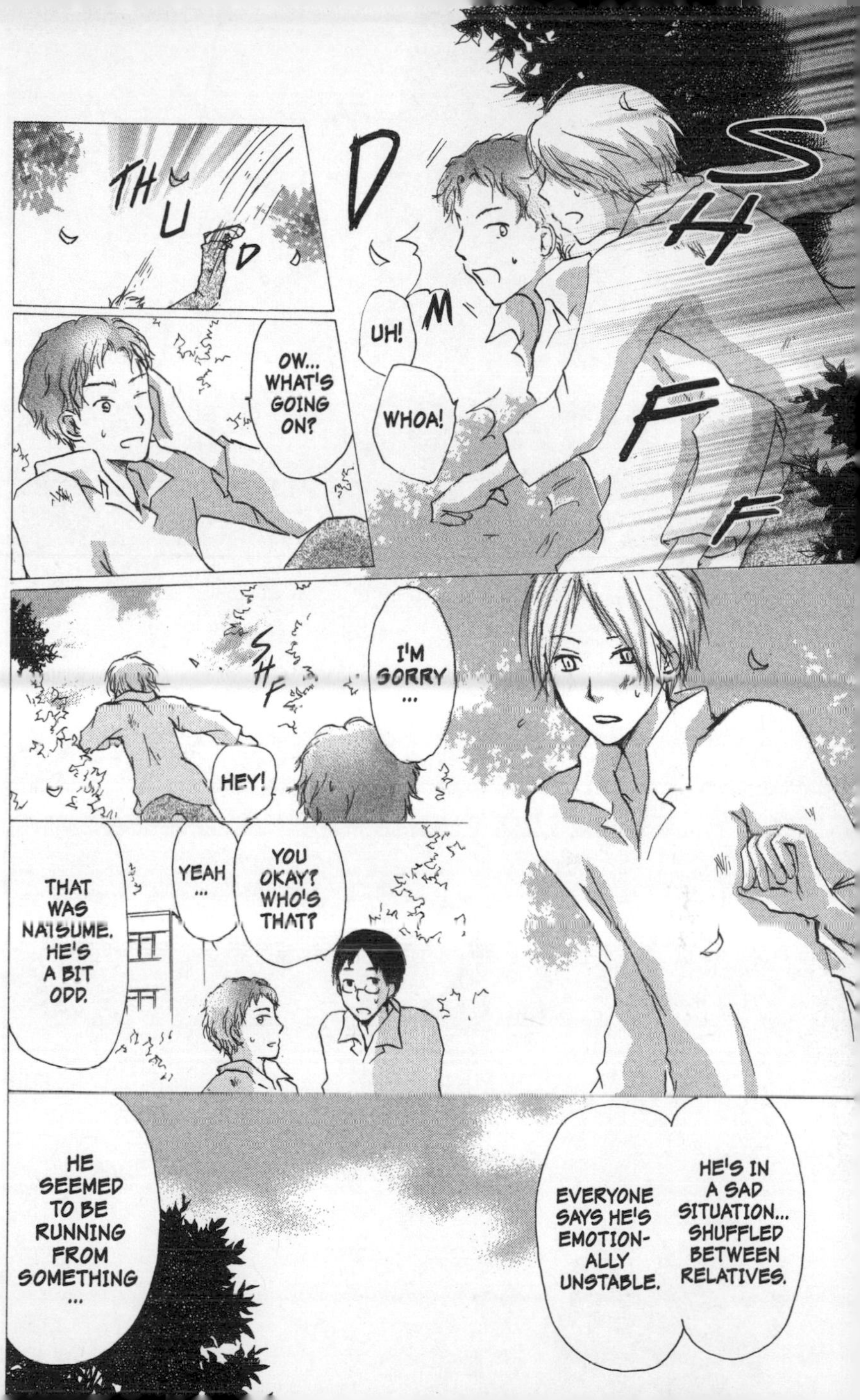
SHFF
UH!
WHOA!
D
M
THUD
OW... WHAT'S GOING ON?
I'M SORRY...
SHF
HEY!
YOU OKAY? WHO'S THAT?
YEAH...
THAT WAS NATSUME. HE'S A BIT ODD.
HE'S IN A SAD SITUATION... SHUFFLED BETWEEN RELATIVES.
EVERYONE SAYS HE'S EMOTION-ALLY UNSTABLE.
HE SEEMED TO BE RUNNING FROM SOMETHING...

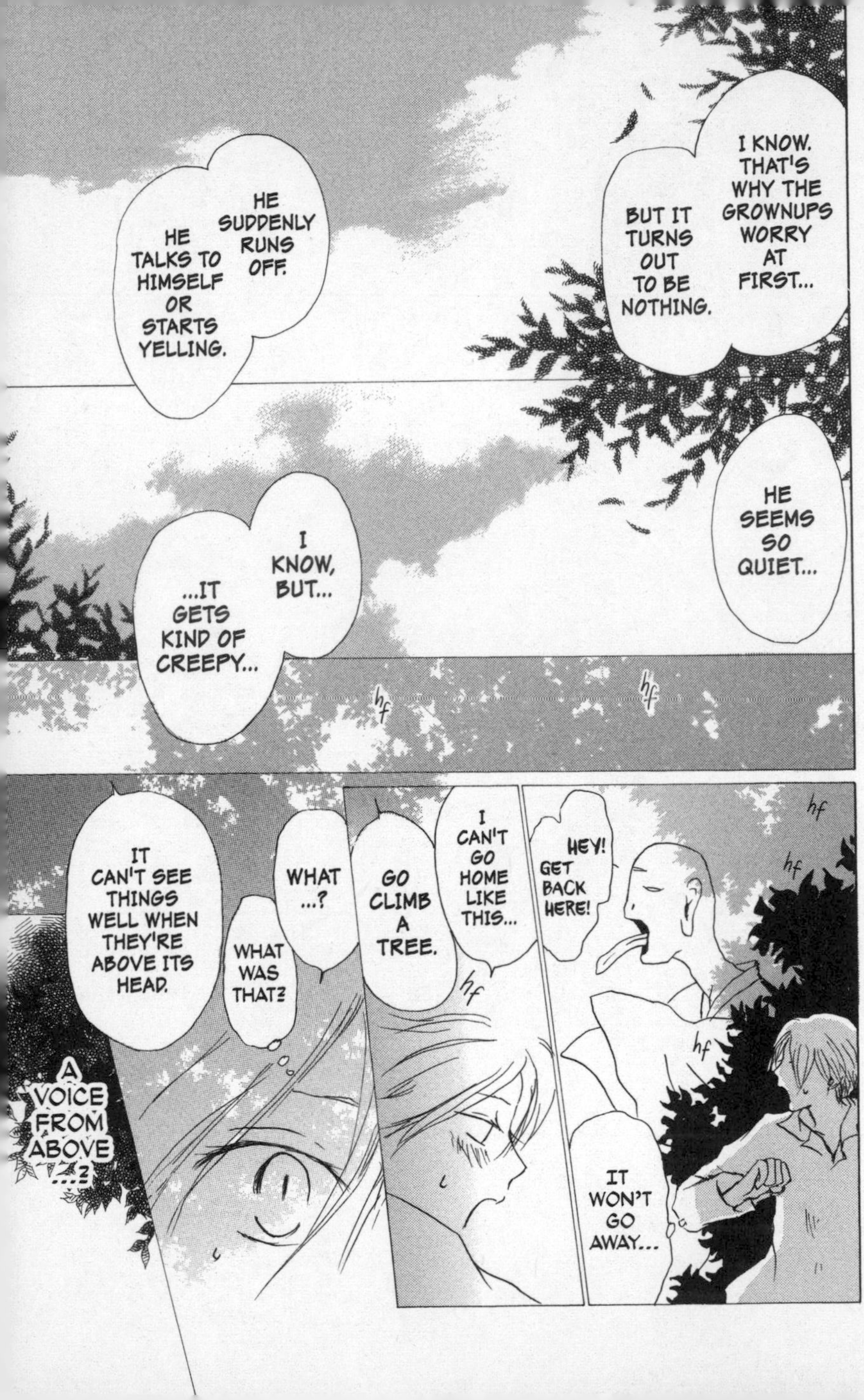
I KNOW. THAT'S WHY THE GROWNUPS WORRY AT FIRST...
BUT IT TURNS OUT TO BE NOTHING.
HE SUDDENLY RUNS OFF.
HE TALKS TO HIMSELF OR STARTS YELLING.
HE SEEMS SO QUIET...
I KNOW, BUT...
...IT GETS KIND OF CREEPY...
hf
hf
hf
hf
HEY! GET BACK HERE!
hf
IT WON'T GO AWAY...
I CAN'T GO HOME LIKE THIS...
GO CLIMB A TREE.
hf
WHAT ...?
IT CAN'T SEE THINGS WELL WHEN THEY'RE ABOVE ITS HEAD.
WHAT WAS THAT?
A VOICE FROM ABOVE...?

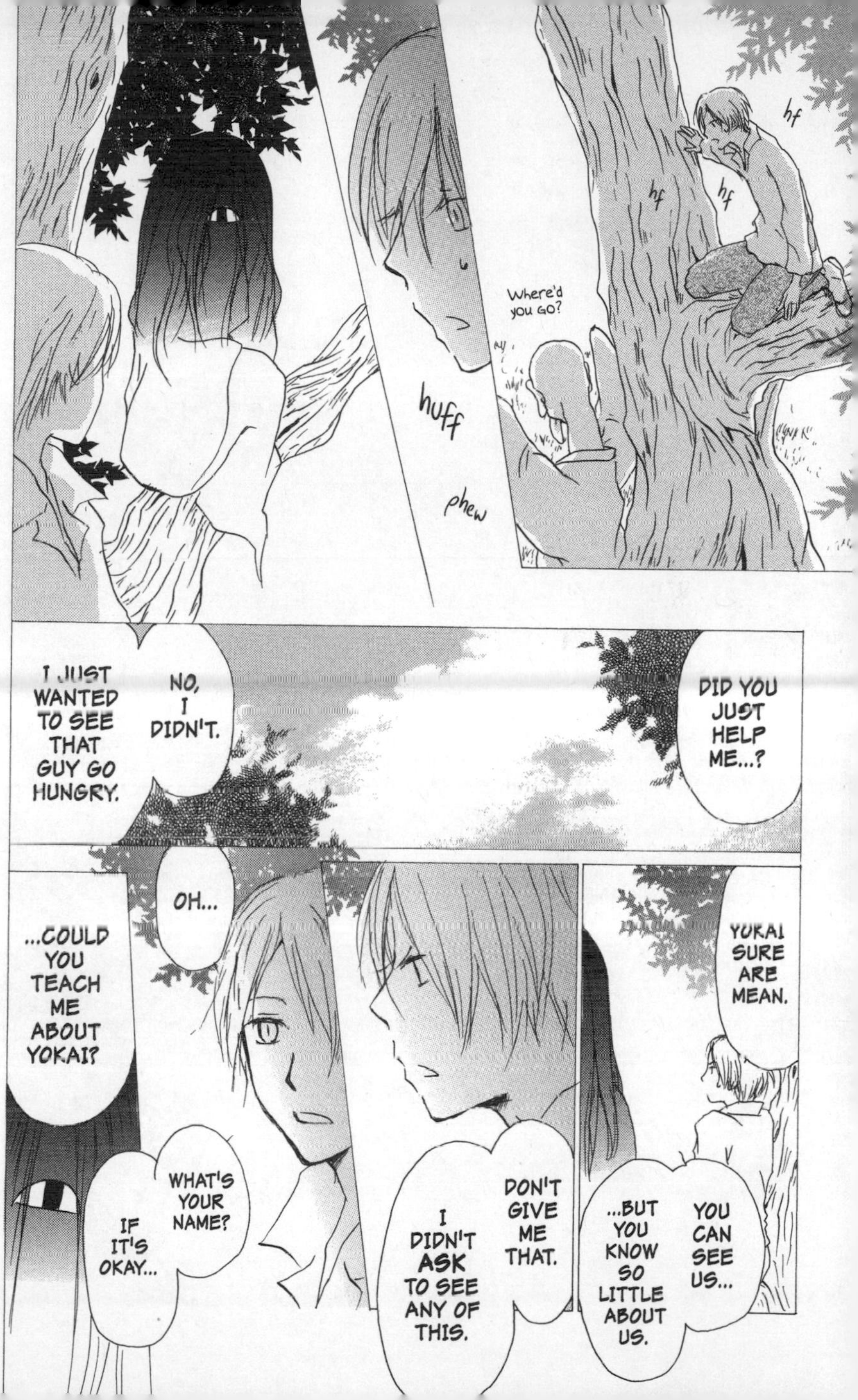
hf
hf
hf
Where'd you go?
huff
phew
DID YOU JUST HELP ME...?
NO, I DIDN'T.
I JUST WANTED TO SEE THAT GUY GO HUNGRY.
YOKAI SURE ARE MEAN.
YOU CAN SEE US...
...BUT YOU KNOW SO LITTLE ABOUT US.
DON'T GIVE ME THAT.
I DIDN'T **ASK** TO SEE ANY OF THIS.
OH...
...COULD YOU TEACH ME ABOUT YOKAI?
WHAT'S YOUR NAME?
IF IT'S OKAY...

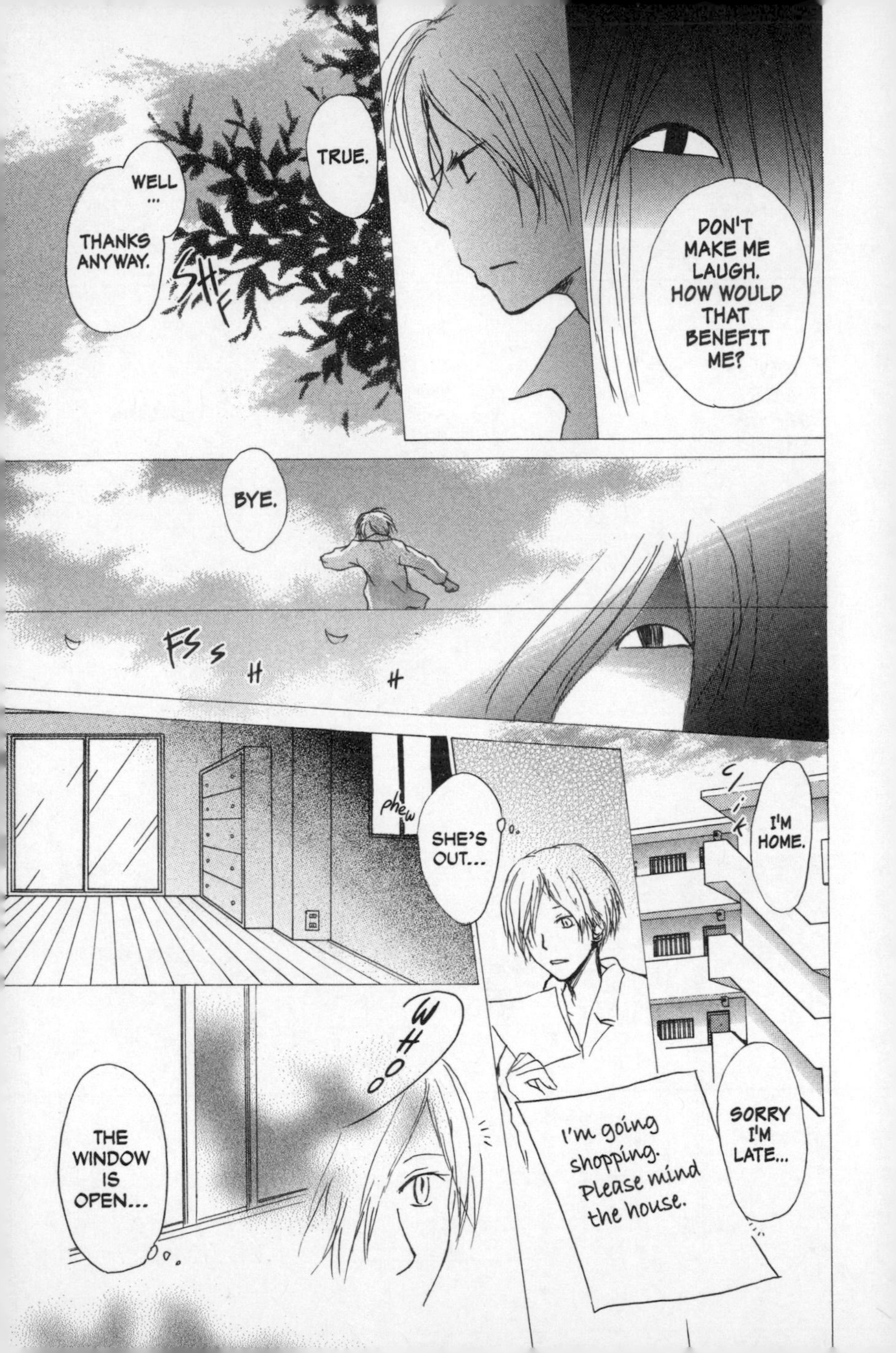
DON'T MAKE ME LAUGH. HOW WOULD THAT BENEFIT ME?
TRUE.
WELL ...
THANKS ANYWAY.
SHF
BYE.
FSSHH
click
I'M HOME.
SORRY I'M LATE...
I'm going shopping. Please mind the house.
SHE'S OUT...
phew
WHOOO
THE WINDOW IS OPEN...

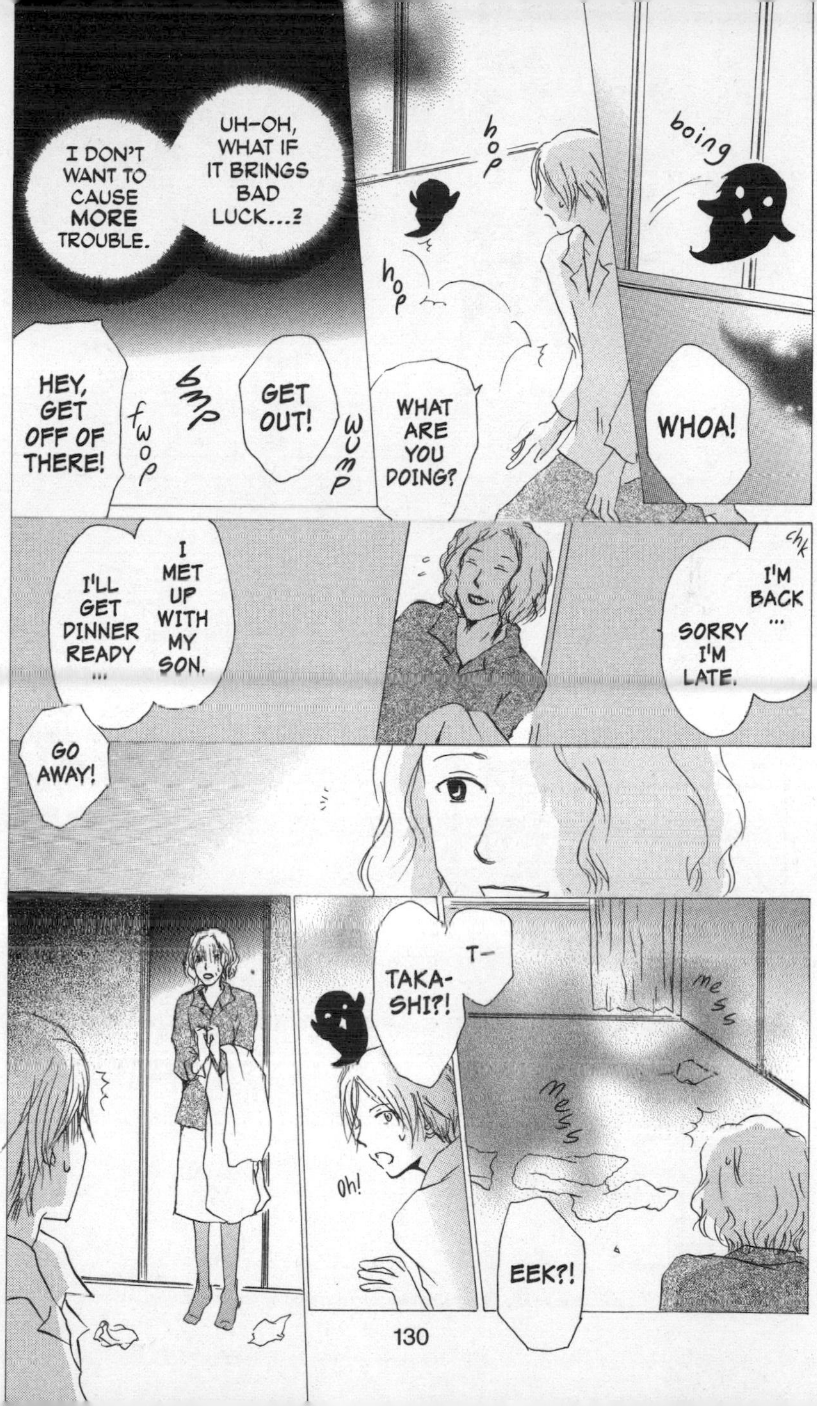
boing
WHOA!
hop
hop
UH-OH, WHAT IF IT BRINGS BAD LUCK...?
I DON'T WANT TO CAUSE MORE TROUBLE.
WHAT ARE YOU DOING?
wump
GET OUT!
bmp
fwop
HEY, GET OFF OF THERE!
chk
I'M BACK...
SORRY I'M LATE.
I MET UP WITH MY SON.
I'LL GET DINNER READY...
GO AWAY!
T- TAKA-SHI?!
mess
mess
Oh!
EEK?!

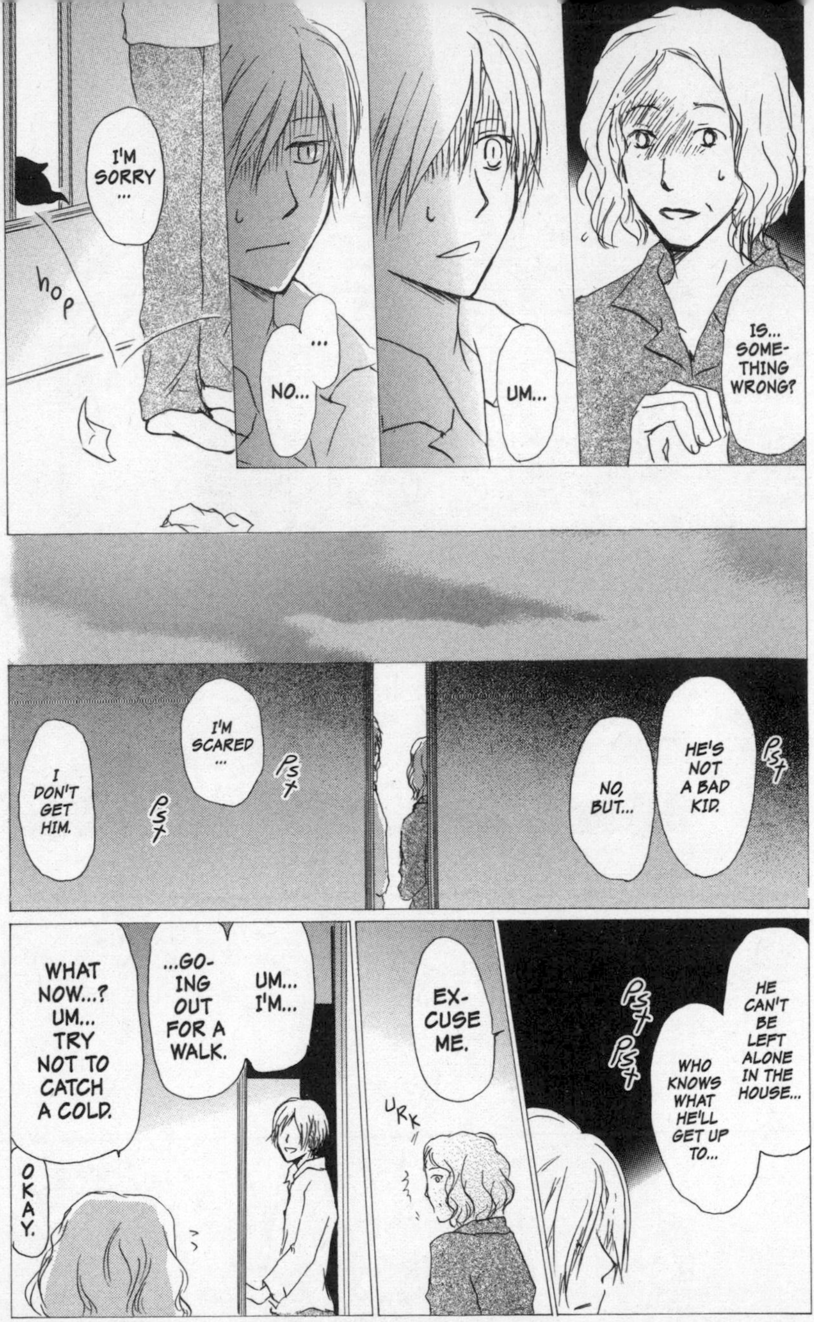
IS... SOMETHING WRONG?
UM...
...
NO...
I'M SORRY ...
hop
HE'S NOT A BAD KID.
Pst
NO, BUT...
I'M SCARED ...
Pst
Pst
I DON'T GET HIM.
HE CAN'T BE LEFT ALONE IN THE HOUSE...
WHO KNOWS WHAT HE'LL GET UP TO...
Pst
Pst
EX-CUSE ME.
URK
UM... I'M...
...GO-ING OUT FOR A WALK.
WHAT NOW...? UM... TRY NOT TO CATCH A COLD.
OKAY.

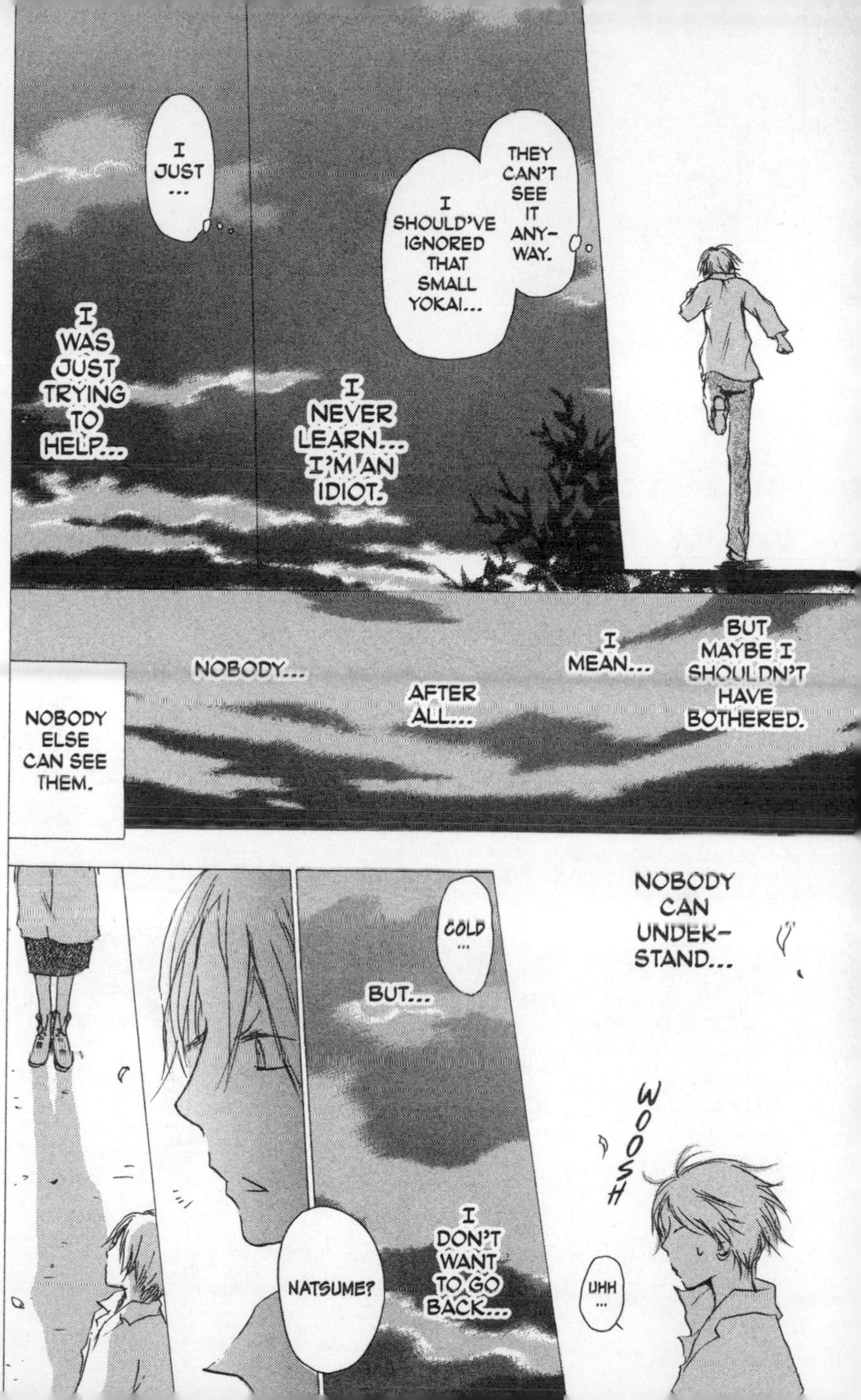
THEY CAN'T SEE IT ANY-WAY.
I SHOULD'VE IGNORED THAT SMALL YOKAI...
I NEVER LEARN... I'M AN IDIOT.
I JUST ...
I WAS JUST TRYING TO HELP...
BUT MAYBE I SHOULDN'T HAVE BOTHERED.
I MEAN...
AFTER ALL...
NOBODY...
NOBODY ELSE CAN SEE THEM.
NOBODY CAN UNDER-STAND...
WOOSH
UHH ...
COLD ...
BUT...
I DON'T WANT TO GO BACK...
NATSUME?

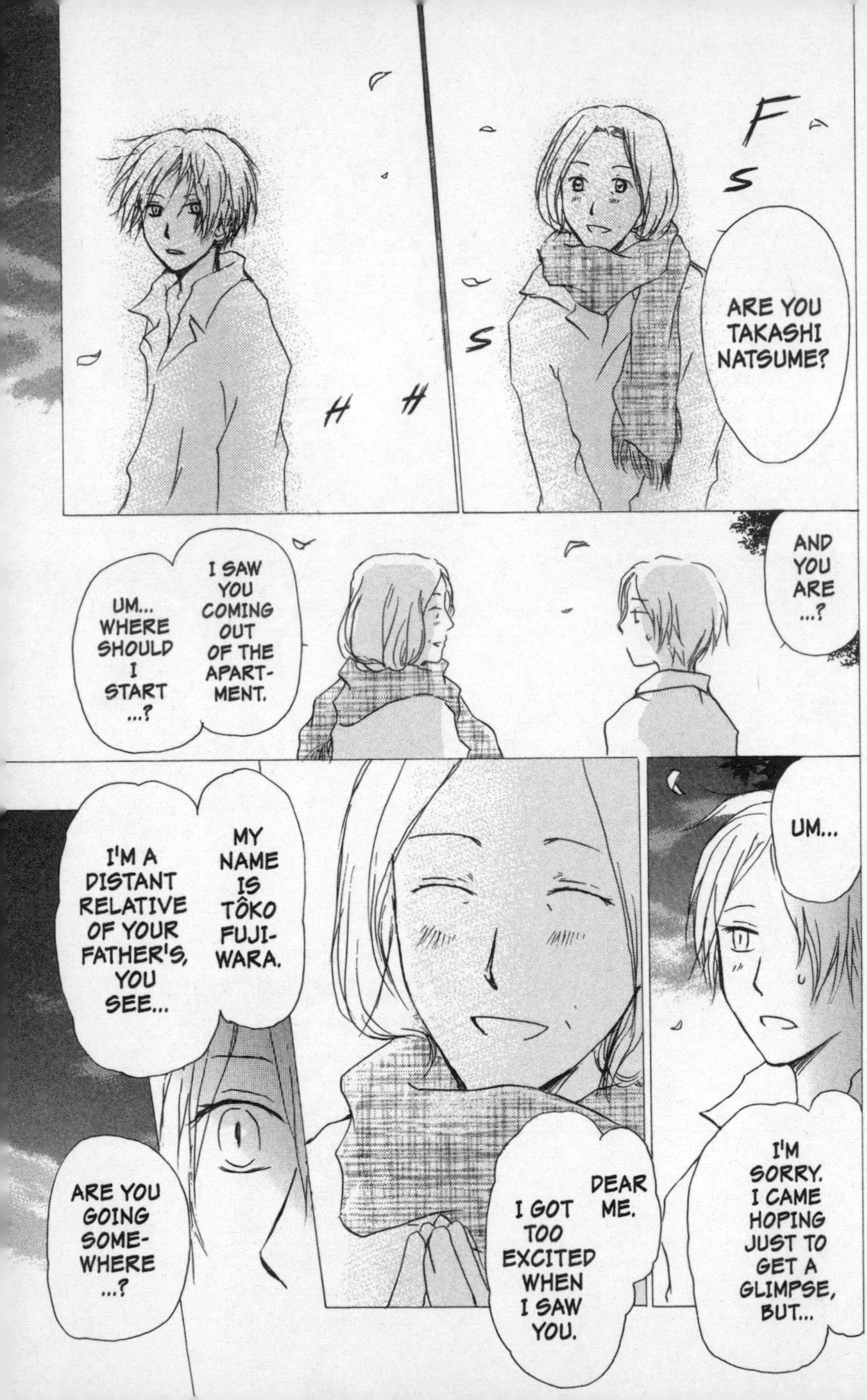
FS
ARE YOU TAKASHI NATSUME?
S
HH
AND YOU ARE ...?
I SAW YOU COMING OUT OF THE APART-MENT.
UM... WHERE SHOULD I START ...?
UM...
I'M SORRY. I CAME HOPING JUST TO GET A GLIMPSE, BUT...
DEAR ME.
I GOT TOO EXCITED WHEN I SAW YOU.
MY NAME IS TÔKO FUJI-WARA.
I'M A DISTANT RELATIVE OF YOUR FATHER'S, YOU SEE...
ARE YOU GOING SOME-WHERE ...?

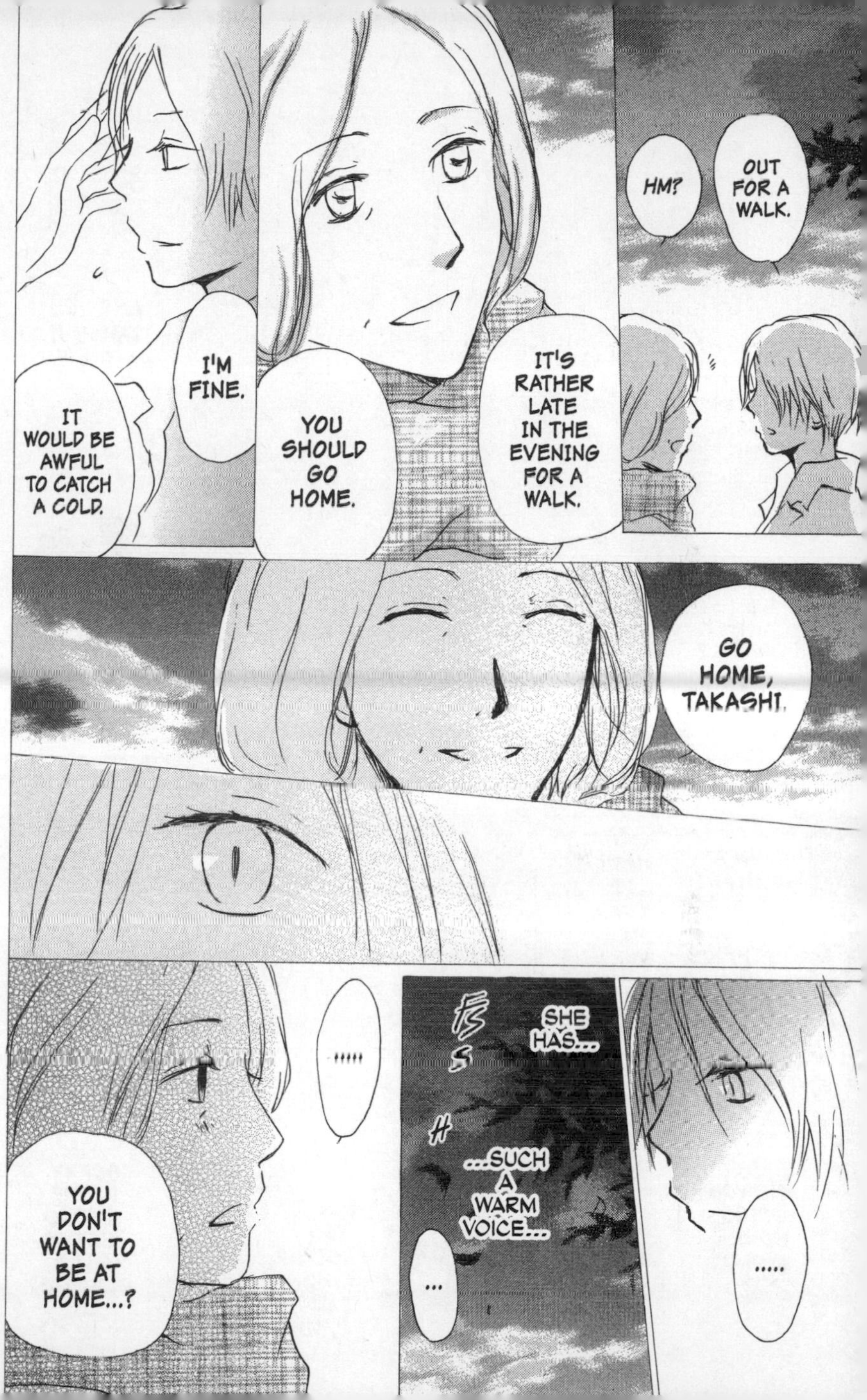
OUT FOR A WALK.
HM?
IT'S RATHER LATE IN THE EVENING FOR A WALK.
YOU SHOULD GO HOME.
I'M FINE.
IT WOULD BE AWFUL TO CATCH A COLD.
GO HOME, TAKASHI.
.....
SHE HAS...
FSSH
...SUCH A WARM VOICE...
...
......
YOU DON'T WANT TO BE AT HOME...?

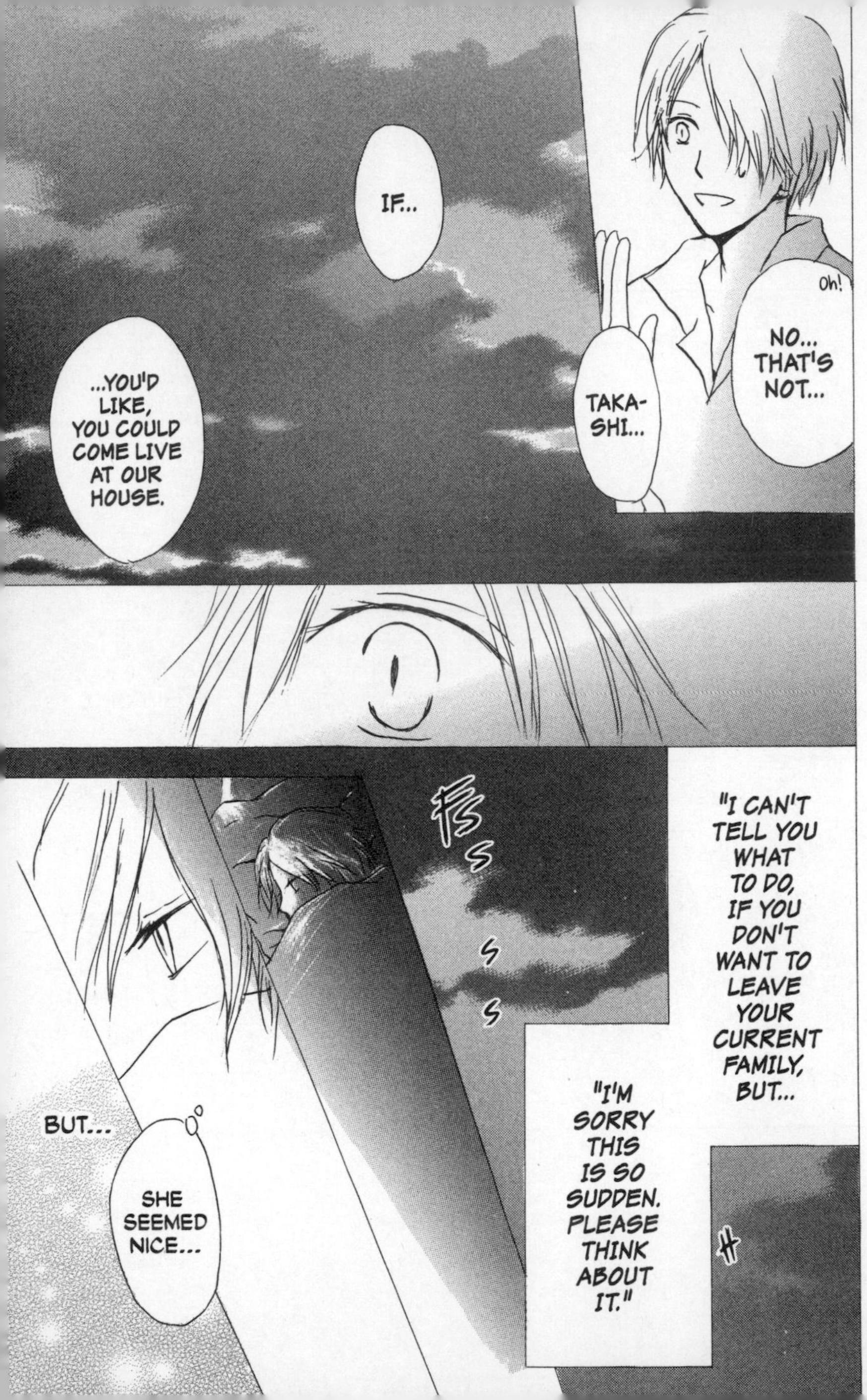
Oh!
NO... THAT'S NOT...
TAKA-SHI...
IF...
...YOU'D LIKE, YOU COULD COME LIVE AT OUR HOUSE.
"I CAN'T TELL YOU WHAT TO DO, IF YOU DON'T WANT TO LEAVE YOUR CURRENT FAMILY, BUT...
"I'M SORRY THIS IS SO SUDDEN. PLEASE THINK ABOUT IT."
BUT...
SHE SEEMED NICE...

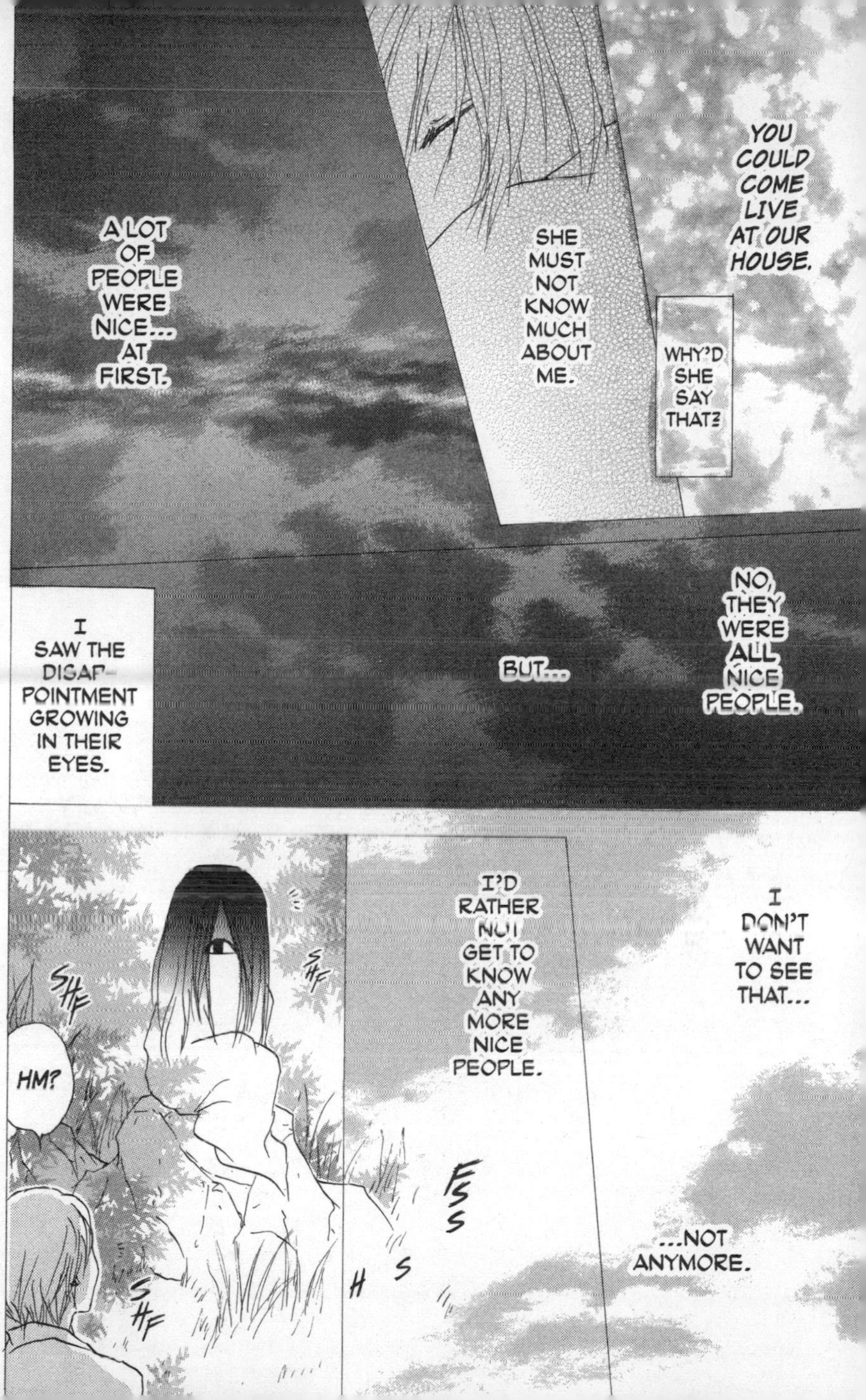
YOU COULD COME LIVE AT OUR HOUSE.
WHY'D SHE SAY THAT?
SHE MUST NOT KNOW MUCH ABOUT ME.
A LOT OF PEOPLE WERE NICE... AT FIRST.
NO, THEY WERE ALL NICE PEOPLE.
BUT...
I SAW THE DISAP-POINTMENT GROWING IN THEIR EYES.
I DON'T WANT TO SEE THAT...
...NOT ANYMORE.
I'D RATHER NOT GET TO KNOW ANY MORE NICE PEOPLE.
FSS
S
H
SHF
SHF
HM?
SHF

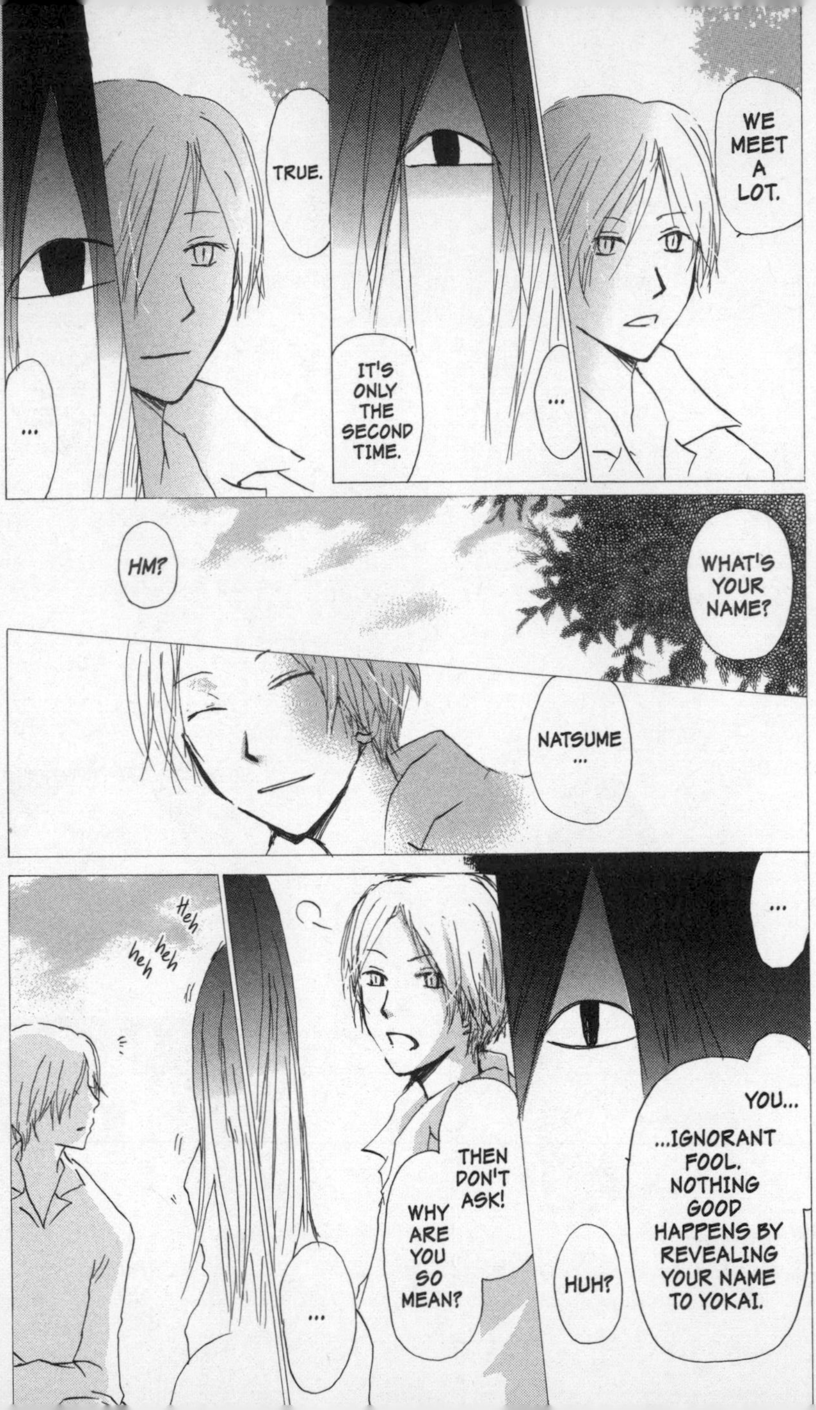
WE MEET A LOT.
...
IT'S ONLY THE SECOND TIME.
TRUE.
...
WHAT'S YOUR NAME?
HM?
NATSUME ...
...
YOU...
...IGNORANT FOOL. NOTHING GOOD HAPPENS BY REVEALING YOUR NAME TO YOKAI.
HUH?
THEN DON'T ASK!
WHY ARE YOU SO MEAN?
...
Heh heh heh

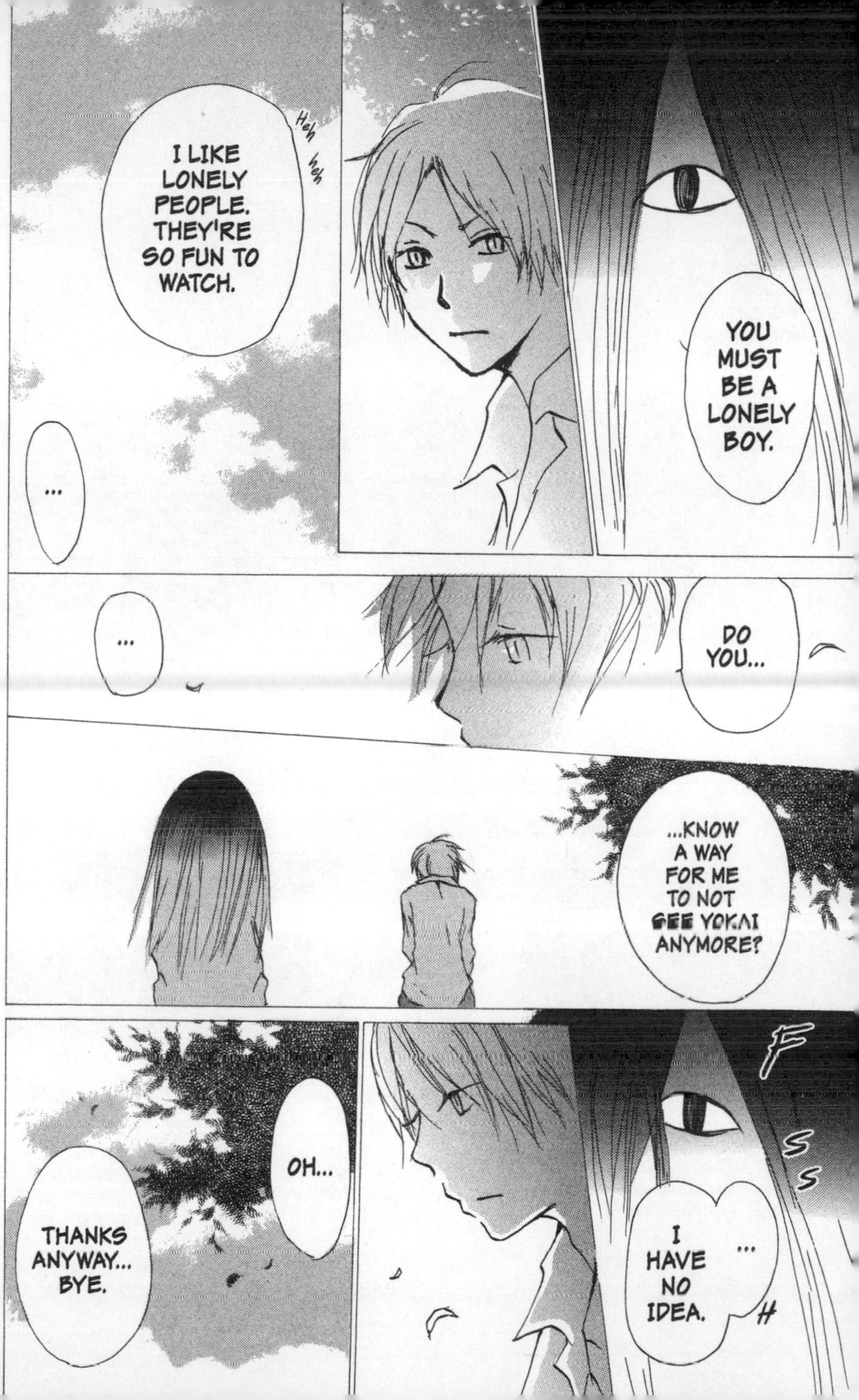
YOU MUST BE A LONELY BOY.
Heh heh
I LIKE LONELY PEOPLE. THEY'RE SO FUN TO WATCH.
...
DO YOU...
...
...KNOW A WAY FOR ME TO NOT SEE YOKAI ANYMORE?
FSSSH
...
I HAVE NO IDEA.
OH...
THANKS ANYWAY... BYE.

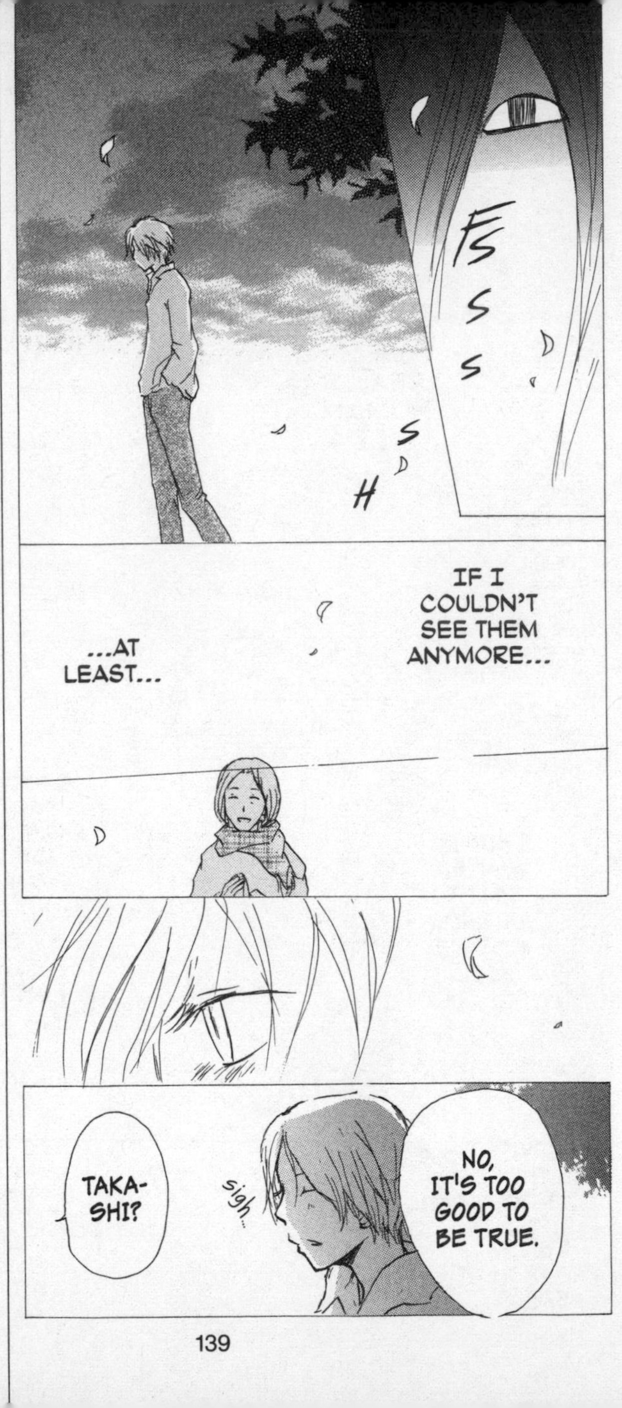
FSSSSH
IF I COULDN'T SEE THEM ANYMORE...
...AT LEAST...
NO, IT'S TOO GOOD TO BE TRUE.
sigh...
TAKA-SHI?

04

❋Tanuma's Bed

His dad bought him a Western-style bed instead of the traditional Japanese bedding on the floor, because it would be too tedious to put it away and set it out all the time when he gets sick so often. I figured Natsume would be a little envious of the bed somehow, but he didn't bring it up because then Tanuma would lecture him to just ask the Fujiwaras for one. It only appeared in one panel, but a few people actually wrote me about it. It made me happy that they found familiarity with beds in Japanese rooms. Thank you for writing.

❋The Natsume anime wraps up

I was truly blessed with a great director, scriptwriter, character designer, music, background, studio, OP & ED animation, all the actors, and everyone else involved. The anime Natsume came to an end.

Continued in part 5

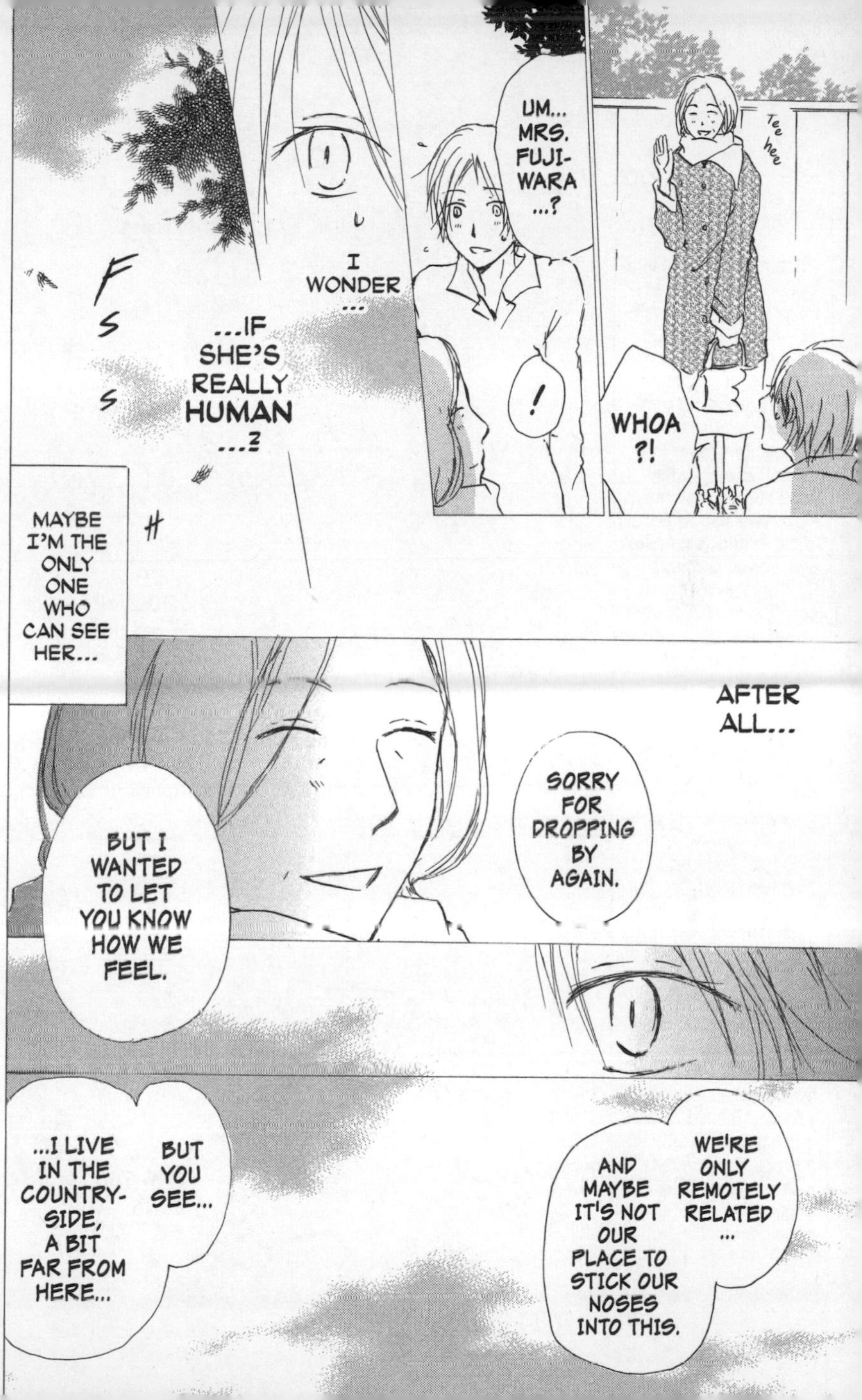
Tee hee
WHOA?!
UM... MRS. FUJIWARA...?
!
I WONDER...
...IF SHE'S REALLY HUMAN...?
FSSH
MAYBE I'M THE ONLY ONE WHO CAN SEE HER...
AFTER ALL...
SORRY FOR DROPPING BY AGAIN.
BUT I WANTED TO LET YOU KNOW HOW WE FEEL.
WE'RE ONLY REMOTELY RELATED...
AND MAYBE IT'S NOT OUR PLACE TO STICK OUR NOSES INTO THIS.
BUT YOU SEE...
...I LIVE IN THE COUNTRYSIDE, A BIT FAR FROM HERE...

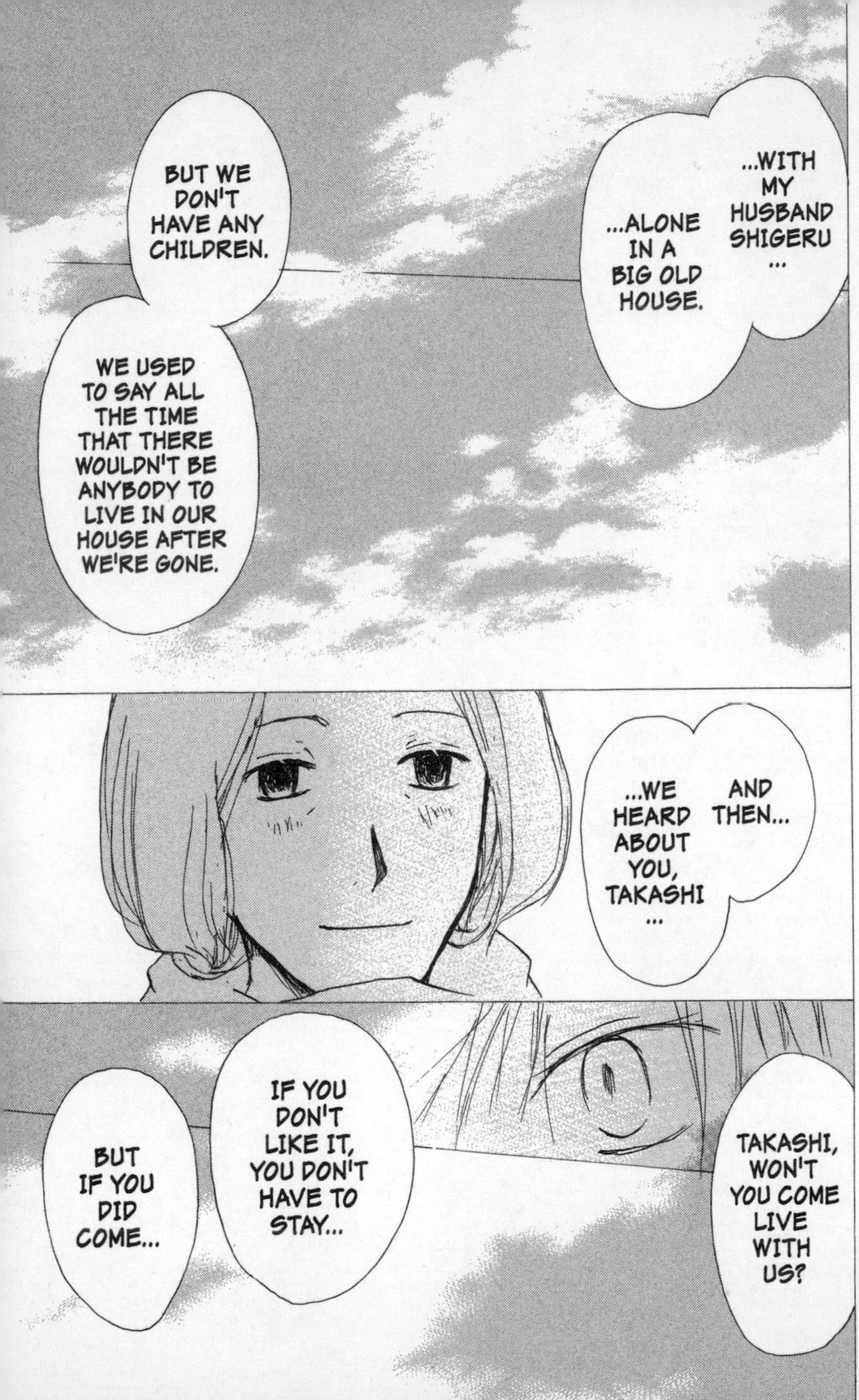
...WITH MY HUSBAND SHIGERU...
...ALONE IN A BIG OLD HOUSE.
BUT WE DON'T HAVE ANY CHILDREN.
WE USED TO SAY ALL THE TIME THAT THERE WOULDN'T BE ANYBODY TO LIVE IN OUR HOUSE AFTER WE'RE GONE.
AND THEN...
...WE HEARD ABOUT YOU, TAKASHI...
TAKASHI, WON'T YOU COME LIVE WITH US?
IF YOU DON'T LIKE IT, YOU DON'T HAVE TO STAY...
BUT IF YOU DID COME...

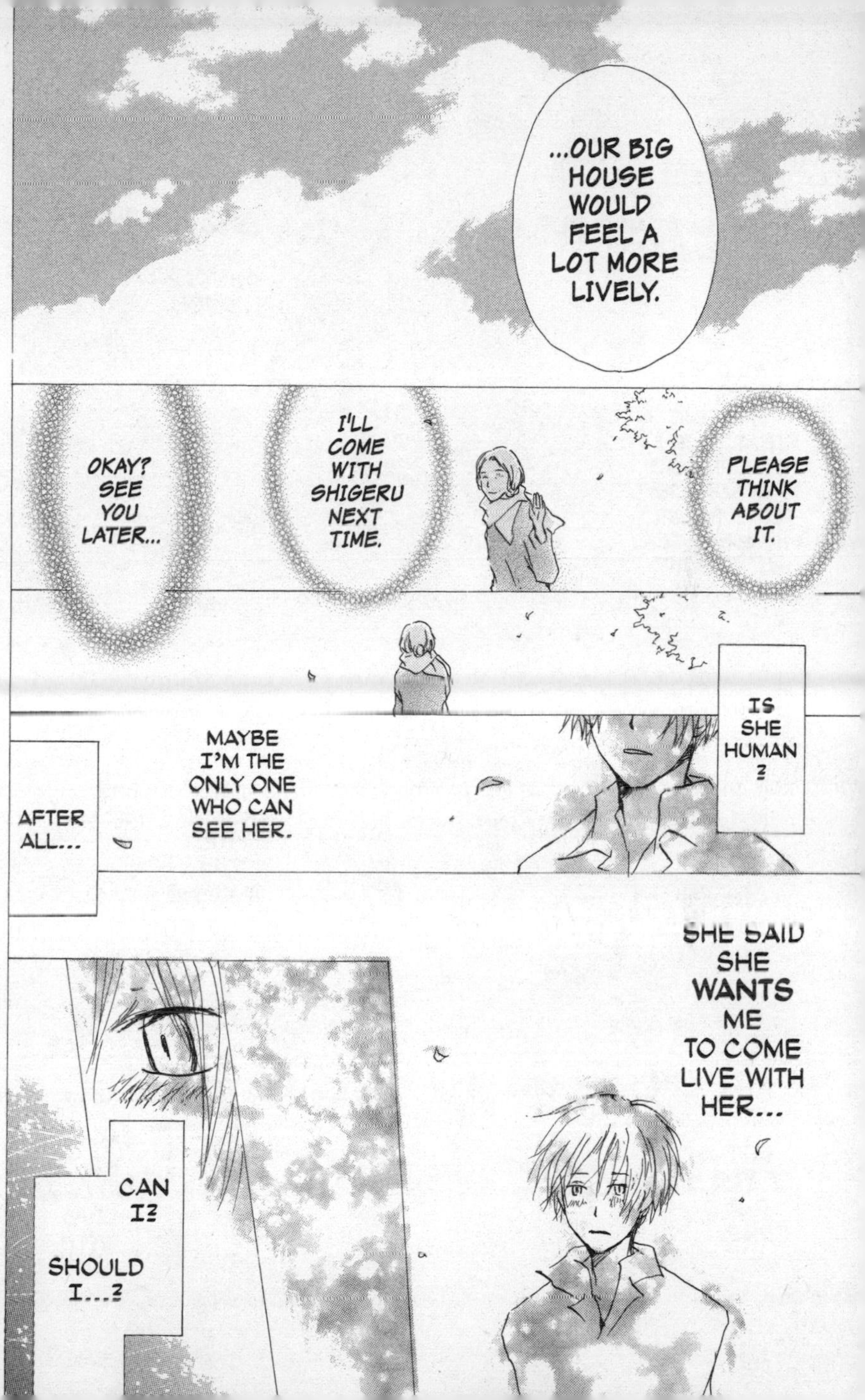
...OUR BIG HOUSE WOULD FEEL A LOT MORE LIVELY.
PLEASE THINK ABOUT IT.
I'LL COME WITH SHIGERU NEXT TIME.
OKAY? SEE YOU LATER...
IS SHE HUMAN?
MAYBE I'M THE ONLY ONE WHO CAN SEE HER.
AFTER ALL...
SHE SAID SHE WANTS ME TO COME LIVE WITH HER...
CAN I?
SHOULD I...?

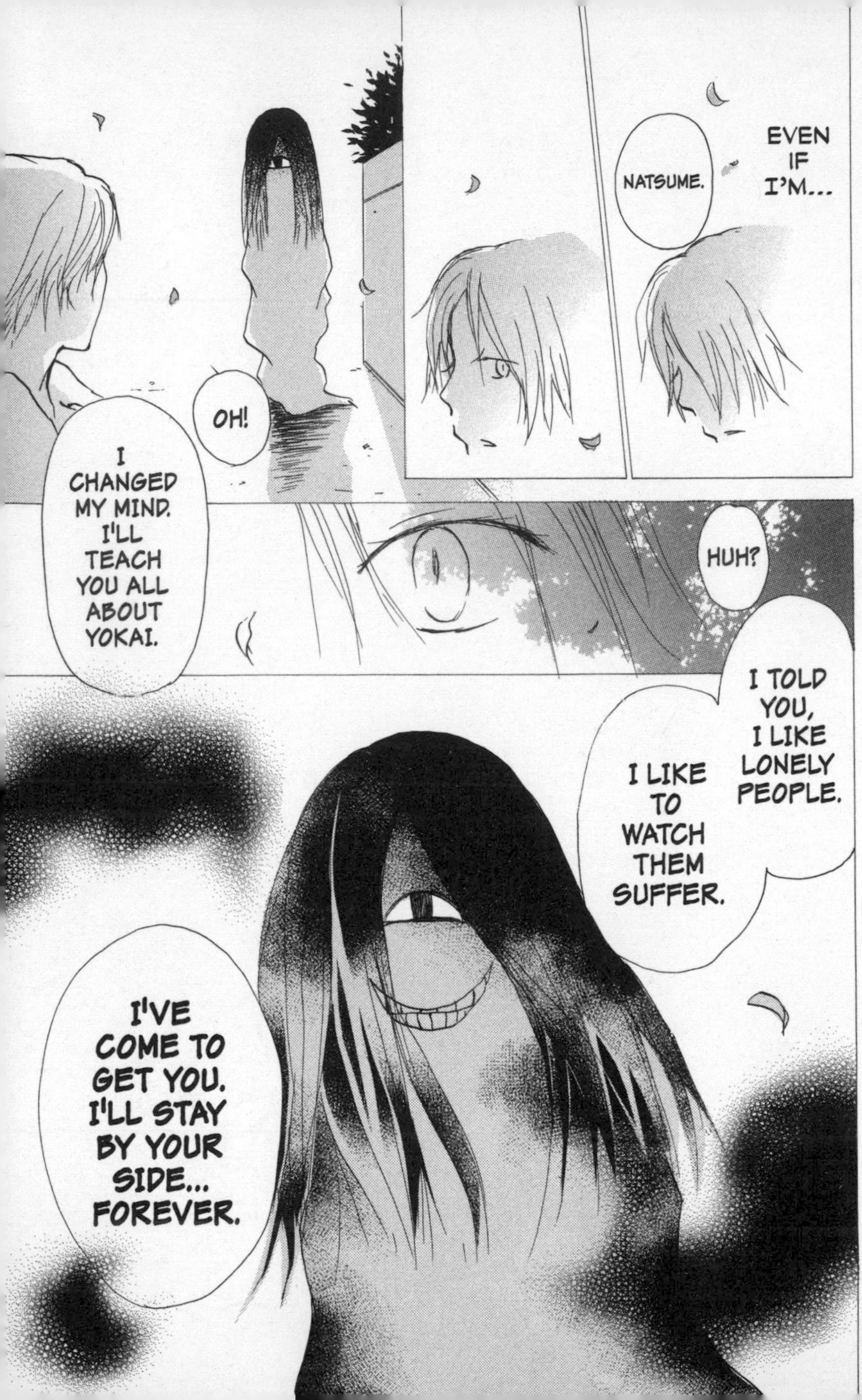
EVEN IF I'M...
NATSUME.
OH!
I CHANGED MY MIND. I'LL TEACH YOU ALL ABOUT YOKAI.
HUH?
I TOLD YOU, I LIKE LONELY PEOPLE.
I LIKE TO WATCH THEM SUFFER.
I'VE COME TO GET YOU. I'LL STAY BY YOUR SIDE... FOREVER.

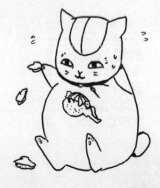

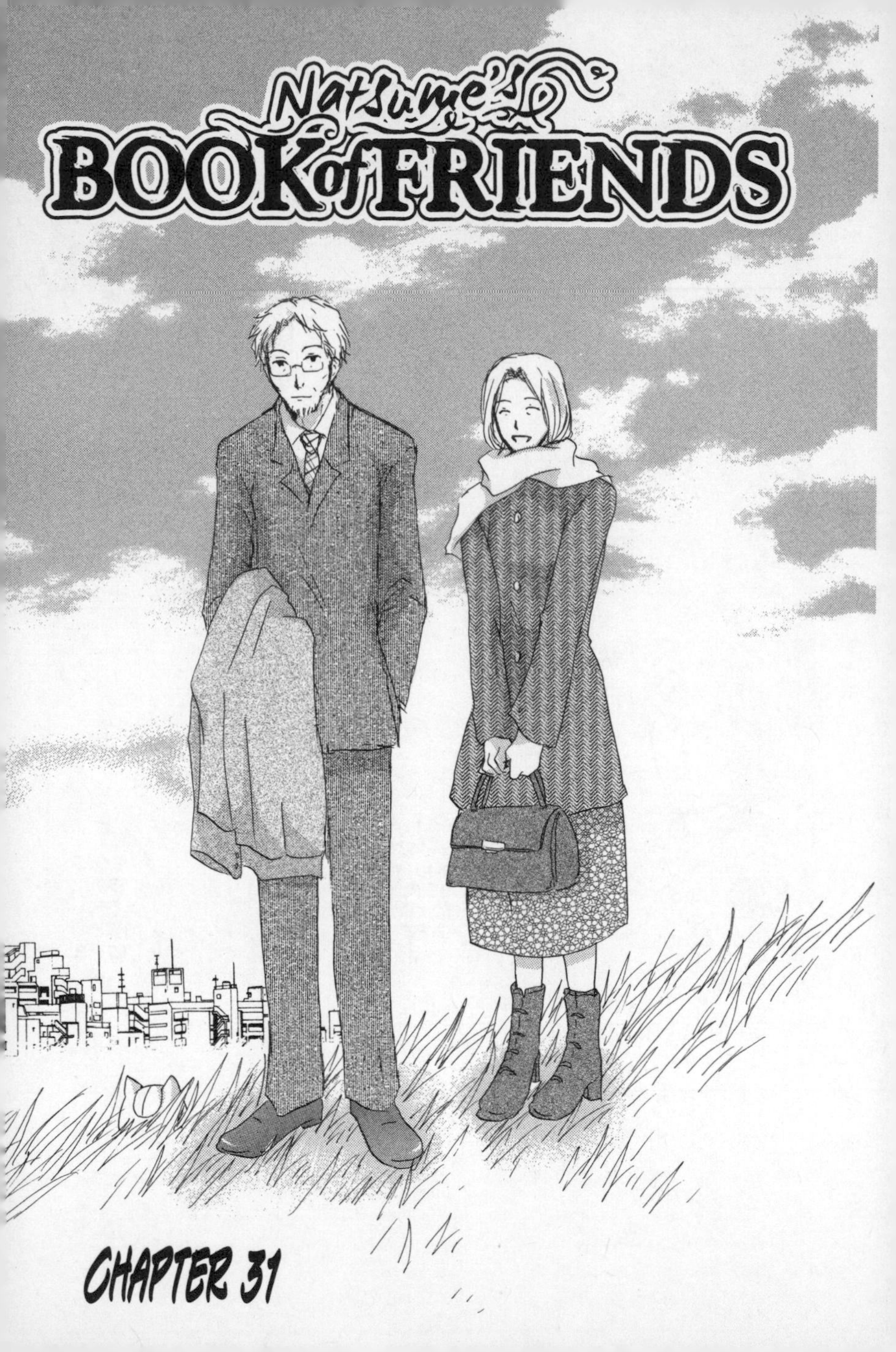
Natsume's
BOOK of FRIENDS
CHAPTER 31

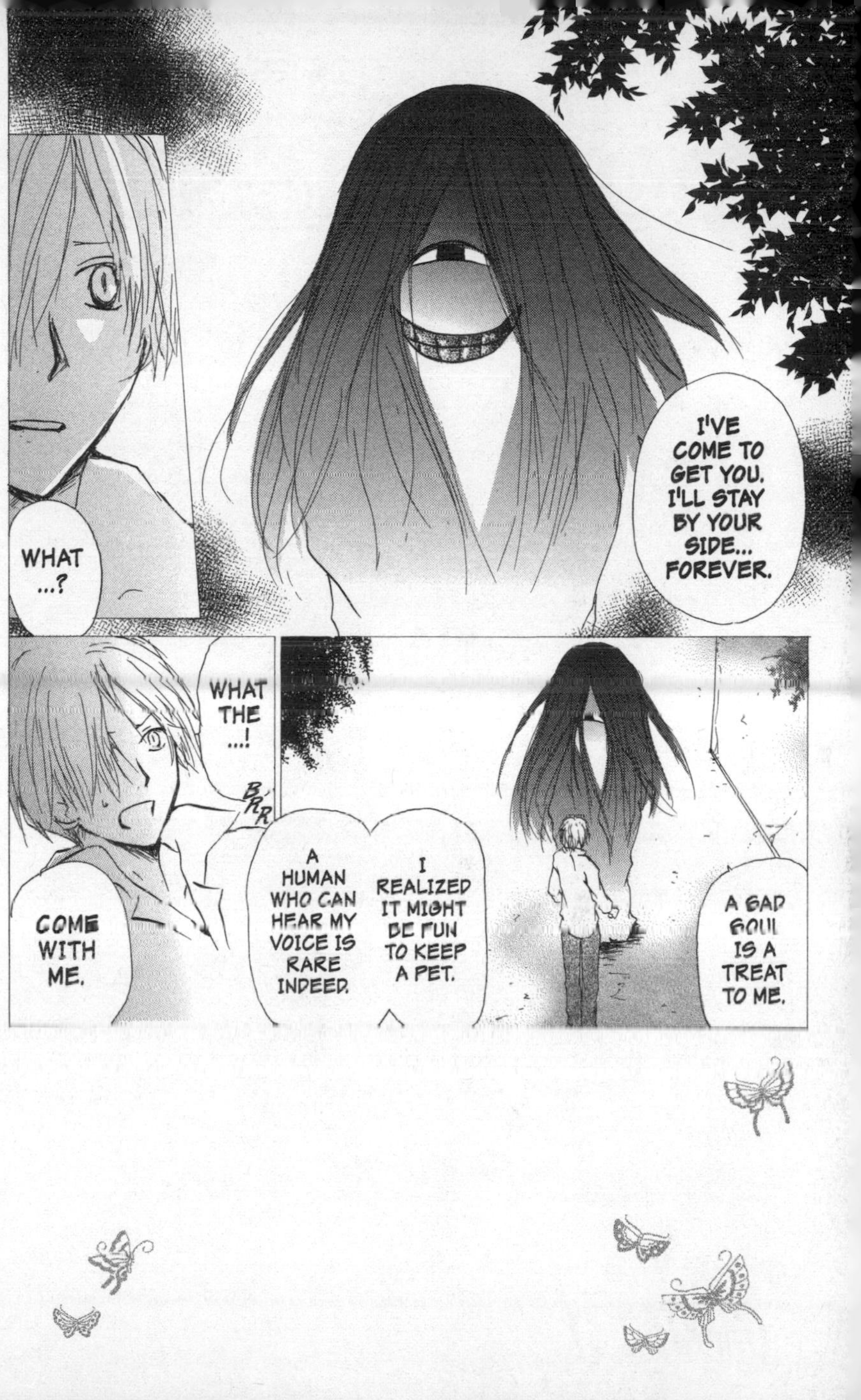
I'VE COME TO GET YOU. I'LL STAY BY YOUR SIDE... FOREVER.
WHAT ...?
A SAD SOUL IS A TREAT TO ME.
I REALIZED IT MIGHT BE FUN TO KEEP A PET.
A HUMAN WHO CAN HEAR MY VOICE IS RARE INDEED.
WHAT THE ...!
BRR
COME WITH ME.

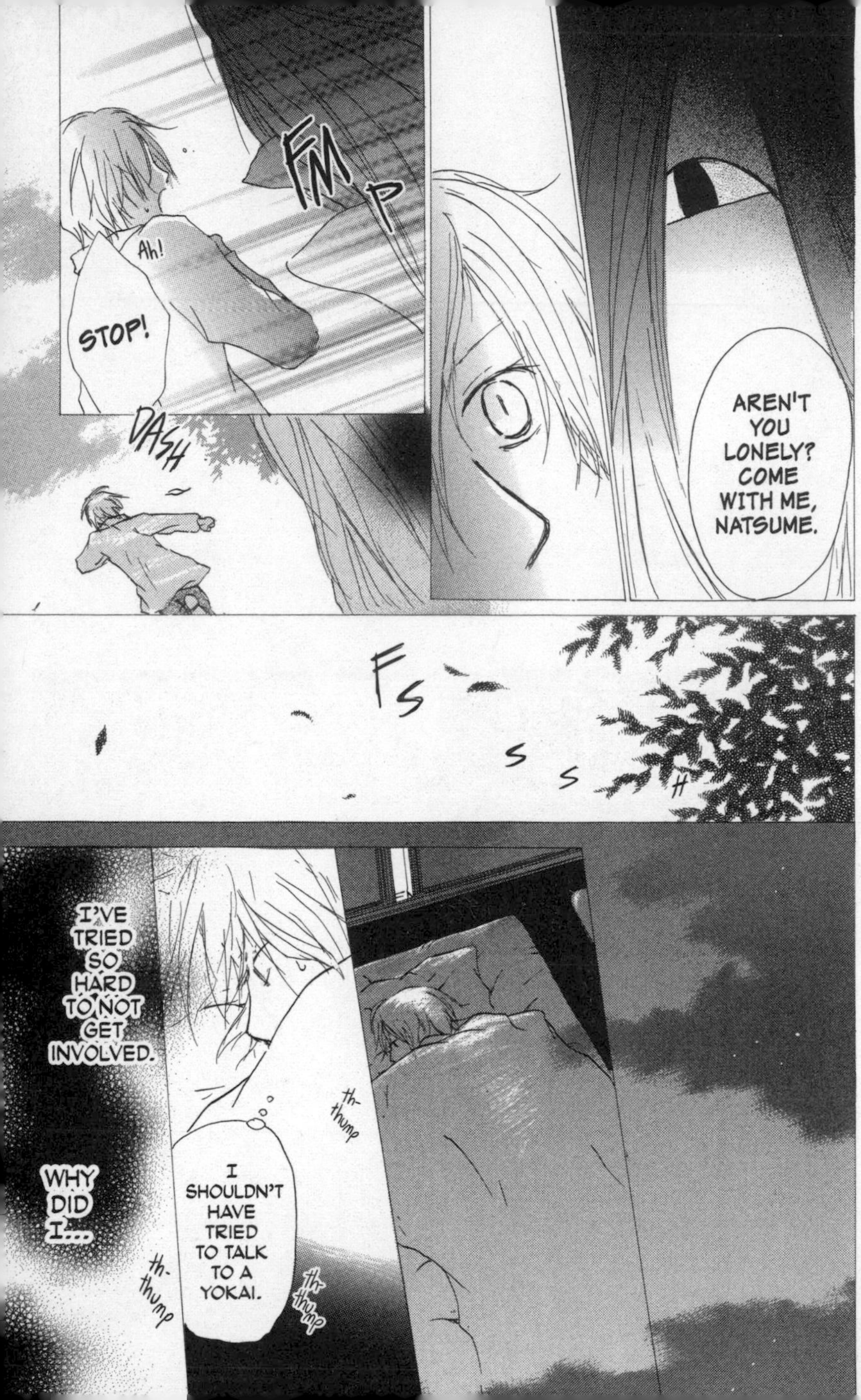
AREN'T YOU LONELY? COME WITH ME, NATSUME.
FMP
Ah!
STOP!
DASH
FSSSH
th-thump
I'VE TRIED SO HARD TO NOT GET INVOLVED.
I SHOULDN'T HAVE TRIED TO TALK TO A YOKAI.
thr-thump
WHY DID I...
th-thump

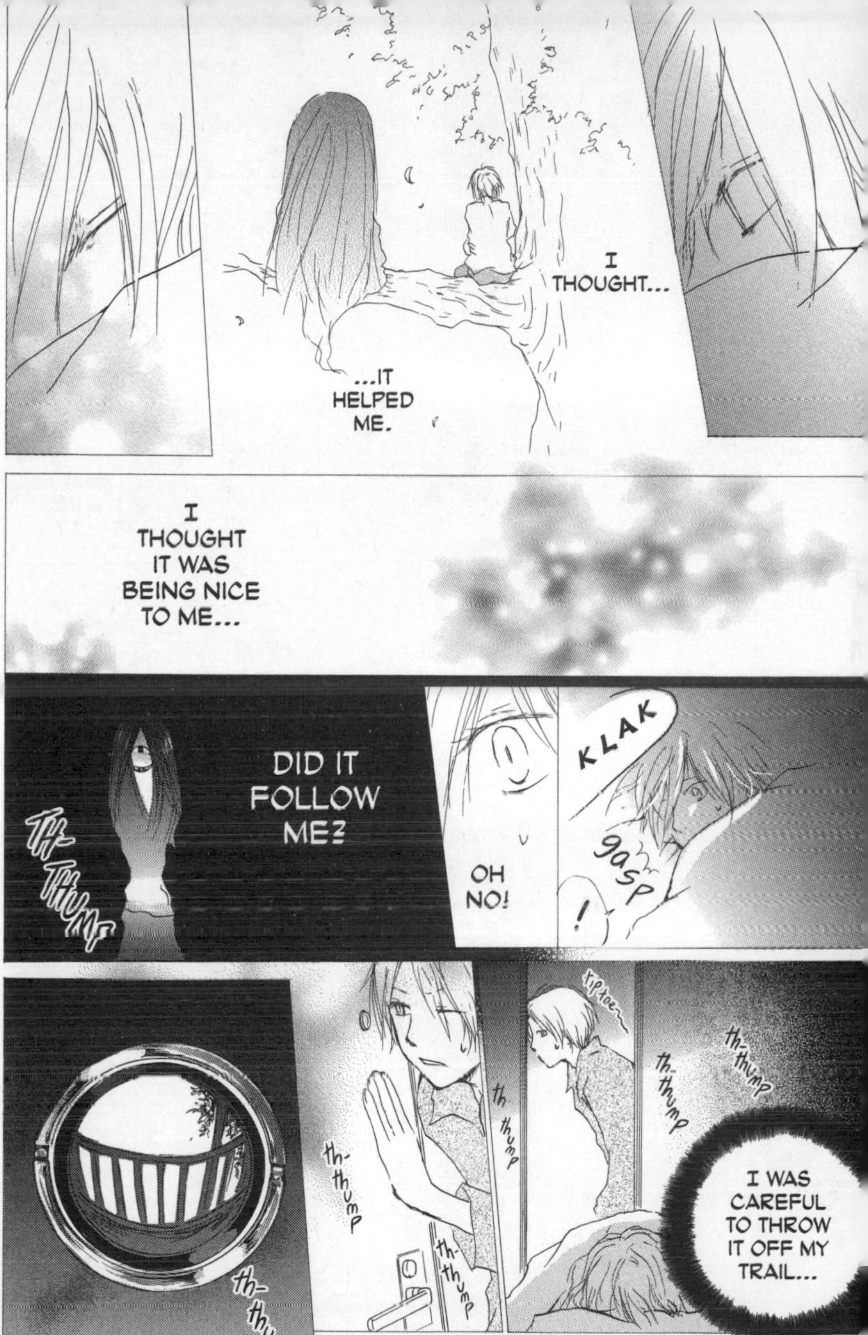
I THOUGHT...
...IT HELPED ME.
I THOUGHT IT WAS BEING NICE TO ME...
KLAK
gasp
!
OH NO!
DID IT FOLLOW ME?
th-thump
tiptoe
th-thump
th-thump
I WAS CAREFUL TO THROW IT OFF MY TRAIL...
th thump
th-thump
th-thump
th-thump

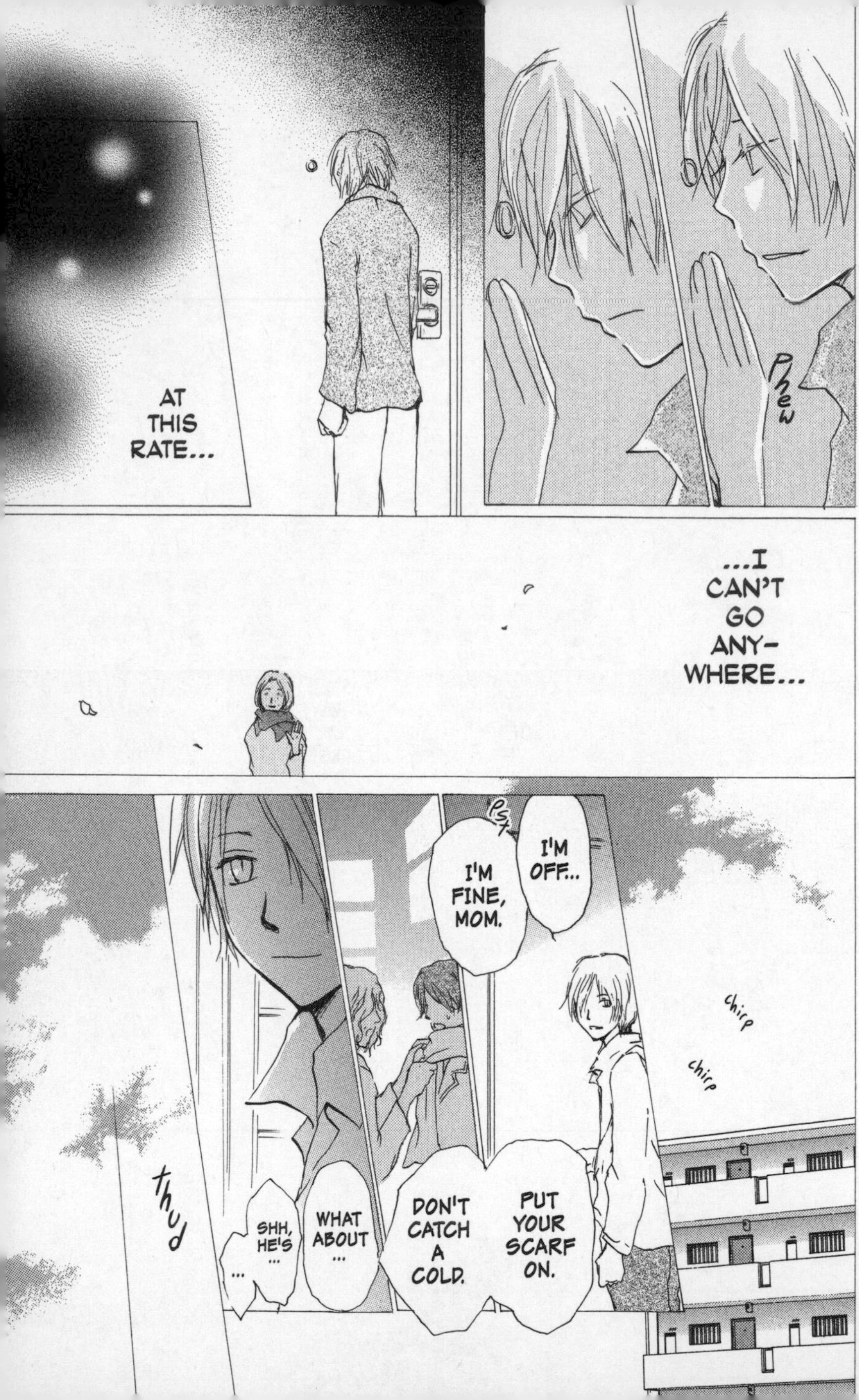
Phew
AT THIS RATE...
...I CAN'T GO ANY-WHERE...
chirp
chirp
I'M OFF...
I'M FINE, MOM.
Psst
PUT YOUR SCARF ON.
DON'T CATCH A COLD.
WHAT ABOUT ...
SHH, HE'S ...
...
thud

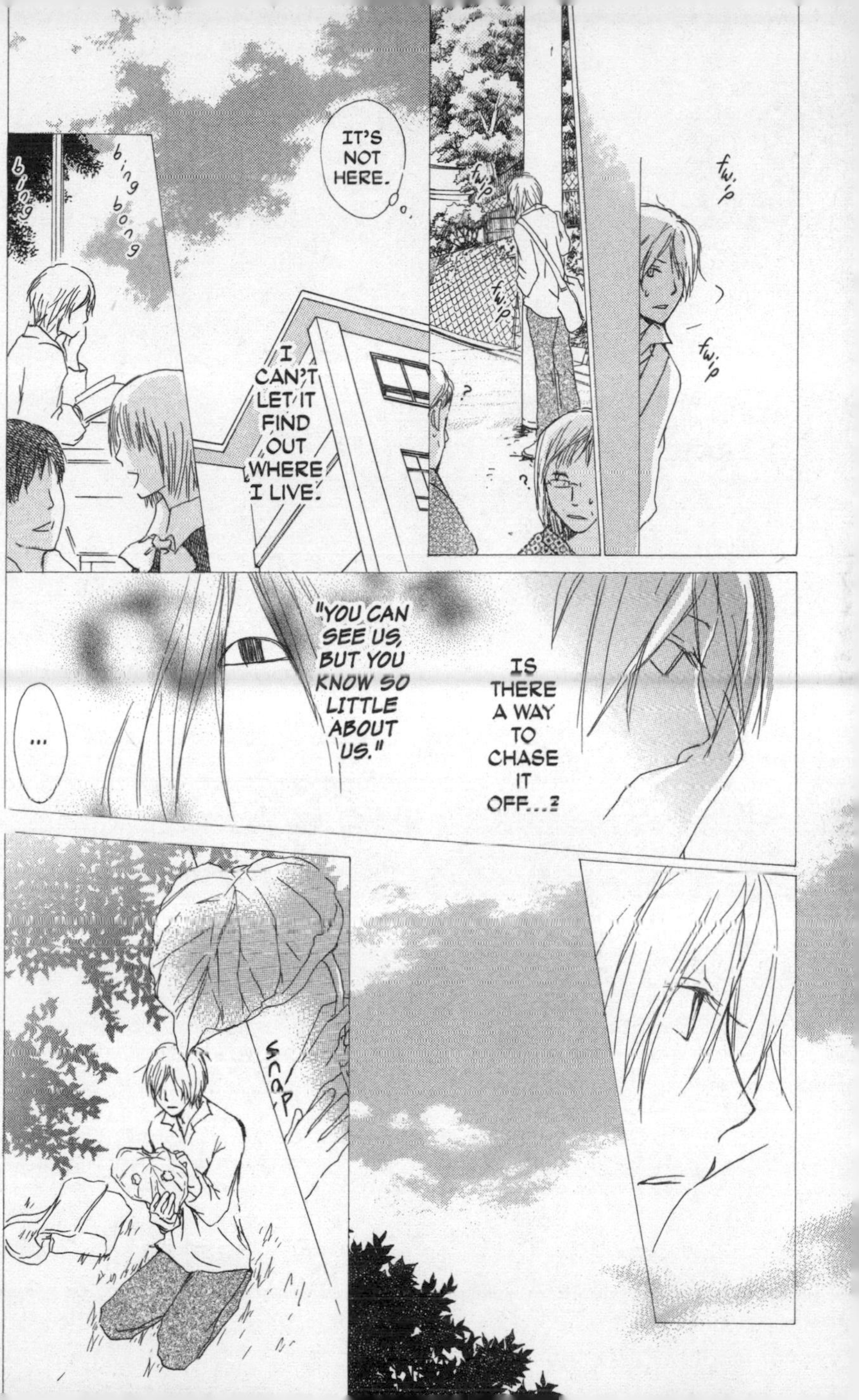
fwip
fwip
fwip
fwip
?
?
IT'S NOT HERE.
bing bong
bing bong
I CAN'T LET IT FIND OUT WHERE I LIVE.
IS THERE A WAY TO CHASE IT OFF...?
"YOU CAN SEE US, BUT YOU KNOW SO LITTLE ABOUT US."
...
scrap

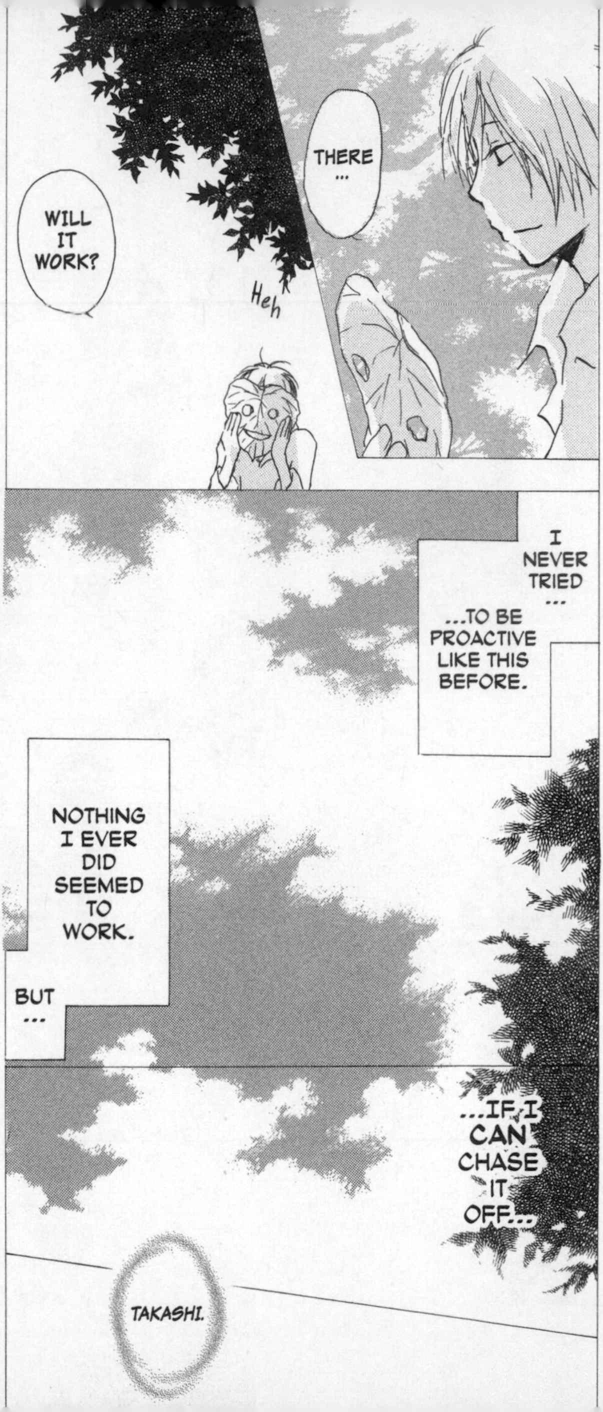
THERE ...
WILL IT WORK?
Heh
I NEVER TRIED ...
...TO BE PROACTIVE LIKE THIS BEFORE.
NOTHING I EVER DID SEEMED TO WORK.
BUT ...
...IF I CAN CHASE IT OFF...
TAKASHI.

05

The opening and ending songs made me emotional every time. I looked forward to the beautiful episode title backgrounds and the kitty antics after the commercial break in every episode. I sincerely enjoyed all of it.

I was so amazed at the wonders of animation in all the little details. How the characters turned, or blinked, or how you could tell that all four limbs were moving even though you could only see one. The scripts were organized for better communication, but were careful to retain their original mood. The various actors had such breadth in their craft to leave room for interpretation. The music kept playing in my mind long after watching. The background art made me feel so much nostalgia. I am so, so happy that I was able to participate in the creation of the Natsume anime. I went to the wrap party, and saw how everyone was so passionate about creating animation. It almost made me cry. Director Ohmori shook my hand at the very end. It's a memory I'll never forget. Thank you so much to everyone involved. I'll keep working hard on the manga!

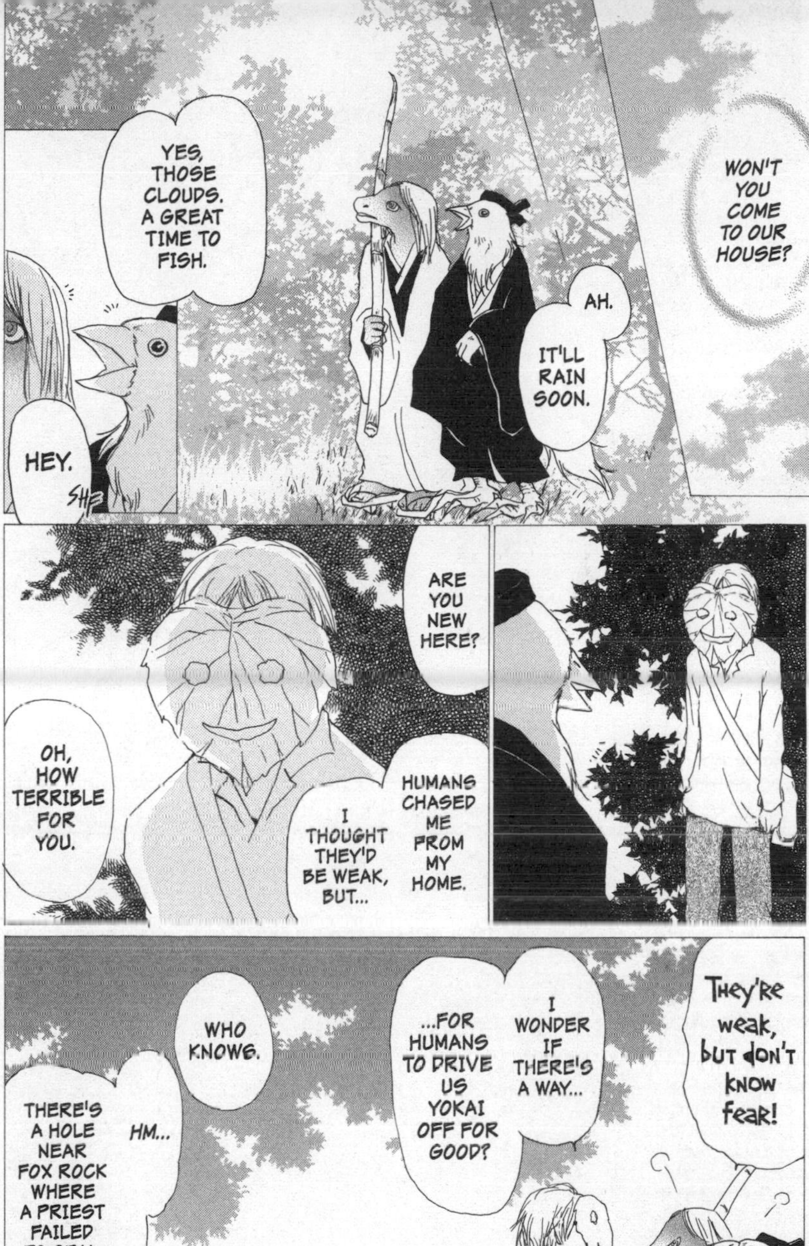
WON'T YOU COME TO OUR HOUSE?
AH.
IT'LL RAIN SOON.
YES, THOSE CLOUDS. A GREAT TIME TO FISH.
HEY.
SHF
ARE YOU NEW HERE?
HUMANS CHASED ME FROM MY HOME.
I THOUGHT THEY'D BE WEAK, BUT...
OH, HOW TERRIBLE FOR YOU.
They're weak, but don't know fear!
I WONDER IF THERE'S A WAY...
...FOR HUMANS TO DRIVE US YOKAI OFF FOR GOOD?
WHO KNOWS.
HM...
THERE'S A HOLE NEAR FOX ROCK WHERE A PRIEST FAILED TO SEAL A YOKAI LONG AGO.

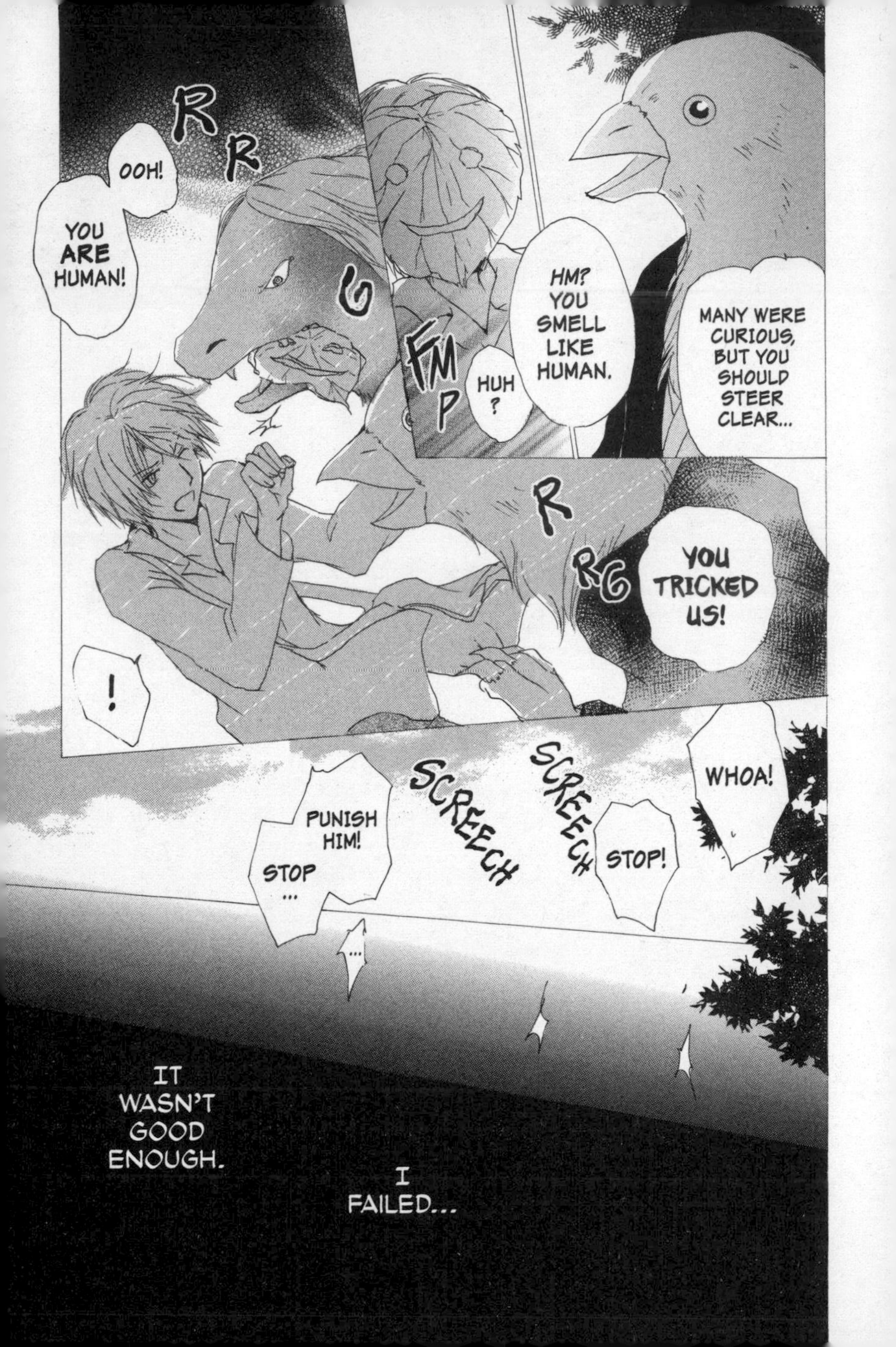
MANY WERE CURIOUS, BUT YOU SHOULD STEER CLEAR...
HM? YOU SMELL LIKE HUMAN.
HUH?
FMP
R R
OOH!
YOU ARE HUMAN!
G
R
RRG
YOU TRICKED US!
!
WHOA!
STOP!
SCREECH
SCREECH
PUNISH HIM!
STOP ...
...
IT WASN'T GOOD ENOUGH.
I FAILED...

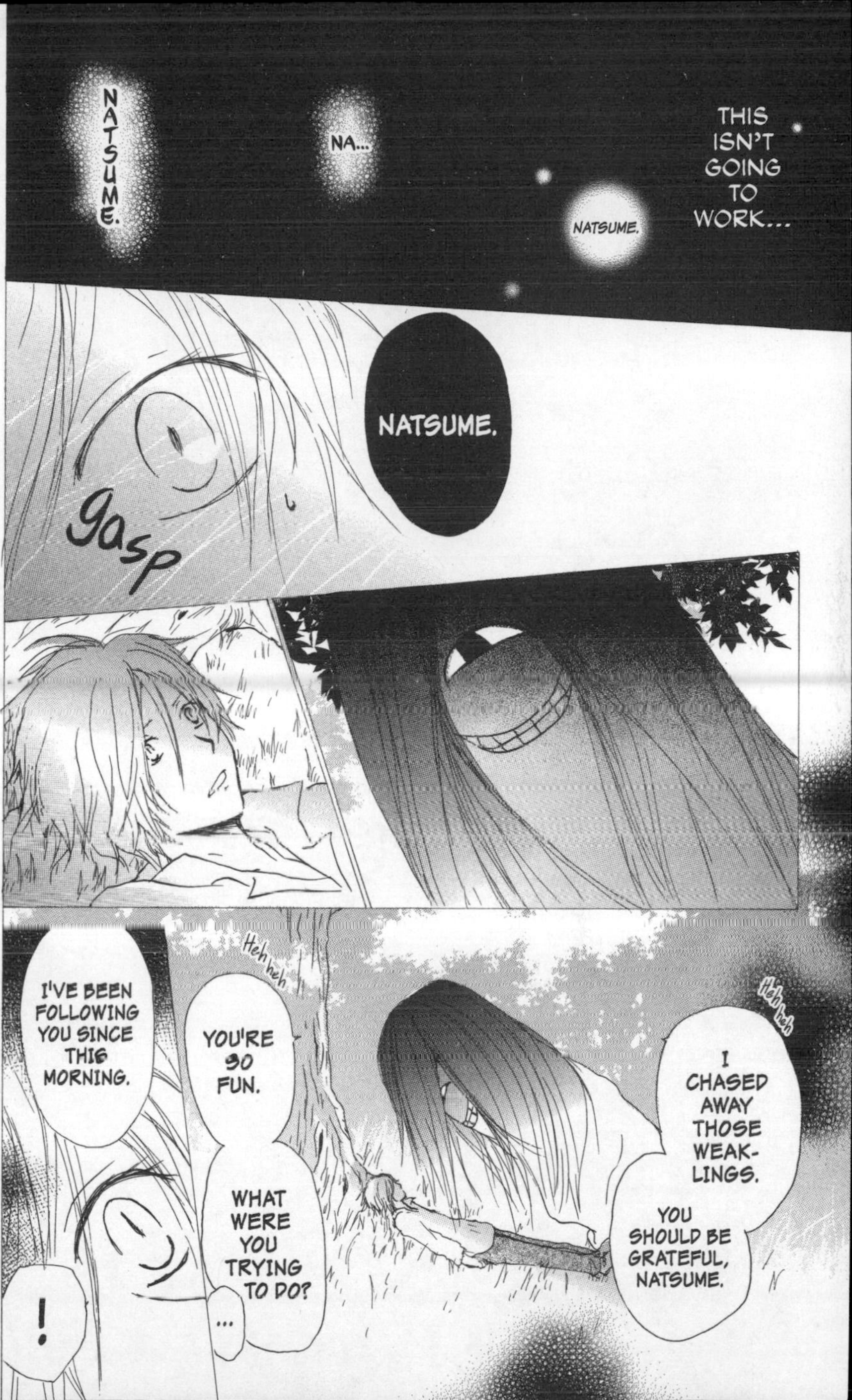
THIS ISN'T GOING TO WORK...
NATSUME.
NA...
NATSUME.
NATSUME.
gasp
Heh heh
I CHASED AWAY THOSE WEAK-LINGS.
YOU SHOULD BE GRATEFUL, NATSUME.
Heh heh
YOU'RE SO FUN.
I'VE BEEN FOLLOWING YOU SINCE THIS MORNING.
WHAT WERE YOU TRYING TO DO?
...
!

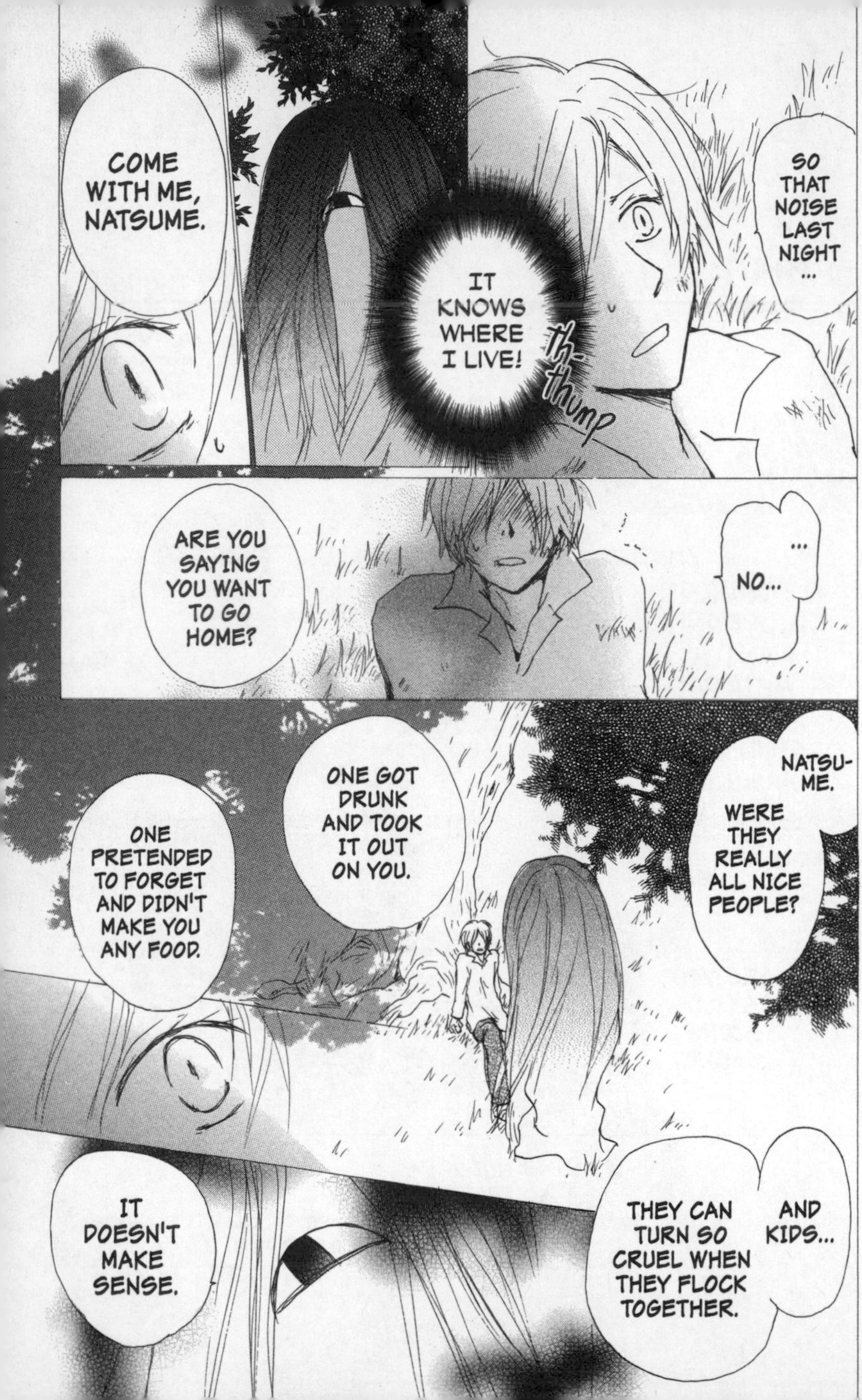
SO THAT NOISE LAST NIGHT...
IT KNOWS WHERE I LIVE!
th-thump
COME WITH ME, NATSUME.
... NO...
ARE YOU SAYING YOU WANT TO GO HOME?
NATSUME. WERE THEY REALLY ALL NICE PEOPLE?
ONE GOT DRUNK AND TOOK IT OUT ON YOU.
ONE PRETENDED TO FORGET AND DIDN'T MAKE YOU ANY FOOD.
AND KIDS... THEY CAN TURN SO CRUEL WHEN THEY FLOCK TOGETHER.
IT DOESN'T MAKE SENSE.

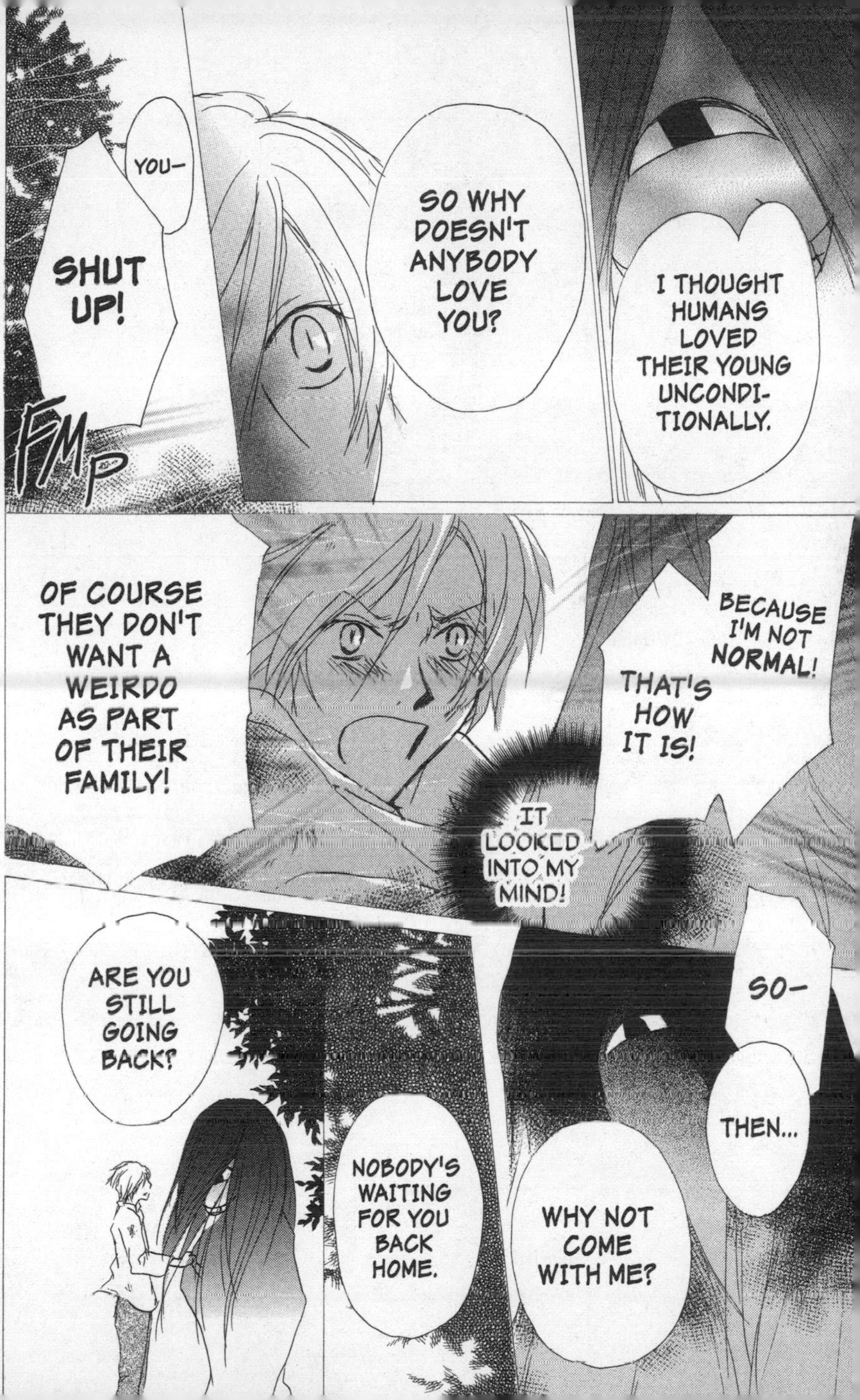
I THOUGHT HUMANS LOVED THEIR YOUNG UNCONDITIONALLY.
SO WHY DOESN'T ANYBODY LOVE YOU?
YOU-
SHUT UP!
FMP
BECAUSE I'M NOT NORMAL!
THAT'S HOW IT IS!
OF COURSE THEY DON'T WANT A WEIRDO AS PART OF THEIR FAMILY!
IT LOOKED INTO MY MIND!
SO-
THEN...
WHY NOT COME WITH ME?
NOBODY'S WAITING FOR YOU BACK HOME.
ARE YOU STILL GOING BACK?

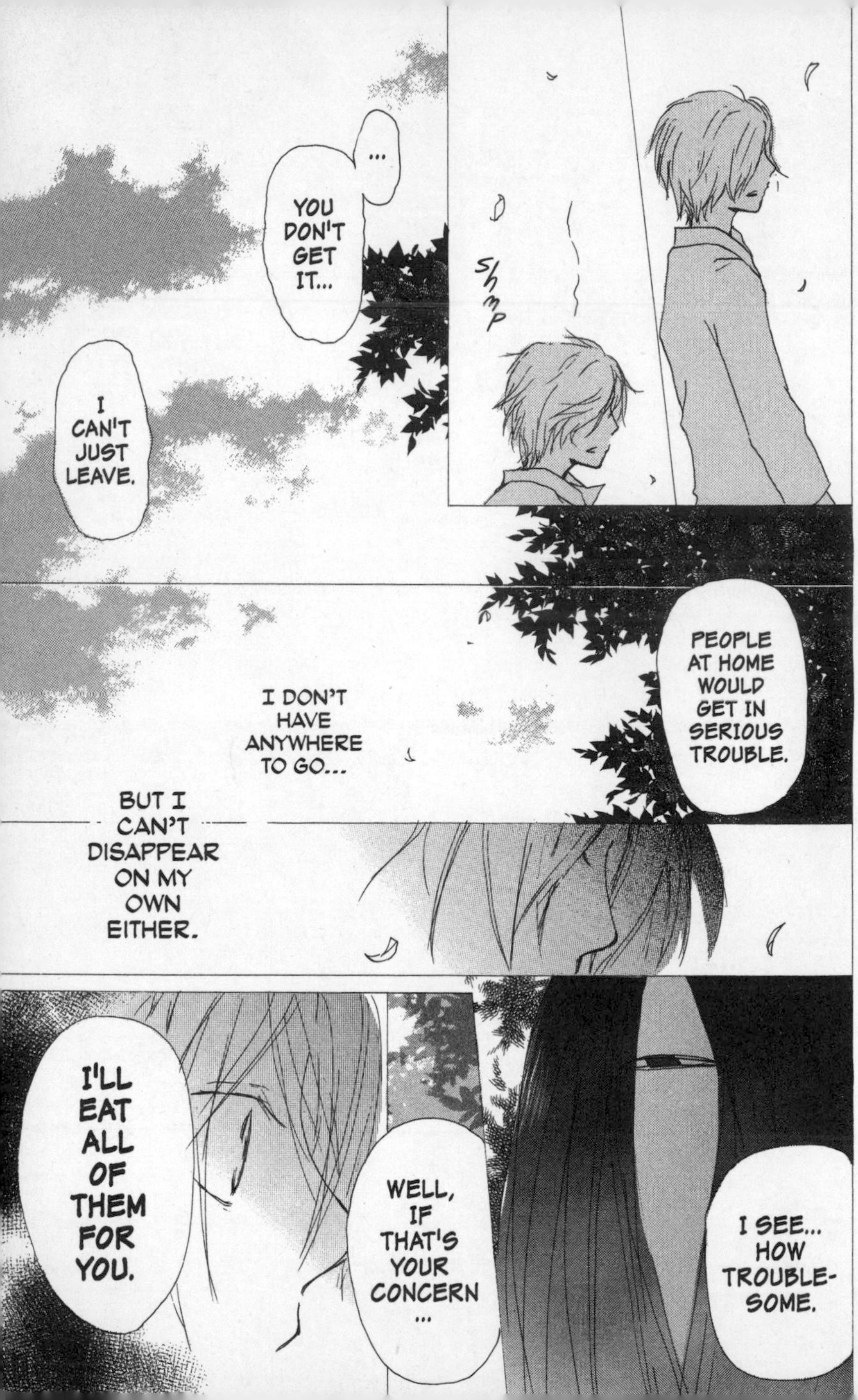
SHMP
...
YOU DON'T GET IT...
I CAN'T JUST LEAVE.
PEOPLE AT HOME WOULD GET IN SERIOUS TROUBLE.
I DON'T HAVE ANYWHERE TO GO...
BUT I CAN'T DISAPPEAR ON MY OWN EITHER.
I SEE... HOW TROUBLE-SOME.
WELL, IF THAT'S YOUR CONCERN ...
I'LL EAT ALL OF THEM FOR YOU.

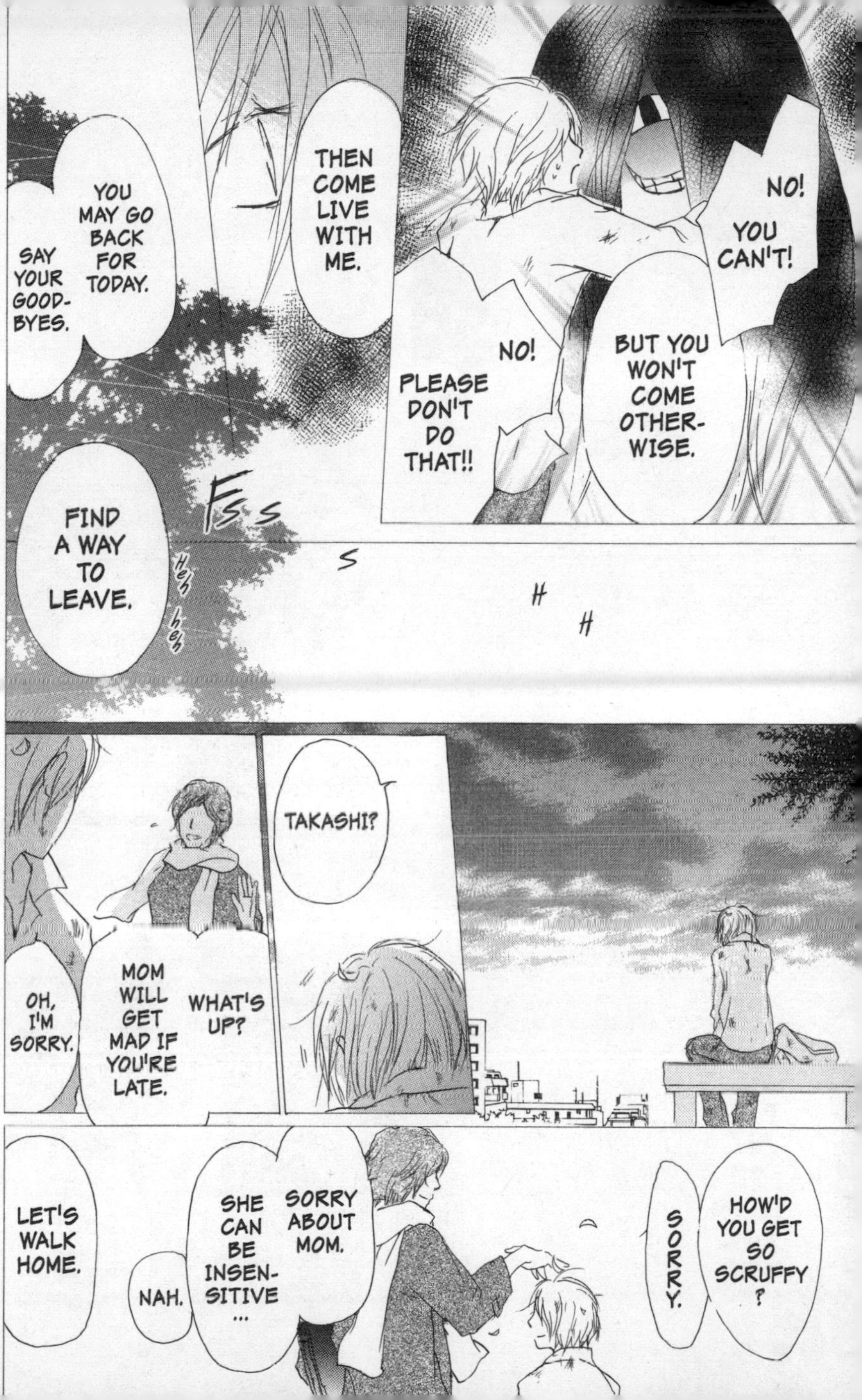
NO!
YOU CAN'T!
BUT YOU WON'T COME OTHERWISE.
NO!
PLEASE DON'T DO THAT!!
THEN COME LIVE WITH ME.
YOU MAY GO BACK FOR TODAY.
SAY YOUR GOOD-BYES.
FSS
FIND A WAY TO LEAVE.
Heh heh
S
H
H
TAKASHI?
WHAT'S UP?
MOM WILL GET MAD IF YOU'RE LATE.
OH, I'M SORRY.
HOW'D YOU GET SO SCRUFFY?
SORRY.
SORRY ABOUT MOM.
SHE CAN BE INSENSITIVE...
NAH.
LET'S WALK HOME.

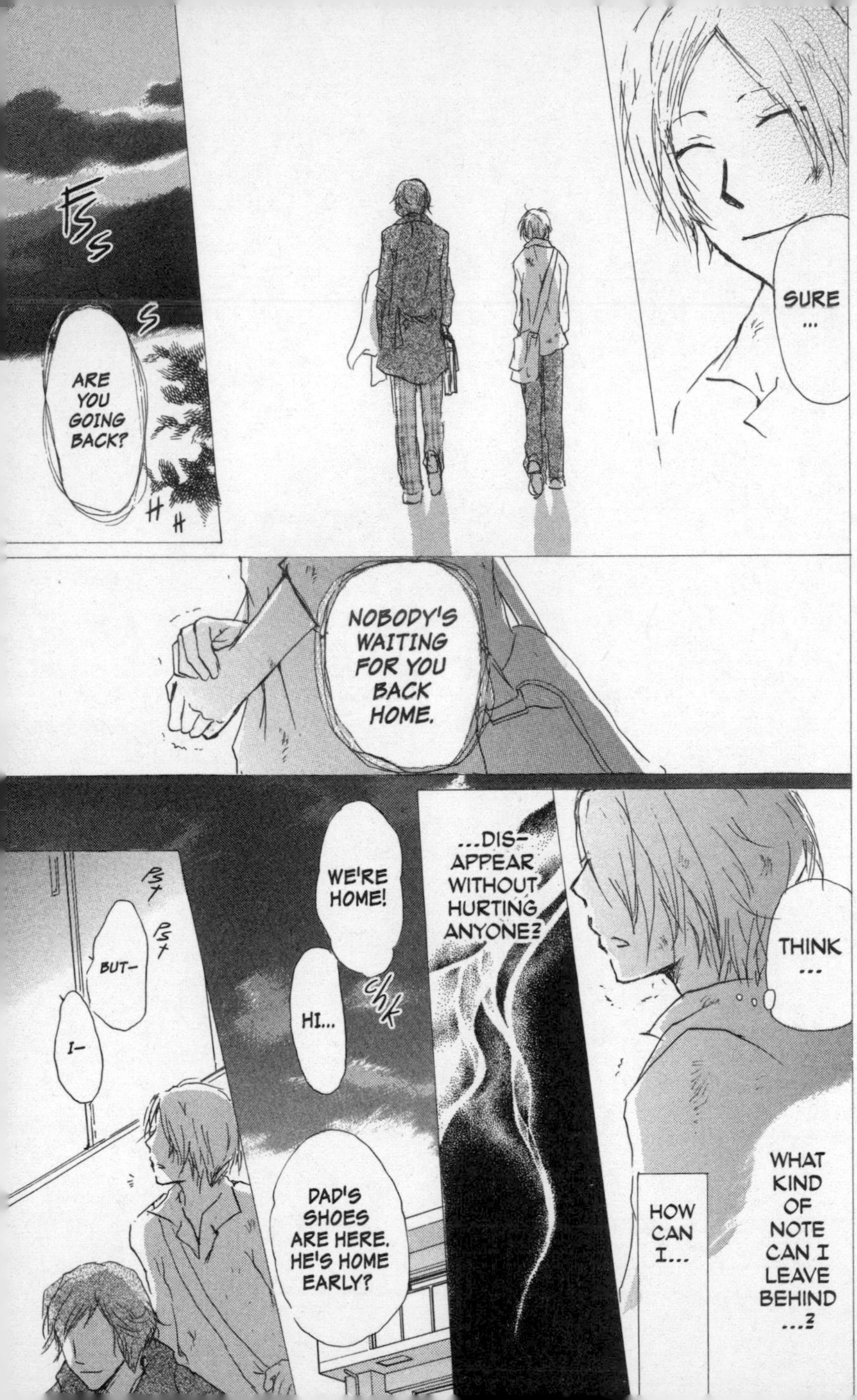
SURE...
FSSS
ARE YOU GOING BACK?
HH
NOBODY'S WAITING FOR YOU BACK HOME.
WHAT KIND OF NOTE CAN I LEAVE BEHIND...?
HOW CAN I...
THINK...
...DIS-APPEAR WITHOUT HURTING ANYONE?
WE'RE HOME!
CHK
HI...
DAD'S SHOES ARE HERE. HE'S HOME EARLY?
PST PST
BUT-
I-

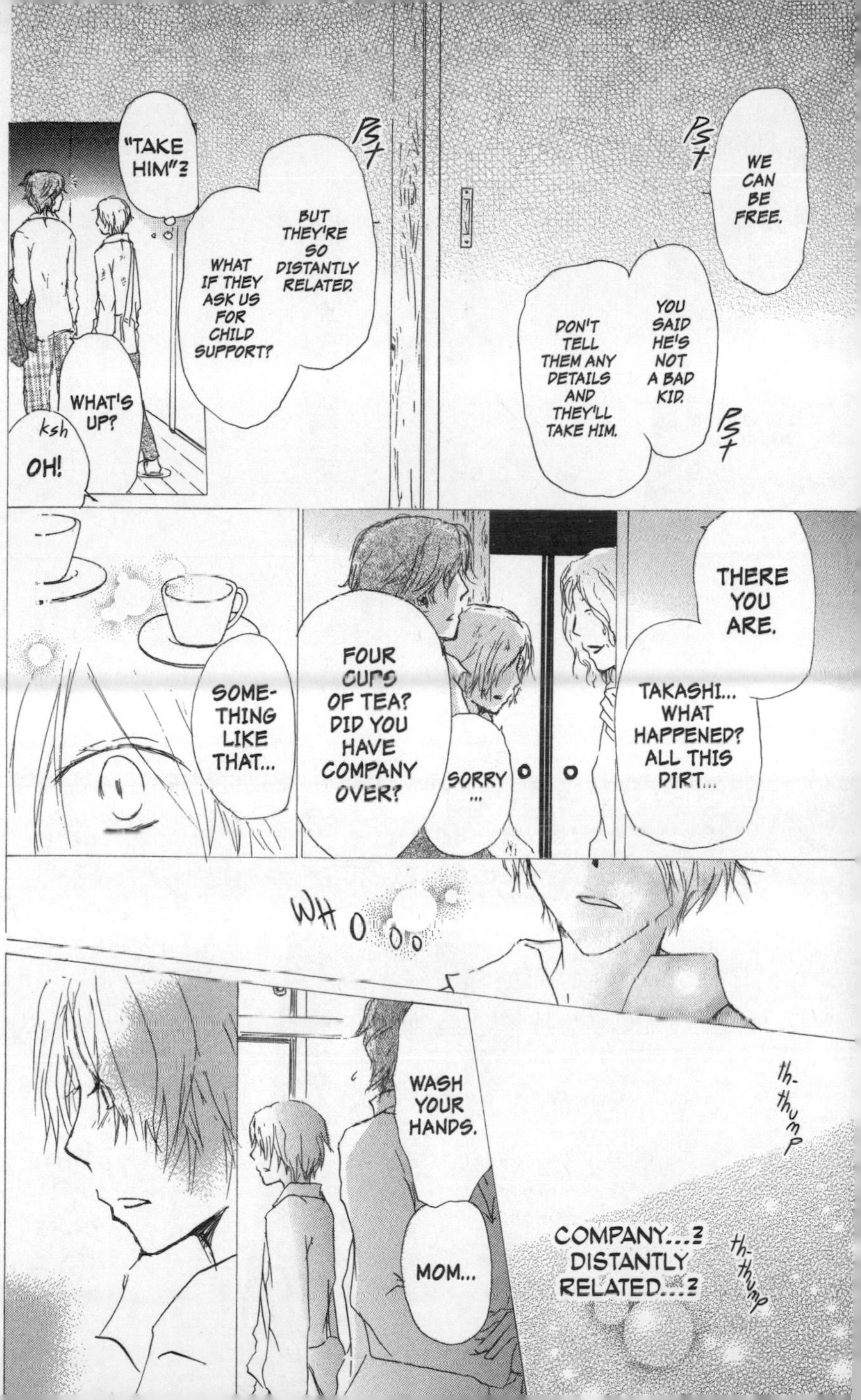
PST
WE CAN BE FREE.
YOU SAID HE'S NOT A BAD KID.
DON'T TELL THEM ANY DETAILS AND THEY'LL TAKE HIM.
PST
PST
BUT THEY'RE SO DISTANTLY RELATED.
WHAT IF THEY ASK US FOR CHILD SUPPORT?
"TAKE HIM"?
WHAT'S UP?
ksh
OH!
THERE YOU ARE.
TAKASHI... WHAT HAPPENED? ALL THIS DIRT...
SORRY...
FOUR CUPS OF TEA? DID YOU HAVE COMPANY OVER?
SOMETHING LIKE THAT...
WHOOOO
th-thump
WASH YOUR HANDS.
COMPANY...? DISTANTLY RELATED...?
th-thump
MOM...

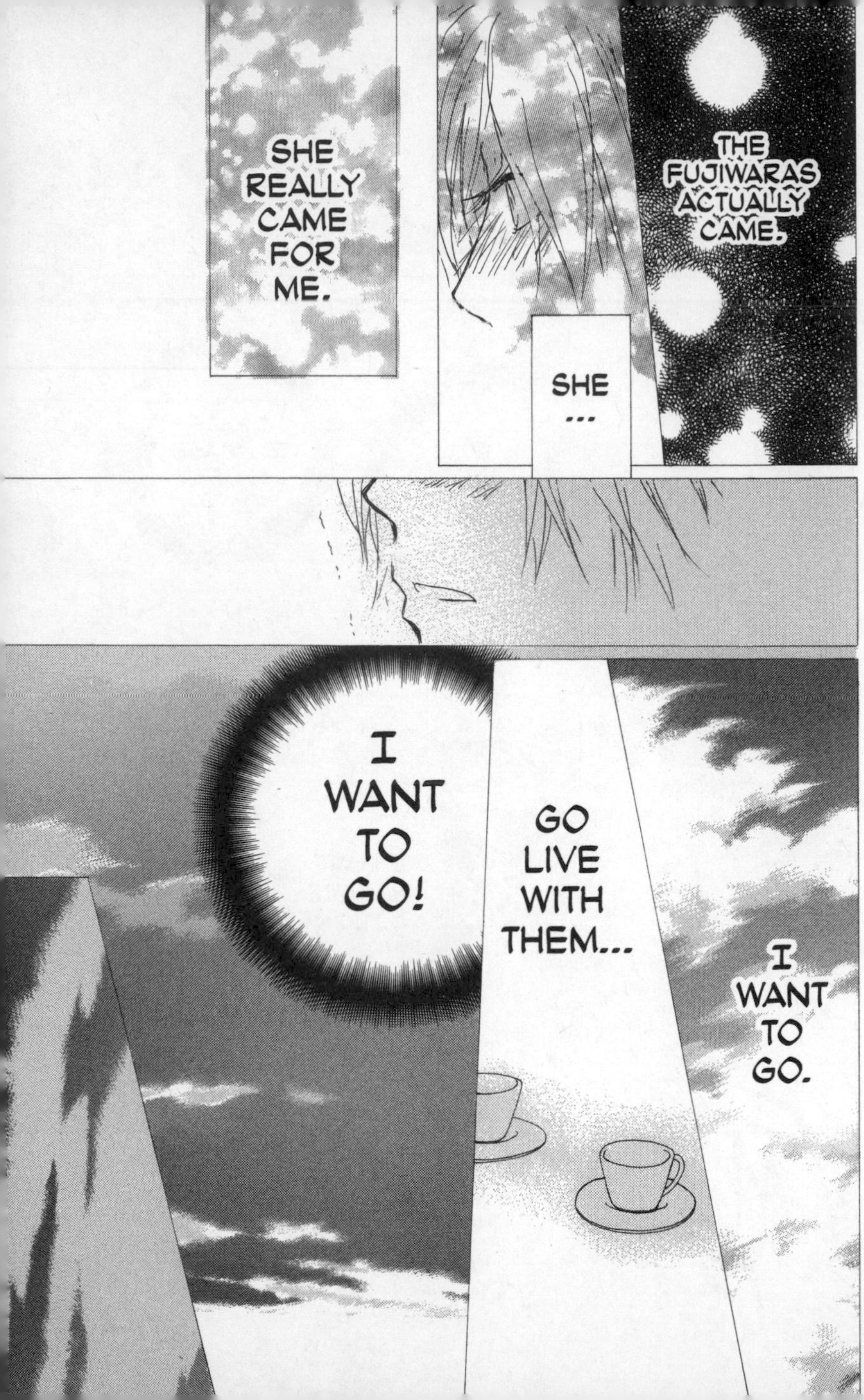
THE FUJIWARAS ACTUALLY CAME.
SHE...
SHE REALLY CAME FOR ME.
I WANT TO GO.
GO LIVE WITH THEM...
I WANT TO GO!

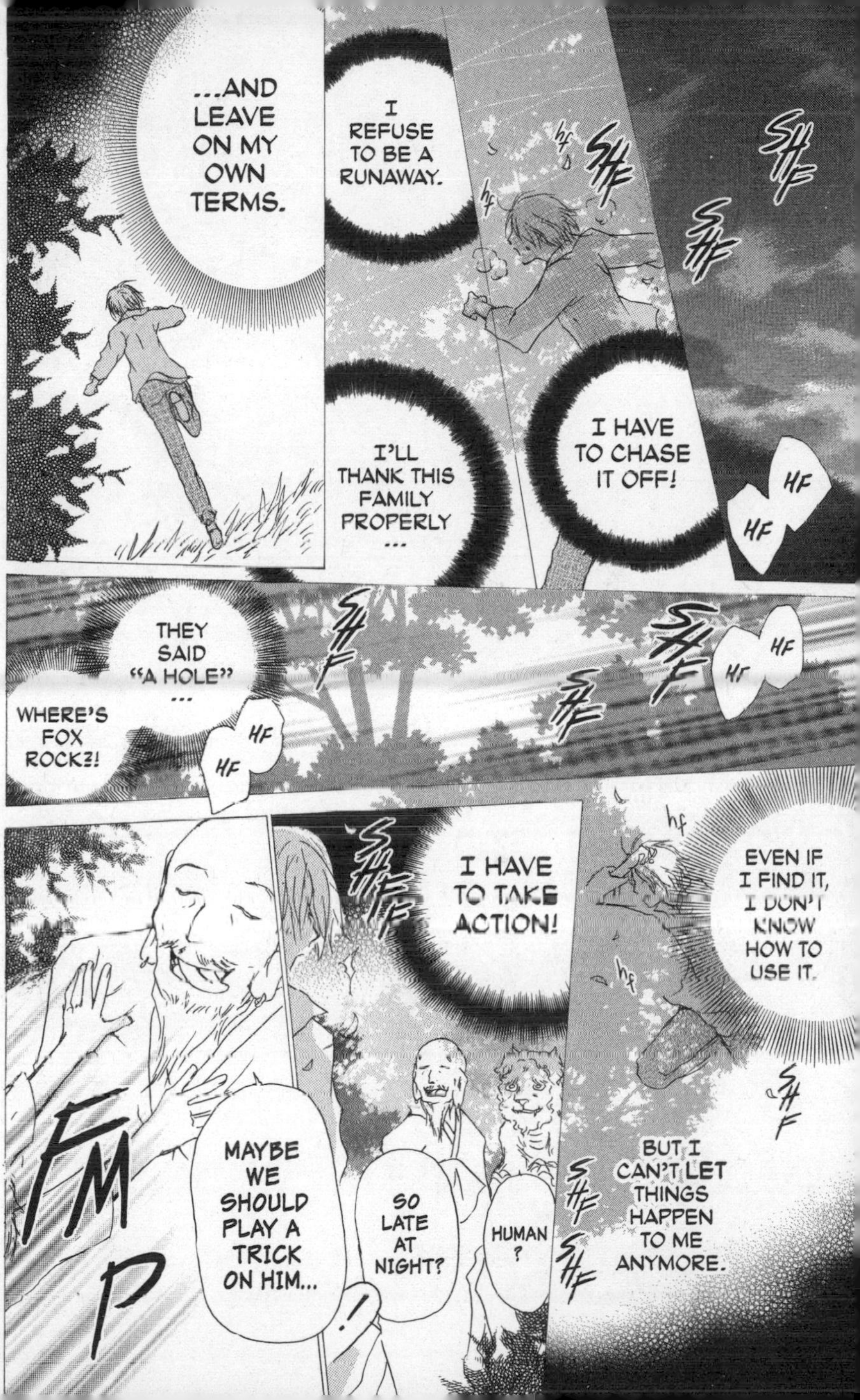
SHF
SHF
I HAVE TO CHASE IT OFF!
HF
HF
hf
hf
SHF
I REFUSE TO BE A RUNAWAY.
I'LL THANK THIS FAMILY PROPERLY...
...AND LEAVE ON MY OWN TERMS.
SHF
HF
HF
SHF
SHF
THEY SAID "A HOLE"...
WHERE'S FOX ROCK?!
HF
HF
hf
EVEN IF I FIND IT, I DON'T KNOW HOW TO USE IT.
hf
SHF
BUT I CAN'T LET THINGS HAPPEN TO ME ANYMORE.
SHF
SHF
I HAVE TO TAKE ACTION!
SHF
HUMAN?
SO LATE AT NIGHT?
MAYBE WE SHOULD PLAY A TRICK ON HIM...
!
FMP

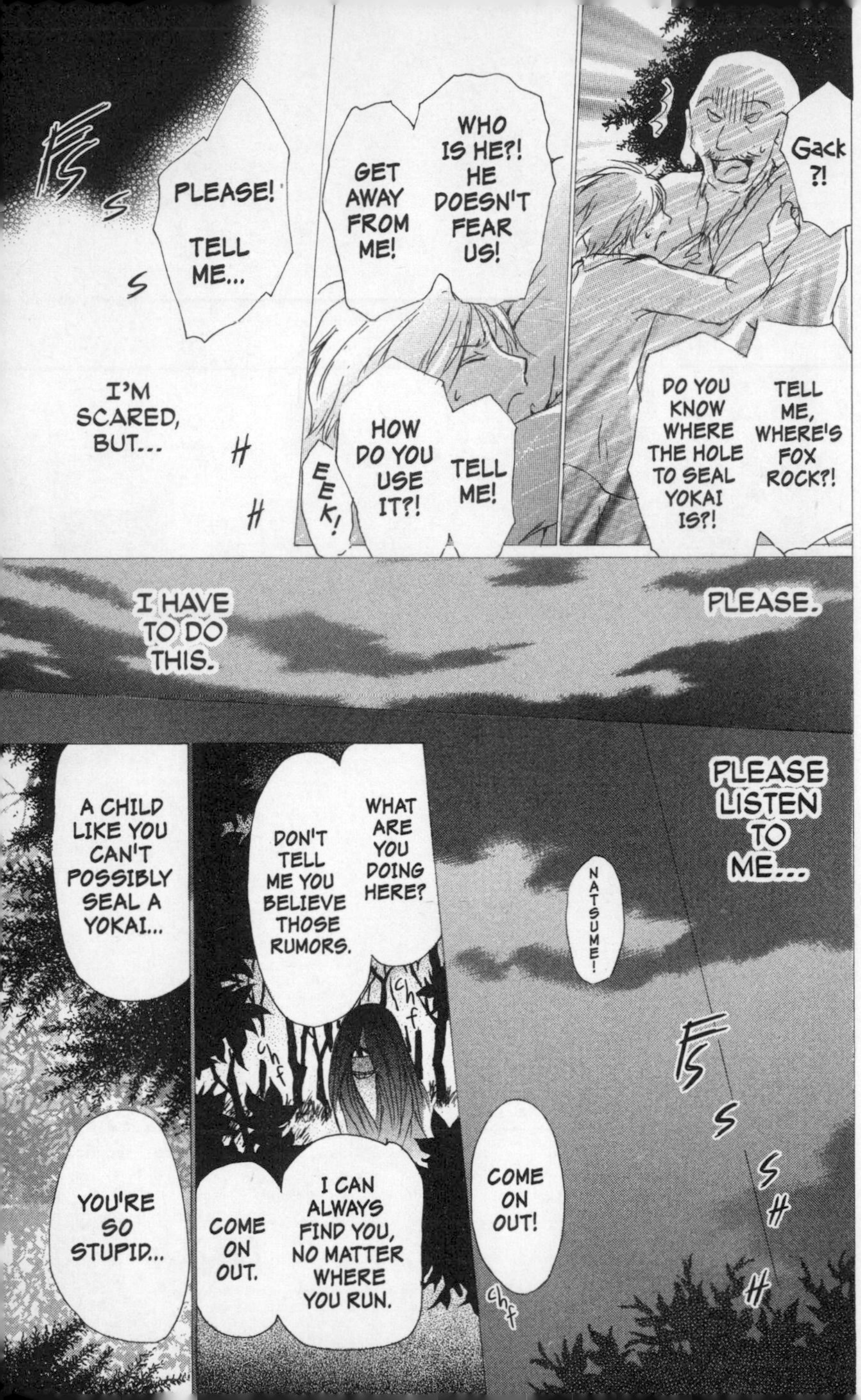
Gack ?!
TELL ME, WHERE'S FOX ROCK?!
DO YOU KNOW WHERE THE HOLE TO SEAL YOKAI IS?!
WHO IS HE?! HE DOESN'T FEAR US!
GET AWAY FROM ME!
TELL ME!
HOW DO YOU USE IT?!
EEK!
PLEASE! TELL ME...
FSSS
I'M SCARED, BUT...
HH
PLEASE.
I HAVE TO DO THIS.
PLEASE LISTEN TO ME...
NATSUME!
FSSSHH
COME ON OUT!
chf
WHAT ARE YOU DOING HERE?
DON'T TELL ME YOU BELIEVE THOSE RUMORS.
chf
chf
I CAN ALWAYS FIND YOU, NO MATTER WHERE YOU RUN.
COME ON OUT.
A CHILD LIKE YOU CAN'T POSSIBLY SEAL A YOKAI...
YOU'RE SO STUPID...

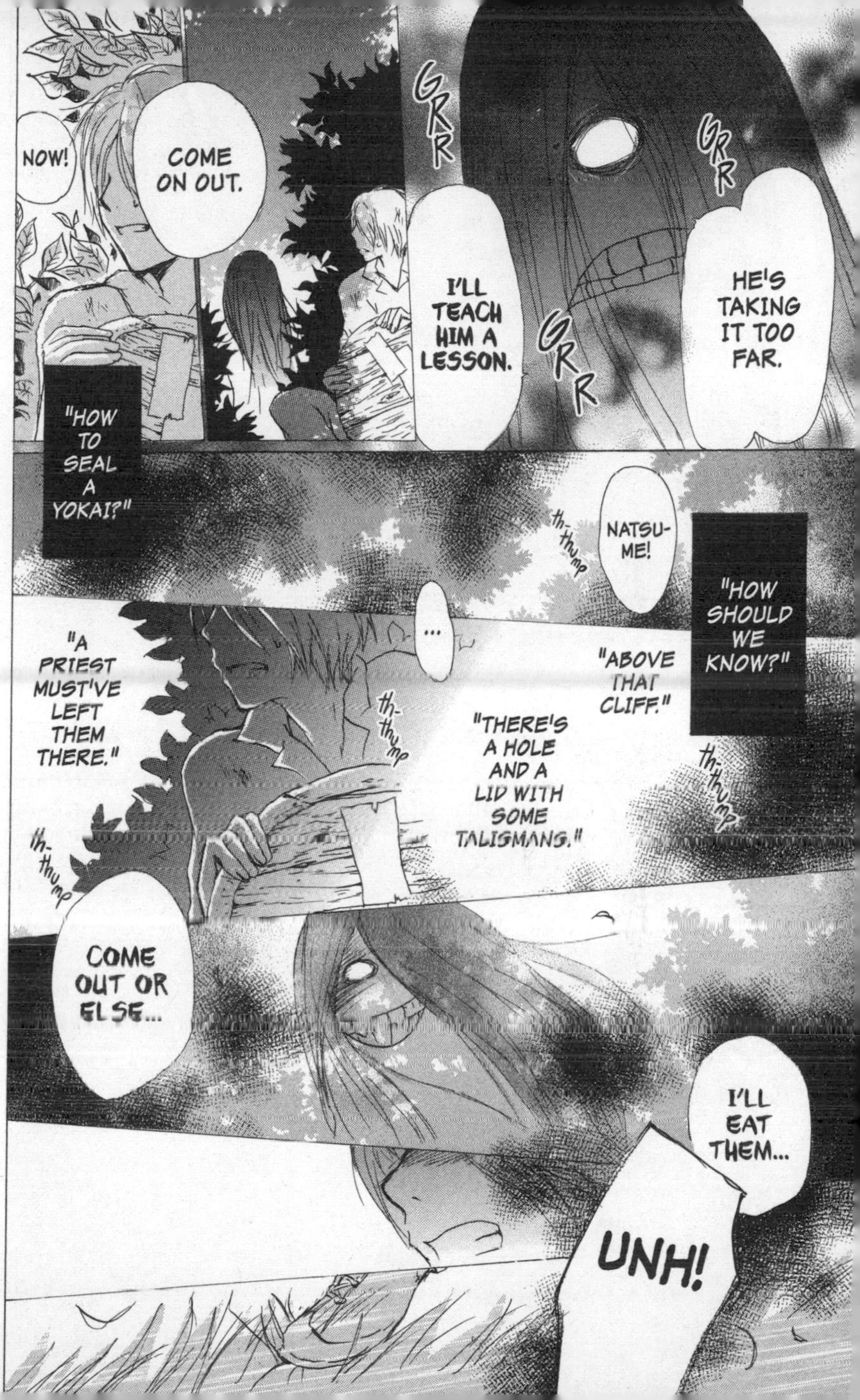
GRR
GRR
GRR
HE'S TAKING IT TOO FAR.
I'LL TEACH HIM A LESSON.
COME ON OUT.
NOW!
"HOW TO SEAL A YOKAI?"
"HOW SHOULD WE KNOW?"
th-thump
NATSUME!
th-thump
"ABOVE THAT CLIFF."
...
"THERE'S A HOLE AND A LID WITH SOME TALISMANS."
th-thump
"A PRIEST MUST'VE LEFT THEM THERE."
th-thump
I'LL EAT THEM...
COME OUT OR ELSE...
UNH!

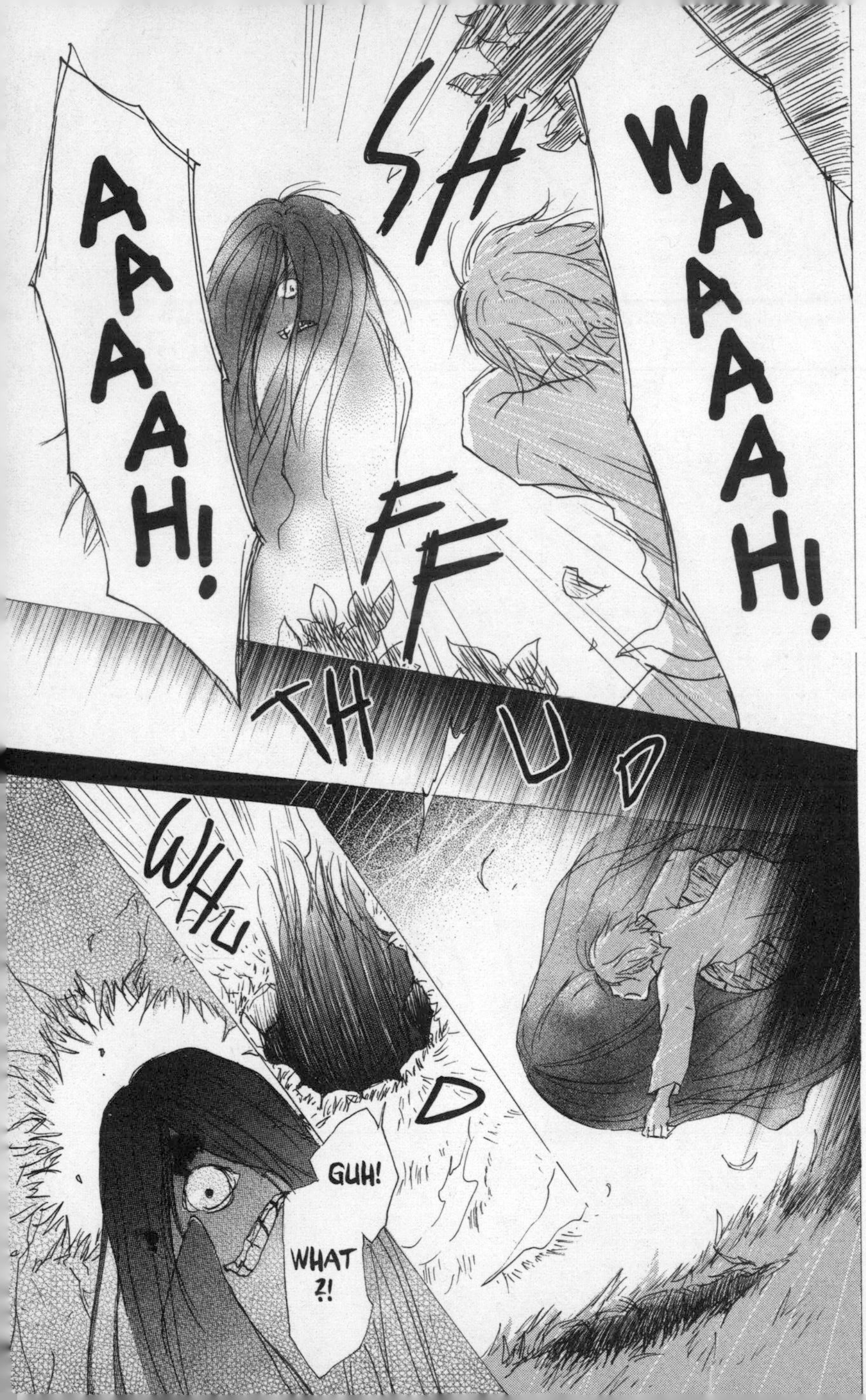
WAAAAAH!
SHFF
AAAAAH!
THUD
WHUD
GUH!
WHAT?!

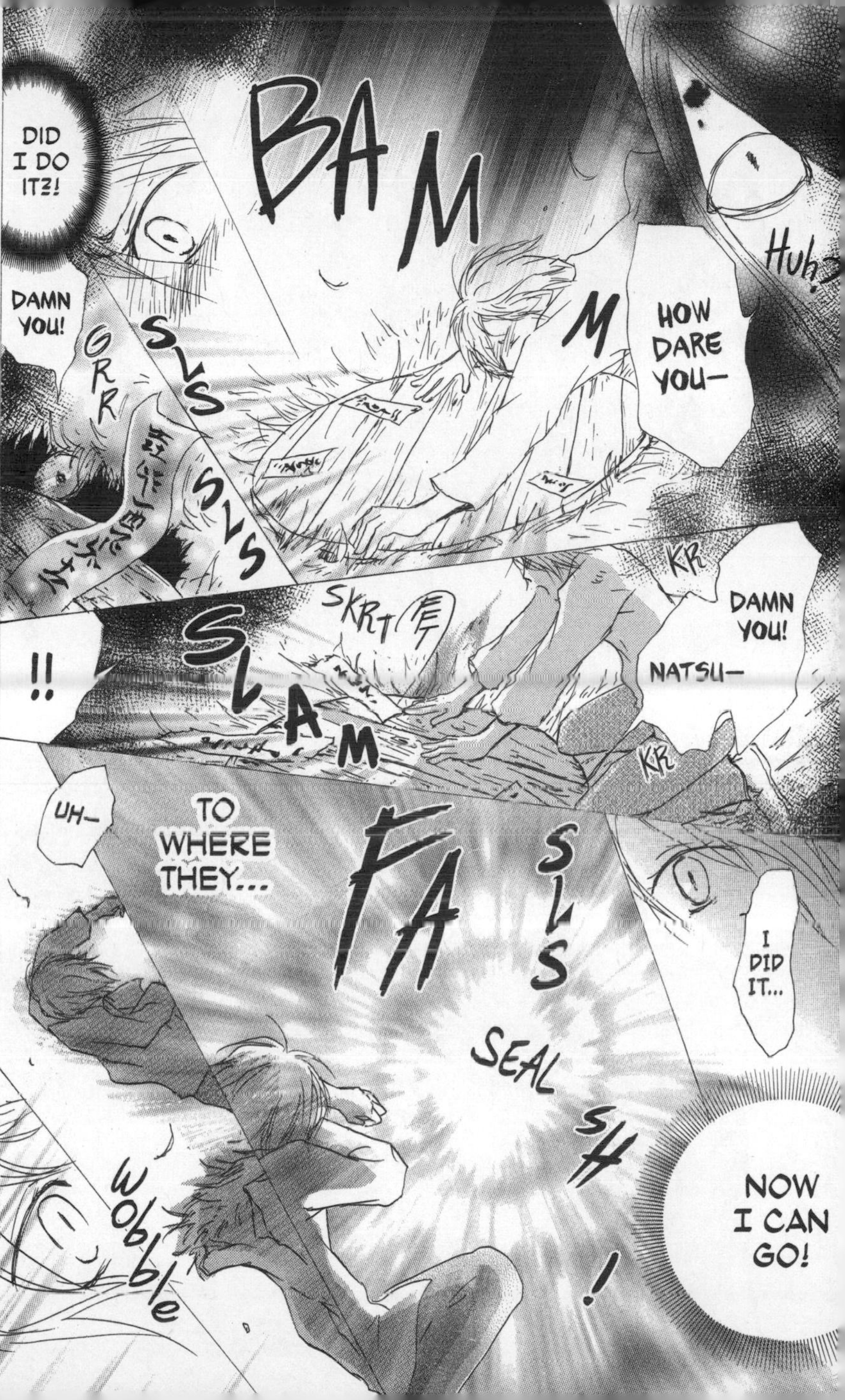
Huh?
HOW DARE YOU—
BAMM
M
SLS
SLS
SLS
GRR
DAMN YOU!
DID I DO IT?!
KR
DAMN YOU!
NATSU—
KR
SKRT
SLAM
!!
I DID IT...
NOW I CAN GO!
SLS
FA
SEAL
SH!
TO WHERE THEY...
UH—
wobble

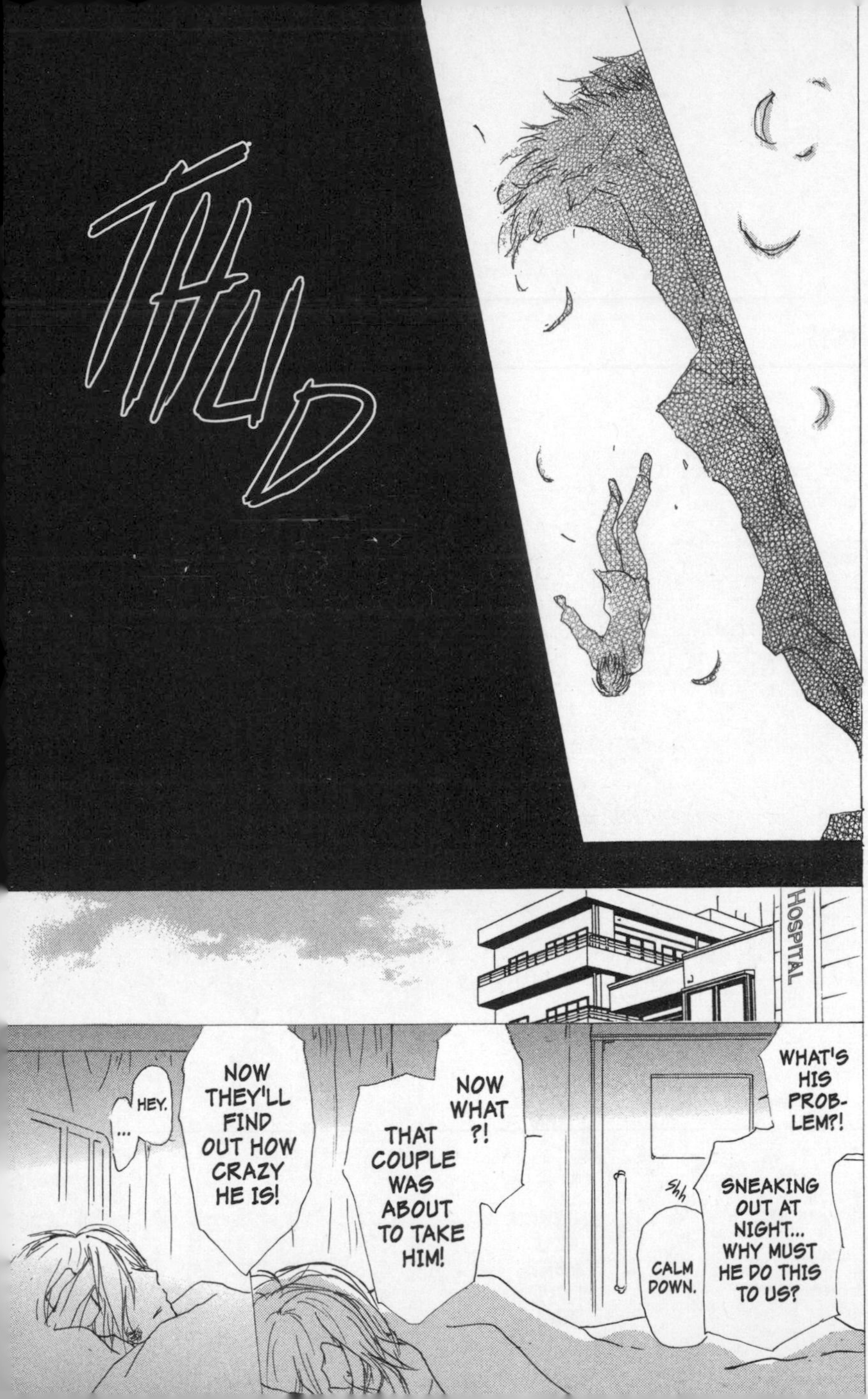
THUD
HOSPITAL
WHAT'S HIS PROB-LEM?!
SNEAKING OUT AT NIGHT... WHY MUST HE DO THIS TO US?
Shh
CALM DOWN.
NOW WHAT?!
THAT COUPLE WAS ABOUT TO TAKE HIM!
NOW THEY'LL FIND OUT HOW CRAZY HE IS!
HEY.
...

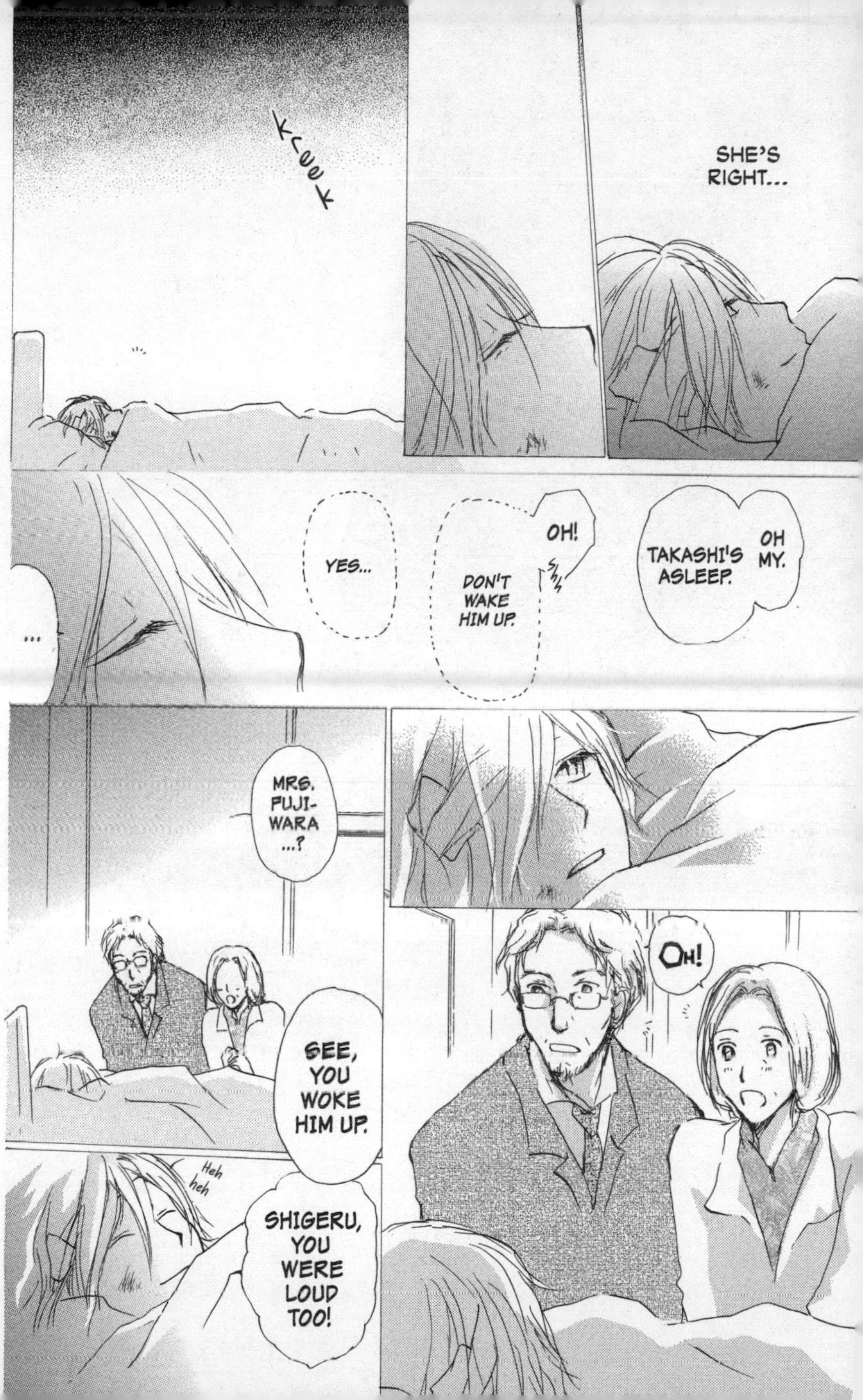
SHE'S RIGHT...
kreek
OH MY.
TAKASHI'S ASLEEP.
OH!
DON'T WAKE HIM UP.
YES...
...
MRS. FUJIWARA...?
OH!
SEE, YOU WOKE HIM UP.
Heh heh
SHIGERU, YOU WERE LOUD TOO!

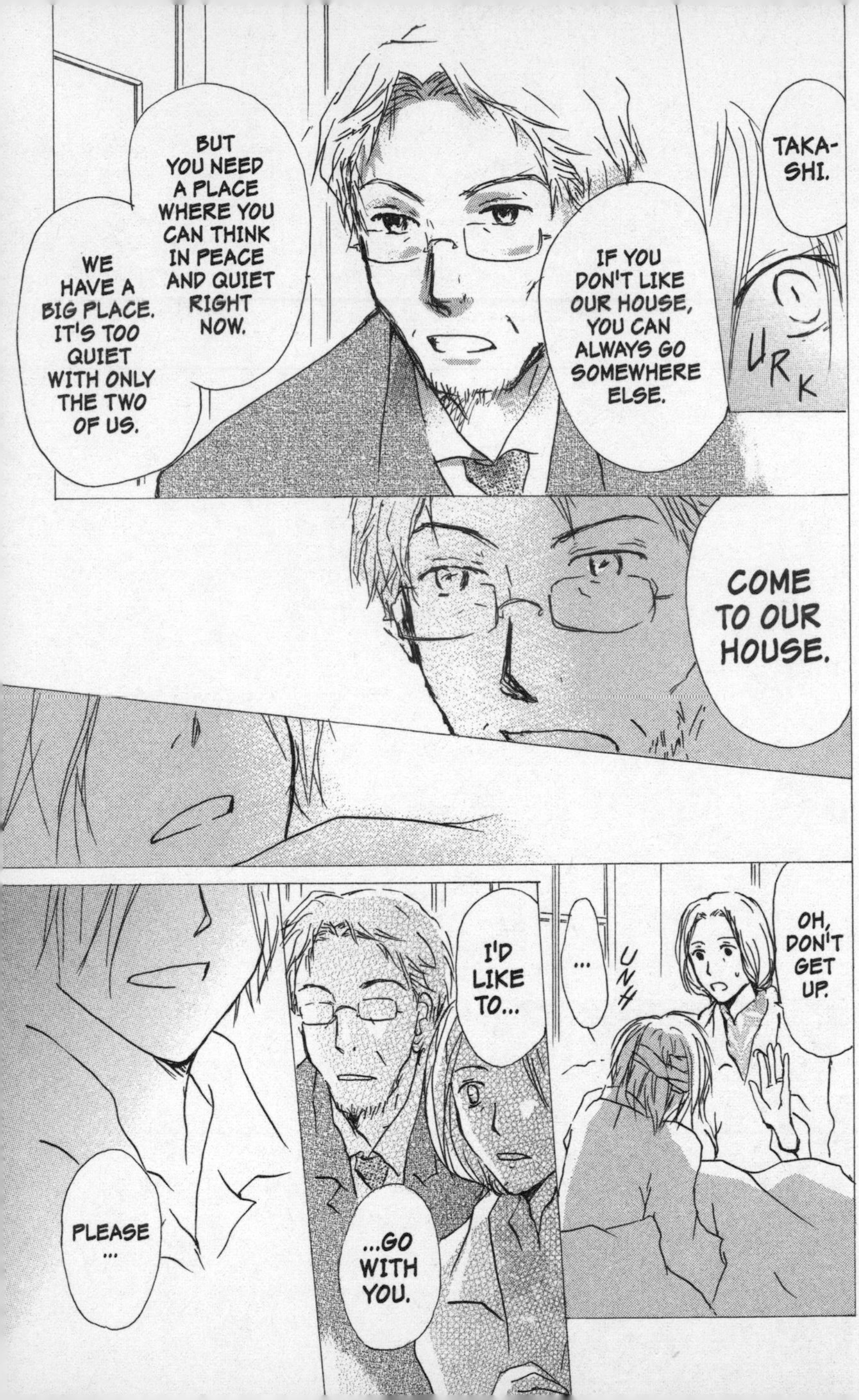
TAKA-SHI.
URK
IF YOU DON'T LIKE OUR HOUSE, YOU CAN ALWAYS GO SOMEWHERE ELSE.
BUT YOU NEED A PLACE WHERE YOU CAN THINK IN PEACE AND QUIET RIGHT NOW.
WE HAVE A BIG PLACE. IT'S TOO QUIET WITH ONLY THE TWO OF US.
COME TO OUR HOUSE.
OH, DON'T GET UP.
UNH
...
I'D LIKE TO...
...GO WITH YOU.
PLEASE ...

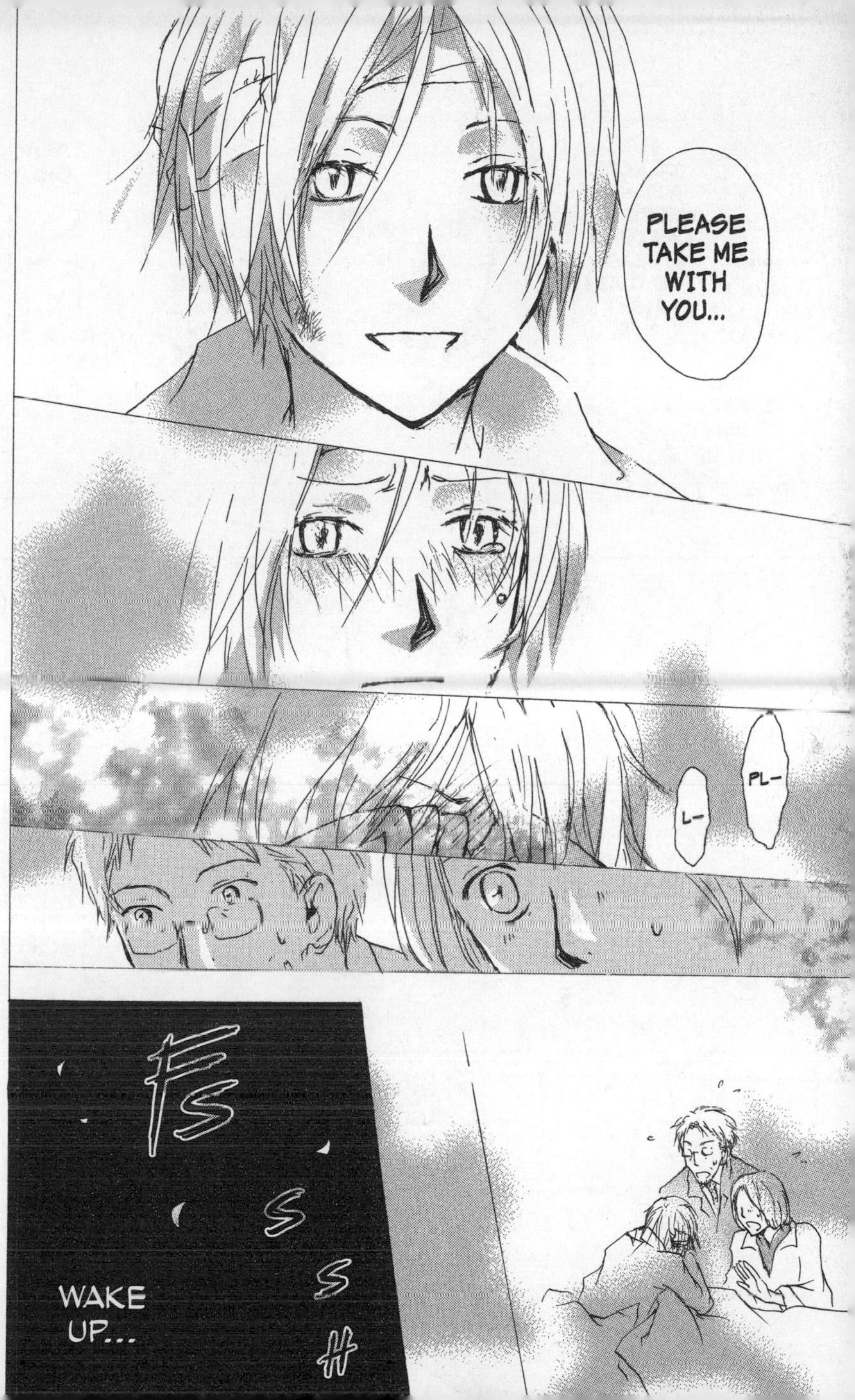
PLEASE TAKE ME WITH YOU...
PL—
L—
FSSSH
WAKE UP...

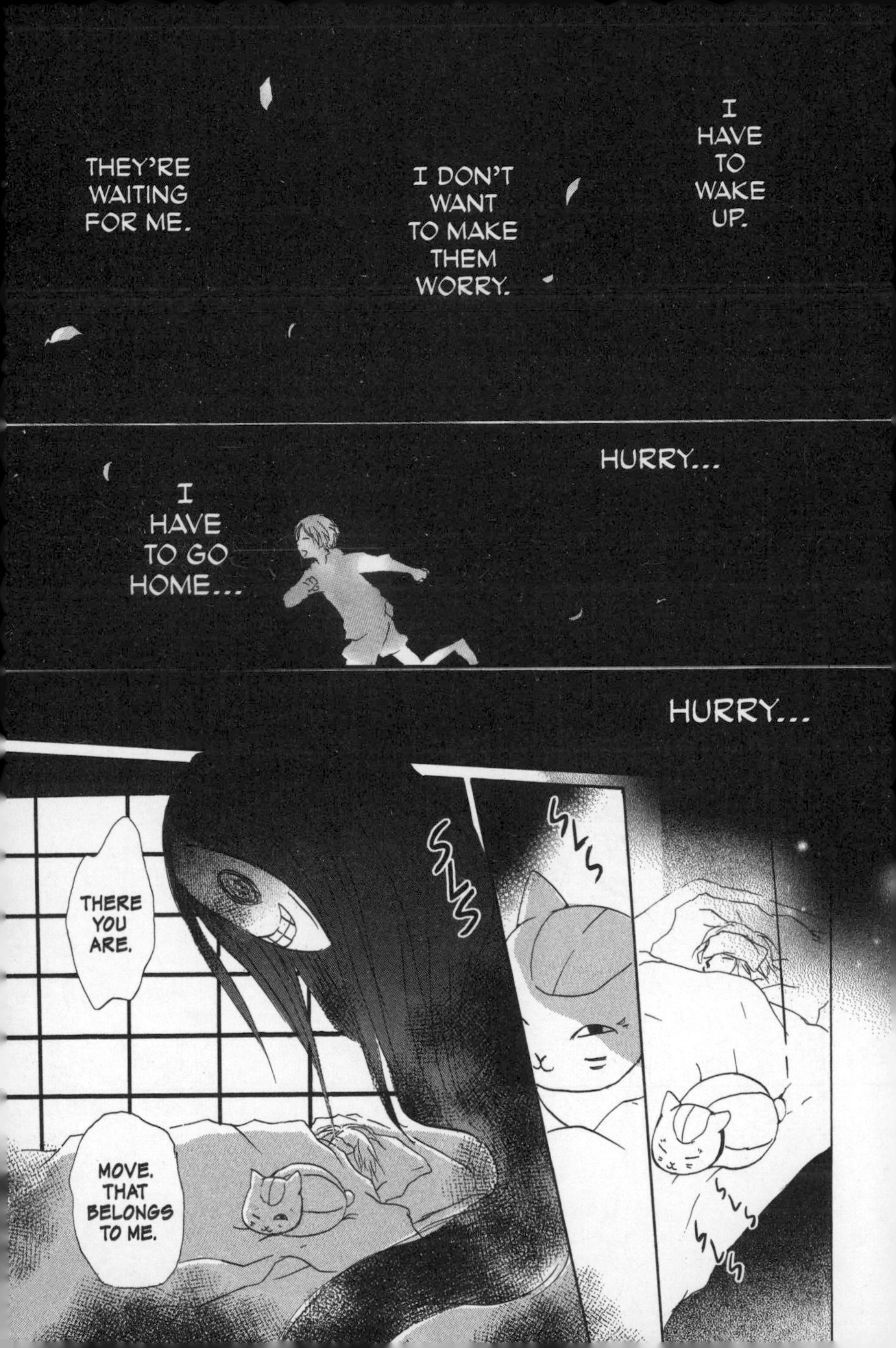
I HAVE TO WAKE UP.
I DON'T WANT TO MAKE THEM WORRY.
THEY'RE WAITING FOR ME.
HURRY...
I HAVE TO GO HOME...
HURRY...
THERE YOU ARE.
MOVE. THAT BELONGS TO ME.

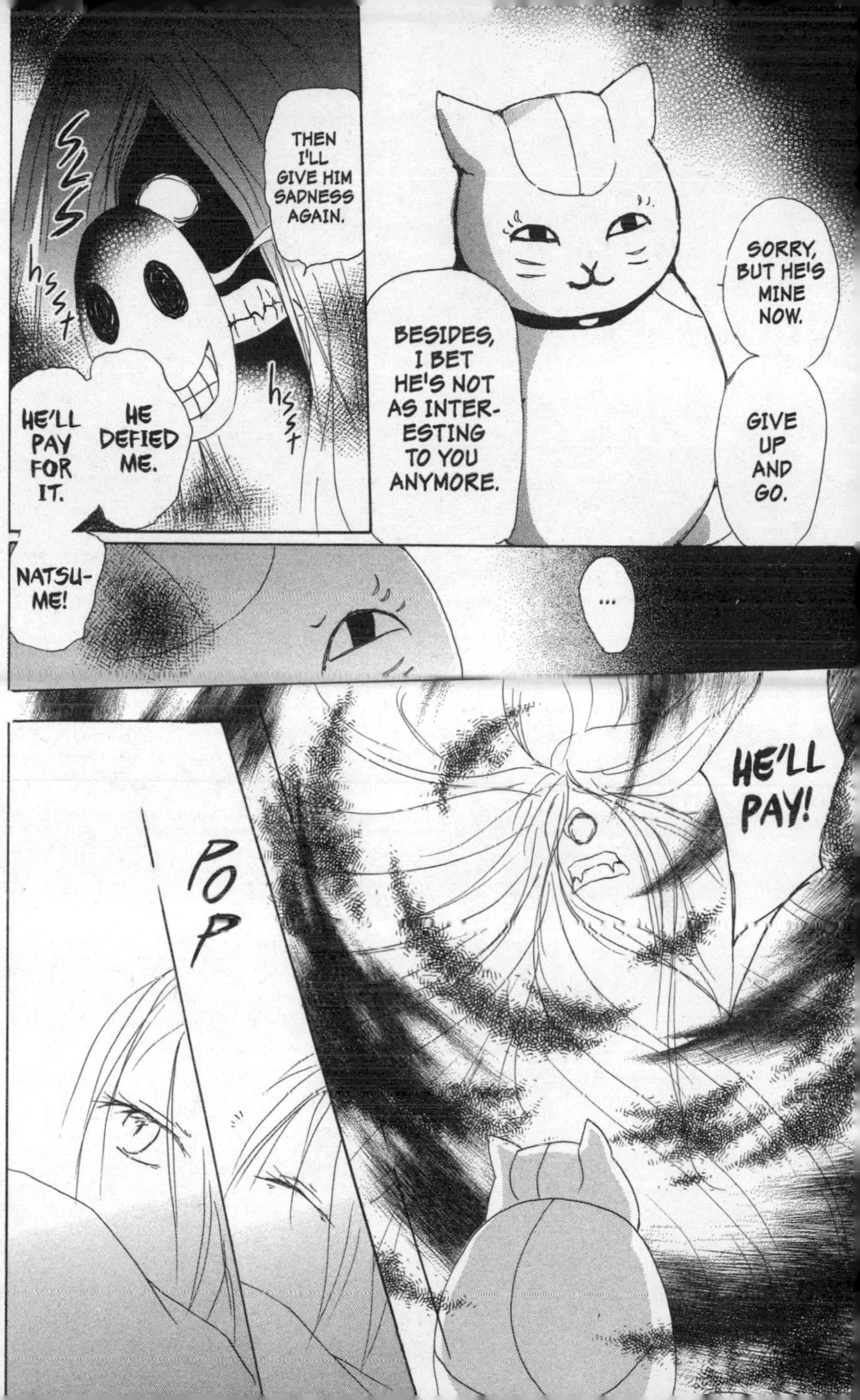
SORRY, BUT HE'S MINE NOW.
GIVE UP AND GO.
BESIDES, I BET HE'S NOT AS INTER-ESTING TO YOU ANYMORE.
THEN I'LL GIVE HIM SADNESS AGAIN.
SSS
hsst
hsst
HE DEFIED ME.
HE'LL PAY FOR IT.
...
NATSU-ME!
HE'LL PAY!
POP

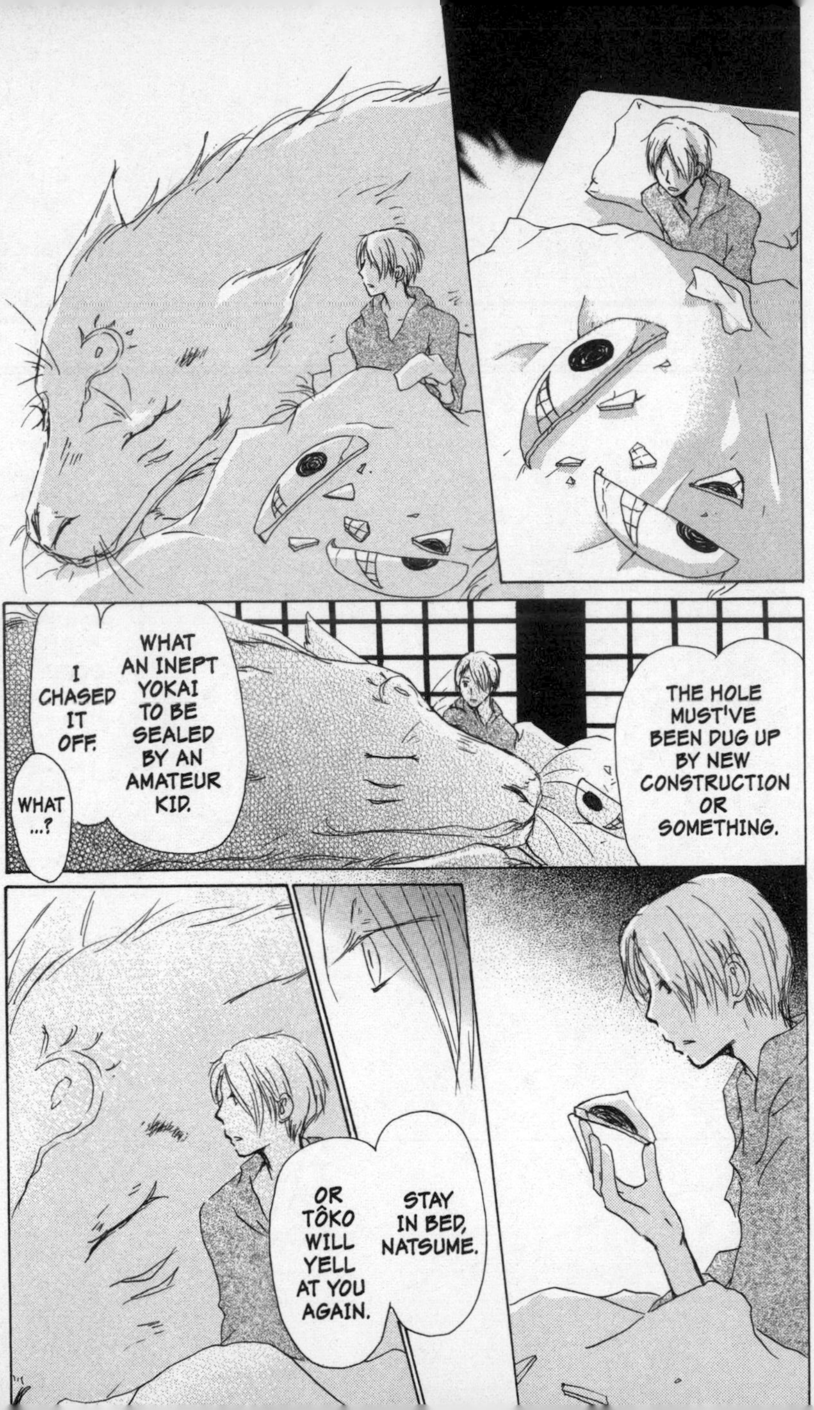
THE HOLE MUST'VE BEEN DUG UP BY NEW CONSTRUCTION OR SOMETHING.
WHAT AN INEPT YOKAI TO BE SEALED BY AN AMATEUR KID.
I CHASED IT OFF.
WHAT ...?
STAY IN BED, NATSUME.
OR TÔKO WILL YELL AT YOU AGAIN.

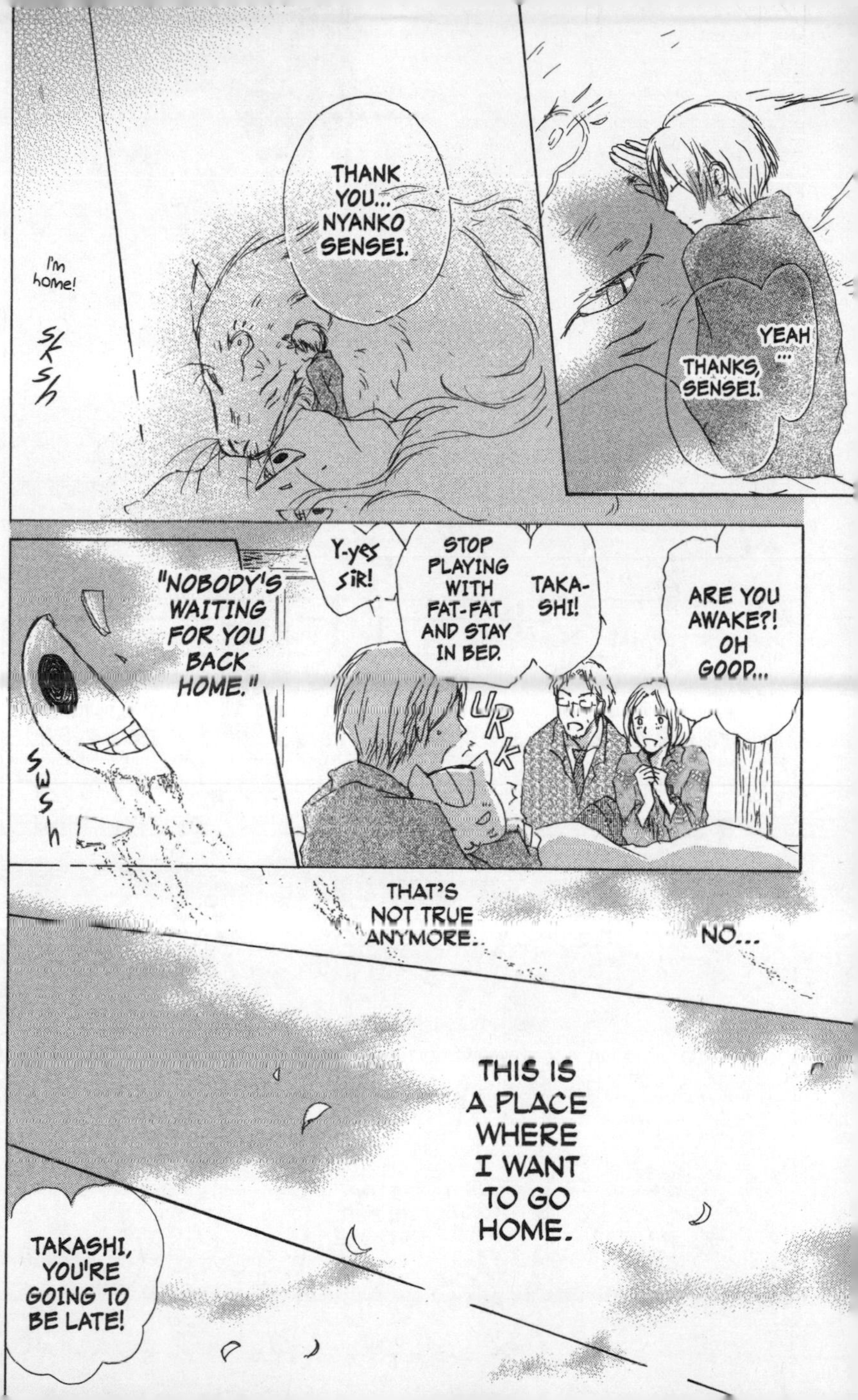
YEAH...
THANKS, SENSEI.
THANK YOU... NYANKO SENSEI.
I'm home!
SKSH
ARE YOU AWAKE?! OH GOOD...
TAKASHI!
STOP PLAYING WITH FAT-FAT AND STAY IN BED.
Y-yes sir!
URK
"NOBODY'S WAITING FOR YOU BACK HOME."
SWSH
NO...
THAT'S NOT TRUE ANYMORE.
THIS IS A PLACE WHERE I WANT TO GO HOME.
TAKASHI, YOU'RE GOING TO BE LATE!

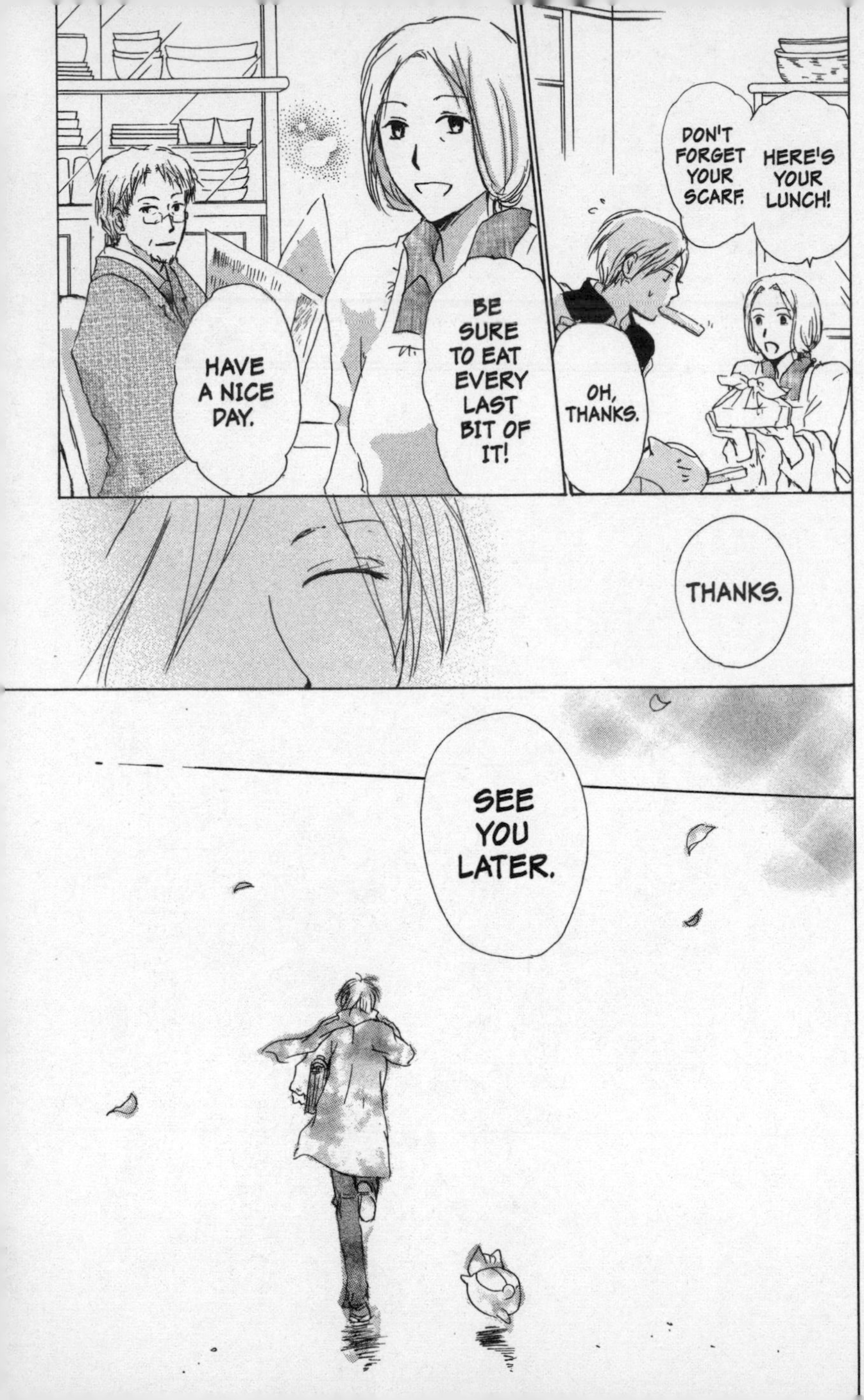
HERE'S YOUR LUNCH!
DON'T FORGET YOUR SCARF.
OH, THANKS.
BE SURE TO EAT EVERY LAST BIT OF IT!
HAVE A NICE DAY.
THANKS.
SEE YOU LATER.

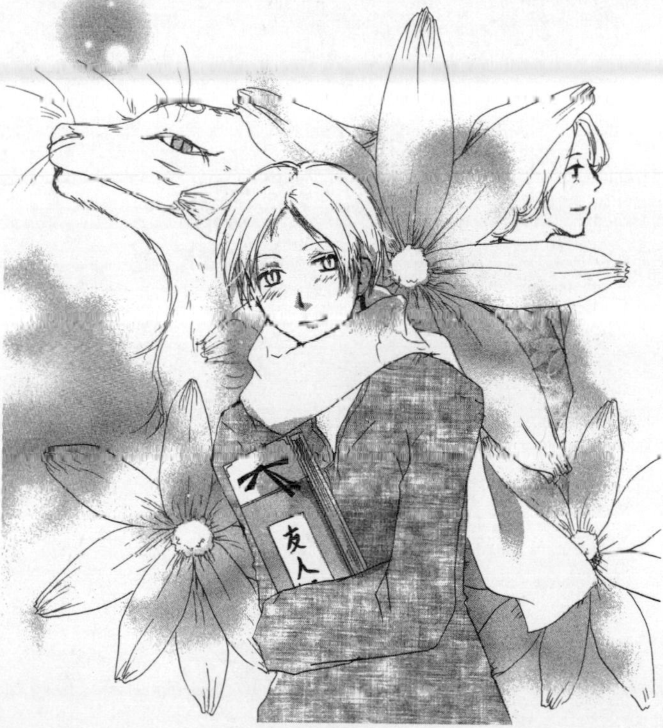
友人

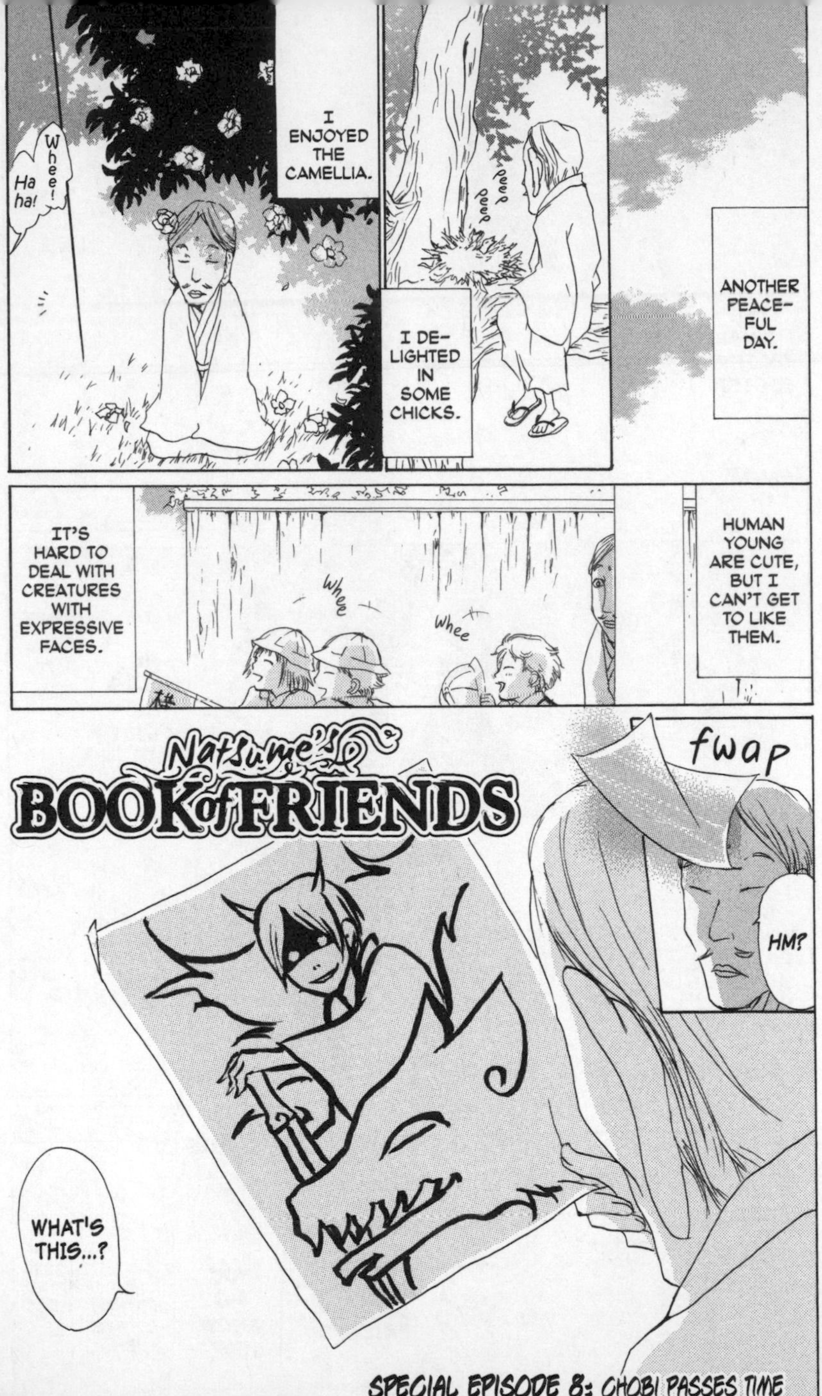
ANOTHER PEACEFUL DAY.
peep peep
I DELIGHTED IN SOME CHICKS.
I ENJOYED THE CAMELLIA.
Whee!
Ha ha!
HUMAN YOUNG ARE CUTE, BUT I CAN'T GET TO LIKE THEM.
Whee
Whee
IT'S HARD TO DEAL WITH CREATURES WITH EXPRESSIVE FACES.
fwap
HM?
Natsume's BOOK of FRIENDS
WHAT'S THIS...?
SPECIAL EPISODE 8: CHOBI PASSES TIME

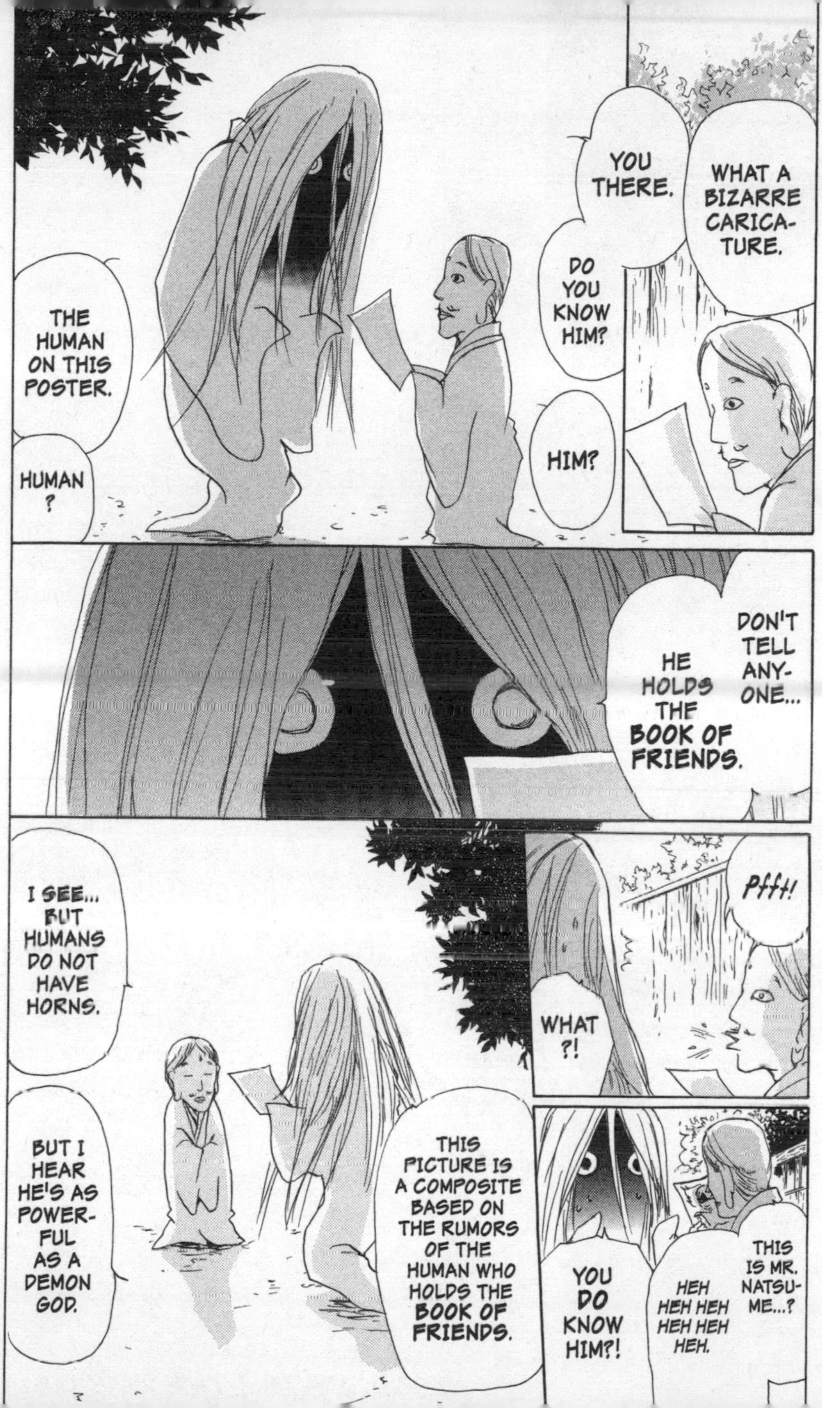
WHAT A BIZARRE CARICATURE.
YOU THERE.
DO YOU KNOW HIM?
HIM?
THE HUMAN ON THIS POSTER.
HUMAN?
DON'T TELL ANYONE... HE HOLDS THE BOOK OF FRIENDS.
Pfft!
WHAT?!
THIS IS MR. NATSUME...?
HEH HEH HEH HEH HEH HEH.
YOU DO KNOW HIM?!
THIS PICTURE IS A COMPOSITE BASED ON THE RUMORS OF THE HUMAN WHO HOLDS THE BOOK OF FRIENDS.
I SEE... BUT HUMANS DO NOT HAVE HORNS.
BUT I HEAR HE'S AS POWERFUL AS A DEMON GOD.

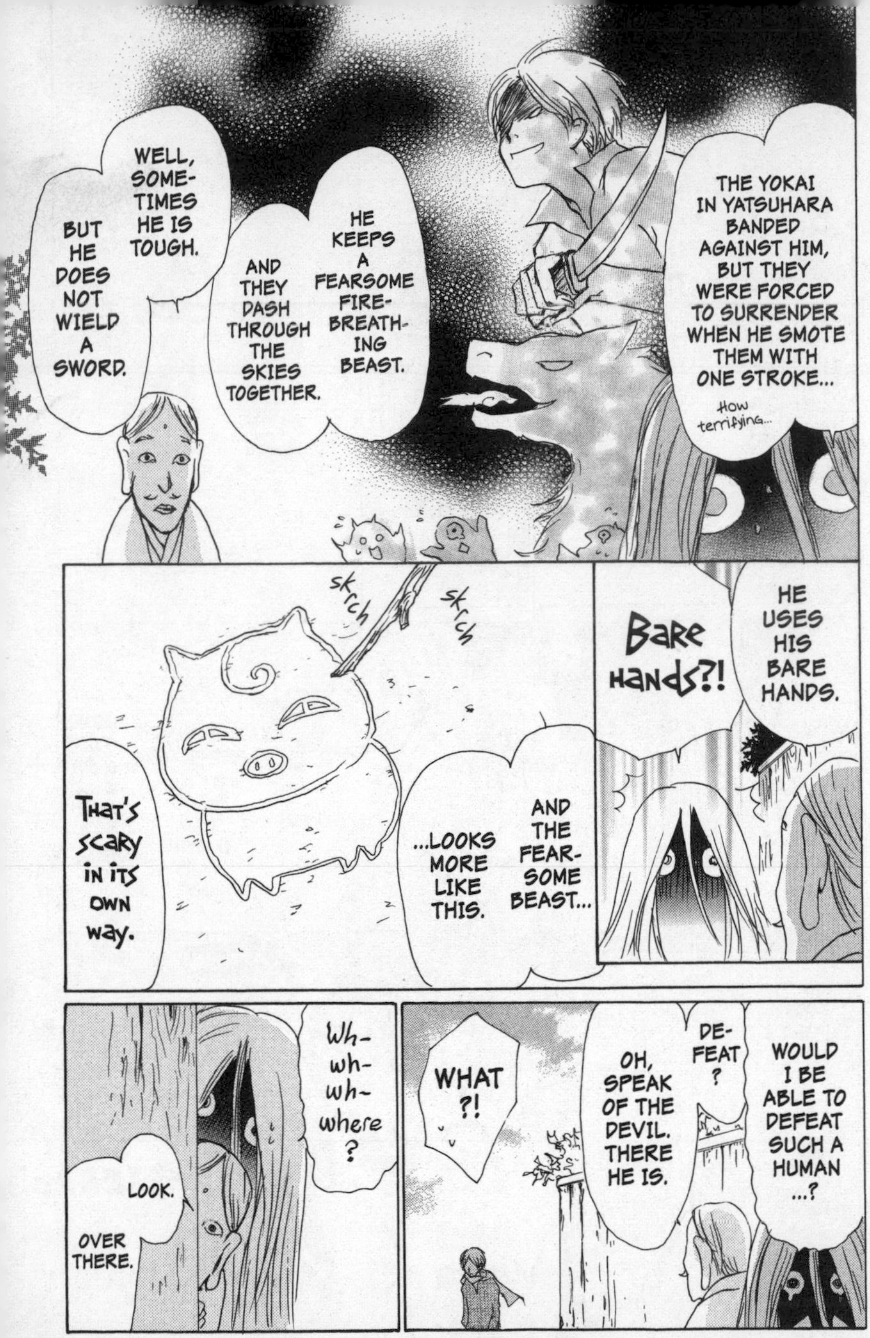
THE YOKAI IN YATSUHARA BANDED AGAINST HIM, BUT THEY WERE FORCED TO SURRENDER WHEN HE SMOTE THEM WITH ONE STROKE...
How terrifying...
HE KEEPS A FEARSOME FIRE-BREATHING BEAST.
AND THEY DASH THROUGH THE SKIES TOGETHER.
WELL, SOMETIMES HE IS TOUGH.
BUT HE DOES NOT WIELD A SWORD.
HE USES HIS BARE HANDS.
Bare hands?!
skrch
skrch
AND THE FEARSOME BEAST...
...LOOKS MORE LIKE THIS.
That's scary in its own way.
WOULD I BE ABLE TO DEFEAT SUCH A HUMAN ...?
DE-FEAT ?
OH, SPEAK OF THE DEVIL. THERE HE IS.
WHAT ?!
Wh-wh-wh-where ?
LOOK.
OVER THERE.

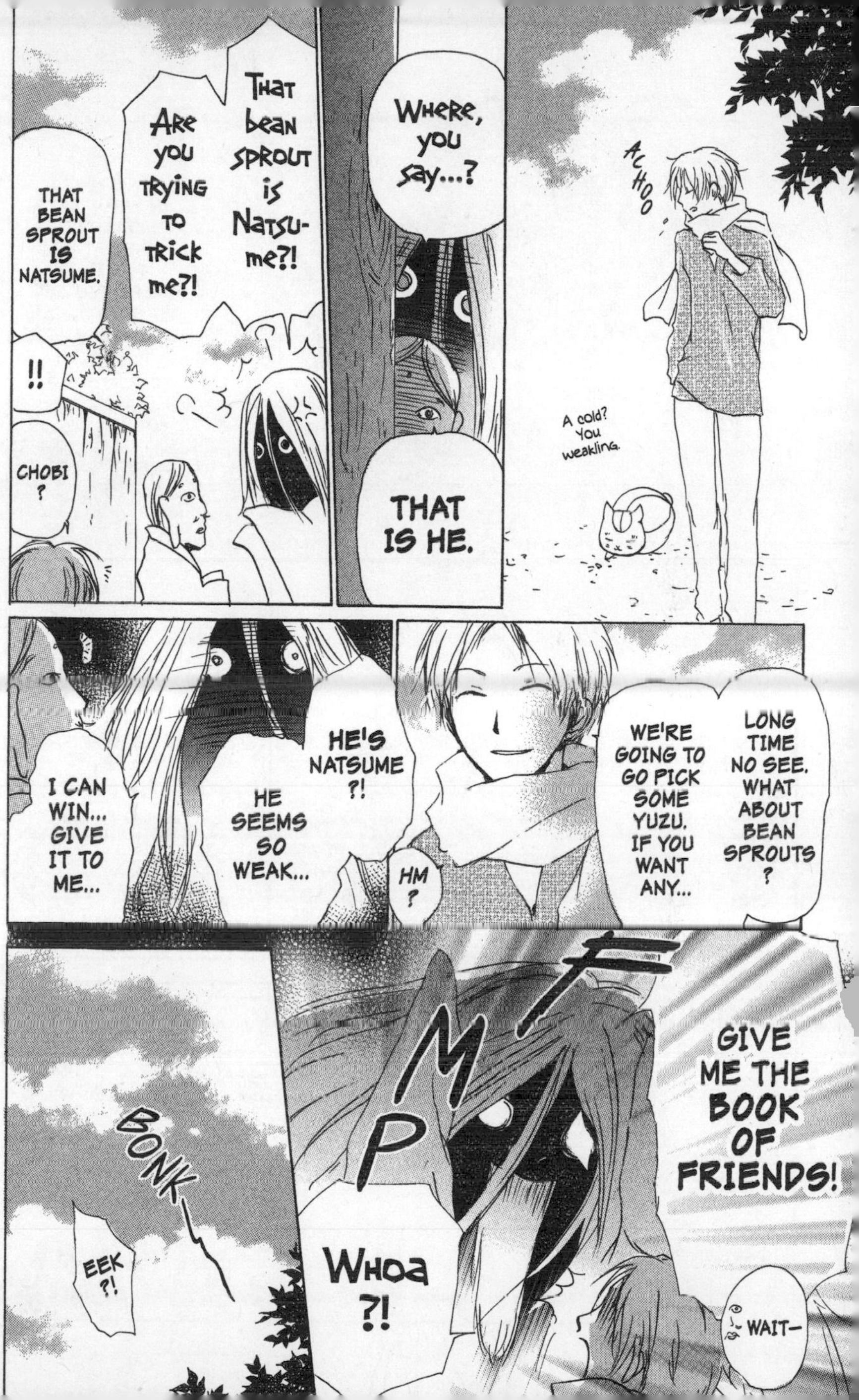
ACHOO
A cold? You weakling.
Where, you say...?
THAT IS HE.
That bean sprout is Natsu-me?!
Are you trying to trick me?!
THAT BEAN SPROUT IS NATSUME.
!!
CHOBI?
LONG TIME NO SEE. WHAT ABOUT BEAN SPROUTS?
WE'RE GOING TO GO PICK SOME YUZU. IF YOU WANT ANY...
HM?
HE'S NATSUME?!
HE SEEMS SO WEAK...
I CAN WIN... GIVE IT TO ME...
GIVE ME THE BOOK OF FRIENDS!
WAIT—
Whoa?!
BONK
EEK?!

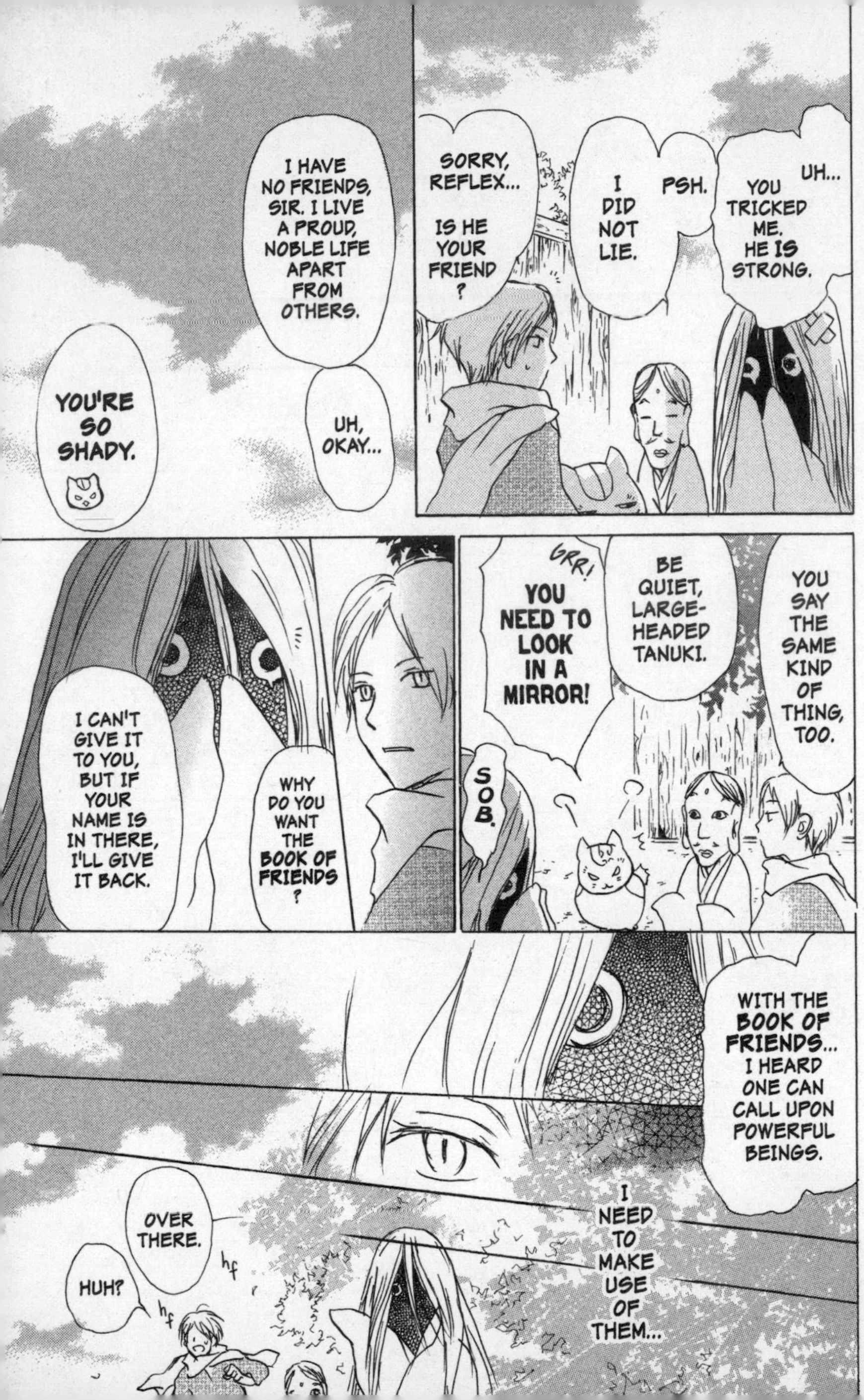
UH...
YOU TRICKED ME. HE IS STRONG.
PSH.
I DID NOT LIE.
SORRY, REFLEX... IS HE YOUR FRIEND?
I HAVE NO FRIENDS, SIR. I LIVE A PROUD, NOBLE LIFE APART FROM OTHERS.
UH, OKAY...
YOU'RE SO SHADY.
YOU SAY THE SAME KIND OF THING, TOO.
BE QUIET, LARGE-HEADED TANUKI.
GRR!
YOU NEED TO LOOK IN A MIRROR!
SOB.
WHY DO YOU WANT THE BOOK OF FRIENDS?
I CAN'T GIVE IT TO YOU, BUT IF YOUR NAME IS IN THERE, I'LL GIVE IT BACK.
WITH THE BOOK OF FRIENDS... I HEARD ONE CAN CALL UPON POWERFUL BEINGS.
I NEED TO MAKE USE OF THEM...
OVER THERE.
hf
HUH?
hf

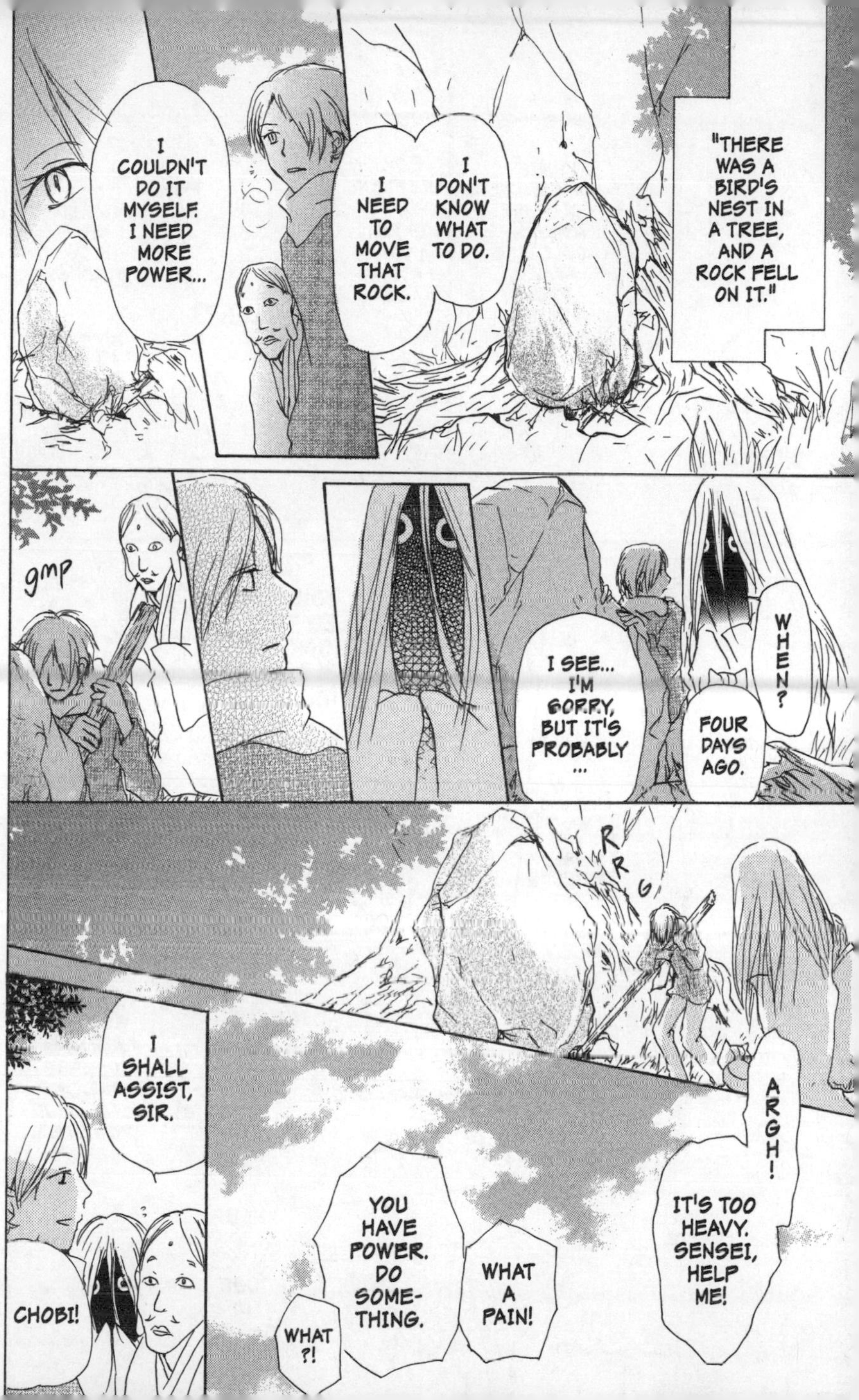
"THERE WAS A BIRD'S NEST IN A TREE, AND A ROCK FELL ON IT."
I DON'T KNOW WHAT TO DO.
I NEED TO MOVE THAT ROCK.
I COULDN'T DO IT MYSELF. I NEED MORE POWER...
WHEN?
FOUR DAYS AGO.
I SEE... I'M SORRY, BUT IT'S PROBABLY ...
gmp
RRG
ARGH!
IT'S TOO HEAVY. SENSEI, HELP ME!
WHAT A PAIN!
YOU HAVE POWER. DO SOMETHING.
WHAT?!
I SHALL ASSIST, SIR.
CHOBI!

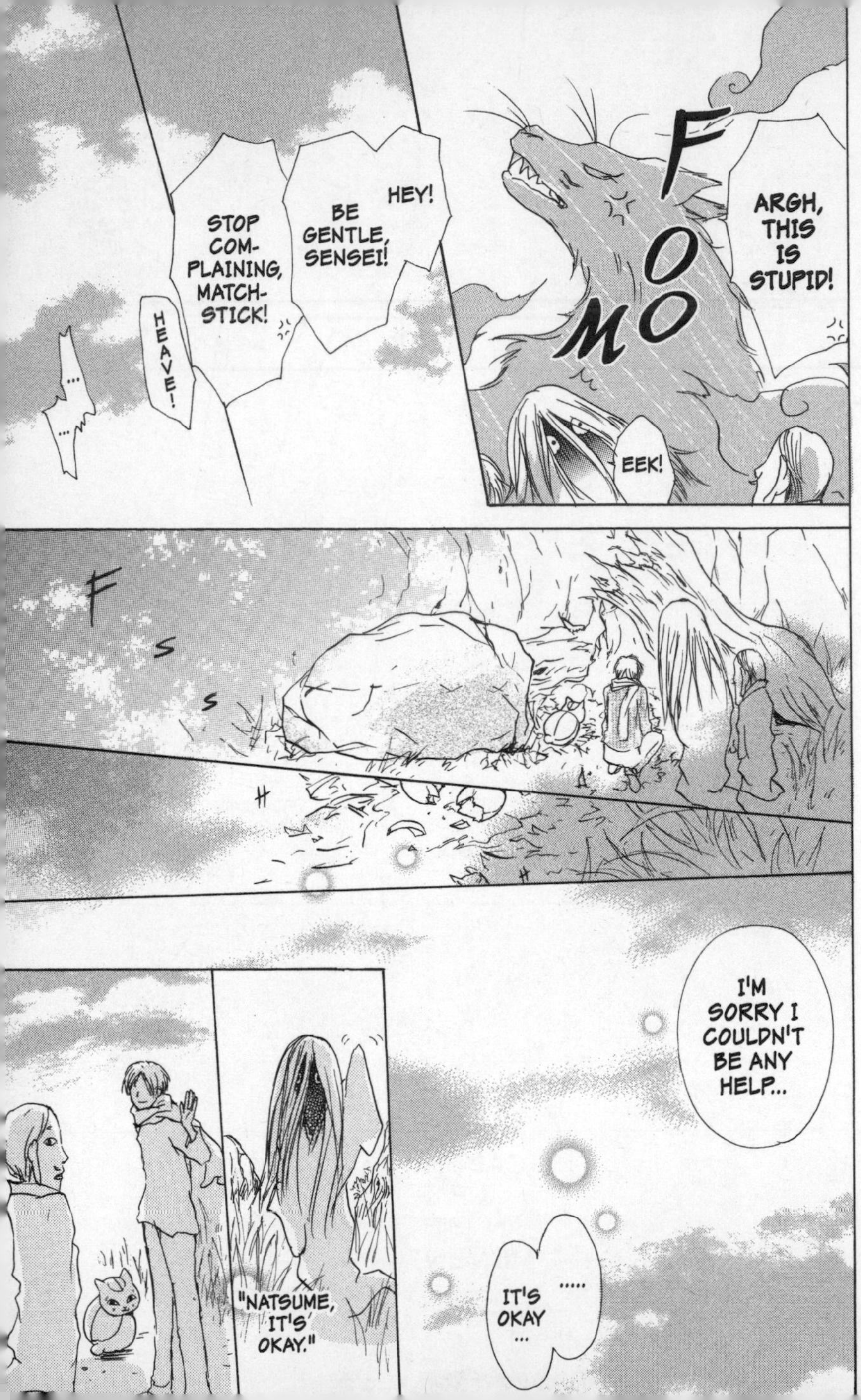
ARGH, THIS IS STUPID!
FOOM
EEK!
HEY!
BE GENTLE, SENSEI!
STOP COM-PLAINING, MATCH-STICK!
HEAVE!
...
...
FSSH
I'M SORRY I COULDN'T BE ANY HELP...
IT'S OKAY ...
.....
"NATSUME, IT'S OKAY."

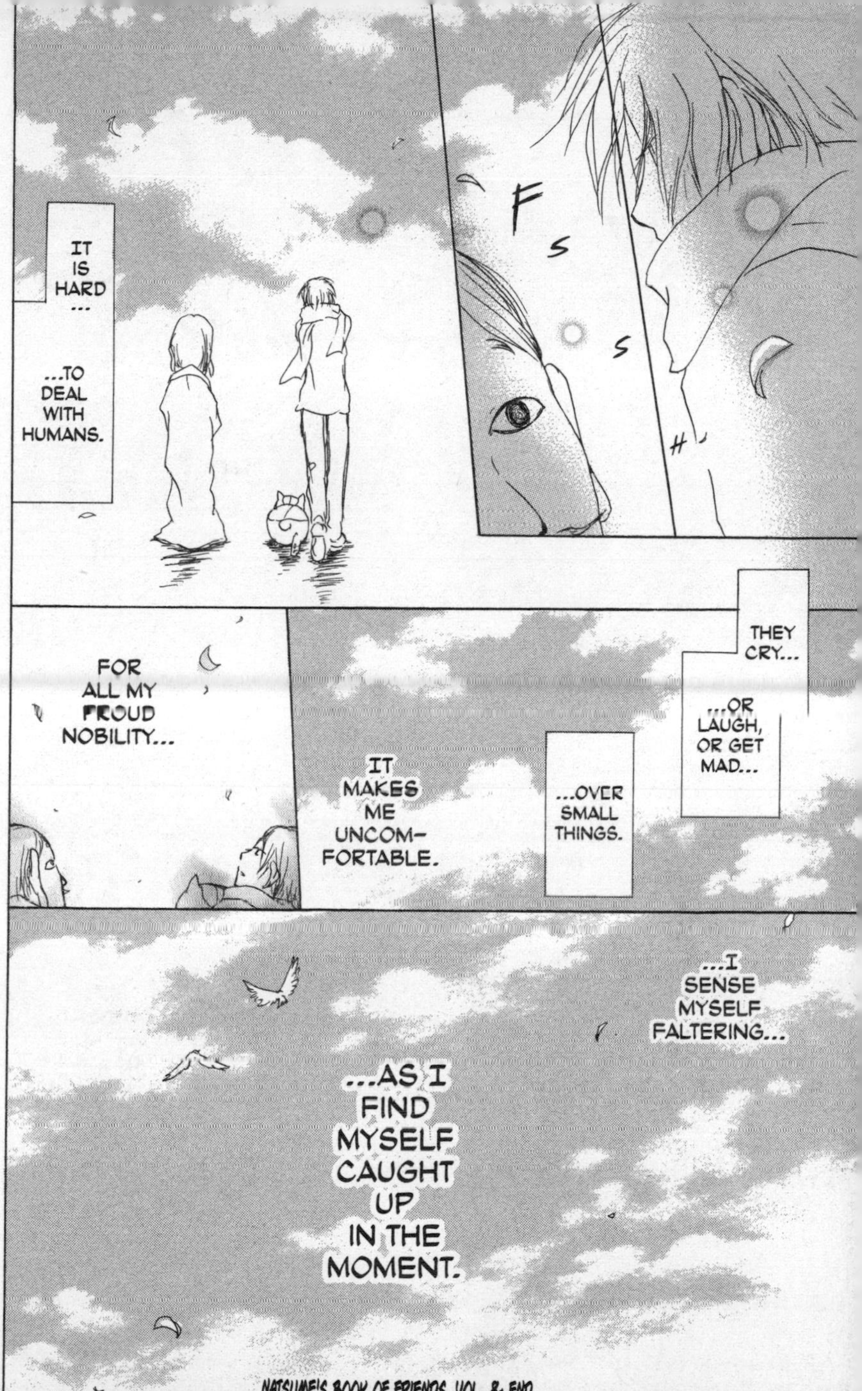
FSSH
IT IS HARD...
...TO DEAL WITH HUMANS.
THEY CRY...
...OR LAUGH, OR GET MAD...
...OVER SMALL THINGS.
IT MAKES ME UNCOMFORTABLE.
FOR ALL MY PROUD NOBILITY...
...I SENSE MYSELF FALTERING...
...AS I FIND MYSELF CAUGHT UP IN THE MOMENT.

AFTER-WORD

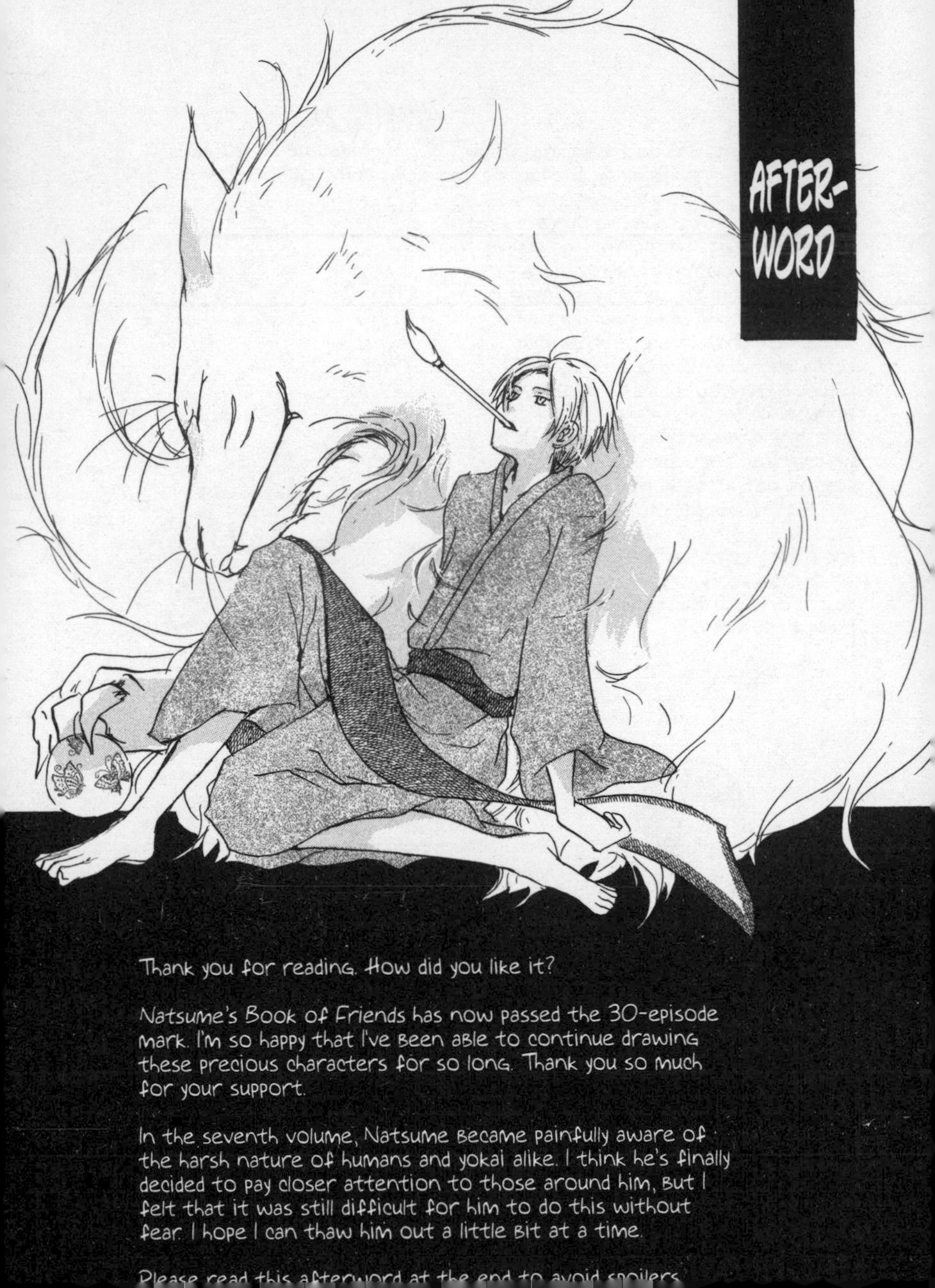

Thank you for reading. How did you like it?

Natsume's Book of Friends has now passed the 30-episode mark. I'm so happy that I've been able to continue drawing these precious characters for so long. Thank you so much for your support.

In the seventh volume, Natsume became painfully aware of the harsh nature of humans and yokai alike. I think he's finally decided to pay closer attention to those around him, but I felt that it was still difficult for him to do this without fear. I hope I can thaw him out a little bit at a time.

Please read this afterword at the end to avoid spoilers.

CHAPTER 27

Natsume Participates in the Culture Festival

I thought I shouldn't write episodes that don't revolve around yokai, but I was given the go-ahead to do a campus story. I was still nervous, but it was so fun to finally include incidents I've wanted to insert for a long time, even if it had to be a side story. I wanted to spend more time on the Culture Festival, but I was worried it would get too human-centric, and I kept running into problems I don't usually encounter. It was a new experience. In my mind, Kitamoto has a cute younger sister, and Nishimura has an older brother that he doesn't get along with. I remember the day I decided on their faces, imagining a former baseball player and a former soccer player. I hope to one day work on an episode describing how the three of them first met.

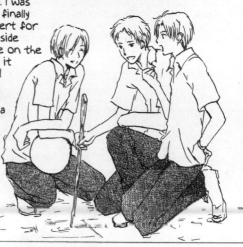

CHAPTER 28, 29

Reflections

I kept missing opportunities to do an episode on Tanuma, because I was afraid I couldn't give him the time and attention he deserves. Then I was assigned a two-part episode, so I knew this was my chance. I feel that Natsume is embarrassed because he wants to get closer, but is just not used to that kind of thing. This time, he found out how it feels to be the one being avoided. These colleagues all know about the existence of yokai, but when he's with Mr. Natori, Natsume wants to take a step forward. With Tanuma and Taki, the difference is a desire to take a step back. I hope I can depict such subtlety. I also realized how fun it is to draw the interactions between students.

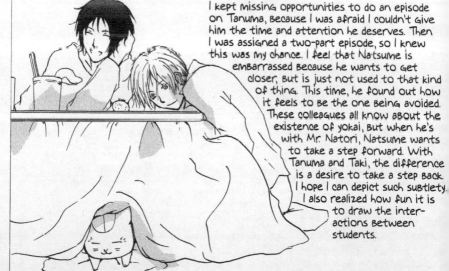

CHAPTER 30, 31

A Place to Belong

This is also a story I've wanted to work on for a long time, so I had fun. It was a strange feeling, like sketching a path from memory which I've walked with Natsume so many times. Without Nyanko Sensei in the story, I felt anxious even as the writer. Natsume feels that the Fujiwaras provided the light when he was lonely, but the same was true for the Fujiwaras. The anime producers made a wonderful episode of Natsume before he came to live with the Fujiwaras for the drama CD that came with the anime DVD volume one of Natsume's Book of Friends. I added a tiny bit of awkwardness to Aunt Tôko. Like she got a little too excited, and she had to be calmed down by Shigeru when she got home. This was a lot of fun.

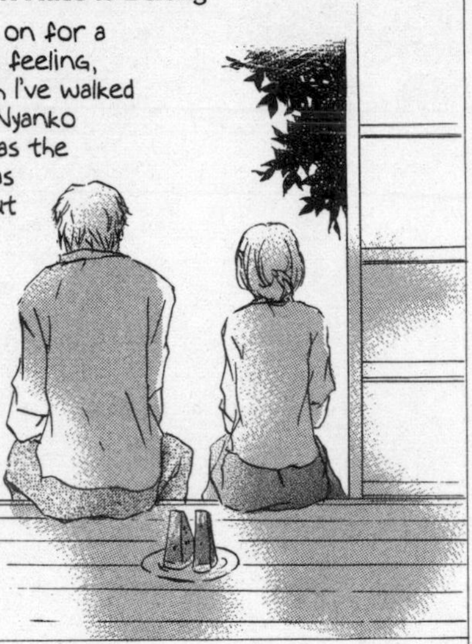

SPECIAL EPISODE

I was given eight pages, so I debated what to write about, and settled on Chobi, with whom I could be the most natural. For some reason I grow calmer when I'm drawing Chobi. Natsume is usually pretty incompetent, but you can't see inside his head from a third-person perspective, so I could draw him being a little cooler.

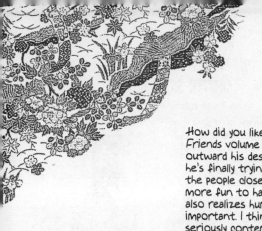

How did you like Natsume's Book of Friends volume 8? Natsume has directed outward his desire to do something, but he's finally trying to pay attention to the people close to him. It has become more fun to hang around yokai, but he also realizes human relationships are very important. I think he's going to start seriously contemplating his future course of action. I'd like to draw all the difficult things and the fun things with the utmost care.

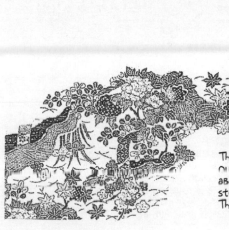

Thank you so much for checking out the book. I'm passionate about drawing interesting stories that you'd like to read! Thank you again.

Special thanks to:
Tamao Ohki
Chika
Mika
My sister
Mr. Sato
Hoen Kikaku, Ltd.
      Thank you.

Please send me your thoughts and comments.

Yuki Midorikawa
c/o Shojo Beat
P.O. Box 77010
San Francicso, CA 94107

AFTERWORD, END

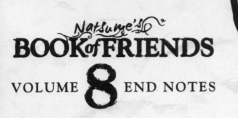

Natsume's
BOOK of FRIENDS
VOLUME 8 END NOTES

PAGE 7 PANEL 2: *Cultural Festival*
Most Japanese schools hold a yearly cultural festival where each class creates a booth, such as a café or rummage sale.

PAGE 53, PANEL 5: *Tanuki*
An animal native to Japan, also called a raccoon dog. In folklore, tanuki are sometimes depicted with big, round bellies.

PAGE 56, PANEL 1: *Day duty*
In Japan day duty is when students take turns recording what occurs in the classroom in a daybook.

PAGE 114, PANEL 4: *Melon bread*
A sweet pastry common in Japanese bakeries, it is a round fluffy bun with a thin cookie crust. The name comes from the crust's crosshatch pattern, which resembles melon skin.

PAGE 139, AUTHOR NOTE: *Japanese bedding*
Traditional Japanese beds are a thin cotton mattress and a comforter that can be folded and put away during the day.

PAGE 180, PANEL 4: *Yuzu*
A Japanese citrus, often used for its zest.

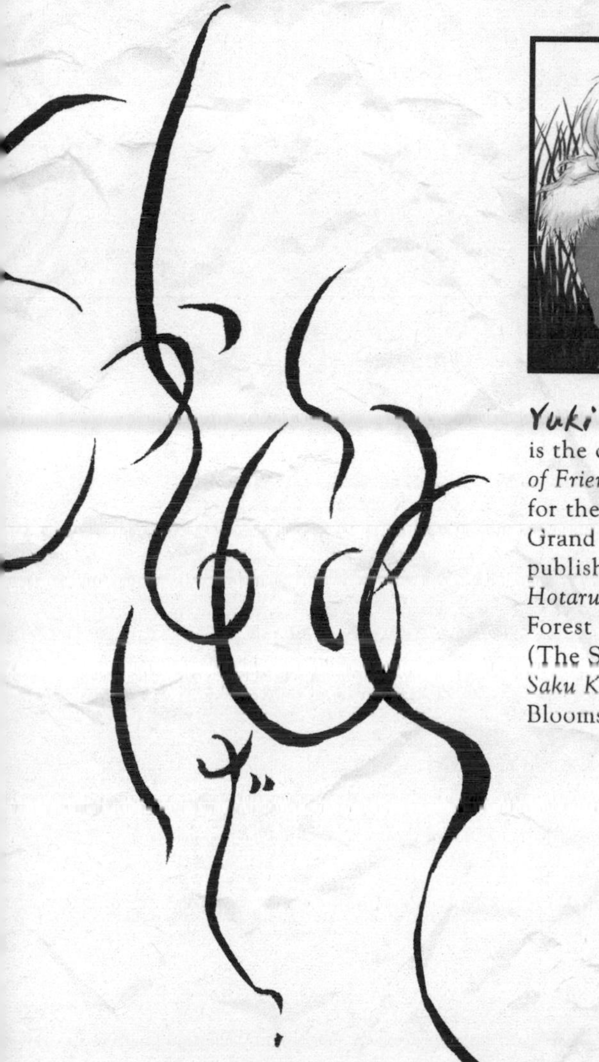

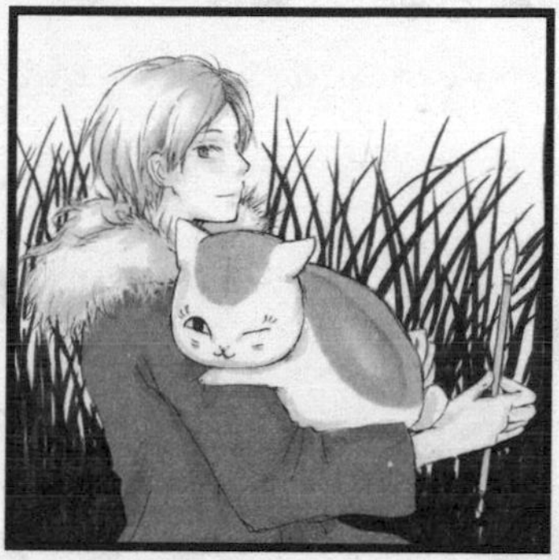

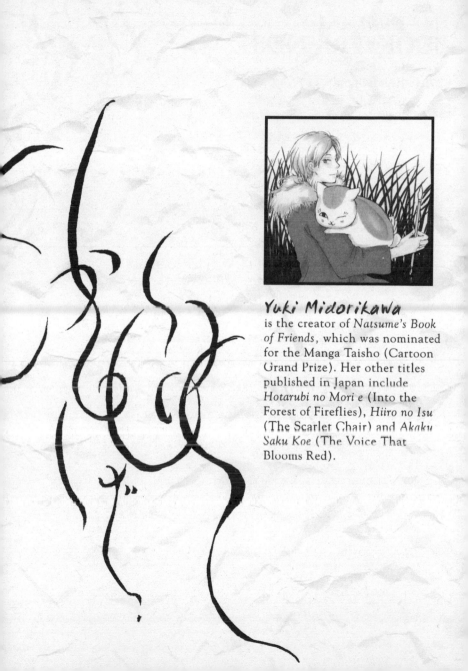

Yuki Midorikawa

is the creator of *Natsume's Book of Friends*, which was nominated for the Manga Taisho (Cartoon Grand Prize). Her other titles published in Japan include *Hotarubi no Mori e* (Into the Forest of Fireflies), *Hiiro no Isu* (The Scarlet Chair) and *Akaku Saku Koe* (The Voice That Blooms Red).

NATSUME'S BOOK OF FRIENDS

Vol. 8
Shojo Beat Edition

STORY AND ART BY *Yuki Midorikawa*

Translation & Adaptation *Lillian Olsen*
Touch-up Art & Lettering *Sabrina Heep*
Design *Fawn Lau*
Editor *Pancha Diaz*

Natsume Yujincho by Yuki Midorikawa
© Yuki Midorikawa 2009
All rights reserved.
First published in Japan in 2009 by HAKUSENSHA, Inc., Tokyo.
English language translation rights arranged with HAKUSENSHA, Inc., Tokyo.

The stories, characters and incidents mentioned in this publication are entirely fictional.

Printed in the U.S.A.

Published by VIZ Media, LLC
P.O. Box 77010
San Francisco, CA 94107

10 9 8 7 6 5 4 3
First printing, August 2011
Third printing, February 2019

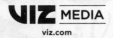
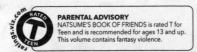

SURPRISE!

You may be reading the wrong way!

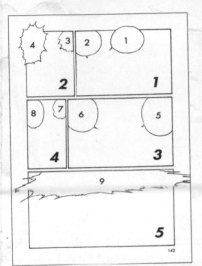

It's true: In keeping with the original Japanese comic format, this book reads from right to left—so action, sound effects, and word balloons are completely reversed. This preserves the orientation of the original artwork—plus, it's fun! Check out the diagram shown here to get the hang of things, and then turn to the other side of the book to get started!

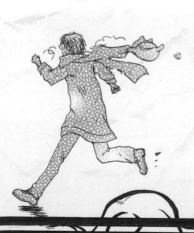

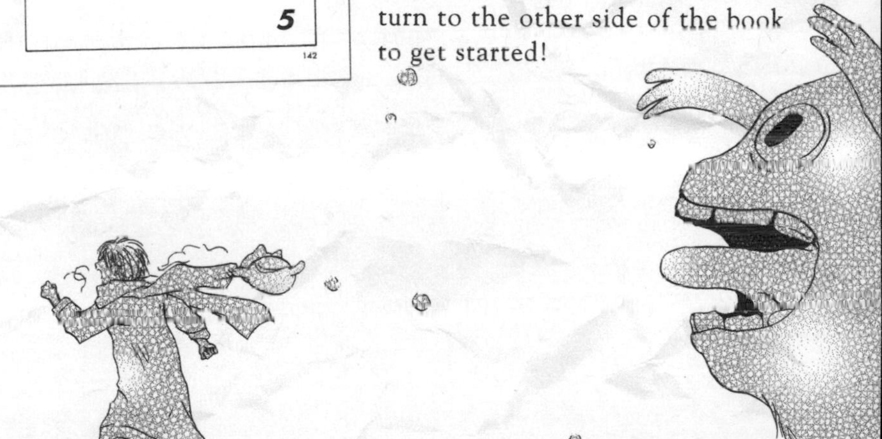